REUTHER

Frank Cormier and William J. Eaton

Prentice-Hall, Inc., Englewood Cliffs, N.J.

ISBN 0-13-779314-6

Library of Congress Catalog Card Number: 71-131869
Printed in the United States of America
Prentice-Hall International, Inc., London
Prentice-Hall of Australia, Pty. Ltd., Sydney
Prentice-Hall of Canada, Ltd., Toronto
Prentice-Hall of India Private Ltd., New Delhi
Prentice-Hall of Japan, Inc., Tokyo

For Marilynn and Margot

Credo

My main point is that the labor movement is about that problem we face tomorrow morning. Damn right! The guys have a right to expect the labor movement to deal with that problem. I can't give them some philosophical baloney and say: "Well, fellows, you know we're operating way up here in the stratosphere and you shouldn't get excited about these little problems that are bothering you every morning."

But to make that the sole purpose of the labor movement is to miss the main target. The labor movement is about changing society. I mean, I don't think I am eloquent when I say to a guy: "What good is a dollar an hour more in wages if your neighborhood is burning down? What good is another week's vacation if the lake you used to go to, where you've got a cottage, is polluted and you can't swim in it and the kids can't play in it? What good is another $100 pension if the world goes up in atomic smoke?"

Look, I think that's a pretty practical look at the thing. Now I may be motivated because I just happen to think that these values are important, and I'm willing to fight for them, and I'm willing to die for them, because I believe in them.

I've had what I think is the richest, most self-fulfilling kind of experience that a human being has. I have been living what I believe. . . . Nobody can be better rewarded. When they say to me: "You're getting a little bit of money compared to somebody else," they don't understand. I'm the best paid guy in the movement, I think, because I'm doing what I want to do. . . . Nobody has to feel sorry about me. The only limitation on what I'm doing is that there's only so many hours in a day and so many weeks in a year.

Walter P. Reuther
Interview, August 20, 1969

Contents

Credo   *vii*

REUTHER

CHAPTER ONE

Father and Son

FIVE VOICES, BLENDING IN ROUGH HARMONY, SANG IN GERMAN THE folk melodies of the Old Country. At 86, Valentine Reuther was dying. His four sons and only daughter, clasping hands and standing in a semicircle around the foot of the bed, sang the tunes that had been childhood favorites of the man they knew as *Vater*. For fleeting moments Valentine Reuther opened his eyes and smiled, as if to express silent appreciation for the final tribute. He closed his eyes for the last time on November 17, 1967.

Seventy-five years had passed since the patriarch of the Reuther family had left his Rhineland birthplace for the United States. Since then, he had been beer wagon driver, labor leader, Socialist candidate for Congress, chicken farmer, real estate broker, life insurance salesman, husband, and father. One of his five children, Walter Philip Reuther, had carried the family name to eminence.

Walter Reuther, heralded by many and cursed with equal fervor by others, even within the ranks of organized labor, owed much to his strong-willed father and to the beliefs and traditions of the Reuther family. These influences were pervasive long past the formative years. The sentimental farewell at the nursing home in Wheeling, West Virginia, seemed a natural and appropriate act, belying the coldness often attributed to Walter in his personal relationships.

Nearly a century earlier Walter's grandfather, Jacob Reuther, had been an agitator of sorts in the village of Edigheim, near Mannheim. Although he never associated with trade union activity, Jacob's strongly held pacifist views and Christian Socialist convictions had marked him as a nonconformist in the small farming community. Quarreling with the policy of the established Lutheran Church, Jacob argued that its doctrine concentrated too much on the hereafter and neglected earthly social conditions. Opposed to compulsory service in the Prussian army and repelled by authoritarianism in any guise, he was outraged when the largest employer in the village, a factory owner named Gross, displayed on election eve a banner reading: "He Who Does Not Tomorrow Vote for Dr. Gross Will Be Out of Work."

Seeking greater freedom from the oppressive political climate, Jacob Reuther sold his small dairy farm and emigrated to the United States, following in the tradition of the Socialist rebels of 1848 after their protest movement was put down. Perhaps, like many others before him, he also sought greater prosperity in the New World; in Germany, the Reuthers had been poor, often making a meal of potatoes and cottage cheese.

With 11-year-old Valentine and two other children, Jacob and his wife sailed for America in 1892. According to family legend Jacob thrust his arm around Valentine as the boat passed the newly erected Statue of Liberty and said, "A man should always fight for freedom and brotherhood."

The family settled on a dairy farm near Effingham, Illinois, then an important rail center, where a cousin had preceded them. To the delight of young Valentine, Indians still camped alongside the nearby Wabash River.

Jacob, a stern-looking man with white beard, continued his fight for better social conditions and for revision of Lutheran doctrine. At times he wrote what he regarded as serious treatises on theology, running to 30 or 40 pages in longhand, delineating his differences with Effingham's Lutheran pastor. Eventually convinced that his polemics would not alter the teachings at the neighborhood church, he began conducting services in his home. He believed strongly that many churches "do too much for God and not enough for man."

Valentine felt that opportunities were limited in southern Illinois, and just before the turn of the century he headed east for Wheeling. A bustling industrial city with a sizable German populace, Wheeling, with nearly 4,000 signed-up union members, had been a labor stronghold as early as 1885, when the Ohio Valley Trades and Labor Assembly was founded there.

Valentine's first work was in a steel mill, at $1.40 for a twelve-hour day. Later he was hired by the Schmuhlbach Brewing Com-

pany to drive a beer wagon. Although his formal education had
been limited, he learned to speak English well and took correspondence courses to broaden his knowledge. Foreshadowing his son
Walter's career, he organized Schmuhlbach workers into a plant-
wide union and served as chief negotiator. Working conditions, as
he knew from his own job, were often rugged. He drove a wagon
over mountain roads for as long as seventeen hours a day, sometimes in snow and sub-zero weather. More than once his body became so stiff from cold that he had to be lifted from the driver's
seat and warmed up before he could walk normally.

Despite the long hours, Valentine found opportunity for romance. He became infatuated with a red-haired German girl who
served free lunch in a beer hall near the brewery. She was Anna
Stocker, 18-year-old daughter of a wagonmaker from Scharnhausen,
near Stuttgart, in the region of Germany called Swabia. After her
father died in his forties, necessity had compelled Anna to help
with the housework for a family of twelve. When she fell in love
with a young man in the village, Mother Stocker disapproved, perhaps because she did not want to lose Anna's services. Rebellious,
the daughter left for the United States to join a brother, a steel-
worker in Wheeling, and found employment as a servant.

Valentine and Anna found they had much in common: German
birth, a Lutheran heritage, and a strict sense of duty and morality.
Their courtship blossomed at meetings of a Beethoven singing society. Because Anna's command of English was limited, the young
couple spoke German together. They were married in 1903. Later,
when teased that he had been Anna's second choice, Valentine asserted, "If I were third, I still would consider myself fortunate."

The newlyweds rented a small second-story flat in the South
Wheeling laboring-class district. Life there was not easy. Anna
awoke at 4:30 A.M. each working day to prepare breakfast for her
husband and get an early start on the housework. His daily wage—
$1.50 by now—did not permit many luxuries. The young Mrs.
Reuther sewed bedsheets from Gold Medal flour sacks and produced homemade soap to keep down costs. She baked her own
pastries and rolls and kept the tiny Reuther home spotless. Her

life revolved around the *hausfrau*'s three traditional interests, *kinder,*
kirche, and *küche*—children, church, and kitchen.

At this point Valentine was rising rapidly in the labor movement.
Elected president of the Ohio Valley Trades and Labor Assembly
in 1904, at the age of 23, he became chief spokesman for 42 trade
unions in the Wheeling area. In this position he led, but lost, a
fight against accepting a library for the city from Andrew Carnegie.
Valentine and others in organized labor held the steel baron responsible for the "Homestead Massacre," in which seven striking
steelworkers had been killed by Pinkertons and twenty others
wounded. Valentine also helped organize coal miners, testified before the West Virginia legislature on labor disputes, and urged
Wheeling officials to use union workmen in building schools and
other government structures.

Although he was a dedicated partisan of Socialist Eugene V.
Debs and Populist Democrat William Jennings Bryan, Valentine
knew how to compromise. Asked late in life about his record of
settling contract disputes without a strike, he answered, "I always
won by politeness. There is an art in negotiating . . . You have to
be diplomatic."

At times he could be boldly outspoken. When a new minister
at the Zion Lutheran Church began delivering a Labor Day sermon
against trade unions, Valentine stood up in his pew and took immediate issue with the cleric. The elder Reuther never returned to
the church, although he did not interfere with his wife's efforts to
raise the children in the faith.

At the West Virginia Federation of Labor convention in 1912,
it was Val Reuther who sponsored a resolution, couched in the best
Marxist rhetoric, that all but endorsed the Socialist Party. It called
for "control of government by the workers, the abolishing of the
exploitation of the workers through the capitalist system, and the
giving of workers the full social value of their toil."

Something of an intellectual among Wheeling's working class,
Valentine prized a personal library that included not only Schiller
and Goethe, but volumes by the British agnostic Thomas Henry
Huxley, and the American atheist Robert Ingersoll. Books were
one of his few luxuries.

The first of Valentine and Anna Reuther's sons, Theodore, was born in 1905. A second son, born September 1, 1907, the eve of Labor Day, was named Walter Philip. When Roy and Victor followed, each two years apart, the family moved to a larger home Valentine built himself at 3640 South Wetzel Street in Wheeling. Grudgingly, the head of the family agreed to build a bathroom onto the living quarters—rather than install an outhouse, his preference —but he insisted it be entered from the porch. By the time Mrs. Reuther persuaded him to provide an indoor entrance, she had to sacrifice a kitchen cupboard to make room for the door.

The upbringing of the Reuther boys was strict and serious, to the extent that elders could prevail. Their mother—they called her *Mutterchen*—required them to bow their heads and say grace at meals. Even in winter they huddled around the stove in nightclothes to say prayers before racing upstairs to unheated bedrooms. Father spurred them with such traditional Teutonic aphorisms as "Work makes life sweet," and demanded instant obedience. What made the Reuther home different from many German-American households of the time, however, was the spirit of social justice that prevailed there.

"At my father's knee," Walter recalled years later, "we learned the philosophy of trade unionism. We got the struggles, the hopes and aspirations of working people every day." Sometimes the message was implanted physically, as when Victor innocently brought home a Hearst newspaper during a labor boycott of Hearst publications. Says Victor: "Dad was furious when he saw me with the Hearst comics. I got a whipping that I really felt."

The red-haired Reuther boys were credited with perfect attendance at the Zion Church Sunday School. But they learned applied Christianity at home. "No matter how little we had to eat," Walter remembered, "Mother and Father always took in every tramp who came along and sat him down at the table. Dad would always say to us, 'I want you to remember that, as long as you have something to eat, you have to share it with others who haven't.' "

The youngsters also learned to eat every scrap off their plates— and to whisper "F-H-B," for family hold back, when guests came to dinner. *Mutterchen* would chide those who left food untouched, saying, "Willful waste makes woeful want and you will live to say, 'How I wish I had that bread that once I threw away.' "

Practicing what she preached, Mrs. Reuther altered Valentine's discarded clothes so they would fit one or another of the four sons. When her prized black umbrella was broken while being used by the boys as a parachute, she made Walter a shirt from the fabric. Pleased beyond measure, he told his friends, "Look, I have a shirt that sheds water!" When *Mutterchen* prepared cherry pancakes, a delicacy, she left the pits in place, to slow the rate of consumption.

Although Walter and his brothers walked three miles to Sunday school, never missing class in seven years, they hardly were little saints. Some neighbors knew Walter as "wiggle-britches," and even his mother thought of him as "hot-headed and stubborn." Only her vigilance prevented an explosion when Walter and Victor, playing with a coal miner's son, brought dynamite into the basement. There was a small blast once, when Walter turned on the gas in the kitchen stove; he was not hurt. He also escaped injury when, on a dare, he leaped on stilts from the roof of a boxcar into a clay mound.

In school Walter did his best work in manual training classes. And he often visited a nearby glass factory where skilled metalworkers prepared elaborate steel molds for bowls and other household wares. He did not leave until the mold-makers gave him a piece of steel, a hammer, and a chisel to try his hand. The experience helped convince him to become a tool and die maker a few years later. Warned by the molders against entering the glass business, he could see even then that machines were capable of stamping out designs faster than the hand craftsmen they were displacing. In a classic example of technological change, the glass factory soon was closed.

Walter began part-time work while still in grade school, delivering the Wheeling *Register* in predawn hours for more than two years. On the way home from his route he paid his trolley fare with a newspaper apiece for the motorman and the conductor—and that included passage for the little red wagon he had built to facilitate his daily chore. On the way home young Reuther also tossed a third free copy into a friend's yard. His aim at the friend's stoop eventually failed and the *Register* crashed through a front window.

Athletics held greater attraction for him than a paper route. Walter and Roy spent much time at the *Turnverein,* the German gymnastic center, and both played basketball in the Luther League. Their team won a three-state tournament. Although Roy was an inch taller, Walter always jumped at center because of the remarkable spring in his legs. In summer they played baseball. Walter pitched and Roy was shortstop. Roy once considered a career as an athletic instructor but *Vater* convinced him it was a frivolous choice.

Amidst the fun and work, adversity struck. Valentine was thrown out of work with the closing of the Schuhlbach Brewery when West Virginia adopted a "prohibition" law in 1914. Trying a new field, the elder Reuther and *Mutterchen* opened a small lunchroom in the basement of a nearby home. They catered to factory workers on their lunch hour. Then, in a freak accident, a bottle of homemade root beer exploded, embedding glass fragments in Valentine's right eye. With all the pain, he resisted anesthesia, fearing the doctors might remove the eye while he was unconscious. Rather than that, he took a gulp of whiskey and clamped his teeth tight while two men held him down and the physician plucked out the glass splinters. The eye had to be removed eventually. It was a shattering psychological blow to Valentine and he could not work for months. Once recovered, he opened an office to sell insurance to his considerable circle of friends and former co-workers.

During World War I the rise of anti-German sentiment was as evident in Wheeling as elsewhere in the country. A can of red paint was splashed across the front door of the Reuther home, reflecting, perhaps, antipathy not only toward the family's German origins but toward Valentine's radical views.

Vater's old Socialist hero, Eugene V. Debs, was convicted of sedition for speaking against American involvement in the war and was sent to the federal prison at Moundsville, West Virginia. Taking Walter and Victor, Valentine Reuther made a pilgrimage to see him. "I remember," said Victor, "the terrible feeling when I saw those enormous iron bars. And then I met this kindly man." As the Reuthers left the prison, Valentine wept—a sight the boys did not forget. Just a few years earlier Valentine had run for Con-

gress, without success, on the Socialist ticket. He had been a passenger on the Debs "Red Special" presidential campaign train. To
Valentine, the fiery Debs symbolized the concern for the downtrodden and the belief in social change that he was championing
on a smaller scale in Wheeling.

After the war, hard times continued for the Reuthers. Eldest
son Ted left school after finishing the eighth grade and took a
job in the paymaster's office at the Wheeling Steel Company. Adding to family troubles, Anna Reuther suffered through a lengthy
illness after the birth of her only daughter, Christine. Valentine's
pride kept him from borrowing money and Victor recalls that, as
a consequence, the family had "many and many a meal when the
menu was boiled potatoes and perhaps a can of tuna fish."

Walter got a part-time job in a bakery shop, and his father hoped
he would learn the trade. The 15-year-old did not care for the
working conditions. As he said later: "I used to start at six o'clock
in the evening and I worked until eight the next morning. At five
o'clock in the morning I had to clean the dough mixer. That is
what discouraged me. I just couldn't see cleaning dough mixers for
the rest of my life."

At Wheeling High School Walter found a greater attraction. "I
was almost totally absorbed in the school machine shop," he said.
"I almost lived in that shop. That's really where my mind and my
heart and my soul were at the time. The result was that I didn't
devote much time to some of my academic studies . . . and I got
a bad mark in algebra."

Brother Ted at about this time learned of an opening at Wheeling Steel for an apprentice tool and die maker, an opportunity that
came only once in four years, normally. Although Walter's parents
were not pleased to see him leave school before finishing his sopho-
more year, they consented and he was hired. The beginner,
naturally, got the dirtiest job—oiling the pulleys that kept the machines going. After a year as handyman, he was transferred to
the tool and die department for instruction. Dies, made from
specially hardened metal with very sharp cutting edges, are used
in many industries to stamp gears and other parts from softer
metals. Precision is a watchword with the elite corps of die makers.

Walter's pay on his first full-time job was eleven cents an hour. "I worked my tail off," he once stated. But he rebelled against Sunday and holiday work. There is a legend that he was fired by Wheeling Steel as the youthful leader of a stay-home strike one Columbus Day. But in fact, he left the company because he was attracted by higher pay offered in Detroit, then as now the automobile capital of the world.

Before leaving Wheeling, however, and at the age of 17, Walter was maimed in a factory accident that probably explains a complaint he registered several years later about inadequate safety precautions in a plant in the Soviet Union where he found employment. With three other workers he was moving a huge die when their hands slipped on its oily surface. The 400-pound object crashed down on Reuther's right foot, shearing through the shoe and slicing off his big toe. Leaving the Wheeling works by ambulance, Walter demanded that his friends bring the severed toe to the hospital. He was fearful that without it his career as a basketball center would be ended. The toe was produced and Walter insisted it be sewn in place, although the surgeon was certain it could not be saved. Like his father, Walter refused any anesthetic because he suspected his wishes would not be followed if he were unconscious. The toe had to be amputated anew a few days later.

The patient also balked at taking prescribed pills, tossing them out a hospital window. Once discovered, he had to take his medicine under the reproachful eyes of his nurses.

Despite the pain, Reuther learned to walk upright again, and even to play basketball. Forty years later, however, a new pair of shoes would renew the pain and remind him of his accident at Wheeling Steel. For the rest of his life, he vowed, he would try to wear soft, comfortable, sometimes shabby, old shoes. "I was lucky," he said. "If the die had crashed a few inches further back, it would have taken off my whole foot."

Walter's earnings helped the family balance the budget, toward which Ted also was contributing, and allowed younger brothers Victor and Roy to finish high school. Their father wanted each of them to learn a trade. Roy became an electrician, specializing in house wiring. Victor thought of becoming a plumber but, perhaps because he was more bookish, gave it up after a summer of digging ditches as an apprentice. He also thought about becoming a lawyer but this did not please Valentine, who regarded the law as a "highbrow" profession; in this case, *Vater* was overruled, if only for a time.

The father's greatest contribution to the education of his four sons, apart from the lessons implicit in daily living, was a series of "bedroom debates" that gave them basic training in oratory and a good grounding in social issues. For several years the Sunday ritual of the Reuther family hardly varied. *Mutterchen* and the children would go to church in the morning, and at noon the family assembled for its biggest meal of the week. After dinner Valentine and the boys adjourned to the master bedroom to practice forensics. The elder Reuther normally assigned debate topics to his sons in advance. The boys argued about child labor, women's suffrage, Prohibition, military conscription, labor's rights, and other issues far beyond the intellectual grasp of most of their contemporaries. They did their homework in the Carnegie-endowed Wheeling Public Library.

A demanding master, Valentine sat behind a small desk at one end of the room and the four sons gathered around a table, two on each side. The father not only acted as moderator but criticized the arguments and kept an alarm clock within reach to help him enforce an equal time rule. To keep the boys alert, he occasionally assigned those who had prepared a negative argument to advocate the affirmative. Sometimes the voices of the participants rose to such volume that little sister Christine thought they were fighting; Mrs. Reuther would comfort her.

"We each had pretty good schooling in soap-boxing techniques," Victor acknowledged later. "We lived in a family where, from the time we learned to talk, we were told social injustice presents each person with a personal responsibility. Our father insisted on getting our point of view on every important development. Once we spoke, he would insist that we defend our positions. By the time we went to work, and then went off to college, we had acquired a zeal for social justice which naturally made the expression of our views in class, at meetings, and later in union organization to be almost an instinctive response."

Walter Reuther's early years were filled with hard work, serious discussion of social issues, and simple pleasures. The father, imbued with an idealism that encompassed deep faith in the essential goodness of man, was the single strongest influence on his personality and thought. *Mutterchen,* the quiet homebody, contributed a gentleness and strong religious faith. Together, the elder Reuthers prepared their sons for the world of organized labor in much the way Joseph P. Kennedy taught his boys how to succeed in the equally competitive realm of politics.

At 19, after three years at Wheeling Steel, Walter felt ready to head for Detroit to exploit his new skills as a tool and die maker. "I hear they need men at Ford's," he told his mother, while munching some of her *apfelkuchen.* "I am leaving for Detroit as soon as you can get me packed, Mother." A friend from the shop accompanied him on his first long trip away from home. Anna Reuther worried about her boy. Valentine assured her, "You'll be proud of him some day." She prayed he was right.

CHAPTER TWO

The Die Leader

WALTER REUTHER PICKED JUST ABOUT THE WORST POSSIBLE TIME to go to Detroit to find work in the auto industry. When he arrived in February 1927, unemployment was massive. Ford had shut down production of its famous Model T and was retooling for the revolutionary Model A. This threw thousands of jobless men into the streets, most of them standing in long lines before factory employment offices. Despite near-zero weather, the lines often formed before dawn because of the desperate competition for the few openings. Ever since Henry Ford's dramatic $5-a-day pay policy began, the auto industry's reputation for high wages had drawn men to Detroit from the Deep South, the mountains of Kentucky and Tennessee, and the farmlands of Ohio and Indiana.

For Walter, the combination of high pay and work in the major industrial citadel was irresistibly attractive. He left Wheeling Steel with co-worker Leo J. Hoars and together they tramped Detroit's sidewalks. Walter's credentials were not overwhelming. Having quit high school after his freshman year and neglecting to complete his formal apprenticeship, he was, moreover, a newcomer to the industry. Also, he appeared very much a country boy. "I was 19 but I looked like 16 with my red cheeks, red hair, and complexion of a 13-year-old girl," he conceded later. "I looked as if I'd just fallen off a green apple tree."

His family's relentless spirit and his own boyish self-confidence kept him going. "I was a very hard kid to discourage," he said. "I stood in line at four in the morning trying to get a job." Persistence paid off and he was hired at the Waterloo plant of the Briggs Manufacturing Company, an auto body firm with a reputation for sweatshop operations. Reuther was put on a thirteen-hour night shift—from 5:30 P.M. until 7:00 A.M. with half an hour for lunch. The pay was 85 cents an hour, the work rough and heavy. When shop backlogs permitted, he worked as many as 21 days without a break. It was a wearying regimen, even for a young man who neither smoked nor drank and who prided himself on staying in peak physical condition.

Two months later Reuther lost little time in replying to a Ford Motor Company advertisement in the Detroit *Free Press* for veteran tool and die men capable of directing groups of their skilled colleagues in retooling work on the Model A. Die leaders, as these specialists were called, usually had some gray in their hair, but Walter was not deterred by lack of years or experience. Hopping a bus for Ford's Highland Park plant, which awed him by its size, he found the employment office closed and a 260-pound guard barring his entrance. When Reuther explained that he was a die leader, the guard scoffed: "Come on, you're just a kid. Get the hell out of here!" Thus began a two-hour conversation during which Walter argued successfully that the guard could not tell for certain he was not a die leader simply by looking at him. "He let me in out of sheer desperation," Walter believed. The hiring officer inside the plant was equally skeptical, demanding, "How did you get in here?" Reuther persuaded him that a higher authority should examine his credentials and Ford's master mechanic was summoned. When this veteran craftsman saw the russet-headed stripling, he exploded, "Look, I'm in no mood for jokes this morning!" Walter, spotting a roll of blueprints under the mechanic's arm, appealed for a chance to be tested on his knowledge. Taken up on the proposal, he answered technical questions well enough to get hired as a bench hand, but only for a two-day tryout period. The delighted Reuther, hurrying back to Briggs to pick up his toolbox, encountered another obstacle, this one demonstrating that his work was valued there. The night superintendent tried to talk him out of quitting, offering a ten-cent raise and day work, but Walter balked. "If you can be arbitrary, I can be arbitrary," vowed the superintendent, refusing to grant clearance for the removal of the toolbox in a last effort to pressure Reuther into changing his mind. Finally, at 6:00 A.M., the supervisor yielded and Ford's newest hire took a taxi, bending his budget, to start work there on time. Although exhausted after Ford interviews and arguments at Briggs that deprived him of sleep for a 36-hour stretch, Reuther passed the tryout test and his starting pay on the new job was set at $1.05 an hour. In April of 1927, that made him an aristocrat of labor. The average manufacturing worker's hourly earnings were but 54 cents at that time.

Despite his relative affluence, Reuther lived modestly. He rented a room in a boarding house and joined the YMCA "to get rid of some of my excessive energy" in the swimming pool and gymnasium, where he began playing basketball again. After finishing his night shift at 1:00 A.M., he often took a long walk and cold shower before going to bed. His closest approach to dissipation was chewing gum.

In these early Detroit days, Walter Reuther was trying to find himself and his life's work. Early indecision on choice of a career was reflected in a questionnaire he filled out when joining the YMCA. Asked, "What is your life's ambition?" he gave two replies: "Labor leader or chicken farmer." Retelling the story, he quipped, "You know, the General Motors Corporation has told me repeatedly that they thought I would have made a damned good chicken farmer."

Another spare-time activity was a flying club composed of Ford employes. After working almost a year to build a glider, but before completing it, they chipped in money to buy a Jenny, a biplane of World War I vintage, to pull the glider. Not long thereafter, two club members, flying the Jenny to Detroit from Chicago and eyeball navigating along the tracks of the Michigan Central Railroad, lost their way in a snowstorm and made an emergency landing in a cow pasture, breaking the propeller. Walter and others went to the scene the following weekend, repaired the plane, and it was flown home. "Then one of the boys was killed in the Jenny and that kind of broke our spirits," Walter said. The glider never was completed and the club eventually disbanded.

At Ford's, Reuther later worked on the first wind tunnel models for the Ford tri-motor, the famous "Tin Goose" of pioneer days in commercial aviation. The models probably were the first ever built for wind tunnel testing, and in those days young Reuther toyed briefly with the notion of becoming an aeronautical engineer.

Throughout the Detroit years Walter maintained his close family ties. He sent half his pay home to his parents until he was 21, when his father returned the first post-birthday contribution and wrote, "I won't take any more money from you." Following his mother's advice, Reuther opened a savings account in Detroit. When he went home for Christmas, *Mutterchen* brought out her red "mother's wine," a sweet vintage made from grapes grown on the family property. Sister Christine, 15 years younger than Walter, begged him tearfully at the end of each visit not to return to Detroit. Moved by the child's appeals but unwilling to leave his work, Walter asked his mother to keep Christine away from the partings.

On the job Reuther never became "one of the boys," although he joined occasionally in the shop enthusiasms that reflected the speculative spirit of the late 1920's. One fellow worker talked him into buying ten shares of Kelvinator stock to ride the Wall Street boom. Another saw riches in real estate so Walter bought a lot in nearby Dearborn in partnership with his older brother, Ted. A baseball fan on the day shift in the tool room failed repeatedly, however, to persuade Reuther to report the Detroit Tigers' baseball scores when relieving him in late afternoon. "Reuther, you're the dumbest bastard I ever knew," was his conclusion.

Management was good to the young redhead. His foreman at Ford's was so pleased with him that he invited Walter to live with his family. Reuther declined, fearing such a move would arouse jealousy in the plant and bring promotions unrelated to performance.

He realized, however, that his failure to complete high school could inhibit his career possibilities and decided, shortly after his twentieth birthday, to complete his education, attending classes during the day and working a shift from 3:30 P.M. until 1:00 A.M. The schedule allowed him only a few hours of sleep on school days since he usually began studying when he arrived home and kept at his books until three or four o'clock in the morning.

Reuther found that most of the students were five years younger than he was. One of his few contemporaries was Merlin Bishop, a former Illinois coal miner who operated a crane at Ford's new River Rouge plant, where Walter now worked. The two decided to form a club of older boys who were working and attending classes. "When I asked who would be president, Walter said he wouldn't be part of any organization he couldn't be president of," Bishop recalled years later. "There was no contest, really. He was elected president and I was elected secretary." Adopting their English teacher's suggestion, they named the organization the 4-C Club, with the C's standing for Citizenship, Confidence, Comradeship, and Cooperation. Club members rented movies and showed them in the school auditorium. They sold candy and soft drinks at football and basketball games. Money they raised was put into a student loan fund to help poor youngsters go to college. The high school principal hailed their efforts and so did the local chamber of commerce. "Walter and I were paraded before the Rotary Clubs and the Kiwanis Clubs as officers of this dynamic organization," said Bishop.

Reuther, the redeemed dropout, proved to be a brilliant student, graduating from Fordson High School at the age of 22. Merlin Bishop became a valued friend and, later, an ally in the pioneer drive to unionize the auto industry. A younger brother, Melvin Bishop, also belonged to the 4-C Club and in time became active in union organizing, although his path and Walter's parted in bitterness a quarter-century later.

At work, Walter was advancing steadily. His pay eventually climbed to $1.45 an hour and he became the foreman of 40 tool and die makers at the Rouge. After getting his high school diploma, he enrolled at Detroit City College with some thought of becoming a lawyer, influenced perhaps by younger brother Victor, who had begun a pre-law course at the University of West Virginia. Walter urged Victor to come to Detroit so they could study for the bar together.

The Reuthers' optimism was shattered, if only for the moment, by the stock market crash that began in October 1929 and deepened the following year. The Great Depression that followed sent unemployment soaring to 12 million or 25 percent of the work force, by 1932. While millions of Americans suffered, most federal government officials churned out cheerful forecasts, with President

Herbert Hoover predicting prosperity "around the corner." Walter
kept his job, but the misery he saw in Detroit had a lasting influence, helping to revive the radical political views preached by
his father. One associate, however, attributed Walter's aroused
political consciousness to the influence of Victor, who moved into
an apartment with his older brother. As Merlin Bishop saw it:
"When Vic came . . . he got Walter all steamed up about the Socialist movement. I think Walter had pretty well forgotten about
it up to that point. . . . He was a very frugal fellow, and invested
his money, so I think at that point he was more interested in making money. His mind hadn't got onto social problems . . . until Vic
came and got him stimulated." It should be noted, however, that
Walter had been motivated earlier to join Bishop in establishing
the 4-C Club.

The Reuther brothers entered City College, then holding classes
in Detroit's Central High School, in the fall of 1930. Beginning
with a pre-law course, they gave that up after a visit to police
courts to watch attorneys in action. Overhearing corridor talk
about stratagems to fool the jury, they were disillusioned and decided to concentrate on sociology and economics.

With Walter taking the lead, a Social Problems Club was formed
at City College. Elected president, he took club members to picket
lines and invited Socialist and pacifist leaders to address them.
Norman Thomas, then the perennial Socialist Party candidate for
President, was one. The club was affiliated with the League for
Industrial Democracy, a campus-oriented national organization that
was founded in 1905 as the Intercollegiate Society of Socialists. At
that time, reformer-novelist Upton Sinclair urged that Socialism be
taught on the campus somehow, since it was not part of the standard curriculum. Clarence Darrow and Jack London helped get the
national group established and early members included Walter
Lippmann and Ralph Bunche. Its name was changed to League for
Industrial Democracy in 1921 because the word "Socialist" had
become decidedly unpopular with most Americans since the Russian Revolution of 1917.

The Reuthers did not lack for causes. Walter took student demonstrators to the picket line at the Briggs body plant, where a union firebrand named Emil Mazey was a strike leader. In a campus fight over the establishment of a Reserve Officers Training Corps unit, the Reuthers rallied opposition in the tradition of pacifist grandfather Jacob. At one anti-ROTC rally Victor made the opening speech and Walter gave the closing arguments. The brothers also fought against a ban on Negro students at a hotel swimming pool used by the college, with Walter organizing a picket line for the first time. The arrangement to use the pool was canceled. The Reuthers even put together a crude book, pasting up pictures and text to show the contrast in living conditions between Detroit's poor and the affluent residents of suburban Grosse Pointe. Merlin Bishop remembers that poverty was ever visible from the apartment he shared with Walter and Vic: "We used to see people walking with nothing but burlap bags on their feet, go into the garbage cans, looking and hoping there would be something there."

Bishop and the Reuthers soon were joined by Roy Reuther in the two-bedroom apartment and, while the others worked, Victor did most of the cooking; all shared in the rest of the household chores.

Walter and Victor developed an unusually close relationship in their studies. "Their minds were like one," Bishop discovered. "Walter would start a theme and then say, 'Vic, you finish it up— I've got to go to work.' " Victor did so under a unique arrangement with their professors that permitted the brothers to submit a single paper.

Occasionally the roommates explored the facts of life more directly. "We used to go on what we called whore-ology tours at night," says Bishop. "After studying until eleven o'clock, we'd go out . . . and, just for interest, talk to these girls on the street. Once we won their confidence and they knew we weren't detectives, they would talk freely. This was quite a revelation." Life in the apartment often was jovial, with the *gemuetlich* Reuthers singing German folk melodies or spurring lively conversation. In a more serious moment the three brothers pledged to remain single and dedicate their lives to the cause of labor. The self-imposed celibacy was short-lived, however; all were married within five years.

As the Depression worsened, Walter Reuther turned to adult political action for the first time. He and brother Victor, along with several friends, jumped into the presidential campaign of 1932 to champion Norman Thomas. President Hoover, who was equivocating about the economy, claimed little more than their contempt, and they saw no real alternative in the Democratic nominee, Franklin D. Roosevelt, who ran on a platform advocating a balanced budget and reduced federal spending. The Reuthers did not believe Thomas could win in 1932 but they felt that Roosevelt, if elected, would be unable to do any better for the nation than the Republican administration. In their analysis, a strong Socialist showing in 1932 could help assure victory in 1936 over the two major parties, which by then, they believed, would be discredited.

Armed with lists of old Socialists compiled in the heyday of Eugene Debs, Walter Reuther and Merlin Bishop planned a tour of Lower Michigan with stops at Lansing, Muskegon, Grand Rapids, and Traverse City. Victor and a friend headed for Upper Michigan. Preparations were thorough. Bishop's seven-passenger Buick brougham was refitted to sleep two persons. A platform was hooked onto the back bumper and an eight-foot wooden sign, anchored to the roof, urged Michigan voters to "Vote for Norman Thomas—Repeal Unemployment." The old Socialists hailed "Comrade Reuther" for his speeches ridiculing Hoover. In heavily conservative areas Walter sometimes was able to overcome resistance through ingenuity. Warned that one city might prevent the holding of a Thomas rally downtown, Reuther told the city manager that he and Bishop wanted to speak on "applied Christianity"—their euphemism for Socialism. The naive city manager gave his approval. Like his father, Walter was an enthusiastic soap-boxer. "He could sit with a chicken farmer and talk economics for five or six hours," says Bishop. "He was very warm that way."

Even in Dearborn, dominated by ultraconservative Henry Ford, Reuther outfoxed the city fathers. Dearborn police predictably refused to issue him a permit for a rally in behalf of the Socialist ticket. Undisturbed, Walter drove his Model A Ford—with custom-built speaker's platform in the rumble seat compartment—onto a vacant lot and began making a campaign speech for Norman

Thomas. "Pretty soon the cops came, as we knew they would, and said that we couldn't make a speech because we were on private property," he recounted. The officers did not know the property belonged to him; it was the lot he and brother Ted had pooled their savings to buy. "I had my deed with me, and so I flashed that. They were rather perplexed." Recovering their aplomb, the police pounded stakes along the lot boundaries, insisting the audience not step beyond them. Later in the campaign, Walter drove back to Wheeling in the car, plastered with Thomas stickers, and organized a West Virginia meeting for his candidate.

With all the exertions of the Reuthers and others, Thomas got only 39,205 votes in Michigan—a tiny fraction of the total.

Even during the campaign Walter worked steadily and was one of the highest paid craftsmen at Ford's, while millions were jobless. As production slumped, wages began to slide, too. One day, pay was cut five cents an hour in the morning and another five cents an hour in the afternoon, infuriating the hapless Ford workers. In his quiet unionization efforts there, Reuther even had learned sign language to communicate with three deaf mutes in his department. Until the double pay cuts took effect, however, they showed little interest in his message. Then one of them slipped him a note: "Let's start the Revolution." It was a not-implausible dream under 1932 conditions.

Early in January 1933, Reuther was fired from his $1.45-an-hour job at Ford's and turned in his badge, Number X-1162, for the last time. Then 25, he never knew whether he was discharged because of union leanings, Socialist campaigning, or a Depression-caused lag in auto production. In any event, he did not brood about the reason because he and Victor already were talking about making a workers' tour of the world.

"I came home that night feeling I had been liberated," he said later. "I told Vic, 'I've been fired. Now I'm free and nothing stands in our way. We can go on that trip.'"

CHAPTER THREE

Europe 1933

BARRED FROM THE ROUGE, WALTER REUTHER SOUGHT A JOB AT a primitive auto assembly plant being constructed near Gorki, in the Soviet Union. A stay in the new Communist state, he thought, would fit perfectly with his plan to travel around the world. The Amtorg Trading Company, the business arm of the Soviet government, was hiring American technicians to teach peasant laborers how to build automobiles. Amtorg already had purchased from the Ford Motor Company a complete set of dies and machinery for producing the Model A, a simple and durable vehicle suited to rugged Russian roads. Although the Ford company would have no traffic with union organizers, it was quite willing, for a price, to deal with the Soviets even though the United States government had yet to accord diplomatic recognition to the U.S.S.R. As part of the Ford-Amtorg arrangement, Ford technicians were sent to the Gorki plant and Russian craftsmen went to the Rouge, all for the purpose of transplanting American mass production techniques.

Already on the Gorki payroll—the plant was known formally as the Molotov Automotive Works—was a dedicated American Communist and former co-worker of Reuther's named John Rushton. Fired from the Rouge for Communist activities, he had been hired by Amtorg and had moved to Gorki with his family. When he learned that Reuther too had been dismissed from Ford's, he recommended the employment of his old acquaintance from Detroit.

Reuther, when approached by an Amtorg representative, was eager; he had been in touch with Rushton and the offer was not a total surprise. Like many American radicals of the day, especially in such centers of Depression misery as Detroit, he still regarded the Communist experiment as offering the workingman some hope of building a bulwark against economic injustice through social planning. As an active Socialist, he also welcomed the opportunity to participate in the Soviet attempt to translate Socialist theory into practice.

Amtorg had reason to take a special interest in Reuther. As a Ford craftsman he had been one of the few skilled enough to be entrusted with such delicate tasks as fashioning dies for the Model A headgasket, work that involved precision cutting of soft brass a mere fifteen-thousandths of an inch thick. Since the Soviets had purchased but a single set of Model A dies, many of which were certain to break down quickly during use, the Molotov Works needed technicians to make replacements and, equally important, to train Russians to do the same.

Reuther's bargaining position was so strong he could insist that Amtorg hire Victor, too, although the younger brother had little shop experience and meager skill.

On the way to Gorki the Reuthers intended to make a "social engineering" tour of Western Europe. Their aim was to visit factories and mines, to exchange ideas with trade union leaders and young Socialists, and to visit their mother's relatives in a troubled Germany coming under Nazi rule.

Victor explained years later why they looked forward to an arduous and prolonged self-exile: "It was the kind of interest and concern that stimulates many of our young people to join the Peace Corps today—to go to Africa, to Latin America, or to India." As for their desire to work in Russia, "there was a lot of excitement about seeing a country that was terribly primitive and backward moving into the modern industrial age." Walter stated: "We planned this world tour to get a practical background for our future work; that is, we felt if we were going to do anything useful in the way of economic sociology, we would have to have a practical background to tie up with our academic training."

After waiting a few weeks for Victor to reach his 21st birthday so he could apply for a passport without parental permission, the Reuthers dropped out of City College, never to complete their courses, although Walter had earned 60 hours of credits. The older brother withdrew bank savings of a little more than $1,600 as a joint travel fund. Two weeks later the governor of Michigan ordered the temporary closing of all banks in the state. Many never reopened.

In early February of 1933 the Reuthers paid a farewell visit to their parents in Wheeling. They had left their Detroit lodgings without wakening brother Roy, who was weary from strike duty at Briggs. Their other housemate, Merlin Bishop, had no inkling they planned to be gone more than a few months or, for that matter, to work overseas.

The brothers, in conversations with the elder Reuthers, broke the news bit by bit. Walter remembered their parents "didn't know where we were going to be, or when, or how long." However, he was convinced "my folks understood the need for young people to reach out and do the things they wanted to do." Victor recalled that the parents "were not terribly happy about the prospect of a lengthy separation."

In the evenings during the home visit Walter took Victor to the machine shop at Wheeling High for a "short refresher course" so he could qualify as an instructor of the Russian peasantry.

On February 16 the brothers sailed third class from New York on a German-operated liner, arriving at Hamburg eight days later. While they were at sea, they later learned, Detroit police broke up Roy's picket line at Briggs, giving him a scar he bore for life when they shoved him into a spiked iron fence.

Using letters of introduction to trade union leaders and young radicals, the brothers arranged free lodgings in Hamburg, spending one night with a jobless dock worker who welcomed them because they brought greetings from a nephew in Detroit. After reading in the German-language press about the mysterious fire that had destroyed the main building of the Reichstag, symbol of short-lived German parliamentary democracy, they hurried to Berlin where they took a Nazi-conducted propaganda tour of the ruined building and saw and heard enough to strengthen their opposition to the Hitler regime.

In Berlin the Reuthers received unexpected and disappointing news about the prospective jobs in the Soviet Union. Through the local Amtorg office they learned they could not proceed to the Molotov plant until housing was available. Although they had anticipated some delay, they now faced the prospect of marking time indefinitely.

With their letters of introduction the brothers found quarters in a communal hostel operated by a group of student radicals. Inas-much as all leftists were prime targets for Hitler's strong-arm squads, Merlin Bishop was not surprised when the Reuthers "wrote us stories how . . . they had to go down a rope from a student's apartment when the Storm Troopers came in the front door." Vic-tor remembers that they jumped from the window. Whatever the precise circumstances, the Reuthers apparently had a close call; Walter remarked that "I'm sure if we had been found there, our passports wouldn't have done us much good."

Among the escapees was a trade union activist named Emil Gross. He joined up with the Reuthers and together they traveled south through Dresden to Nürnberg and thence to Stuttgart, close by the native village of *Mutterchen* Reuther. From there Gross crossed the frontier to Switzerland and safety.

Through Gross, the Reuthers were enlisted as helpers in an un-derground anti-Nazi network. Because they were fluent in German, held American passports, and had warm testimonials from radicals in the United States, they were recruited to carry secret messages across the German frontier. Gross moved to Amsterdam, set up an underground group he called "The New Beginning," and dispatched the Reuthers on errands that Walter recounted in melodramatic, spy-tale fashion:

> We would leave London, where we had made a contact, and we would go to a designated bookstore in a small Ruhr town. We would ask, just as if we were ordinary customers, for a certain very rare, unusual book. The bookseller would tell us, "I'm sorry but I don't have that book." We would pretend sur-prise. "But," we would tell him, "we were recommended to you. We were told we could buy the book here." The bookseller would insist he was sorry, there must have been some mistake; he had never carried such a book. "Well," we would say then, "we are very anxious to get this book. Do you know another bookseller who might have it?" Then he would give us a name and we would go on to the next bookseller and begin all over again. Sometimes we would make as many as eight contacts in this fashion before finally we reached the person we were sup-posed to see and deliver our message to.

Gross later returned to Germany to contine his work in opposition to Hitler. He was arrested and sent to a concentration camp. The Reuthers had presumed him long dead when, in the winter of 1958, he turned up at Victor's Washington office; by then he was a prominent publisher of trade union periodicals in West Germany.

One of the first major stops in Germany for the Reuthers was their mother's native Scharnhausen. There they found that their relatives were strongly opposed to Hitler and Nazism, except for an uncle who was vice-mayor of the village. With him, Walter recounted, "we had some very rough arguments."

Being young and unattached, the brothers were delighted to find two girls, their cousins, who gladly accepted invitations to accompany them to a *kino* in Stuttgart. The Reuthers went because the featured film was the first big Nazi propaganda effort in that medium. They wanted to see for themselves this facet of Hitler's appeal to the Germans. At the conclusion the swastika emblem was flashed on the screen and the audience rose to give the stiff-arm, palm-down Nazi salute and sing the *"Horst Wessel"* song. The two Americans kept their seats and the girls did the same. It was a bold challenge to the emotionally charged audience and, in retrospect, probably an unwise one. Patrons at first murmured at the nonconformists, then began shouting: "They're Communists! Throw them out!" The Reuthers quickly began jabbering to each other in loud English, hoping their American accents would establish their identity. There was a good bit of pushing and scuffling and, as Victor tells it, "We got our cousins to hell out of there as fast as we could." He concluded that, even in those earliest months of the Hitler regime, the choice facing Germans was to "conform or pay the price."

The "most horrible" personal experience came in May of 1933 when the brothers witnessed a Nazi ceremony atop a hill overlooking their mother's village. Scores of Storm Troopers tossed trade union banners onto a bonfire, proclaiming they would build their Third Reich upon the ashes. When union men reached toward the flames to save their flags, Victor reports, "they were brutally beaten in front of the whole village." He recalls the "pained expression" on the face of the Lutheran pastor who, though disapproving, felt powerless to intervene. The two Americans noted that Hitler's terrorism was evident not only in Berlin and other cities but "even in this most remote village."

In Stuttgart the Reuthers bought bicycles and set out on a continental tour that took them through eleven countries by the end of the year. Victor remembers:

> . . . It was a rather inexpensive way of travel. They were ordinary bicycles we bought in Germany. No motors. We used the muscles in our legs. We traveled about sleeping in very inexpensive inns and, wherever possible, youth hostels. Sometimes, when weather permitted, we would sleep in fields or haystacks. I remember one unfortunate experience in France, in the battlefield areas of Verdun. French farmers were not very happy about wandering youths sleeping in their haystacks; they were fearful of cigarettes igniting them. So we were always very careful to turn off the lights on our bicycles before heading for a haystack. It was very dark this particular night and we thought we clearly saw the outline of a haystack. Dead tired, having cycled more than 100 kilometers that day in rather bad weather, we stretched out our tarpaulin only to discover—the next morning—that we'd been sleeping on a manure pile.

The Reuthers pedaled through France and into Italy, arriving in Rome during the Fascist exposition and hearing Mussolini orate from the balcony of his palace. It was their second exposure to authoritarian rule. Next stop was Vienna, where the brothers marched proudly in what proved to be the last wholly free May Day demonstration before the Nazi *Anschluss.*

Returning to Germany, as they did repeatedly during the year, the Reuthers visited Munich's *Hofbrauhaus,* where Hitler and his followers had met in the 1920's to plan a *putsch* that failed. Victor recalls, "We had arrived in Munich late in the evening . . . and were rather tired, and our diet was slim. Neither one of us was a drinker, but, when in Munich do what the *Muencheners* do. So we always wanted to see this enormous beer hall and we went there. . . . I rather jokingly challenged Walter to drink a full litre of heavy bock beer. We both downed one, but I think that if either of us had entertained any inclination to become a drinker, that cured us—that one experience that night." Walter often cited the Munich experience as prompting his almost total abstinence from alcohol, unusual among labor union leaders. Victor remained the more convivial of the two.

Cycling through France again, the Reuthers boarded a channel steamer for England. Says Victor:

> Sometimes we had to eat a lot of the dirt of the road if we followed behind a heavy truck. . . . It was a bit dangerous. I remember in England, on the outskirts of Stratford-on-Avon, we were cycling on a road which had been freshly covered with very fine stone but not wetted down with tar. The stones were loose. We had learned the tricks of taking advantage of air suction, or lack of air resistance, behind a huge truck or van. On a good road it was reasonably safe to take that advantage and cycle close behind a big truck. But we made the mistake of doing this on a road that was freshly graveled. The truck swerved and Walter had to turn his cycle sharply. It ripped off the front tire and he went head-over-heels into the road, and he got a terrible gash on his arm. . . . I dragged him aside and flagged a passing car, which took us into the nearest village for medical care for Walter. For at least three weeks thereafter I would hold the handlebar of his cycle, which we'd had repaired, and sort of help him get seated on it and give him a push, because he had one arm in a sling. I cycled beside him until we came to a hill and he couldn't cycle any more. I'd grab the handlebar and hold it until he got off. . . . We didn't have the money to stay in one place [while Walter's arm healed]; had to just keep going along. . . . There were many times, even in that first year, when we were sort of tempted to turn back.

Despite the accident, the brothers got full satisfaction from their tour of England. They visited the Ford, Austin, and Morris auto plants, saw mines and textile mills. Also, they attended the annual Trade Unions Congress at seaside Brighton and were struck by what they regarded as almost total apathy toward the Nazi threat from Germany. Walter associated the apparent lethargy of the British labor movement, as evidenced at Brighton, with the lackadaisical attitude back home of the established American Federation of Labor.

After their travels through England and Scotland, with stops along the way to exchange views with like-minded workers, the Reuthers returned to the Continent and, after cycling through the Low Countries, were back in Germany in the autumn. They were in time for the first national elections under the Nazi regime—the first in which voters had no choice but to vote *ja* or *nein*.

The brothers were keeping in touch all the while with John Rushton at the Molotov plant, they imploring and he seeking to find a way through the bureaucratic maze that was delaying their planned journey to the East. Rushton did what he could, which apparently was considerable. Soviet visas were forthcoming in December 1933, barely days after Franklin D. Roosevelt established diplomatic relations with the Communist state. Without Rushton's help, said Walter, "we might have had to wait two or three months longer." Their cycles in tow, the Reuthers boarded a train that would carry them across Poland and all the way to Moscow.

CHAPTER FOUR

Russian Adventure

THE TEMPERATURE IN MOSCOW STOOD AT 35 DEGREES BELOW zero when the Reuthers arrived for an overnight stay between trains. "We had no proper winter clothing with us," Victor relates. "We were wearing knickers and long but thin stockings. It was not a very pleasant arrival." Next stop was Gorki, the old city of Nizni Novgorod on the Volga River some 250 miles east of the Soviet capital. There they pushed their way aboard a rickety streetcar bound for the factory site six miles up the intersecting Oka River. The lurching vehicle was so crowded that some passengers sat on the roof. With knapsacks on their backs and suitcases in hand, the Reuthers stood in the aisle, immobile in the crush. "When we got off the tramway at the edge of the construction," says Victor, "both of us found that our jackets had been very neatly slit open and the contents taken out. Fortunately, we didn't have very much money in there at the time, and no important documents; our passports and such little money as we had were carried in belts under our clothing."

Through deep snow, the brothers walked about a mile and a half to a village of two-story wooden barracks built to house foreign workers. It was called the Commune Ruthenberg or, more informally, the "American Village." Scores of Detroiters had preceded them there, forming the backbone of the skilled labor force at the Molotov plant. Also living in Ruthenberg were British engineers, Finnish experts in concrete construction, and political refugees from Italy, Austria, and Germany. Some lived with their families in quarters barely larger than a single room. There were no kitchens in the barracks and residents shared cold water taps in the hallways and common lavatories. In short, it was a jerry-built international settlement set down beside a very old peasant village dominated by onion-shaped church towers.

"There was very little in the factory when we arrived excepting the power plant and a couple of shells of structures . . ." reports Victor. "It was just a big construction area." The Reuthers were assigned to the tool room, where 25 to 30 other foreign technicians already were employed. Since the newly arrived Americans spoke no Russian, they conversed with Soviet workers—the peasants they were hired to train—through other foreigners, who spoke German and Russian. One interpreter was Leo Dvorny, who had worked in the Western Electric plant at Cicero, Illinois, before moving to the Commune Ruthenberg in 1931. Dvorny was an elected deputy to the Gorki Soviet. Victor has described the types of Americans they found at the Molotov Works:

> You had the straight technician who was there because he was hired to do a job. He may have been interested in a unique kind of experience but he had no political attachment or political commitment. Then you had some who had a Communist background in the United States, or a political sympathy with the Soviet Union. This was especially true of some of the . . . Finnish-Americans who went there. It was true of some others of Russian background, Polish background. And some native-born Americans went there because they believed in the Soviet concept. They were not many in number.

The Reuthers were the youngest foreign employes in the plant and worked an eight-hour day, six days a week. The factory operated around the clock, with three shifts. Walter and Victor were paid in rubles, which were valueless outside the country. Pay was based on skill and production. "In some months," says Victor, "Walter made as high as 400 rubles and I made 280 to 300. A sweeper during that period . . . was getting somewhere around 80 or 90 rubles a month."

At the outset, working conditions were primitive in the extreme. Recalls Victor: "The only heat in the whole building was in the small heat treatment department where metals were tempered. Otherwise temperatures were 30 to 35 degrees below zero at the workbench. We found those early weeks very difficult. We'd work for half an hour and then go into the heat treat room for a few minutes and come back again." The Reuthers wore large felt boots over flannel swaddling wrapped around their feet. Heavy wool gloves and fur caps that covered the ears also were part of their daily uniform that first winter, and with the arrival of trunks they had shipped before entering Russia, they enjoyed the warmth of sheepskin coats purchased in a Detroit pawnshop.

Walter worked on major die-making projects. Victor's task was to teach simpler chores to peasants out of backward Volga villages. "Most of them," he says, "hadn't seen anything more complicated than a wheelbarrow or a pitchfork before. To teach them to work with precision instruments—height gauges and micrometers—and to build precision tools that would function within tolerances of a tenth of a thousandth of an inch was no easy matter under those primitive conditions. But they did learn, and they did build the automobile." Eager students, the Russians were extremely warm and friendly toward their American teachers.

As foreigners, the Reuthers enjoyed a somewhat better food ration than their Soviet co-workers. Even so, they went without butter and fresh meats for months at a time. Victor regarded the special cafeteria for the foreign colony as the most pleasant place in the entire settlement: "One day the Italian immigrants would cook and we'd have spaghetti. The next day it would be the Poles' turn and so we had some variety." During breaks for meals during the working day, however, the Reuthers ate with their Russian colleagues, ". . . out of, I suppose, youthful enthusiasm and a display of camaraderie." The Russian diet was spartan: "The normal meal was a big chunk of black bread which would stay moist for six months, I think, and a bowl of cabbage soup, or a cereal the Russians call *kasha*." Another advantage enjoyed by the Reuthers and other foreigners was access to a special store offering some items not then available to Soviet citizens.

The Reuthers began their new life with tremendous enthusiasm, doing volunteer work, participating in an endless round of meetings after their shifts ended, patronizing the "Red Corner" social center. Their excitement was expressed by Walter in a letter published in the English-language Moscow *Daily News* about a month after his arrival:

> I have always pictured the Soviet Union as a beehive of social and industrial activity, but it was not until I arrived that I realized that even in my most imaginative moments I had underestimated the scope of Socialist construction.

At the Gorki Auto Plant model building a vast amount of technical machinery greeted us. Here, as in all other socialized industries, is an industry with unlimited possibilities and potentialities.

There are so many striking things here that I dare not attempt to enumerate them all: the Red Corner, shop library, the numerous shop meetings where serious problems are discussed, the frank criticism exchanged between the workers and the administration, and the multiplicity of cultural activities connected with shop life.

I must confess that all these things are foreign to me as one who has received his training in a capitalist auto plant.

                                              WALTER F. [sic] REUTHER

Walter's enthusiasm, at that point, apparently was not dampened by the fact that the plant, after three years of construction, was producing very few automobiles. In fact the dies and machines to make the Model A were hardly in place, inasmuch as the Ford Motor Company did not part with them until, from Ford's standpoint, they were made obsolete by the introduction of the revolutionary V-8. Earlier, the Molotov Works had been nothing more than an assembly point for knocked-down Model A's shipped from the United States. Reuther was not blind to Soviet failings, however, and sent a lengthy complaint to the Moscow *Daily News*:

> The shortcomings responsible for the greater percentage of inefficiency in the Gorki Auto Plant are administrative in character. This is the conclusion I had formed after working for one month in the plant and keenly watching how the work is organized.
>
> Let us take the question of the monthly program. On the first of the month our department, to take one example, is given a list of dies that it has to construct as its contribution to the monthly program. The brigadier receives the list on the first of the month but the blue prints, castings and steel with which to construct the dies may be received any time from a week to two weeks later.
>
> Sometimes 90 percent of the job is received but the entire job must lie dormant because of the missing 10 percent. As a

result of this "system," the first half of the month sees inefficient work and the second half a mad rush to complete the program with quality being sacrificed.

If we filled our shop with the most competent and highly skilled or specialized die makers, we would still be faced with the month-end jam and inefficiency, as this problem lies beyond the sphere of technology and can be solved only through proper administration.

Instead of trying to build dies on a distinct monthly basis why not stagger the program so that there is a constant flow of new work into the shop and a steady flow of finished dies out.

This would ensure sufficient work for both bench and machine men at all times and result in higher quality as well as increased quantity.

Another glaring example of administrative inefficiency is the matter of part prints (this is a print of the part of the auto that the die is to make, such as hub cap, radiator cap, head gasket and so on). The part print is indispensable in the construction of dies, being more important than the print of the die itself.

In highly organized shops such as the Ford Motor Company when the question of design or construction arises, the part print is always consulted for the final decision. I am amazed to find that in the Gorki plant, part prints were available for less than 25 percent of the dies constructed. As a result, many dies have to be reworked and often rebuilt.

The furnishing of these part prints is not a technical problem; the prints are already made and on file in the engineering department, it is merely a question of seeing that a copy of the part print is sent to the shop along with the die prints.

Disregarding safety measures is another matter reflecting on administrative laxity. The administration seems to be under the illusion that safety measures are entirely divorced from efficiency, something more or less superfluous.

In our department, for example, heavy dies and castings are moved by a heavy crane. In every efficiently organized shop, safety holes are drilled in heavy dies and castings to allow for the use of lifting hooks. I could not find a single die in which these holes had been drilled.

What is the result? I watched a crane man and two hook-up

men trying to put a heavy casting on a machine; they struggled for an hour trying to get the casting to balance on the cable. Several times it slipped and fell to the floor. At last they hoped it would stay balanced and held their breath as they watched the crane man swing the casting over towards the machine.

As the casting swung over the edge of the machine, the jerk of the crane stopping threw the casting off its balance and it came crashing down on the machine, and as the machine man jumped aside to safety, the casting fell to the floor. It might have cost thousands of rubles had the casting fallen on the vital parts of a delicate machine, or it might have cost a life. Two rubles at the most would have been the cost of putting safety holes in this particular casting.

If the situation is to be altered then it must be done through the administration. Somebody must be made responsible for the enforcement of this question.

W. REUTHER

EDITOR'S NOTE: Such cases should be taken up with BRIZ (Bureau of Workers Inventions.) We are sending a copy of this letter to the Gorki Auto Plant BRIZ.

Reuther's complaints were of a kind with those expressed by Charles E. Sorensen, production expert of the Ford Motor Company, following a 1929 visit to the Soviet Union in which he negotiated the arrangement for creating the Gorki plant. Sorensen found that "a few weeks as consultant in Soviet Russia gave me a liberal education in how not to do things and forever erased from my mind the fear that bureaucratic Communism can successfully compete with free men." Victor tells that Walter's letter of complaint "created some unpleasant moments for the factory management, but they learned the hard way on these things." As Walter put it: "The way to beat the bureaucrats was to get Moscow's ear. They had respect for technicians there." That he succeeded in getting a Moscow forum for his suggestions is evident from a series of his letters published in the *Daily News* in the ensuing months. A second critical letter was followed by a report in the Moscow daily that the head of the foreign bureau at Gorki had been reprimanded by the presidium of the trade union committee for being impolite in dealings with alien workers; he was warned "that energetic measures would be taken against him should there be any repetition of this."

Reuther's published attacks on the managers of the plant had no ideological content. He wrote as a craftsman dismayed at the contrast between the Molotov Works and the Rouge. There was, however, a heavy ideological background to life in the factory. When the Reuthers exceeded their production quotas, small red banners would be placed on their workbenches. Those who lagged felt the moral pressure of working beside little burlap flags. Ideology also played an important part in after-hours' shop meetings. For example, most foreign die workers—and the course the Reuthers took on this matter was never disclosed—signed the following pledge at one shop session:

> We the foreign workers and specialists of the die department of the Gorki Plant, having read Stalin's report to the 17th Congress of the CPSU [Communist Party of the Soviet Union], pledge ourselves to further study this report and make it our guide in our future work in the building of the classless socialist society.
>
> In answer to Voroshilov's report we pledge ourselves to do all in our power to assist in the speedy upbuilding of the auto industry both by transference of our knowledge and skill to our Russian comrades and by honest *udarnik* work [meaning that performed by skilled shock troop workers], so that the Red Army will not suffer want of cars or trucks to crushing any foreign imperialist army that violates the borders of the workers' and peasants' fatherland.

When May Day came the Reuther brothers were in Moscow's Red Square for the parade marking Communism's big holiday. They stood with a delegation from Gorki "a very short stone's throw from Joseph Stalin." Walter was interviewed by the Moscow *Daily News*: "I arrived last year, and have been impressed by the scope of technical and social activities here. Imposing as the plant is, its human aspects are, to a Ford worker especially, bound to be even more absorbing. In the Red Corner at lunch intervals a wonderful spirit of camaraderie is to be found among the workers. A foreman produces a guitar, strums a few chords. A greasy mechanic and a red-kerchiefed *Komomolka,* forgetting work, swing into gay dancing. Everybody keeps rhythm, shouts, and laughs. I enjoy every moment here!" He pronounced the Molotov Automotive Works superior to Citroen in Paris and Mercedes-Benz in Frankfurt, two of the factories he and Victor had visited. "It is the best plant on the continent." But he drew contrasts between managerial inefficiency and red tape at Gorki and the way things were done at the Rouge. He said die production quotas were "irrational," worthwhile suggestions from workers were pigeonholed, and foremen lacked needed powers to make decisions. He also grumbled about needing a sleeve for a machine during night work: "The department had fifteen such sleeves, but the tool crib was found with none. Workers had taken them and locked them in their drawers. We found ourselves unable to do a rush job for want of an essential tool—yet our department has more tools per worker than Ford's." He suggested that tools be checked in at the end of each shift and that if any was missing, a man's time card be lifted until it was returned; that's the way it was done at the Rouge, he reported.

A few days later the Moscow newspaper claimed production at Gorki had climbed to 130 vehicles a day. By June the Molotov Works was making its own wheels. Unreported went the fact that secret tooling was underway for a different type of vehicle—the military tank. The Reuthers found themselves making many dies having military application. Victor recalls: "It was openly discussed in meetings that the rise of Hitler posed a very direct military threat against the Soviet state and the Soviet people. It is amazing that that early, already, there was widespread concern among the people." The die workers' pledge was a reflection of that.

At about this period Reuther was quoted in the *Daily News* as saying the plant had experienced an "earthquake" that supposedly would ensure speedier consideration of suggestions. However, he viewed the reformation with considerable cynicism, fearing it would represent "only a short spurt" and soon be forgotten.

The Reuthers were driving as hard as ever to make the plant a carbon copy of the efficient Rouge. They were honored as *udarniks,* or shock troop workers. Walter was proclaimed a "Hero of Production" and became the *Stakhanovite* leader of a 16-man shock brigade. As the Moscow *Daily News* made evident in an editorial, the brothers were members of the working-class elite in the supposedly classless society: "Nothing is more honorable in the U.S.S.R. than the name of an *udarnik,* no method of work is more creative than shock brigade work and Socialist competition." This type of competition could have its comic aspects, as Victor has related:

> There was much to-do inside the factory about the fact that the Soviet society was concerned with creating more than just material wealth; it was trying to develop a new kind of human being, one who had a cultured life and good social outlook. So there was a great promotional campaign that sometimes took on rather curious aspects.
>
> The department we worked in, the tool room, challenged the neighboring brake drum department to what the Russians called "Socialist competition." Which department could contribute most to elevating the cultural level of their workers? Well, many weeks passed and nobody had come up with any great ideas. There were many, many meetings and discussions, speeches, and so forth. Finally, the brake drum department sent a delegation out looking for something that would add a touch of culture. They sent a group with a truck all the way to Moscow, which was quite a distance, and they came back with a load of artificial palm trees. They put these all through their department. . . .
>
> Well, we were put to shame in our department because we hadn't yet come up with anything quite so dramatic to raise the cultural level. . . . We put our heads together and decided that, gee, if we could just get some metal spoons for the cafeteria, so that when we ate the soup and *kasha* we didn't have to use old wooden peasant spoons . . . it would be a symbol of the cultural progress being made.
>
> We sent a committee out to try to find spoons—and where do you find them? They weren't available in the whole Volga area. . . . So we decided on our own free time to build a die to stamp soup spoons out of scrap fender metal. We didn't have any

tumbler to take the burr, or rough edge, off. But otherwise they looked like a regular American soup spoon. . . . We ran off enough for the whole department, and there was a great celebration when we took these up to the cafeteria. The brass band was out, and special banners were made and speeches were delivered that this marked another significant step forward in raising the cultural level.

I must admit that the following day I returned to the cafeteria with considerable new enthusiasm because I relished the thought of eating with a more sanitary metal spoon. I got back there and there wasn't a damn spoon in sight. They'd all taken them home with them.

There was another big meeting, with protests made about stealing state property, the workers' property. But everyone knew we couldn't supply the whole Volga countryside with soup spoons. Henceforth a new procedure applied. One would enter the cafeteria, surrender his factory pass which had his picture on it, and he would get a soup spoon. Going out you would return the soup spoon and get your pass back.

We won the Socialist competition with the brake drum department.

Late in July the Reuthers and other foreign *udarniks* at Gorki were rewarded for loyal work with a 22-day boat trip down the Volga to the Caspian Sea and back. The regime granted this type of reward instead of pay increases. Before returning to the Commune Ruthenberg, the brothers had seen the Donbas Basin, a mining area, and such cities as Yalta, Batum, and Baku. Years later Walter found occasion to tell Nikita Khrushchev about the trip:

> In the stores there was always one kind of canned goods we could readily buy—*Amerikanski* corn, because the Russians did not eat corn. When we got to Baku we bought four cans of corn, took it home, and found it was pork and beans. The cans were so old the labels had worn off. We went back and asked for eight more cans, specifying we preferred ones without labels. The man at the store said it was the same with the paper or without. . . . We again found they were all pork and beans. As a result, we lived like capitalists for a while.

The spring and summer of 1934 marked an especially pleasant period for the Reuthers. They lived within easy walking distance of the Oka, where there was a fine beach and excellent swimming. (Ford's man Sorensen had been startled on his visit to the prospective plant site to see men and women swimming nude together.) The brothers also enjoyed departmental picnics, and outings aboard small boats powered by Model A engines.

With the passing of the months came some facility in the Russian language and development of warm friendships with Russian workers and their families. The Reuthers had a particularly close relationship with one Vladimir Vladimirski, a trainee who subsequently became leader of the tool room. Victor remembers him as "a very bright, very intelligent and very sensitive human being." They also enjoyed the company of Russian girls for, as Victor puts it, "Walter and I were both single and the Russian winters are very long and the Russian nights are very much longer still." But he says neither developed any serious attachment.

Victor got his first date by asking interpreter Dvorny how he might learn Russian more quickly. "Oh," said Dvorny, "you pick up a young *dyevochka,* you go walking with her, and you will learn very quickly." Victor tells the rest:

> I had my eyes on a little *marushka* who issued height gauges and micrometers. With Dvorny's encouragement I consulted my *knizhka,* my dictionary that I carried around in my pocket, to learn the words to ask her, "Would you like to go walking?" She said she would be delighted.
>
> Then I thought, well, perhaps if it rains we should make plans to go to the club house or the theater. I wanted to ask, "What should we do in the event it rains? *Yesli dozhd budyet?*" But instead of saying *dozhd,* I said *doch.* I discovered I had asked her, "What shall we do in the event there is a daughter?"
>
> Well, despite all the stories of the immorality of Russian girls, this one blushed purple with indignation and turned angrily on her heels and wouldn't speak to me. . . . Down the craneway I went looking for Dvorny. . . . *"Durak,* you fool!" he said, "you'd better apologize." . . . So I went back to her. But by that time it had occurred to her that I was just another stupid for-

eigner. And we went walking and there was neither *dozhd* nor *doch*. I learned a little Russian—and whatever else I learned has not complicated my life.

A quarter-century later, after Walter had a rather acrimonious dinner meeting in San Francisco with the visiting premier of the Soviet Union, Khrushchev got his revenge in the pages of the trade union newspaper *Trud*. Under the headline, "GET ACQUAINTED WITH MR. REUTHER, LACKEY OF THE MONOPOLISTS," Walter's old friends Rushton and Vladimirski, still living in Russia, were quoted as describing him as an evil, avaricious man. Moreover, a woman identified only as "N" related that at age 19 she had married Walter Reuther in Gorki after an acquaintance of one week. She was quoted:

> . . . He vowed his love at first sight. He said he had dedicated his life to the workers and needed a true girl friend.
>
> He spoke about the chains of capitalist labor which must be broken, about bloodthirsty exploiters—my God, what he didn't talk about. Anyone's head would have been turned, let alone an inexperienced girl.
>
> Soon after we got married he stopped talking about politics and I no longer heard beautiful speeches about class struggle. There was next to me merely a miserly, reticent man. He reiterated without end that one must be careful with money.

After they had lived together eight months, the account went on, Walter announced, "I am leaving for America," and promised to write but never did. In a formal statement Reuther replied that the *Trud* attack was "based on complete fabrication and falsehood." Editorially, the Detroit *News* summed up the reaction of most Americans: "The Russians, who have a talent for abuse that approaches genius, have surpassed themselves in their vilification of Walter P. Reuther. The UAW president has been assaulted with a variety of unkind nouns and adjectives in his own country, but it took Moscow to decide that he is a bigamist."

On October 4, 1934, the Moscow *Daily News* published a rare

Reuther letter—rare because it contained no complaint about management of the Molotov factory:

> The international Commune Ruthenberg at Gorki has just had a harvest festival.
>
> Blistered hands, stiff backs, and aching muscles, all free gifts of the day's potato digging *subotnik,* were all forgotten in the swing and rhythm of the songs and dances.
>
> The American group pepped up the evening by singing several popular songs. The Italian group came back with *"O Sole Mio,"* and everyone caught the spirit of the occasion and thunderously rendered several Russian numbers. There were also several vocal and instrumental numbers given by some of the talented members of the group.
>
> Each week during the spring and summer, members of the commune, body builders, designers, die specialists, and other workers would go out to our garden armed with spades and hoes and do their share in the struggle to win from nature the fruits of the soil. Our well-supplied commune table is sufficient testimony to our success.
>
> Besides a good supply of tomatoes, beets, carrots, and other vegetables that the commune enjoyed all summer, the commune gardeners were able to report a harvest of two and a half tons of potatoes, over 500 head of cabbage, and about 50 pumpkins.
>
> We are sure that as a result of the experience we acquired this year, our success for the coming year should be even greater.
>
> WALTER REUTHER

This was part of a volunteer labor program that became all too familiar to Gorki workers. Because the plant was draining labor from nearby farms, factory workers were drafted to plant, cultivate, and harvest. When unskilled labor was needed to build a "Socialist City" beside the plant, the Reuthers helped level the ground and plant trees and flowers. In the plant itself they worked overtime without pay to finish rush projects. "During the early months following our arrival," says Victor, "we were perhaps more impressed by the degree of response than we had reason to be. . . . We later came to realize that there was considerable moral pressure brought to bear, and people were afraid to be looked on as laggards and shirkers." Volunteer work was a key to advancement and to membership in the Communist Party. After a time, there seemed to be a perpetual state of emergency requiring volunteers. Many of the workers joked about it. Even so, Walter and Victor saw merit in the system. "I think we both genuinely felt," relates Victor, "that much of this was in the interest of the nation's development. We weren't there just to teach them how to build tools and dies. We were anxious that they get good housing and that they have an opportunity to begin some kind of cultural life. . . . We understood full well that this country was going through a very difficult period."

In October the Reuthers had an opportunity, relatively unusual for Americans, to sit through a Communist Party "cleansing" at the plant. Victor explains it:

> Those who are members of the Party, those who are supposedly the elite, are compelled to sort of stand public trial by their contemporaries in the shop and be answerable for their conduct, and also to respond to specific questions . . . about political matters and political theory. . . . The actual interrogation of course is done by the shop leaders of the Communist Party and they sort of put them over the hurdles in the presence of their colleagues in the shop, who may or may not be members of the Party.

As a result of the cleansing, the Moscow *Daily News* reported, nearly 15 percent of the 3,719 Party members and candidates at the plant were expelled. "The chairman," said the newspaper, "criticized the situation in the factory, pointing out that stoppages amount to 13 percent of working time, that spoilage this year is higher than in 1933. . . ."

In November the Reuthers visited Leningrad, just days before the assassination of Sergei M. Kirov, once a close associate of Stalin's and a Party boss in the city. The murder of Kirov, now widely believed to have been staged by Stalin agents, signaled the start of the bloody purges of the late 1930's that ultimately claimed an estimated three million victims. In the Gorki plant, as in others throughout the Soviet Union, a mock trial was held, supposedly using the same evidence produced in a Leningrad courtroom against the alleged assassin. Party chieftains in the plant, with the Reuthers and others looking on, tried to relate events in Leningrad to the Molotov Works—to convince the laboring force that enemies of the state may lurk anywhere and should be ferreted out, with their cooperation. A continual search for saboteurs, already in progress before the Reuthers arrived, was given new impetus.

Walter talked later about seeing women and children appearing puffy-eyed in the cafeteria, the breadwinner mysteriously absent: "The others in the dining hall knew that any gesture of comfort to the stricken family, even just asking them what had happened, would be interpreted as sympathy, and they might well be the next victims just because of such a gesture." One night the Reuthers heard the knock of the secret police on a neighbor's door. Victor says:

> He was an Italian political immigrant and married a young Russian woman. He took out Soviet citizenship and was working in the factory. I worked with him every day on the bench. He had the room just next to Walter and I. We knew him very, very well. The knock on the door came at three o'clock in the morning. We couldn't help but hear it. As a matter of fact, we opened the door to see what was going on. The secret police came and arrested him—took him away. No explanation was given to his Russian wife. No explanation was given to anyone. The word was circulated in the plant the following day that it was discovered he was in league with Trotsky. But there was no trial, and nothing was ever heard of him again. . . .

Although such experiences were a source of disenchantment with some aspects of the Soviet experiment, the Reuthers were not totally disillusioned. As Victor has said: "It was a very inspiring thing to see people out of very remote peasant villages getting technical training in trade schools, acquiring skills in factories, moving into much more modern and comfortable apartments which were being built. . . . To see people who had been so long denied and suppressed . . . awakening to new opportunities in this century was a

very exciting thing. But it was at a great price." Progress, if modest
by American standards, was evident nearly everywhere. The factory
now was well heated. The Reuthers had won a battle to equip tool
room workers with aprons designed to prevent their baggy clothing
from getting snagged in the machines. After their arrival the
brothers were disappointed that it took several months to produce
a single stamp or die. But after 22 months on the job, and with only
two or three foreign specialists still in the shop, Russian labor was
turning out three and four dies a month. Here is how Walter sum-
marized the experience:

> We were enthused over the eagerness of the workers to learn
> technique. They were in a new world, building factories and
> machines. They were like kids in toyland. But we were disillu-
> sioned by the workings of bureaucracy. There was a tremendous
> power down below, on the workers' level—lots of pioneer en-
> thusiasm. But the power of the state interfered. There was a
> Party secretary in every department of the plant, and he had
> more power than the superintendent of the department. This
> went on clear from the bottom up, until there was no considera-
> tion at the top for the people down below. Vic and I had Amer-
> ican passports and could leave. Unless you've been there, you
> don't fully appreciate what it means to have to stay.

Armed with rubles they could not spend elsewhere, the Reuthers
left the Soviet Union at a leisurely pace, making an 18,000-mile
tour of the country. Because of their *udarnik* work, they were permitted to visit areas normally closed to Americans. For nearly three
months they hiked through the Caucasus from Tiflis to Ordzhoni-
kidze, skirted the borders of Turkey, Iran, and India, traveled by
bus and train to Tashkent, Samarkand, and Bukhara, lived with
peasants, coal miners, and steelworkers, and crossed the Kara-Kum
desert. Because they wanted to traverse Siberia by rail, they had
to backtrack to Moscow to board the Trans-Siberian Railroad.
The Russians permitted them to use rubles to buy tickets for the
entire ten-day train trip to Harbin in Manchuria, recently occupied
by the expansionist-minded Japanese and now called Manchukuo.
    The Reuthers found themselves sharing the journey with a very

pleasant traveling companion, a talkative Englishman named Hayley Bell, who said he operated an aluminum plant in the Far East. During the long ride he quizzed them at length about the Gorki plant and their experiences in the Soviet Union. They welcomed the opportunity to discourse to the appreciative listener.

At the Manchurian border the English-speaking trio was detained by Japanese authorities. The border guards told Bell his visa was not in order. When the Reuthers pointed out that theirs were the same as his, all three were taken off the train. By the time the American brothers were able to convince the Japanese they were innocent tourists, the train had left and they were forced to wait several days for another. Not until after World War II did they learn why they were detained. Winston Churchill, in the House of Commons, paid tribute to the late Hayley Bell as Britain's principal secret service agent in the Far East before the war. The ostensible aluminum magnate was a lieutenant colonel in His Majesty's Service —and he had pumped the Reuthers dry of everything they knew about Gorki and the Soviet Union. Bell was the grandfather of British actress Hayley Mills.

Proceeding to Harbin, the Reuthers ran short of travel funds and cabled their parents to cash in some insurance policies and forward the proceeds. Their route then took them to Mukden, Peking, and Nanking, where they boarded a riverboat for Shanghai. Walter once told a *New York Times* Forum:

> I was going down the Yangtze River at the height of the 1935 flood and they were evacuating flood refugees from one side of the river to the other. There was a Chinese junk that had about 40 men and women and children in it, and our boat hit that Chinese junk and threw all of these Chinese people into the water and they all drowned before our eyes.
>
> My brother and I protested that and the Chinese captain of the boat laughed at us. He was very philosophical and he said, "You don't understand China." We said, "We may not understand China, but it's wrong to let people die when not a finger is raised to save them." He said, "Six million people will starve in China this year because the crops have been destroyed."

When men in search of food tried to leap aboard the steamer as it left Hankow, Sikh deck hands clubbed them to death and threw the bodies overboard.

The Reuthers had hoped to visit India but, through letters from Roy and others back in Michigan, they learned that the trade union cause was moving forward in the American automobile industry. Boarding a boat in Shanghai, they sailed across the East China Sea to Japan, where they bought bicycles and make a quick tour— followed much of the time by police who had been alerted, apparently, to their association with Hayley Bell. Says Victor: "At every inn we stayed in there were three cups of tea served. Walter and I became accustomed to it because one was for him, one for me, and one for the policeman who was sure to come."

Looking back across the years, the Reuthers may have tended to romanticize about the interest shown them by the Japanese authorities. It seems quite plausible that the Japanese wanted from them—after their nearly two years in the Soviet Union—no more than Hayley Bell had already gotten.

In Yokohama, the brothers contacted the American consul and, through him, secured employment on the homeward-bound cruise ship *President Harding*. Victor was a deckhand and Walter worked in the engine room. They returned to Wheeling, West Virginia, in the autumn of 1935, spending their sea pay for cross-country tickets from San Francisco. They had been away nearly three years.

CHAPTER FIVE

Open Shop Town

WHEN THE REUTHER BROTHERS RETURNED TO DETROIT LATE IN 1935, the city still was an "open shop" citadel despite efforts by the American Federation of Labor and the fledgling Roosevelt Administration to aid the workingman's cause. Caution and lack of familiarity with mass production industries hampered the AFL. And Franklin D. Roosevelt's assistance was inconsistent during his first years in the White House because of his limited insight into the realities of industrial relations, and the fact that other national problems commanded more urgent attention. However, Walter and Victor Reuther noted several encouraging developments that had occurred during their work and travels abroad. The Wagner Act, endorsing collective bargaining and providing machinery for representation elections, was put on the books, although many employers felt confident it would be struck down by the Supreme Court. The worst of the Depression seemed past. And John L. Lewis, breaking with the staid AFL leadership, had committed himself to organizing auto, steel, rubber, and electrical industries.

Yet, as the brothers checked around Detroit, they found the scene rather discouraging: Unions were weak or nonexistent in the giant auto corporations. Elaborate spying systems were being used by employers to penetrate the few labor organizations that did exist and to report promptly to management any sign of union sentiment in the shops. Thousands of unemployed provided instant replacements for workers who did not toe the company line. Job security and seniority were not part of the industrial vocabulary. The handful of strikes that had been called were smashed, usually with the aid of the Detroit police. Occasionally, skilled craftsmen walked off their jobs, only to discover that splinter strikes did not halt production. A reputation for high pay, traceable to Henry Ford's dramatic $5-a-day offer in 1914, drew enough new recruits to Detroit to serve as an effective strikebreaking force.

Leon Henderson, a federal economist, made one of the most

intensive studies of the auto industry for a 1935 report to the National Recovery Administration. Of assembly line workers, Henderson wrote: "The fear of layoff is always in their minds. . . . The speedup is thus inherent in the present situation of lack of steady work and an army of unemployed waiting outside. . . . The automobile industry has set a new low age for displacement of workers. Men near 40 find great difficulty in securing jobs with the industry or being rehired after layoffs. Labor unrest exists to a degree higher than warranted by the Depression. The unrest follows from insecurity, low annual earnings, inequitable hiring and re-hiring methods, espionage, speedup, and displacement of workers at an extremely early age." Backing up his findings on espionage, Henderson reported General Motors had paid $419,000 to the Pinkerton Detective Agency in less than three years. Chrysler had paid another detective firm $211,000 and Ford had enlisted 3,000 men in a "Service Department" that discouraged union loyalties.

The assembly line itself had been another source of hostility for many years. Men felt chained to this "iron horse" that knew no fatigue and dictated the pace of their working lives. The sheer boredom of auto factory life has been summed up this way: "One man may, for example, hold six bolts for another man to tighten on each car as it moves by. That may mean roughly 250 bolts an hour; 2,000 bolts a day; 500,000 bolts a year. How does this affect a man's life if he keeps at it year after year?"

Historically, Ford's paternalism and unrelenting hostility toward unions had set the tone for Detroit's labor relations. Ford's suppliers had followed his lead and even his competitors were influenced by his conservative philosophy.

Long before the Reuther brothers appeared in Detroit, Henry Ford's pioneering decision to use the assembly line led to the first labor strife in the industry, with the shop hands' cause being championed by the radical Industrial Workers of the World. When the Model T was introduced in 1908, the jack-of-all-trades mechanic was the key production worker. But Ford hired a factory expert, Walter E. Flanders, to modernize his plant and, within a year, was exploiting the essentials of scientific mass production.

Ford turned out 10,000 cars in 1909, a record at the time. The Flanders system was a bonanza for management but the work force suffered. With the advent of the new techniques, Ford abolished bonuses for good production and returned to flat hourly wages. For the average man in the plant, the pay dropped to $2.34 a day, the prevailing wage in the area.

The assembly line system proved unpopular and Ford's workers began leaving in large numbers. By 1913, Ford conceded, turnover was tremendous. The company had to hire 963 men to keep 100 on the payroll. Constant supervision, monotonous jobs, fewer rest breaks, and a crowded plant led thousands to quit.

The IWW, or Wobbly movement, began to concentrate its fire on the Highland Park plant. In speeches outside the gates, IWW agitators labeled Ford a "speedup king" who operated a "sweat shop." Although many Wobbly speakers were arrested as soon as they hit the soapbox, their campaign for an eight-hour day and unionization persisted. The word on the grapevine was that the Wobblies would strike the plant in the summer of 1914.

Ford's business manager, James Couzens, provided a dramatic solution. Faced with labor unrest and the Wobbly threat, Couzens conceived the Five-Dollar-Day wage and, disclosing it on January 5, 1914, made it seem solely a humanitarian gesture: "We believe that social justice begins at home." The response was greater than Ford and Couzens had anticipated. The next morning 10,000 job seekers practically stormed the gates. A migration of clerks, farm boys, lumberjacks, miners, and sailors headed for the Ford plant. In the bitter cold of daybreak a week later, thousands of men were jammed together outside the hiring office, walling off the entrances by weight of numbers and unintentionally preventing Ford workers from getting to their jobs. When police tried to clear a path, the crowd became a mob and fought for two hours before being dispersed by icy jets from fire hoses. Stones and bottles pelted police and factory windows were smashed in the melee.

Once the $5-a-day system was put into effect, turnover nosedived and absenteeism was virtually eliminated. Management had its pick of the labor force and increased the speed of the assembly line. Efficiency soared. In his autobiography Ford stated, "The payment of $5 a day for an 8-hour day was one of the finest cost-cutting moves we ever made. . . ." Not all workers got the $5, however. Excluded were women, unmarried men under 22, married men involved in divorce suits, new employes, and others regarded by Ford as undeserving.

Ultimately, Ford's move brought higher pay and a faster pace to the entire auto industry. Workers' resentment was subdued during the prosperous 1920's, although a Communist Party publication, *Ford Worker* priced at a penny a copy, had a circulation of thousands in the Ford system. In 1926 the AFL convention directed President William Green to unionize the auto industry. Paul Smith, a professional organizer, was put in charge and cautiously tested sentiment in Detroit, Chicago, Milwaukee, and St. Louis. A report from the latter city was typical: "Eight men who had signed an application at our meeting Friday night were discharged Saturday morning." Worker militancy was further undermined when Ford's discontinuance of the Model T threw 100,000 men out of work in 1927. About 60,000 in the Detroit area alone were idled for six months to a year while the company retooled for the Model A.

Detroit's greatest shock was, of course, the Depression that followed the October stock market crash of 1929. Henry Ford emerged from a White House conference a few weeks later with an announcement intended to build confidence: a $7-a-day minimum wage in his plants. But the magic effect of the original $5-a-day plan was missing. Auto production skidded. In 1929, before the crash, more than 470,000 men had worked in Detroit's auto plants. By 1931 the employment total fell to 257,000 and the city's relief rolls climbed to 211,000. Another 150,000 workers had gone back to farms or small towns to wait out the Depression. Those who kept their jobs took pay cuts that lowered the average wage to $17.57 a week.

A Chevrolet assembler recalled conditions in a Buffalo plant in those days: "It was always speedups. . . . You were hired in the morning and could be fired at noon. You would start at 50 cents an hour. . . . If you got up to 70 cents an hour you'd come back after layoff at 50 cents. . . . A fellow would work there five or six years and he'd be laid off, . . . unless you'd be painting the boss's house or cutting his grass."

Emil Mazey, who later became secretary-treasurer of the United Auto Workers, belonged to the Citizens' Unemployed League in the early Depression years and has described some of his anti-poverty activities: "We had a squad of men who were experts on the light meters. We'd go around to the houses of people who'd had their lights turned off and we'd jump the meter and turn them on again. We could do it with the gas, too, but that was a little harder. After a while the company fixed us by pulling the pipes out. We didn't think we were breaking any law."

In March 1932 the Communist Party sponsored a mass march on the Ford plants at Dearborn to dramatize Depression depriva-tion. The election of liberal Frank Murphy as mayor of Detroit had led to reduced restrictions on radical protests, and the Com-munist "Hunger March," as it was called, formed in Detroit with several hundred jobless men of all political persuasions in the ranks. The announced goal was to present a formal petition to Ford man-agement for jobs or company-financed relief. Detroit police es-corted the peaceful procession to the city limits, where Dearborn police waited with tear gas bombs and a warning that force would be used to disperse any marchers who crossed the boundary line. After rally leaders decided to go forward, tear gas shells were pumped into the marching column. Demonstrators retaliated with bricks, stones, and frozen mud. The main battle came at Gate Three at River Rouge. Ford executive Harry Bennett ordered plant police into the fray, then was hit and seriously injured by a flying brick as he stepped from his car. Moments later, police opened fire on the crowd. Four marchers were killed and a score or more were wounded.

The funeral of the four men was a Communist propaganda show, yet it attracted thousands who were neither Party members nor sympathizers. At least 10,000 persons marched in the cortege and spectators stood four deep in respectful silence along Detroit's sidewalks to view the red-draped caskets. Some mourners wore red armbands or red berets. Before another crowd of 30,000 in Grand Circus Park, leftist orators praised the Communists and trade unionism. The dead were lowered into nearby graves to the tune of the "Internationale."

Labor strife began to increase. An early union target was the Briggs Manufacturing Company, a major Ford subcontractor, where a citizens' committee found some workers had been paid as little as ten cents an hour for a fourteen-hour day. To Henry Ford, it was "the biggest surprise of my career" that Briggs workers walked off their jobs. As noted earlier, Roy Reuther was an active participant. In 1933 more than 100 plants were shut down by strikes, if only briefly, despite massive unemployment.

The AFL's latest auto organizer, William Collins, found militant workers clamoring for action. He counseled restraint in most instances, and the auto unions complied. Under the terms of their AFL charters, local officers depended heavily on Federation resources for financial aid and for guidance, especially where strikes were concerned. In one meeting where strike fever was high, an AFL leader reacted by turning off the lights in the meeting hall and gaveling a quick adjournment. Another weakness of the AFL approach to the auto industry was its insistence that workers in a plant be parceled out into as many as a dozen separate craft unions that claimed jurisdiction over them. Auto workers felt this fragmentation undercut their bargaining power.

Franklin D. Roosevelt's inauguration offered new hope to the downtrodden. The National Industrial Recovery Act, with its famed Section 7-A broadly guaranteeing labor's right to organize, was enacted in the New Deal's first "Hundred Days." John L. Lewis of the Mine Workers was quick to place his own interpretation on the new law, telling labor: "The President wants you to unionize. It is unpatriotic to refuse." Lewis did not mention the lack of machinery to protect workers against employer reprisals, and most AFL leaders, suspicious of government intervention of any kind in union concerns, held back; they sent only one organizer to Detroit for still another try at breaking the united front of the auto industry. To ward off any concerted AFL drive, which probably bulked largest in the imaginations of employers, many companies set up management-dominated unions to create a facade of compliance with Section 7-A.

Richard T. Frankensteen, a trim operator making 49 cents an hour at Chrysler's Dodge plant in Detroit, became an employe representative on a works council set up by the company after NRA took effect. He found that many of his co-workers on the council were more interested in currying favor with management than voicing grievances. Dealing only with minor issues, the council ignored Frankensteen's well-researched analysis showing that pay scales would not provide a decent standard of living even if workers held their jobs on a year-round basis. "When it came to economics you might as well have talked to the moon," Frankensteen said.

One Dodge unionist with a reputation for militancy, John Andrews, became a close friend of Frankensteen's. They took a summer vacation together with their families, and Andrews' uncle bestowed gifts on Frankensteen's child. It was only after the La-Follette Civil Liberties Committee began an investigation of employer espionage that Frankensteen learned that Andrews and his uncle were Chrysler spies and had reported his every move and conversation.

The NRA, headed by General Hugh S. (Ironpants) Johnson, dealt a blow to auto unionism in its first code of fair competition for the industry. It included a "merit clause" that allowed employers to hire, retain, or promote workers on the basis of individual merit, decided by the employer alone, without regard to membership or nonmembership in any organization. The AFL charged that companies used the clause to blackball union men but F.D.R. rejected a plea for revision of the code.

Even so, Henry Ford refused to sign the document because he would not agree to bargain with representatives of his workers as the code required. Ford diligently abided by code provisions for wages and hours and his sales did not suffer despite the lack of NRA's symbolic "Blue Eagle" on his cars.

A year after Roosevelt's inauguration, leaders of AFL unions in General Motors and Hudson plants in Detroit, Cleveland, and St. Louis went to Washington to protest alleged discrimination against union members. A strike was called for March 21, 1934, but the President intervened personally and produced a settlement that created an Automobile Labor Board. The Board was to conduct elections among workers to select bargaining representatives and make binding decisions on complaints of anti-union discrimination. A system of proportional representation was set up, encouraging a variety of small unions to seek a voice rather than granting exclusive negotiating rights to one union if it could win a majority of workers' loyalties. Naively confident despite the arrangement's inherent shortcomings, Roosevelt exulted: "In the settlement there is a framework for a new structure of industrial relations—a new basis of understanding between employers and employes. I would like you to know that in the settlement just reached in the automobile industry we have charted a new course in social engineering in the United States."

The President selected Leo Wolman as the neutral member of the three-man Board. Wolman had close ties with organized labor. But AFL officials retained grave doubts about the agreement, complaining that it was drawn up mainly by General Johnson and spokesmen for the auto companies. The Board soon lost all of labor's confidence because its procedures were cumbersome, time-consuming, and ineffectual. It was disbanded in June 1935.

Once the New Deal won a renewed mandate in the 1934 Congressional elections, Sidney Hillman of the Amalgamated Clothing Workers joined with AFL President William Green, and Lewis, in demanding a federal investigation of labor conditions in the auto industry, to be conducted by Leon Henderson. On the same day, Walter Chrysler and General Motors' Alfred P. Sloan insisted that F.D.R. extend the life of the NRA code. Trying to please management and labor, Roosevelt extended the code provisions for 90 days and named Henderson to study labor relations in the auto plants.

Inside the labor movement, lines already were forming for a titanic clash between John L. Lewis and his militant, industrial-minded allies and the more conservative craft union leaders who were reluctant to challenge the nation's corporate giants. In June 1934, delegates from 77 auto locals convened under AFL auspices and, in a burst of defiance, banned AFL representatives from the floor. They also sent out feelers to Lewis, who was on the verge of his industrial union drive. Lewis later pleaded their cause at the AFL convention, but without success.

A federal poll of auto workers resulted in an 88 percent "no union" vote in the spring of 1935, interpreted by many as a repudiation of the AFL rather than a reflection of lack of union sympathies. Wildcat strikes erupted in Toledo, Cleveland, and Norwood, Ohio, and in other auto cities, until 30,000 workers were off their jobs. The AFL's chief organizer in the auto industry, Francis Dillon, accepted an arbitrated settlement opposed by many strike leaders, including fiery George F. Addes of Toledo's Auto-Lite plant. It was another blow to AFL prestige.

A consolidated auto union finally was set up in August 1935, and Dillon was appointed president by the AFL. A former preacher from Kansas City, Homer Martin, was named vice-president. When the AFL convention met in Atlantic City that autumn, John L. Lewis again proposed the chartering of new, self-governing unions for mass production industries, these to receive massive financial backing from the federation. In an eloquent appeal, Lewis thundered, "Heed this cry from Macedonia, that comes from the hearts of men. . . ." His resolution was voted down by a margin of nearly two to one. The bitterness in the convention was dramatized when Big Bill Hutcheson of the Carpenters, a six-foot-three heavyweight, objected to recognition of speakers from the new auto and rubber unions. Chided Lewis, "This thing of raising points of order all the time on minor delegates is rather small potatoes." Hutcheson shot back: "I was raised on small potatoes. That is why I am so small." When Lewis persisted, Hutcheson replied in anger, using the word "bastard." The powerfully built Lewis knocked him to the floor with a single blow.

Deciding to go ahead on his own, Lewis formed the Committee on Industrial Organization (CIO) with like-minded leaders such as Charles Howard of the Typographical Union, Sidney Hillman of the Clothing Workers, and David Dubinsky of the Ladies' Garment Workers. A slight, red-haired young man, Walter Reuther, was in Atlantic City for the historic moment but took no part in the meetings.

Lewis resigned as an AFL vice-president and rejected federation directives to disband the committee, saying he sooner would see his fellow labor barons wearing "asbestos suits in hell." Threatened with expulsion, he remained defiant, saying, "The American Federation of Labor is standing still, with its face toward the dead past." The CIO unions were placed on trial the following summer and were formally expelled from the AFL on October 1, 1937. The expulsion was an anticlimax. By that time the CIO was on the march in auto, steel, electrical, and other industries where unions had been unknown or impotent under AFL tutelage.

To serve as his lieutenants, the personally conservative Lewis often turned to radicals, Socialists, and Communists, who viewed the organizing drive as a step toward larger social and political goals; Lewis felt he needed their effective activism. President Roosevelt also contributed to the CIO cause by belatedly endorsing legislation introduced by Senator Robert F. Wagner of New York, thus giving a federal blessing to unionization and collective bargaining. Early in the New Deal F.D.R. seemed indifferent to the concept of exclusive representation by a union with a majority backing in a plant. Workers, he said in 1934, should be free to choose the Ahkoond of Swat, the Royal Geographic Society, or the Crown Prince of Siam to represent their interests. He did not recognize that a variety of minority union spokesmen would weaken workers in dealing with management. When the Supreme Court struck down the National Recovery Act, including its guarantee of the right to organize, union leaders urged Roosevelt to apply White House pressure for passage of the Wagner Act. Employers were solidly against it, with Alfred P. Sloan warning, "Industry, if it has any appreciation of its obligation to future generations, will fight this proposal to the very last." After F.D.R. embraced the Wagner measure, it sailed through Congress in July 1935.

"In this curious way Roosevelt and labor first became partners," one contemporary observer wrote. Certainly the shift of attitude at the White House gave Lewis reason to press for F.D.R.'s reelection in 1936. The CIO chieftain sparked the formation of Labor's Non-Partisan League early that year, eventually contributing a million dollars to Roosevelt's campaign, with $500,000 coming directly from the United Mine Workers' treasury. Lewis later boasted that his union and the CIO "paid cash on the barrel for every piece of legislation that we have gotten," adding: "Is anyone fool enough to believe for one instant that we gave this money to Roosevelt because we were spellbound by his voice? . . . Certainly there was a *quid pro quo*—the right of labor to organize."

In a campaign speech on Labor Day eve, Roosevelt showed a strong interest in the same objective, declaring: "There are those who fail to read both the signs of the times and American history. They would try to refuse the worker any effective power to bargain collectively, to earn a decent living and to acquire security. It is these shortsighted ones, not labor, who threaten this country with that class dissension which in other countries has led to dictatorship and the establishment of fear and hatred as the dominant emotions in human life."

Roosevelt may have been referring to General Motors, Standard Oil, U.S. Steel, Du Pont, and other corporations that had formed a special committee early in 1936 to fight the burgeoning CIO. Saul Alinsky, the radical community organizer, later wrote, "In the last analysis, the greatest organizers of the coming automobile workers' unions were the executives and owners of the industry."

CHAPTER SIX

Reuther Organizes

THE YEAR 1936 WAS A TURNING POINT IN THE LIFE OF WALTER Reuther. He got married, attended his first union convention, was elected to the UAW Executive Board, ran a sit-down strike, and established a power base on Detroit's West Side. After an initial flirtation with radical political groups, he devoted his entire time and effort to the United Auto Workers. The landslide reelection of Franklin D. Roosevelt and Michigan's elevation of liberal Democrat Frank Murphy to the governor's chair were bright omens for the growth of the infant union and Walter Reuther's own success as an extraordinarily effective and daring union leader.

As the year began, however, Walter and Victor Reuther were just two of the unemployed masses who searched in vain for jobs in the auto plants. After returning from their world tour in the fall of 1935, the brothers first went home to Wheeling for a reunion with their parents, then visited Roy Reuther, who was teaching at Brookwood Labor College in Katonah, New York. Brookwood was a training center for union leaders in an unlikely setting— a magnificent estate on the Hudson River north of New York City. Financed by wealthy liberals and the more progressive AFL unions that formed the nucleus of the newborn CIO, it had a strong pacifist, Socialist orientation. Most of the courses, however, were in such prosaic subjects as parliamentary law, public speaking, and basic economics. While there, Walter and Victor spoke to the student body and were briefed by Roy on developments in Detroit labor circles.

"When we first got back, the employment outlook was pretty bleak in Detroit," Victor recalled. "Walter and I decided to move around the country and do a bit of lecturing on our travels." They made a few appearances for lecture agencies but usually spoke to campus chapters of the League for Industrial Democracy or other student organizations. "Rarely did we get a fee," said Victor. "Normally we got transportation and lodging." In Flint, Michigan,

Walter spoke on "Russia's Economic Position Today" to the Young People's Socialist League. The three brothers attended a conference in Columbus, Ohio, at which the Communist and Socialist student groups were merged into the American Student Union. Victor spoke at a rally to raise funds for the Spanish Loyalists, appearing on the platform with the American Communist writer Anna Louise Strong, who had been a regular contributor to the Moscow *Daily News* during their stay in the Soviet Union. "There is no secret that Walter and I felt very strongly about the defense of the duly elected government in Spain, which was a democratic government, and were very much opposed to the Fascist takeover," Victor said later. His own activities were diverse: Working for a Quaker group, the Emergency Peace Committee, he lectured trade unionists on the dangers of war. He spent several months doing research and writing at Brookwood, under the direction of Tucker Smith. In the summer of 1936 he taught at the Southern Workers Anti-War School at Commonwealth College, Mena, Arkansas.

Walter, after hitchhiking to radical meetings throughout the Midwest, settled in Detroit. Boarding a homebound streetcar early in 1936, he encountered a young woman he had not seen in more than three years. She was May Wolf, a red-haired physical education instructor in the Detroit schools who was trying to organize her colleagues for the American Federation of Teachers. The streetcar romance flourished. Soon Walter and May were meeting almost nightly on the trolley, discussing labor causes. Like Walter, Miss Wolf had a history of radicalism that included membership in the Proletarian Party, a small left-wing group in Michigan.

Their courtship lasted three months and culminated in marriage on March 13, 1936. "On our wedding night we took a drive out of town somewhere," May recalled. "Walter had to make a speech." The newlyweds led a spartan life, often skipping meals to get to evening meetings on time and, too frequently, not returning to their apartment until near midnight. "I never knew people to eat less," said May. "I was so thin the mattress hurt my hips." Her husband added, "We hardly ever slept."

The struggle to build a union of automobile workers soon occupied Reuther's full attention. Embracing trade unionism with all the fervor of a dedicated priest, he was ready to make any sacrifice for his new calling. Associates found him motivated by a crusading spirit and idealistic commitment to which physical comfort and security and personal ambition were completely secondary.

His decision to join the fledgling United Auto Workers coincided with a surge of militancy in the ranks of mass production laborers. Shaking off the worst effects of the Depression, they were ready to respond to new leadership in a popular revolt against oppressive factory life.

Although the majority of workers had yet to join a union, in many cases out of fear of employer reprisals, few failed to feel the mounting spirit of rebellion. And among the pioneering membership of the UAW, there was increasing restiveness under the conservative, cautious leadership of AFL-appointed president Francis Dillon. Homer Martin, the vice-president, wrote a Cleveland unionist: "The situation in Detroit is the most pitiful I have ever seen. Dillon has completely betrayed the automobile workers, in my opinion. It is going to take a lot of hard work to straighten these matters out." Early in 1936 Martin and secretary Ed Hall seized control of the international union offices from Dillon. Explaining their action to David Dubinsky, an AFL vice-president, Martin wrote: "Dillon has pursued a positively impossible policy. If he is allowed to remain in his present position he will only further destroy the automobile workers' unions." Martin asked Dubinsky to seek Dillon's ouster.

Wanting autonomy for the UAW, Martin and his followers decided to wrest all power from Dillon at the union's second convention at South Bend, Indiana, in April 1936. The auto unionists also were impatient with the limitations on organizing rights in their AFL charters.

It was a scrappy group that assembled in the Indiana city, home of the Studebaker plant and its well-established local union. One of the scrappiest was Walter Reuther, then 28 years old, who arrived with a delegate's credential from UAW Local 86, which represented employes of the General Motors Ternstedt plant in Detroit. Here is how he remembered his entrance to South Bend:

> I checked into the LaSalle Hotel. It is not like the Statler. It is true they had plumbing if you were willing to stand in line down at the end of the hall in the morning. I said to the room clerk, "I would like to rent the widest double bed you have." He said to me, "Young man, all of our double beds are standard-sized." What he didn't know was that there were six of us who slept in that room, although I was the only guy registered. We ate hamburgers and we didn't have any money, but we had belief in an idea and an ideal. We believed you could organize workers and together they could solve their common problems.

Later in his career, Walter told how he was chosen to be a convention delegate:

> The constitution of our union said you had to have fifteen members to have a charter. We had only thirteen. We paid for two people by taking up a collection every month for two guys who hadn't joined yet. . . . I was elected by acclamation. I stood before this great mass meeting of organized workers—there were five others there besides myself—and thanked them for the great honor.

Then, he said, a motion was approved to give him the money in the local treasury to finance the trip to South Bend. "But the financial secretary thought the boys were getting reckless with the local union money," Reuther added, "so she amended the motion to read that upon my return I was obligated to reimburse the local with any money left over. . . . Whereupon she opened her purse and handed me a five-dollar bill. That is all the money we had."

The truth is that Walter Reuther did not have a valid credential for the South Bend meeting. Several other UAW delegates challenged his right to be seated, claiming he never had worked at the Ternstedt plant and therefore was ineligible to represent its employes in the convention. Walter told the Credentials Committee he had worked in the plant under an assumed name in December

1935 and January 1936. The Committee upheld his right to a
delegate's badge and the convention seated him without debate.
More than 30 years later Reuther gave his version of the episode:

> I might say that my credentials were highly in question. I
> never did work at Ternstedt. I couldn't get a job there. [But]
> it was felt that I could do a more effective job in the local union
> that was tied in with Ternstedt. . . . What we thought was,
> tactically, the active guys . . . ought to be associated with organ-
> izational efforts in the plants where we thought we might break
> through and make a base, and then, with that base, go to Ford.
> This was kind of the strategy. . . . We just made a tactical
> decision that I would be associated with Ternstedt. . . . The
> point is that all the guys that really were working [in the union]
> knew exactly where I was and why I was there. I didn't make
> that decision. . . . I got that as an assignment. I didn't care
> where I worked. It was really an unimportant detail where you
> were because all the locals put together weren't very much.

Reuther was a member of the strong left-wing group at the South
Bend convention. That accounted for the suspicions he aroused
among some of the old-line trade unionists. As he put it, "There
were a few guys I would think were more conservative, kind of
orthodox trade unionists who looked at us like a bunch of young
punks, you know, and they challenged us at every turn."

Once past the initial barrier, Reuther plunged into the work of
the convention. In his first speech he supported a plan to elect three
vice-presidents so each major center of the auto industry would be
represented. But he showed his frugal upbringing and habits by
demanding an $8-a-day ceiling for travel expenses, noting with
disgust that the union had paid a daily tab as high as $52 for one
officer. "We do not want to start creating big, fat jobs," said the
slim, ascetic Reuther.

His next oratorical target was a popular one within the union
movement, the Hearst press. Just as his father had denounced the
publisher in years past, so did Walter. The occasion now was a
headline in Hearst's Chicago *Herald-Examiner* that declared the
auto union had quit the AFL. Reuther condemned the press ac-

count and shouted, "Let us destroy Hearst!" He won unanimous adoption of a resolution denouncing the Chicago newspaper for its "infamous lie" and pledging UAW loyalty to the AFL.

Homer Martin appointed Reuther to the convention's Education Committee. The seven-man panel recomended yearly spending of $6,010, a large amount for the time, on such activities as summer schools and a union chorus, the latter budgeted at $250 for the year. While the program was largely the work of Brookwood's Tucker Smith, it reflected Reuther's zeal for schooling.

Reuther displayed some anti-AFL sentiments when the convention began debating the jurisdictional limitations imposed in the UAW charter issued by the Federation. Taking a defiant but realistic view of labor conditions at the time, Walter said: "We have certain jurisdictional limits . . . but in actuality we can go out and get all the people that work in our respective plants, and get them in our organization, and they will stay there. We care nothing for what is on black and white. . . ."

The industrial union spirit was echoed in convention speeches by Powers Hapgood of the United Mine Workers and Rose Pesotta of the International Ladies' Garment Workers. The AFL's William Green got a tepid reception, even though he announced the Federation was relinquishing control over the UAW's membership and its treasury of $20,000. Green claimed there were 35,000 on the UAW rolls but those in the know said the dues-paying membership was closer to 10,000. The AFL president lamented that the auto locals had cost the Federation about $68,000 in subsidies.

Frank Winn, the first public relations director for the auto union, recalls that, at the time, the membership harbored "a skepticism and a suspicion about the militance and the good faith of the AFL." The convention delegates looked to the CIO for help in organizing, says Winn, but nevertheless wanted to remain within the AFL family provided they had freedom to run their own union. Green's grant of autonomy, coupled with an announcement by Francis Dillon that he would not seek the UAW presidency, meant that the militants in the auto union had prevailed.

The degree of CIO influence at South Bend was displayed soon after the delegates, apparently influenced by Communist and Socialist blocs, unexpectedly refused to endorse Franklin D. Roosevelt for reelection. This enraged John L. Lewis, who got word of the UAW action at his Washington headquarters. One account had Lewis threatening to withhold $100,000 promised by the CIO for an auto organizing drive unless the convention reversed itself and backed F.D.R. At the urging of Lewis, and pressed by CIO stalwarts in the hall at South Bend, Homer Martin ordered a second vote shortly before adjournment and the delegates agreed to support Roosevelt in November. Walter Reuther did not take an active part in the contretemps. Winn has pictured him as an "enthusiastic campaigner" for F.D.R. in 1936 despite his Socialist ties. Victor Reuther concurs in the recollection.

When it came time to elect officers, the delegates were united in their choice of Homer Martin, the 34-year-old former Baptist preacher, to be the first president of the autonomous auto workers. George F. Addes, the shrewd, swarthy young man who had led Toledo's bloody Auto-Lite strike, was elected secretary-treasurer. Wyndham Mortimer, identified with the Communist bloc in the White Motor Company local in Cleveland, was chosen to be one of three vice-presidents. The other two were Ed Hall and Walter N. Wells.

Executive Board members were selected by the delegates in regional caucuses, and then routinely ratified by the convention. With its vast potential membership, Michigan was allocated four seats on the Board. Acting as temporary chairman of the Michigan caucus, Reuther was a candidate and turned the gavel over to Ed Hall, who conducted the election. In the balloting the newcomer Reuther was elected to the Executive Board with 30 out of a possible 38 votes, tieing for high-man honors with Lester Washburn, a conservative unionist from Lansing. The same critics who objected to Reuther's seating as a delegate complained about the caucus choices. Delmer E. Minzey of Local 29, along with two others, charged that "undemocratic" methods had been used to select three men from Detroit and another from Lansing, excluding Flint and other auto centers from representation. They asked the convention to nullify the Michigan caucus results. Reuther jumped into the debate, saying it was "sheer nonsense" to claim the procedures were undemocratic. Michigan tapped three Detroiters only because it wanted "the best men" for the Executive Board jobs, Walter said. Homer Martin sided with Reuther, declaring from the chair, "I can't help it if certain minorities do not have enough votes to elect the people they favor." After the caucus minutes were read into the record, Martin upheld the legality of the Michigan proceedings and the convention voted to sustain his ruling by what Martin announced as a "very large majority."

That did not end the bickering, however. Delegate Dewey Smith of Local 84 snapped at Reuther, "I don't know what he ever accomplished," and accused "progressives" of controlling the Detroit vote. As adjournment approached, Martin again felt it necessary to defend Reuther. The charter of Ternstedt Local No. 86, he said, was not issued until late November or early December of 1935 and Reuther became a member in early January, "therefore only lacking one month of actually fulfilling the technical qualifications" for holding UAW office. He recalled Reuther's employment at the Ford plant starting in 1927 and noted that Walter gained as many votes as anyone in the Michigan caucus. Said Martin: "We state . . . that the place of Walter Reuther on the General Executive Board from the state of Michigan should remain in the minds of all unquestioned, that he stands clear . . . as a qualified officer of the International." But even the presidential blessing did not silence Roy Speth, chairman of the Credentials Committee, who continued to voice doubts about the legitimacy of Reuther's presence.

Walter's principal critics came from the conservative UAW forces close to the discredited Dillon leadership. Most delegates paid little heed to the squabble and, in truth, there were many among them whose credentials were equally questionable. To the union activists, militancy and energy were what mattered.

One of those who joined in questioning Reuther's election to the Executive Board was H. H. Richardson, a delegate from Flint whose motive was apparent. Having been appointed to the Board as a Michigan representative by AFL President Green in 1935,

Reuther to Richardson was an upstart who had usurped his place in the UAW hierarchy.

Said Walter, "I suppose any guy willing to work day and night for free was welcomed." Homer Martin tempered the welcome, however, despite his sturdy defense of Reuther before the delegates. Alone among Board members, Reuther was not assigned a geographic region by Martin, placed on the payroll of the international union, or given a staff to help with organizing. As a result, Walter had to improvise, which he did with remarkable success in less than a year's time. It was on-the-job training for him and, more important, a realistic test of his talent and idealism. Seldom has any union leader met an equivalent challenge and been able to show such dramatic results.

Although he worked very briefly at his tool and die trade during the period, Reuther opened an office in one of the many impressive buildings vacated by Detroit banks that went broke during the Depression. He picked the corner at 35th and Michigan because thousands of Ford workers changed streetcars there on their way to and from the River Rouge plant. Considering that his personal finances had been exhausted by his travels abroad and at home without benefit of regular employment, it was an exceedingly bold and risky move. Borrowing $300 from a friend, Reuther hired a sound truck and furnished his one-room office with a secondhand desk, a typewriter, and a mimeograph machine. Mrs. Reuther, who had been earning $60 a week as a teacher in the public schools, joined her husband as "the lowest paid secretary in the city." Her new salary was $15 a week, which she returned regularly to the local treasury. She also moonlighted by trying to organize an office workers' union. Living near May's parents in a small apartment on LaSalle Boulevard, the couple ate in cheap restaurants after evening speeches to West Side workers.

"As the curtain rose on CIO, injustice was as commonplace as streetcars," Walter found. "When men walked into their jobs, they left their dignity, their citizenship, and their humanity outside. The very idea that a worker could be wronged seemed absurd to the employer."

One of Reuther's first acts was to build a broad organizing base and, at the same time, a base of political strength within the UAW. "The first thing I did," he said, "was to try to get the Fleetwood local, the Ford local, the Universal Cooler local, the Ternstedt local—there were six local unions—to agree that none . . . in isolation could get anywhere on its own. Therefore we ought to create an amalgamated local union and pool our membership, our resources, and our efforts to try to do something meaningful in terms of organizing the unorganized. When we put together those six local unions, they had a combined membership of 78 members—so you can see the trade union base we had." Reuther became the first president of the consolidated union. It was chartered as UAW Local No. 174 and quickly became known throughout the UAW as the West Side Local.

At about this time, Reuther was hired by the Coleman Tool and Die shop in Detroit. It was his first steady job since returning from abroad, but within two months the boss found out that Walter was a union officer. Here is Reuther's recollection of his last hours in the private enterprise sector:

> At the end of 30 days I completed a perforating die. It had 200 perforated punches which had to pierce 12-or 15-thousandths-thick brass. I put this die in the press for the tryouts and the chief inspector put a sheet of the *Free Press,* the Detroit *Free Press,* under the die, and brought the die down. It pierced all the punches clean without a burr. He said to me, "Man, that is one of the best jobs we have put out in this shop in some time."
>
> I said, "Don't waste your praise on me. Tell it to the boss, because I'm going to demand a wage increase."
>
> And the boss came over. He was called "Highball John." Not because he played basketball. It was because he rode the guys hard. I said to Highball John, "If that job is as good as the chief inspector says it is, I ought to get a ten-cents-an-hour raise." He said, "I will talk to the old man." He meant Frederick Coleman, who owned the shop.
>
> The next morning at seven o'clock, Highball John came over and said, "We are giving you a ten-cents-an-hour increase."

I said, "Thank you." At nine o'clock, I was discharged for being incompetent, because I was organizing that shop. I said to Highball John, "I'm going to finish the job of organizing this shop before you physically throw me out of the plant." And I did, and that was my last job.

There was plenty to do without holding a factory job. Walter has described the pro-union fever that developed in Detroit about that time: "A guy we never heard of would call up and say, 'We shut down such-and-such a plant; send us over some coffee and doughnuts.' So we'd send over the stuff. . . . Our organizing committee was in session continuously. That's how we grew. It was a real industrial revolution."

The UAW also grew by absorbing formerly independent unions, such as the Automotive Industrial Workers Alliance formed at Chrysler plants by Richard T. Frankensteen. A onetime football tackle at the University of Dayton, Dick Frankensteen was widely admired for his physical courage and political sense. To win over the many auto workers among Polish Catholics from the Detroit suburb of Hamtramck, he enlisted Father Charles E. Coughlin, the "radio priest," to address union meetings. Walter Reuther formally proposed that the Executive Board bring Frankensteen's organization under the UAW banner, and it was Reuther who also moved that the new recruit be named an organizer, although he did not have that status yet himself.

Frankensteen's AIWA was the largest and most important of three major independent auto unions in Detroit. The merger of these independents into the UAW was a top-priority objective of the new leadership.

Like Frankensteen, Reuther called mass meetings in Detroit's parks so workers could mingle with the public without being spotted by employer spies. He distributed handbills and spoke often at factory gates. There was a new spirit of militancy in the air, a feeling that the CIO affiliation and more aggressive UAW leadership would hasten strike showdowns with some of the auto giants.

Reviewing target companies on the West Side, Reuther focused on Kelsey-Hayes Wheel Company. It had a work force of nearly

5,000, and several members of Local 174 were, unknown to Kelsey-Hayes, on the payroll. Walter sent for Victor, who was in Philadelphia at a Quaker peace conference. "They are beginning to hire," Walter told his kid brother. "If you are interested, now is the time to come back." Victor immediately sent a message to his wife, Sophie, saying: "I'm going straight to Detroit. I'll send for you." Renting a room in a Polish neighborhood near the plant, Victor was hired on the second shift, earning 22½ cents an hour running a punch press. Other UAW loyalists who infiltrated the plant included Walter's former roommate, Merlin Bishop, and George Edwards, a Harvard graduate who had joined labor's ranks.

Fearing that open unionization efforts would be crushed through the firing of UAW leaders, Reuther decided to employ the sit-down technique that had been highly effective in Akron rubber strikes a year earlier. He was familiar with use of the tactic by workers in France and other countries, too. The heart of the sit-down idea was that a few strategically placed union adherents could disrupt an assembly line and yet not expose strikers to the violence that might be used against a picket line outside the plant. Also, maintenance of union positions inside a factory gave assurance that strikebreakers could not be brought in to do the work.

UAW leaders in Detroit felt confident they could secure widespread rank and file backing for unionization if they could begin winning benefits through the sit-down technique and, at the same time, protect activists against management reprisals. As Frank Winn recalls their mood: "They were gambling on whether or not they could hold out long enough—possibly in the face of hired strikebreakers, company police, city police, or troops—to overcome management's determination not to recognize the union. That was the chance they took."

The Kelsey-Hayes plans were laid in a series of meetings in the homes of UAW members and in the LaSalle Boulevard apartment where Walter and May Reuther were living. Roosevelt's second-term victory was a morale booster, and a quote attributed to the President—"If I were a factory worker, I would join a union"—was displayed on every UAW leaflet. Reuther's plans were advanced when auto workers in South Bend pulled a sit-down strike at the Bendix Products Company in November 1936. Although the dispute was settled in ten days, it prompted the Ford Motor Company to remove its brake shoe dies from Bendix and install them at Kelsey-Hayes, considered a more dependable supplier. The time was ripe for UAW action because Ford now depended entirely on Kelsey-Hayes for brake shoes.

Reuther arranged a conference for December 11 to discuss union grievances over a speedup with the president of Kelsey-Hayes, George W. Kennedy. The day before the scheduled meeting, however, Reuther's followers staged their first preplanned revolt. A woman in Department 49, one of the largest in the factory, threw down her tools and collapsed in a "faint." Reviving, she urged her co-workers to stop their labors until the production line was adjusted to a slower pace. Within minutes, the department was shut down. Work also stopped on the floor below, where Victor Reuther was the key agitator. Summoned to the plant, Walter Reuther convened a meeting of workers inside and listened to their demands for higher pay and a slower production line. The company's personnel manager, tugging at Walter's pantleg as he stood on a soapbox, asked the union leader to deliver a back-to-work plea. Reuther replied, "Well, I've got to organize them first." Reuther subsequently assembled a committee to join him next day in the talks with the boss and everyone went home. At the appointed hour, Kennedy refused to discuss the workers' complaints and the unionists called a sit-down on the spot. Many workers, angry because they had not been consulted on the strategy, left for home. About 400 sitters remained in the plant until Reuther and the personnel manager arrived in the evening with word that Kennedy had agreed to see a union delegation two days later provided the plant was evacuated. The second sit-down was ended on that basis.

The next move by Reuther and his supporters was to capture a rival, company-sponsored union. With an overflow crowd on hand, the UAW elected one of its own men as chairman of the Kelsey-Hayes union. With Victor speaking to those outside from a sound truck, more than 4,000 workers gave the UAW a vote of confidence and hundreds joined the union.

Nevertheless, Kennedy proved adamant about considering UAW grievances and a third sit-down was called. In a short time the plant was closed down tight. When the employment manager threatened to fire anyone who did not leave at once, all but 200 sit-downers walked out of the plant. Others, arriving for the second shift, went home after tossing their lunch bags over the fence to those inside.

The strikers settled down for a long stay, with sentinels assigned around the clock. Women strikers occupied a ladies' rest room and imposed an 11:00 P.M. curfew. The union leadership showed its regard for the proprieties: "A committee was sent to the management to ask that a matron be on duty through the evenings so that the company would have no cause for complaint and to protect the girls against adverse publicity." A union doctor paid daily visits and two strikers served as barbers, using a wheelbarrow instead of a barber's chair. On one sunny morning, the strikers held a square dance at the front gate. Two Christmas trees were set up and decorated with chrome auto parts in case the sit-in lasted through the holiday. To pass time, men fashioned checkerboards from cartons and used washers as pieces. Musical instruments were brought into the plant and a barbershop quartet was formed. Radios provided music for a nightly dance in a corner of Department 49.

Despite efforts to preserve high morale, boredom, loneliness, and gloom began to haunt the plant. George Edwards later recounted his feelings: "On the ninth day . . . we were a rather grim-faced crew. Christmas was only two days away and we felt sure we were due to eat our holiday dinner in the plant and that Santa Claus would have to come down the Kelsey-Hayes smokestack." To add to their woes, the Ford Motor Company was threatening to remove its dies from the plant, an action that would reduce pressures on the company for a settlement.

Walter Reuther and Frankensteen decided to use massed humanity to forestall any effort to move the dies. Frankensteen arranged for the defenders to be joined by the rugged "Flying Squadron" from the Dodge local. Reuther telephoned a tough little Teamster, Jimmy Hoffa, and a platoon of truck drivers showed up to help. Inside the plant, Edwards directed barricade builders. "The main gates were blocked by a solid 3-foot-high wall of steel formed from a dozen carefully placed steel containers," Edwards said. "We loaded each container with a couple of tons of hub castings. Behind the barricade we set a dolly load of 18-inch T-irons." Confronted by this formidable obstacle, not to mention thousands of UAW supporters outside the plant, Ford withdrew its raiding party. The dies remained in the plant, disassembled and hidden by the strikers, who did not intend to give them up even had their defenses been breached.

A shortage of brake parts began to put a crimp in Ford's production, with the result that some workers on the night shift at the Rouge had been sent home for several nights. Harry H. Bennett, Ford's personnel director, told Kelsey-Hayes to settle the strike before Christmas or Ford would buy its brakes elsewhere. George Kennedy grudgingly agreed and Bennett's middleman, John Gillespie, called Frankensteen and worked out a settlement scenario. The union should stick with its demand for a 75-cent hourly rate for both men and women, Gillespie said, but must drop the demand for union recognition because that was intolerable to Henry Ford. Frankensteen and Reuther, who had been sleeping on benches at Local 174 headquarters during the sit-down, hurried to the bargaining table. As Frankensteen played his role, as directed by Gillespie, Kennedy approved the 75-cent rate despite objections from a surprised representative of the Detroit Manufacturers' Association. The settlement also provided for recognition of stewards and establishment of overtime standards. A contract was signed at the Ford offices, a measure of the power of Henry Ford in the auto making community.

"The Kelsey-Hayes workers were so fired up with these successes," said Frank Winn, "that Walter had difficulty in persuading them to settle on these terms. . . . He had to do it on the basis that this was really just an armed truce, because we had to clear the decks for General Motors."

An overwhelming majority of Kelsey-Hayes employes and others rushed to join Reuther's West Side Local, pushing its membership to 30,000 by the following Christmas.

For Walter Reuther, his first battle in the industrial wars of the 1930's was a triumph, dramatizing the eagerness of factory workers for union organization once they were assured they would not lose their jobs because they insisted on their federally guaranteed rights. The sit-down technique had proved to be nonviolent and highly effective, an appropriate and heartening dress rehearsal for what was to come. From a personal standpoint, Reuther's risk in opening a UAW office on borrowed money could be regarded now as a wise and prudent move. The testing period over, he was placed on the union's international payroll.

The reaction of many of the Kelsey-Hayes strikers was one of pure amazement. Twenty-four hours before getting word of the settlement, they had been braced for hand-to-hand combat with Ford's invasion force. George Edwards summed up the moment of triumph: "When we finally swung the gates open and marched out of the plant we had held so long, into the flashing light of the news cameras and the waves of sound of 5,000 throats singing 'Solidarity,' we were all universally bewildered. The change from desperate determination to the hysteria of a victory parade was too sudden."

Walter Reuther realized what they had accomplished and he joined in the labor hymn with gusto:

> They have taken untold millions, that they never toiled to earn,
> But without our brain and muscle not a single wheel could turn.
> We can break their haughty power, gain our freedom when we learn
> That the union makes us strong!
> Solidarity forever! Solidarity forever!
> Solidarity forever! For the union makes us strong!

CHAPTER SEVEN

Flint

INCREDIBLY, THE NEXT TARGET OF THE INFANT UNITED AUTO Workers was gigantic General Motors, an international combine with resources so vast that, seemingly, it could readily crush the union's still infinitesimal membership. By reliable estimates, only one of every 275 auto workers belonged to the UAW in Detroit. In Flint, heart of the General Motors empire, the figure was more like one in every 400. Company spies had penetrated the inner circle of the auto union, often being elected to local office and attending conventions as representatives of the workers. Records indicate that membership in the Flint local plummeted from 26,000 to less than 200 between 1934 and 1936. GM's resources were immense. Controlled by the Du Pont family, it had, 261,977 persons on its payroll in 57 cities in 1936. Its capital assets exceeded a billion dollars and it was producing more than two million cars and trucks each year. Compared to those of other heavy industry, GM wages were relatively high. The average auto worker was paid 80 cents an hour, or slightly more than $36 a week. A typical steelworker at the time was earning less than $29 a week and the average industrial wage was 62.4 cents an hour.

Walter Reuther and his union colleagues, however, were certain the masses of factory workers would rally behind organized labor's leadership if the UAW could establish a firm beachhead in the auto plants. Reuther and others felt it was the right time to capitalize on a new spirit and momentum favoring labor's cause. The surprising success of Kelsey-Hayes and other sit-down strikes sent union confidence soaring. John L. Lewis, the beetle-browed commander of the CIO, was an inspiring symbol. Harold L. Ickes, Secretary of the Interior in the New Deal cabinet, said of Lewis at the time: "His strength is almost overpowering. A great, huge bull of a man, he gives the impression that nothing can stop him short of his objective." Lewis' goal was clear—organization of the mass production industries—and his intended first target was Big Steel.

Energetic auto unionists compelled Lewis to alter his timetable. They began by sending two skilled organizers to Flint: Roy Reuther, then 27, and Robert Travis, handsome and personable, soon to fall under Communist influence. Working in Flint's company-town atmosphere, they soon focused on the assembly line as GM's Achilles' heel. The fast-moving "iron horse" transformed 15,-000 parts into a completed automobile—a miracle of modern production. The assembly line also made men into virtual robots, each performing a simplified task repetitively, with a consequent steady drain on their physical and emotional systems. Few jobs required much skill. Most could be learned in three days. "No one, not even an infantry private, is more easily replaceable than an assembly line worker," concluded two observers. With company supervisors in control of production, many workers protested against "speedups" in the line, but with little recourse except to move faster or quit. "I ain't got no kick on wages," said one, "but I just don't like to be drove."

The UAW's showdown with GM was set for January of 1937, when production of new models would be at a peak. The company, however, got a preview of what was in store on November 13, 1936, at its Fisher No. 1 Chevrolet Body Plant in Flint. Time cards of three welders, all union members, were pulled from the rack and the men were told they had been fired. A fourth union man who dared to protest was fired on the spot. On his way out of the plant, the protester gestured to Bud Simons, a union militant, to join him on his "last mile." Simons followed and, as he moved along the assembly line, his glance conveyed a message: put down tools. Soon 700 men were sitting down on the job. Confronting the plant manager, Simons announced, "You are now talking to a union." Quickly, the company agreed to rehire the four UAW adherents and forget about docking the sit-down strikers for lost time.

Since General Motors was far more centralized in the 1930's than it is today, the UAW strategists directed their organizing efforts at key plants in Flint and Cleveland. The theory, argued by the Reuthers and others, was that effective shutdowns of these factories would, in a short period, cripple GM production since essential parts would not be available for shipment to remote assembly plants. Furthermore, New Deal measures by 1937 had helped revive the economy so that GM and its competitors were in the happy position of facing a record demand for automobiles.

UAW leaders feared that a conventional strike and picket line would be broken easily. The union was not strong enough to draw enough workers, accustomed to the union-busting tactics of the employer, out of the plants to halt the building of cars. Only if it could occupy the factories would a shutdown be assured. Successes at Kelsey-Hayes, Bendix, and Midland Steel in Detroit virtually dictated that this method be tried again in the approaching crunch with General Motors.

After sporadic strikes in Flint plants, and a longer walkout in Atlanta, GM's Executive Vice-President William Knudsen said on December 18, 1936, that the corporation believed "collective bargaining is here to stay." Perhaps too well aware of Ford's dilemma in the then ongoing Kelsey-Hayes strike, Knudsen said General Motors did not want to discourage union organization but believed that negotiations "ought to take place before a shutdown rather than after." Four days later, Knudsen granted a conference to Homer Martin, the erratic and youthful president of the UAW, and George F. Addes, the union's No. 2 man. The GM official termed it a "personal interview," thus signaling that he was not even extending informal recognition to the United Auto Workers; he was temporizing. His advice to Martin was to "take up matters with the plant managers." This was the same answer GM might give to any complaining employe. It would mean slow death for the UAW, as one analyst explained: "If General Motors could force the union to deal on an individual basis with each plant, it would never complete its organization. Since all local plant policies were determined on a national scale by the top-level executives of the company, it would fight the union in its many plants, plant by plant. In each plant a relatively small number of workers would be forced to face the entire strength of GM." From the UAW standpoint, the pattern the corporation intended to establish was all too clear: plant officials could deal with their employes while arguing that major bargaining problems were matters to be handled by the topmost GM executives, an unlikely recourse for any union that agreed to a plant-by-plant negotiating pattern.

Inexperienced in industrial warfare, young in years, and perhaps impressed by rubbing elbows with a man at the apex of the corporate heap, Martin announced that his meeting with Knudsen was "completely amicable." In Washington, John L. Lewis cursed as Martin's words were reported to him, then delivered a verbal spanking to the UAW president and the corporation, saying: "That's not collective bargaining. That's just evasion of responsibilities on the part of GM. It will be unsatisfactory to the union." Chastened, Martin sent a letter to Knudsen demanding a national conference of GM management and labor. His request was ignored.

As the old year ran out, and despite Knudsen's courtship of Martin, the historic confrontation began. On December 28, 1936, the UAW struck the Fisher Body Plant at Cleveland under the direction of union vice-president Wyndham Mortimer, a Communist-line activist. Mortimer had organized a strong local at the Ohio factory, a key one because it stamped turret tops for GM cars. Nearly 1,000 workers in Cleveland sat down. And on December 30, workers on the night shift at Fisher No. 1 in Flint noted that vital dies were being shipped out of the plant, presumably to locations where the union was not as strong. Bob Travis, now in charge for the UAW in Flint, and union members agreed they must halt the shipments to save their jobs. Voting to sit down, 1,000 men occupied the plant in a festive atmosphere. A homespun parody to the tune of "The Martins and the Coys" celebrated the event:

> *Now this strike it started one bright Wednesday evening,*
> *When they loaded up a boxcar full of dies,*
> *When the union boys, they stopped them,*
> *And the railroad workers backed them,*
> *The officials in the office were surprised.*

Those 4,000 union boys,
Oh, they sure made lots of noise.
They decided then and there to shut down tight.
In the office, they got snooty,
So we started picket duty.
Now the Fisher Body Shop is on strike!

The same morning, Fisher No. 2 was forced to close when fewer than 50 UAW members sat down, disrupting production, after GM attempted to transfer two unionists to other jobs. In actuality the sit-down was a pretext to occupy the plant and support union demands for national bargaining. In each plant, as it turned out, the original militants were joined by scores more and several hundred remained inside overnight. GM executives clearly were startled by the bold takeover of the Fisher plants. Soon more than 6,000 workers were idled, including those in a strike-free Chevrolet assembly plant cut off from its supply of car bodies by the sit-downs.

In Cleveland the Mortimer-led strike was so solid that the UAW decided it no longer was necessary to continue the sit-down. In advance of a planned New Year's Eve party inside the factory, UAW loyalists marched out wearing paper hats and blowing noisemakers. "General Motors will never try to run this plant with the kind of picket line we'll set up," a union spokesman vowed. He was right.

In Washington, John L. Lewis was stunned by the developments. At first he tried to check the sit-down fever but soon rallied to the cause as if he had planned this particular assault on the property system. "The sit-down strike is the fruit of mismanagement and bad policy towards labor," Lewis thundered. "Employers who tyrannize over employes, with the aid of labor spies, company guards and the threat of discharge, need not be surprised if their production lines are suddenly halted." And he maintained the pressure for national negotiations, saying, "Obviously, attempts to settle this widespread confusion through local plant conferences and with plant managers devoid of authority would be a futile waste of time." The stakes in the struggle were high, as one CIO official recognized: "It's the CIO against downtown New York"—a struggling auto labor pygmy against the financial power symbolized by Wall Street.

In the White House President Roosevelt was as puzzled as anyone by the dramatic new organizing technique. Since it obviously violated the law, by virtue of its occupation of private property, he could not express even moral support for the strikers. Yet he was reluctant to condemn them. F.D.R. became a benevolent neutral, much to the annoyance of Lewis, who had supported him so generously in 1936. Frances Perkins, then Secretary of Labor, described Roosevelt's reaction at the time to the sit-down tactic. "Well, it's illegal," she quoted the President as saying. "But what law are they breaking? The law of trespass, and that is about the only law that could be invoked. And what do you do when a man trespasses on your property? Sure, you order him off. You get the sheriff to order him off if he tries to pitch a tent in your field without permission. . . . But shooting it out and killing a lot of people because they have violated the law of trespass somehow offends me. I just don't see that as the answer. The punishment doesn't fit the crime. There must be another way. Why can't these fellows in General Motors meet with the committee of workers? Talk it all out. They would get a settlement. It wouldn't be so terrible."

General Motors thought it might be terrible. When the UAW spurned its demands for evacuation of the Fisher plants, the corporation went into court, on January 2, and obtained an injunction from Circuit Judge Edward D. Black, in Flint, directing strikers to leave the premises at once. Sheriff Thomas Wolcott, deputizing 100 Flint policemen and 60 GM plant guards to enforce the order, was laughed out of Fisher 1 and Fisher 2 by the 500 union stalwarts remaining there. The sheriff retreated in the face of boos and catcalls from strikers who were voters and, in some cases, neighbors. However, GM guards regained control of the factory gates while strikers were distracted.

Lee Pressman, the young general counsel for the CIO, tried a flank attack on the injunction, and it worked spectacularly well.

Acting on a hunch, Pressman asked a friend to scan the list of GM stockholders to see whether Judge Black held any General Motors stock. A few hours later Pressman got his answer. "I was practically bowled over with joy when I was informed that . . . he possessed 3,365 shares of General Motors stock currently valued at $219,000. It was a real break for us." The disclosure, accompanied by UAW demands that Black be impeached, discredited the court order. GM had lost the first round.

In advance of the union victory, however, Homer Martin as UAW president had declared that the injunction would be obeyed. He added that he would be willing to deal with plant managers if GM's top executives would begin to discuss "broad principles" on seniority, speedup, hours, and protection for union activity. In effect, Martin was conceding defeat on the UAW's chief objective— national recognition. Beginning to question Martin's ability even before this, John L. Lewis grumbled that a couple of husky auto workers sitting on Homer's mouth would be almost as vital as those sitting down in GM's plants.

With all the ups and downs, spirits were high when the union's Executive Board—Reuther present—convened in Flint on January 3. The union created a Board of Strategy and authorized strikes against every GM plant in the country. Representatives from 50 locals demanded a 30-hour week. John Brophy, a CIO organizer, claimed the UAW had more than 100,000 members. About a thousand unionists formed a 150-car motorcade past the Fisher plants, tooting their horns to encourage the sit-downers inside. Sheriff Wolcott conferred with UAW leaders but neglected to serve the injunction he still carried in his pocket. "There were too many folks around," was his lame excuse.

By then, however, General Motors had switched to a hard-line policy. The corporation rejected all union demands, began a back-to-work campaign, and requested federal help to clear its plants of the unwanted residents. Alfred P. Sloan, Jr., the GM president, posted notices on company bulletin boards and purchased full-page advertisements in daily newspapers to describe the only issue as he saw it: "Will a labor organization run the plants of General

Motors Corporation or will the management continue to do so?" Sloan insisted the firm would not bow to "union dictatorship" and he ridiculed the charge that GM discriminated against union men: "Nothing could be further from the truth."

Asked about the labor-dictator charge, the usually uncertain Homer Martin wryly responded, "Well, I get $3,000 a year and he gets $374,475 with his bonus." By this time plants in eight cities were affected by the strike and 43,800 workers were idled, willingly or not. GM, trying to put the best possible face on its unexpected predicament, claimed there were less than 900 sit-down strikers, with at least 700 in Flint and the rest divided between a lamp plant in Anderson, Indiana, where Victor Reuther had been an organizer, and a transmission plant in Toledo.

At this point an anti-strike organization calling itself the Flint Alliance was formed by George Boysen, former mayor of Flint and once a Buick paymaster. In opening a headquarters to enlist workers and townspeople as members, Boysen piously asserted, "We merely wish an enrollment for its moral effect toward soothing the strike movements and restoring peace in Flint and men and women to their jobs." GM workers, he said, "resent the prospect of prolonged idleness and the suffering it means for them and their families, just when they are getting back on their feet after the years of their depression." A New York public relations man was imported to spread the message. The Alliance later accused UAW officials of Communist loyalties, denounced the strike as the work of outside agitators, and called on Flint citizens to drive them from the city. The immediate response seemed impressive. The Alliance claimed 15,000 members in its first 24 hours of operation.

The UAW's counterattack came quickly. Speaking over a public address system to nonstriking Chevrolet workers changing shifts, Roy Reuther denounced the Flint Alliance as a company union inspired and financed by General Motors. As he talked, someone touched off a small riot by ripping down the loudspeakers. Eight men were injured before police quelled the disorder and the union speaker resumed. The battle led to a call for a mass meeting at Flint's labor temple, and Roy Reuther urged a march on the jail to demand the release of two UAW adherents arrested earlier in the day. "We'll show these police they're not dealing with children!" Roy shouted. "If they want trouble, they'll find 10,000 men marching on Flint." Police armed with tear gas guns routed the union crowd and set up roadblocks to halt caravans of UAW huskies arriving from Detroit and Toledo. The events of January 7 showed how flammable the situation in Flint had become.

Walter Reuther next day flexed his muscle at GM, calling a sit-down strike that halted production at the Cadillac plant in Detroit. Another 4,800 GM workers were idled. In Flint, Boysen's Alliance heralded signatures of more than 11,000 Chevrolet employes, denouncing the strike and proclaiming satisfaction with the status quo. In all, General Motors boasted, 47,000 out of 57,000 in ten plants had signed "loyalty" petitions. And the Reverend Charles E. Coughlin, forgetting his earlier alliance with Frankensteen, appealed for labor peace in the New Year, warning against "false leaders who . . . sow seeds in your souls of capturing factories and dictating to capital how to run its business." As for management, Father Coughlin implored that it "carry religion into the counting room." In Washington, John L. Lewis attempted, successfully, a clever ruse to give the impression that Franklin D. Roosevelt was on the union's side. Arranging a January 9 appointment with the President to discuss the sit-downs, Lewis later met at the Willard Hotel with Edward McGrady, F.D.R.'s labor troubleshooter who had arranged the White House session, and the CIO chief took pains to tip off reporters about the Willard meeting. McGrady, surprised to see reporters when he emerged, muttered only a "no comment." Lewis, equally noncommunicative, simply assumed a pose of mystery and triumph. In Flint the UAW staged a morale-boosting parade outside the two Fisher plants, complete with the ceremonial hoisting of an American flag atop one of the buildings to the notes of a bugle. Children of the sit-down brigade carried banners, one toddler bringing up the rear proclaiming, "My daddy strikes for us little tykes."

Inside the plants the union exercised tight discipline over the strikers. When the sit-downs began, liquor flowed freely on New

Year's Eve and one report said two prostitutes came across the lines. UAW leaders took charge, ejecting outsiders, sending for reinforcements, banning whisky and smoking, and mounting around-the-clock guards. Workers slept in unfinished auto bodies or made beds of car cushions, labeling them "Hotel Astor" or "Hotel Sloan," the last in nose-thumbing honor of GM's executive. A "chief of police" inspected for cleanliness and ordered daily showers for all. Fire drills were held. And for hours at a time strikers practiced hurling car hinges at makeshift targets, just in case they later faced invaders.

Miss Ellen Wilkinson, a member of the British Parliament, was one visitor impressed by sit-down discipline: "So far as a motor plant can be kept spotless they are keeping it so. The cafeterias are neat and clean. The sleeping quarters are tidy."

There was ample time for recreation, too. Hillbilly bands and barbershop quartets were formed. A sit-down song, lyrics by Maurice Sugar, the UAW's lawyer who was close to the Communists in the union, became instantly popular:

> *When they tie the can to a union man,*
> *Sit down! Sit down!*
> *When the speedup comes, just twiddle your thumbs.*
> *Sit down! Sit down!*
> *When the boss won't talk, don't take a walk.*
> *Sit down! Sit down!*

Culture came to Fisher No. 2 in the form of the Union Dramatics Club of New York City, which performed a labor morality play entitled *Virtue Rewarded*. A sample bit of dialogue:

BOSS: Now Bill, your job has been eliminated so now you haven't any seniority rights. But if you can cut the buck on this new operation, your seniority rights will be restored.
BILL: That isn't right.
BOSS: I know, but that's the way we do things here!

Merlin Bishop, as first educational director of the UAW, went into the plants and taught classes. "I turned them into a labor college," Bishop recalls. "Parliamentary law, public speaking, history of the auto industry, labor history. The idea was to occupy their time and take their minds off being isolated."

The sit-down squeeze in key plants was working. After two weeks GM no longer was producing Chevrolets, Cadillacs, or LaSalles. Pontiac and Oldsmobile output was sharply curtailed. The mammoth industrial empire gradually was being strangled by an estimated 600 men in two Flint factories. When Bill Knudsen was asked how much profit the corporation was losing, he replied, "I hate to think about it." Meanwhile, negotiations were stalemated, if not nonexistent.

General Motors decided to try a get-tough approach at Fisher No. 2, where rank and file strikers led by William (Red) Mundale were considered the less staunch of the two UAW occupation forces. Without notice, on the evening of January 11 the heat in Fisher 2 was shut off by the company. A few hours later Flint police who, in effect, were an adjunct of GM security forces, surrounded the entrance, forbidding any further shipments of food into the plant.

Victor Reuther, manning one of the union's sound trucks, was making routine evening rounds to play music and report on the fruitless bargaining. Picket captains rushed toward the truck, shouting, "They've shut off the heat and they've stopped the food going in, and they're trying to freeze our guys and starve them out of the plant!" The sound truck raced to Fisher 2, where Victor and Bill Carney, on loan from the United Rubber Workers, pleaded with the Flint police to allow the food to go through. The appeal was rejected. Shortly before 7:00 P.M., on Victor's command to "take the gates," a determined band of pickets swept the police aside and moved coffee and bread into the beleaguered plant.

About two hours later 50 club-wielding policemen attacked the pickets and, with careful aim, fired a tear gas canister into the plant through a broken window. The battle was joined. Police next fired buckshot and tear gas into pickets and strikers, to be met with stones, pipes, nuts and bolts, soda pop bottles, and coffee mugs. Clubs and knives were used in hand-to-hand encounters. Victor

Reuther ordered a barricade of cars to guard the picket line and sent a crew to the roof of Fisher 2, armed with crude slingshot catapults made potentially lethal by stretching inner tubes between crisscrossed iron pipes. "Our boys let loose a barrage of pound-and-a-half hinges from the roof," Victor recalls. "They were a hell of a lot better shots that I ever dreamed they would be." At the same time, the wind favored the strikers, blowing most of the tear gas back into police ranks. The fighting continued for three hours, with Victor exhorting his troops from the sound truck: "We wanted peace. General Motors chose war. Give it to them!"

Sheriff Wolcott drove to the scene and, within minutes, his car was overturned by pickets supporting the men inside. Three other police cars were captured by the union, and UAW defenders tore up asphalt to get "ammunition" for the fray. When police massed for a fresh attack at midnight, strikers turned a GM-owned high pressure hose on their antagonists. As the stream of icy water whammed into their ranks, the police retreated across an overpass. With that, the fighting was over.

Thirteen strikers were taken to hospitals with bullet wounds. At dawn, however, a defiant chorus of "Solidarity Forever!" was proof that the strikers continued to occupy the plant. Red Mundale, no doubt disappointed that the men inside had been forced to carry the battle, wrote a note to a picket captain outside: "Don't worry about my chin hanging. . . . You know me better than that. But when I see I'm losing the fight and ask for action from the outside, see to it that I get it."

The riot went down in UAW history and legend as "The Battle of Bulls' Run." It proved to be the only attempted use of force to remove the sit-down battalions. It even brought an apologetic statement from GM's Knudsen: "The riot in Flint . . . is very much to be deplored. . . . We are not going to attempt to shut off heat, light, and water. We never intended to. We are not going to encourage violence because we do not believe that labor disputes can be helped by violence." Privately, both GM and UAW sources blamed Flint police for making a touchy situation worse.

The most important result of the battle was a decision by Gover-

nor Frank Murphy to send the National Guard to Flint to preserve
order. About 2,000 troops, plus the governor, arrived in the early
hours of January 12, quite possibly forestalling further bloodshed.
Flint police had set up machine guns but had not yet fired them.
Rejecting demands that the National Guardsmen remove strikers,
Murphy ordered General Motors to stop trying to halt food deliver-
ies to the UAW-captured plants.

Flint judges signed about 300 "John Doe" warrants authorizing
the arrest of men inside the plants on charges of criminal syndical-
ism, inciting to riot, kidnaping, and destruction of property. None
was served.

The encounter at Fisher 2, hailed as a smashing victory by the
United Auto Workers, produced still another sit-down song:

> *Oh, it was a jolly sight,*
> > *On that wintry, chilly night,*
> *When the bulls came out*
> > *To throw us from the fort.*
> *But with bruises, bumps and jolts,*
> > *From the storm of nuts and bolts,*
> *They just turned about*
> > *And made a line for port!*

At the scene of the fracas several thousand union sympathizers
staged a rally the next day in Chevrolet Street, between Fisher 2
and a Chevy plant. In Detroit Walter Reuther pulled the pin at
the Fleetwood Division of Fisher Body, which provided bodies for
Cadillacs, with yet another sit-down strike. With Reuther declaring
it was a sympathy gesture for the Flint strikers, it pushed the total
of idled GM workers past 112,000.

At Fisher 2 a reporter found fewer than 200 men in the plant.
Detroit's Roman Catholic Bishop Michael J. Gallagher saw red
in the sit-down strategy. "We're fearful," he said in a cathedral
sermon, "that it's Soviet planning behind it. The Communists advocate these strikes—often followed by riots—as a smoke screen
for revolution and civil war."

The UAW mobilized hundreds of men from Toledo, Akron, Detroit, and other Midwest cities to prepare for any repetition of the Battle of Bulls' Run. National Guard troops moved into a four-story abandoned schoolhouse and sentries barred the public from the grounds. In their late teens or early twenties, most of the weekend soldiers regarded duty in Flint as a lark and complained only about the frigid weather. However, many were from GM plants or had relatives employed by the corporation, and they were not unsympathetic to the strikers.

General Motors and its allies began putting more pressure on Governor Murphy to act against the strikers. At a meeting of the Flint Alliance, Chairman Boysen won approval of a resolution praising city police in their battle with pickets and strikers and declaring: "We maintain that a small minority—less than 5 percent—has no legal or moral right to deprive the great body of the majority from earning their living." And General Motors had other allies. County Prosecutor Joseph R. Joseph, brushing aside union complaints that he owned 61 shares of GM stock, named Roy and Victor Reuther as those who "directed the combat" at Fisher 2. Also accusing Bob Travis and four others, Joseph promised to bring all the UAW men to trial. At Chevrolet's Gear and Axle Division some 9,000 employes were reported to demand an end to the strike. In Saginaw 3,500 attended an anti-strike rally. Russell B. Porter, *The New York Times* correspondent in Flint, concluded that the strikers probably numbered no more than 2,000 of the 42,000 hourly workers in the city. According to Porter, the others wanted to get back on the job. *Times* coverage of the strike had a pronounced pro-management flavor.

It was at this critical point that Governor Murphy began playing a peacemaker's role. A handsome Irish Catholic who abhorred violence, Murphy had the confidence of the labor leadership because of his liberal record as mayor of Detroit. Capitalizing on this font of good will, the Governor prevailed on UAW officials to evacuate the GM plants as a prelude to negotiations. In return, General Motors would pledge to refrain from operating the factories.

Murphy's mediation was accepted grudgingly by each side and the resulting truce was announced at 3:00 A.M., January 15. By terms of the arrangement, bargaining on all issues was to begin three days later, once the plants were emptied. "We have arrived at peace," said Murphy. And with flying banners and brass bands, Walter Reuther and Richard Frankensteen led 650 workers out of the Cadillac and Fleetwood plants in Detroit into the arms of their wives and children. With Reuther directing the chorus, the unionists sang a variation of a familiar World War I song:

> *The boss is shaking at the knees,*
> *He's shaking in his BVD's.*
> *Hinky, dinky, parley voo.*

Townspeople in Flint rushed to stores and restaurants after hoarding their cash during the strike. "This is a happy town tonight," wrote one reporter. "The agreement is like the end of a depression in its psychological effect upon residents."

But in one of those quirks that often seem to influence history's course, the truce fell apart because of a reporter's curiosity. William H. Lawrence, covering the sit-down for the old United Press, dropped by the office of the Flint Alliance press agent, Larry Williamson, only hours before the plants in Flint were to be evacuated. Entering the open door, Lawrence spotted a press release on the table. It said that General Motors had agreed to negotiate with the Alliance and that there would be a meeting between Knudsen and Boysen. Williamson confirmed that the release could be used. Accompanied by fellow reporter Paul Gallico, Lawrence went to UAW headquarters to arrange coverage of the march-out from the plants. He told Bob Travis about the Alliance press release but the union leader said only, "Oh, don't pay any attention to Boysen." Lawrence and Gallico then entered Fisher 1 and joined in a festive lunch before the evacuation. They were spooning ice cream with Robert Morss Lovett, a union sympathizer from the University of Chicago faculty, when Wyndham Mortimer appeared at the top of the stairs and shouted: "The evacuation is off. We've been doublecrossed." The bewildered newsmen asked for a reason and Mortimer told Lawrence: "You should know. You told us."

The union hierarchy interpreted GM's promise to deal with Boyson as rejection of its major demand for exclusive bargaining rights even before the negotiations began. Lawrence telephoned the story to his office after rechecking with Williamson on the details. Then he repeated the developments to Felix Bruner, General Motors public relations man in Flint. Bruner denied that Knudsen had ever talked to Boysen. Lawrence volunteered to take this message to the UAW Executive Board, then meeting in emergency session. Even as he appeared before the union leaders, however, Gallico broke in to say GM had released a telegram announcing that Knudsen and Boysen had agreed to negotiate. That blew up the deal which had been so carefully arranged by the Governor. The sit-down strikers angrily scrapped plans to leave the plants and called for reinforcements instead.

Were it not for Bill Lawrence's early warning, the UAW would have abandoned its strongholds for far less than it had expected to get. With the strikers still sitting, the National Guard canceled demobilization plans and stayed in town. The mood of Flint went from ecstasy to gloom. "GM was caught in a barefaced violation of the armistice . . . but the union will protect itself," Lewis said.

Turning to Roosevelt for help, Lewis publicly reminded the President of the help he had received from labor in the 1936 campaign when F.D.R. had been the target of conservative business elements. "The same economic royalists have their fangs in labor," said the CIO leader in his florid style. "The workers of this country expect the administration to help the workers in every reasonable way." Roosevelt, aware of the anger in Congress and the nation at the sit-down technique, promptly issued a statement that was widely interpreted as a rebuke to Lewis: "I think, in the interests of peace, there come moments when statements, conversations and headlines are not in order." Secretary of the Interior Ickes sympathized with Lewis but said the open plea for help was a tactical blunder. Monied interests had been demanding similar favors for years, Ickes said, but they had been more tactful about it. Franklin P. Adams, then a popular columnist, sent F.D.R. an epigram by a seventeenth-century

English writer, Matthew Prior, that summed up the state of Roosevelt-Lewis relations:

To John I owed great obligation
But John unhappily thought fit
To publish it to all the nation;
Sure John and I are more than quit.

For the moment, the union looked to Governor Murphy as the workers' savior. Murphy refused demands from the Flint Alliance and others that he use bayonets to force evacuation of the plants. He also directed the state welfare department to provide relief for the strikers on the basis of need, an action that was of great importance to the beleaguered union members. By January 21 the relief rolls in Genesee County had soared. More than 40 clerks were added to handle applications being filed at the rate of several hundred a day.

The CIO also moved to increase pressure on General Motors by calling off strikes in the aluminum and glass industries to assure a flow of materials to Ford, Chrysler, Packard, Nash, Studebaker, and other competitors.

With Murphy continuing to urge that Knudsen agree to negotiations with the UAW, tensions in Flint were rising. Thousands of "loyal" GM workers roared approval of anti-strike resolutions on January 26 and hailed the reopening of one Chevrolet plant with a payroll of 12,000. One nonstriker told the rally, "I don't think it should be necessary to have to fight for my job but I'm a man, and not a mouse, and I'll fight for it if I have to." Union spokesmen promised there would be no violence from their side but warned that reopened GM factories would be targets for sit-downs.

GM management decided to go to court once again for an injunction to get the strikers out of Fisher 1 and 2, properties it valued at $15 million. This time, however, the corporation appeared before a judge without a major financial stake in its profitability. Judge Paul V. Gadola directed an evacuation by 3:00 P.M., February 3, a new zero hour for the union.

Even before the latest get-out order was issued, Roy Reuther met with the UAW's hard-core leadership to consider the bleak outlook. The only key plant still operating was Chevrolet No. 4, where engines were made. Drawing on the back of a shirt cardboard with a blue pencil, Roy Reuther devised a plan to put a further crimp in GM output and simultaneously boost union morale through a seizure of Chevy 4. Rether's battle plan called for a feint attack on Chevrolet No. 9, a ball bearing factory, to attract the company's guards and clear the way for a surprise takeover of the union's real objective, Chevy 4. Aware that the UAW harbored an ample number of company spies, Reuther and Travis made it part of their strategy to capitalize on this fact. The plan to take Chevy 9 would be made known to union headquarters—with the certain knowledge that the word would get to GM—but only a few of the most trusted UAW leaders would be told about Chevy 4.

A heavy GM security force was ready when union men stopped work inside Chevy 9. A 30-minute battle between company police and strikers ensued, with tear gas filling the plant. Women of the UAW Emergency Brigade, in dashing red berets, smashed factory windows from the outside to let the gas escape. Chevy 9 unionists were driven into the street—but only after their diversion had succeeded.

Before a skeleton crew of GM guards at Chevy 4 could summon help, the union commandos had taken control. One of them was Walter Reuther, called in secretly from Detroit to help carry out the scheme. Walter took charge, directing the erection of barricades. "I drove those guys," he recalled. "It took them three days to tear down what we had built up in a few hours." Outside, the women's brigade locked arms and told police, "Nobody can get in except our men."

General Motors was outraged and Governor Murphy, for the first time, acted against union interests in reaction to the UAW deception. He ordered the National Guard's 126th Infantry to set up camp around Chevy 4, and he considered driving the strikers from the building. Finally he ruled that only Chevrolet employes could remain inside, which meant that Walter and Roy Reuther had to leave.

The Guard set up machine guns and howitzers. UAW sympathizers, arriving in Flint from Detroit, Toledo, and other Midwest cities, carried clubs and blackjacks. Inside the plants, nuts, bolts, and car door hinges were stacked high for use in the event an effort was made to force an evacuation. When the court injunction was issued, the strikers wired the Governor a warning that any attempt to make them leave would bring a "bloodbath." CIO attorney Lee Pressman telephoned John L. Lewis at three in the morning to appeal for his appearance in Flint. "I am coming," said Lewis, who subsequently mystified reporters at Union Station in Washington by quoting a line from Tennyson as he boarded a Michigan-bound train: "Let there be no moaning at the bar, when I put out to sea."

Inside Chevy 4 union morale was strong. "It was like we was soldiers holding the fort," said one striker. ". . . Yes sir, Chevy No. 4 was my Alamo." Others took a less heroic view, as this letter reveals:

> Dear Emma,
>   I am very sorry I cannot keep my date with you Thursday but I am in the Chevrolet Factory No. 4 on a sit-down strike. . . . All we have to do is sit! Eat! Sleep! Wash dishes! and Guard! I guess you will have to find a temporary boyfriend because I am staying till we win.
>
>   TONY

"We have the key plant of the G.M. and the eyes of the whole world are looking at us," wrote another, "and we shure [sic] appreciate the cooperation and support we are getting from the outside."

When Lewis arrived in Flint, he played upon Murphy's compassionate nature like a virtuoso, trying desperately to counter public pressure for National Guard eviction of the sit-down strikers.

"What kind of bayonets do you think that you'll use?" Lewis asked the Governor. "You know, if they use the flat, sharp kind, they can push them in a long way, but they can't twist them. . . . On the other hand, if you use the square kind, they can twist them around and make a big hole, but they can't push them in so far."

At another critical point, Lewis told the agonizing Murphy he would enter Chevy 4 himself to urge defiance of an evacuation order: "I shall then walk up to the largest window in the plant, open it, divest myself of my outer raiment, remove my shirt and bare my bosom. Then, when you order your troops to fire, mine will be the first breast that those bullets will strike."

The psychological warfare tactic was effective on Murphy and also served to rally union members solidly behind the Lewis leadership.

At the White House, President Roosevelt spoke to CIO leader Sidney Hillman at a white-tie-and-tails party, then telephoned Lewis in Michigan to propose a compromise settlement. F.D.R. backed a plan calling for GM recognition of the UAW for one month. Rejecting the offer, Lewis said, "Mr. President, my people tell me it's got to be six months." Their talk came to nothing that night.

By this time Lewis was negotiating with William S. Knudsen and, as these contacts dragged on, tensions in Flint became almost unbearable. Prodded by the mayor, both sides agreed to stop walking the streets armed with "sundry pieces of wood and missiles." But it was no secret that thousands of union "shock troops" from outside the city had arrived well armed to resist any use of force to clear out the plants. Walter Reuther was in Flint at the time. A scrawled yellow paper in the Labor History Archives at Wayne State University shows that Bud Simons authorized a pass for Walter Ruether [sic] to enter Fisher 1 "with crew to get pads from cushion room for bedding."

On February 3, the evacuation deadline set by Judge Gadola, about 5,000 UAW loyalists circled in front of Fisher 1 carrying crowbars, stove pokers, pipe, clothes trees, sticks, and clubs. The men inside the plant wore flimsy strips of cheesecloth as makeshift gas masks. Windows were barricaded with steel plates, leaving only small openings for high pressure water hoses. The deadline passed and Governor Murphy sent word to the sheriff to take no action. Instead, bargaining was resumed at President Roosevelt's request.

On February 7, GM's directors met and cut dividends in half. The firm's biggest stockholder, Pierre S. du Pont, was said to have lost $2.5 million by that action. Other auto makers were having a field day at GM's expense. But hard-line advocates in the General Motors hierarchy again prevailed and the corporation once more shut off the heat in the occupied plants. Strikers threw open windows, allowing the fire-fighting equipment to freeze, and let it be known they would burn oily rags to keep warm. GM, faced with possible cancellation of its fire insurance policies, which was precisely what the UAW intended, finally backed down.

Inside the bargaining room Knudsen produced a telegram from President William Green of the AFL declaring that his federation was opposed to any grant of exclusive recognition to the outcast UAW. Rising calmly, Lewis walked to a closet and silently put on his hat and coat. With a cold stare at Knudsen, he said, "Now that Mr. Green and the AF of L have entered into this picture, I suggest that you gentlemen also invite Haile Selassie, because he certainly has as much of a following among your workers. . . ." Even Knudsen burst out laughing and dropped the issue of AFL representation.

Eventually, an agreement was reached. It was written in eight paragraphs on a single page. GM agreed to recognize the UAW as bargaining agent for employes who were members and promised no interference with the right to join, no reprisals against strikers, and the dropping of lawsuits in Flint and Cleveland arising out of the sit-downs. John L. Lewis has described the denouement:

> At three o'clock in the morning on one of the high floors of the Statler Hotel, Mr. Knudsen, the president, Donaldson Brown, chairman of the finance committee of the board, and John Thomas Smith walked into my room, when I was in bed. And they had on their overcoats, and they had their hard hats in their hands, and their gloves on because the room was so cold. I didn't get up, and they said that they would sign the contract at 11 o'clock that morning in Governor Murphy's office. And they did.

Lewis saluted the auto union and paid tribute to Murphy. Knudsen's reaction was terse: "Let us have peace and make cars." And so they did. The industry turned out nearly 400,000 more cars in 1937 than in 1936 despite sit-downs, slowdowns, and conventional strikes. The UAW doubled in size almost immediately and the CIO scored a great follow-up victory three weeks later when U.S. Steel agreed to recognize the Steel Workers Union without a day's work lost. The triumph at Flint was hailed as "unquestionably the greatest, and, by all means, the most strategic victory ever won by American labor and . . . opened all of America's heavy industries to unionization." Interviewed 30 years later, Victor Reuther gave this appraisal: "When we won in Flint, I think this was finally the straw that broke the opposition. From then on, we were on our way."

The crisis also made it clear that the union's new president, Homer Martin, was a rather weak figure. At a crucial point in settlement efforts, he wandered away for hours, attending a movie without leaving word of his whereabouts. John L. Lewis finally exiled him on a speaking tour and Martin heard about the strike settlement when a reporter telephoned him the news in a Chicago hotel room.

Murphy suffered from a citizen backlash against sit-down strikes, losing office in the November 1938 elections. The reaction of Flint-area voters was obvious first in a statewide primary on April 5, 1937, shortly after the sit-downs ended. The city and surrounding Genesee County gave majorities to every Republican candidate on the state ticket, in sharp contrast to the November 1936 results, when Democrats carried all but eight precincts in the county.

For the Reuther brothers, the agreement was a glorious breakthrough for their union, not yet a year old, and marked personal triumphs, particularly for Roy and Victor who had been in the thick of the fight from the start. Walter, who had joined them on the battlefield at critical moments, such as the seizure of Chevrolet Plant No. 4, shared in the glow of victory. The campaign ribbons they earned in Flint would carry them far in the hierarchy of the United Auto Workers. But their personal gains were small compared to the advances scored by their union and the CIO.

"It is a satire worthy of the gods," wrote Saul Alinsky, "that thousands of wearied men, angry and bitter with standing for hours beside an inhuman, constantly speeded-up assembly line, should achieve their triumph by the simple act of sitting down."

Clay Fountain, fired from Chevrolet Gear and Axle Division for union activity, marched back with a UAW-CIO button on his shirt: "This tiny trinket, about the size of a two-bit piece, made of tin and covered with gaudy celluloid, was my badge of honor. It gloated louder than words over the downfall of a proud and mighty corporation."

The immediate reaction in Michigan was more sit-downs. About 60,000 Chrysler workers, led by Richard Frankensteen, struck on March 8, 1937. The union's major problem was to dissuade most of them from remaining in the plant. When police roughed up sit-downers in strikes at other Detroit factories, the UAW showed its power by rallying 150,000 people in Cadillac Square to protest against police abuses. Chrysler signed up with John L. Lewis on April 6.

CHAPTER EIGHT

Bloody Rouge

ON A CHILL DAY THAT SAME MONTH, APRIL OF 1937, A SMALL plane groped aloft through bumpy skies from the old Detroit City Airport and, with the pilot "flying by the seat of his pants," bucked its way across town until it was above Henry Ford's River Rouge plant, probably the most impressive and diversified industrial complex in the nation. Its payroll numbered in the tens of thousands, barely a handful of them union members. At low altitude, the craft circled the citadel of mass production, loudspeakers under each wing beaming earthward a message intended to convince Ford workers changing shifts below that the United Auto Workers represented the wave of the future. Giving voice to the union message were Walter and Victor Reuther, handling the microphone much as if they were back in an earthbound sound truck in Flint.

Although Walter Reuther had been most careful in preparing for his aerial adventure, the laws of physics were not cooperative. The pilot flew as low and as slowly as he dared, but the plane's progress remained so swift that Reuther's impassioned words were blowing in the wind—unheard by the men below.

The flight could not be counted a failure, however. The unique attempt at union proselytizing from the skies attracted the public attention Reuther sought for the UAW drive to organize Ford, last holdout among the Big Three auto makers. Reuther also succeeded in dramatizing the plight of a union that, blocked by Ford labor spies and bully boys on the ground, had to take to the air to appeal to Rouge workers. Finally, the airborne expeditionary force, whatever its inadequacies, underscored the elemental fact that Walter Reuther henceforth would have to be included in any assessment of the UAW leadership; he was young and imaginative, ready to experiment with untried techniques.

The April flight was among Reuther's first demonstrations of an ability to seize upon a simple stunt, a catchy slogan, or an ambitious and carefully conceived program to enlist sympathy both for the UAW and his own leadership qualities.

Before the takeoff, Reuther issued a public statement that boasted, too bravely, perhaps, about several thousand Ford workers already on union rolls. At the same time, he announced grand plans for a public mass meeting and other organizing efforts that, he suggested, would bring Henry Ford to his knees. It was fine publicity for the UAW—and for Walter Reuther. That day, for the first time, he won a place in *The New York Times Index,* several weeks after Victor and Roy had been accorded mention by virtue of brushes with the law in Flint.

Barely a week before the flight, Henry Ford had tossed a direct challenge to Reuther's union in a newspaper interview: "We'll never recognize the United Automobile Workers Union or any other union." Reuther had no cause to doubt the total sincerity of the declaration; Ford, after all, had been born during the Civil War and was the champion of a muddle of social ideas equally antique. Ford's antipathy toward organized labor was expressed even more pungently in another public statement that month:

> Labor unions are the worst thing that ever struck the earth, because they take away a man's independence. Financiers are behind the unions and their object is to kill competition so as to reduce the income of the workers and eventually bring on war. . . . I have always made a better bargain for our men than any outsider could. We have never had to bargain against our men, and we don't expect to begin now.

Just in case his thousands of employes overlooked a carefully plotted series of newspaper interviews, all subsequent to the UAW's victory in Flint, Ford had well-muscled operatives of the Ford Service Department—his private army—place stacks of the *Ford Almanac* at the Rouge gates early in April. The Service men made certain each worker carried away at least one copy. If they read nothing else in the paperbound volume, it was hoped the employes would study an article titled "Musings of Smoke-Stack Joe":

> SHILLBERG—HA HA! I'll bet when he hears Ma's gone he'll be over to the house tryin' to join me up to this labor racket. None of THAT FOR ME either. Why should I pay money to a

gang FOR NOTHING? They can't give me a single thing MORE'N I ALREADY GOT.

Never had to pay to work before—why start NOW.

'Specially when they won't show me the books and let me see what they do with MY MONEY.

IF I PAY money for groceries, I GET GROCERIES in return. If I pay money for a suit, I GET A SUIT in return. Why should I pay money to this crowd for NOTHING?

And look who's asking—all these fellows who got their labor movement education in Russia. . . . It all looks and smells like COMMUNISM to me. . . .

It is worth noting that the anonymous author of "Musings" began with an anti-Semitic reference and then, with Walter and Victor Reuther surely in mind, attempted in his less than literate style to find a link between the UAW and Communism; the Reuther brothers were the only men of prominence in the union who had ever seen the Soviet Union. Within three months the senior counsel of the Ford Motor Company was to try publicly to uncover the identical link.

Confronted with both company muscle and company propaganda, Walter Reuther argued for a new organizing idea that, if hardly startling, merited consideration because no one else had anything better to offer. He proposed a distribution of union handbills at the Rouge gates by enough sympathizers to make a show of force and help foster the idea that the UAW had significant support inside Ford's sooty acres.

Reuther could lay claim to the Rouge because it fell within the geographical jurisdiction of his West Side Local, the home local of the few Rouge workers who had braved company reprisal to sign up with the union. Because of the geography of his UAW power base, he also was a member of the Ford Organizing Committee. His committee position was not preeminent, however. Rivals abounded. All knew that the individual ultimately credited by the men in the shops for getting Ford's signature on a union agreement would achieve instant acclaim that, quite probably, would carry him into the presidency of the UAW.

Both politically and physically, Reuther's strongest rival was Richard Truman Frankensteen, the former University of Dayton football player who, six months older than the young man from Wheeling, was UAW organizing director for the entire city of Detroit. More important, Frankensteen had been duly designated as leader of the Ford organizational drive.

After receiving formal permission from Frankensteen for a hand-bill distribution, and promising him full participation, the Reuther forces prepared a leaflet they called "Unionism Not Fordism," a play on words intended to capitalize on company-sponsored "Ford-isms"—small pasteboards handed to Rouge workers at the plant gates by Service Department personnel. The Ford cards featured anti-union arguments of the most simplistic cast:

—"Figure it out for yourself. If you got into a union they have GOT YOU—but what have YOU got?"

—"Our men ought to consider whether it is necessary for them to pay some outsider every month FOR THE PRIVILEGE of working at Ford's."

Reuther realized the planned leaflet distribution could result in a violent confrontation between the union forces and the strong-arm crews of the Ford Service Department. The head of the department was Harry Herbert Bennett, a former Navy boxer whose ring name was "Sailor Reese." The bantam Bennett, one of Henry Ford's closest advisers, wielded power within the company that could be vetoed only by Ford himself, a prerogative the proprietor rarely exercised. For all practical purposes the Service Department chief was "the law" at the River Rouge. His word came close to being unquestioned law in all of the neighboring city of Dearborn, where the police chief, Carl Brooks, was an honorably discharged veteran of Ford Service.

In 1937 *The New York Times* described Ford Service as the largest private quasi-military organization in the world. To an astonishing degree, Bennett had peopled it with athletes, former convicts, discharged police officers, and prizefight promoters.

Reuther did not want trouble from this menacing source and did what he could to avoid it. Throughout preparations for the demonstration he emphasized to his associates that union people must not allow themselves to be maneuvered into a position in which they could be accused of causing violence; Ford would have to do that. To make certain the UAW was clearly within its rights, he went to the city clerk of Dearborn, outlined his plans, filed a copy of "Unionism Not Fordism," and, perhaps to his own consternation, was granted a permit to distribute the handbills during the afternoon change of shifts on May 26, 1937.

The demonstration was to focus on Gate Four of the Rouge, where an elevated bridge crossed Miller Road for the convenience of workers using the streetcars that stopped across the highway from the plant. The Ford Company had built the bridge and had leased it to the Detroit Street Railway Commission. It was not posted as private property and was used freely by vendors and others having no connection with the company. Reuther and his associates visited the bridge, or overpass, twice in advance of May 26 to survey the terrain. No one bothered them.

The ease with which preparations were accomplished was deceptive. Spies kept Harry Bennett informed about Reuther's plans and, behind the scenes, the boss of Ford Service got busy. With first word of the intended UAW foray, some men were reassigned from production and other work to temporary duty in the Service Department. An inspector of connecting rods was told to station himself daily inside an auto parked near one of the Rouge gates and to report anything that "didn't look right." Later, as he told it, his orders were amended: "If I caught anybody passing handbills, beat him up and bring him to the Service office."

On May 24, shortly before Reuther arrived at the Gate Four overpass on one of his survey trips, photographer Arnold Freeman of the Detroit *Times* recognized a lounger there whom he had recently photographed at police headquarters in connection with a holdup.

"I see you are back to your old tricks again," Freeman remarked.

"We were hired, as far as I know, temporary," the man replied, "to take care of these union men that are to distribute these pamphlets."

The lounger reported that Ford Service planned to assign four of its hired thugs to each UAW man who appeared.

Another news photographer, sensing there would be trouble on May 26, tried to take some general views at Gate Four in advance. One man detached himself from a knot of idlers nearby and chided, "You know how it is—the boys don't want their pictures taken." A reporter, aware of Ford's preparations, inquired at Bennett's office whether the company planned any countermove against the union demonstration. He was told Ford would not interfere in any manner but "maybe some loyal employes might resent it."

Because of the potential for trouble, the Senate Civil Liberties Committee sent staff observers to the scene. Reuther invited representatives of the Conference for the Protection of Civil Rights; one Chicago clergyman, the Reverend Raymond Prior Sanford, responded and arrived, just in time, after an overnight train trip.

Shortly after noon on May 26 Reuther presided at a meeting of more than 100 union members and sympathizers at headquarters of the West Side Local. He told the group he carried a city permit for the demonstration in his pocket and did not anticipate violence. To minimize the chance of a physical clash, the meeting voted to assign the task of actual handbill distribution to the women volunteers, with a few men going along to lend moral support and, should the need arise, physical protection. Women outnumbered men at the meeting by a ratio of four to one, evidence enough, it would seem, of the intimidation of the men who worked at Ford's. Most of the women belonged to the West Side Local Auxiliary: wives, mothers, and girl friends of union members who, for the most part, felt they had to remain undercover. Others were from an Emergency Brigade that Reuther had patterned after one in Flint; these women wore green berets.

Shortly before 2:00 P.M. Reuther and Dick Frankensteen drove to Gate Four in separate autos. Several UAW organizers and the Chicago cleric went with them. The women were to follow by streetcar, arriving in time for the main change of shifts in mid-afternoon.

As Reuther approached the stairway leading to the overpass, a swarthy, dark-haired man stepped forward and demanded, "Who are you?"

"I am an American citizen," Reuther responded, then mounted

the stairs without interference. News photographers were waiting on the bridge. So too were several dozen rough-appearing men, none wearing the badge of a Ford employe or carrying a lunch pail. Slouching against the railings, they seemed unconcerned as the photographers snapped pictures of Reuther, Frankensteen, and others in the UAW group.

Ted Greis, a Ford Service man and wrestling referee, climbed the stairs and approached Reuther and Frankensteen. So did Sam Taylor, a Ford foreman who was president of the right-wing Knights of Dearborn, and Wilfred Comment, another foreman, who had a pair of handcuffs hooked to his belt. As the trio walked forward, the idlers sprang to life and converged on the union leaders.

"This is private property!" a voice yelled. "Get the hell off of here!"

Reuther and Frankensteen exchanged wordless glances, then turned to leave. Reuther, in uncontroverted testimony at a subsequent federal hearing, related what happened next:

> I had taken about three steps, no more than four, and I was slugged in the back of the head from the rear. And then I was immediately surrounded by twelve or fifteen men and I was pounced upon, and all that I did was—I made an attempt to protect my face by shielding my face with my crossed arms. In the meantime I was being pounded in all parts of the head and upper body. . . .
>
> Then I was knocked to the ground, where I was kicked and also beaten on the head again. And then at the instruction of the fellow who was leading the group, he gave the command, he said, "That is enough, fellows." Then I thought I was going to be released and I was raised to my feet by my shoulders. And then some fellows picked my feet and they held me parallel to the concrete; I would say about three and a half to four feet off the concrete. . . . And at a signal from the leader I was thrown on my back on the concrete. After I was on my back again I was kicked again in the head, temples, all parts of the upper body, and an attempt was made to hold my legs apart to kick me between the legs, but I squirmed

enough so that they were not able to do that very successfully. . . .

Q. Well, about how many times were you raised and knocked
down? Can you estimate that?

A. I would say seven or eight times that I was raised up
parallel with the concrete and thrown down on my back. . . .
I finally found myself lying beside Richard Frankensteen, who
at that time was lying face down with his coat up over his
head. . . . I was permitted to lie there while I was being
kicked and punched . . . and then from there I was dragged
by the feet over near the north stairway. I was raised up very
roughly by my shoulder, by my collar, by my coat, and I was
thrown down the stairway. As I got to the top of the stairs I
was able to get my grip on the two railings and I held on there
to brace myself, and then someone else from the rear—several
fellows from the rear—were able to wrench me loose . . . and
throw me down the first flight of iron steps. . . . And then I was
kicked down the other two flights of stairs in the cinders. . . .

While lying dazed in the cinders at the side of Miller Road, with
his temples swollen to the point where they nearly covered his eyes,
Reuther got no reprieve. Four or five men jumped him and, after
he had struggled to his feet, pursued him in and out of cars parked
along the highway, striking blows as they adjusted their pace to his
faltering run. Reuther gained freedom only when his pursuers
noticed the arrival by streetcars of the handbill-bearing women,
and decided they were a more inviting target.

Frankensteen remained a prisoner of the Service Department's
professional tormenters—because he did not wholly subscribe to
Reuther's doctrine of passive self-defense. Struck from behind, he
fought back. Asked at the later federal hearing if he had resisted
assault, he testified, "Yes, I did, in trying to ward off blows; I did
attempt to push away my assailants." *The New York Times* next
morning quoted witnesses as saying that because Frankensteen put
up a scrap, he "was more severely pummeled than the others." Es-
sentially, however, his fate paralleled Reuther's:

I should judge that I had not taken at the most four steps
when I received a thud on the back of the head. I turned to

defend myself . . . and a volley of blows just rained on me. . . .

Q. Did you remain on your feet during this attack?

A. Not for very long, no. . . . I was knocked down several times and picked up. . . . Kicking was quite the practice. They at one point put their heel into my stomach and twisted on it, and at another point they held my legs apart and kicked me in the groin. And then a man whom I have since learned was Taylor would say, "That is enough—let him up." They would stand me on my feet and Mr. Taylor would then proceed to knock me over again. . . .

Q. How did you get off the bridge?

A. I was bounced down. . . . After we had reached the bottom of the stairs, there at the cinders between the car tracks and the fence, they continued to drive me and slug me the rest of the distance. I was knocked down several times on the cinders. At one time my coat was thrown . . . over to the car tracks. Taylor . . . said, "Go pick up your coat." I tried to reach it and as I bent over to reach it, Taylor kicked me and then proceeded to slug me again after I had been knocked down again.

A photographer testified Frankensteen was beaten so severely "I didn't think he would ever get up again." The union leader hardly disagreed. "It was the worst licking I've ever taken," he said.

Reuther and Frankensteen, both bloodied and dazed, found each other after escaping the Service thugs and flagged down an auto driven by photographer Freeman of the Detroit *Times.* "For God's sake, get me to the hospital, Freeman," cried Frankensteen, "I'm hurt." The photographer did not have to be told. "Mr. Frankensteen was bleeding from the mouth and nose. His shirt was torn. He had no coat on. And Walter Reuther's head on both sides was swollen right over—over his eyes. . . ." Freeman drove the two men and Robert Kanter, another UAW organizer who had been beaten on the overpass, to the office of Dr. Eugene M. Shafarman. X-rays revealed no broken bones. Ice packs, bandages, and bed rest were prescribed.

With the most prominent UAW leaders out of the way, the Ford toughs set upon others in the union contingent. As the women tried to get off the streetcars, Ford men blocked the exits—shoving, punching, kicking, and shouting such niceties as, "Why don't you get your citizenship papers before you come fucking around here . . .!" A few women got off the cars but, unable to pass out their leaflets, tossed them into the air.

Catherine (Babe) Gelles, a UAW volunteer, was not intimidated by the Ford Service man who braced her as she tried to dispose of her pamphlets. With tears in her eyes, she traded punches with him as if she were a man, while he shouted, "You little devil! You little hellcat!"

Another woman, kicked in the stomach, vomited at the feet of the Reverend Sanford. The clergyman implored a mounted policeman to intervene. The officer judiciously cautioned the attackers: "You mustn't hurt these women." It was more an appeal than an order. Mrs. Gelles demanded that an ambulance be summoned for the woman who had aroused Mr. Sanford's sympathy. "Let her get back the way she came out here," the policeman replied. "We didn't ask her out. . . ."

William Merriweather, a UAW member assigned to help escort the women, was seized from behind and, as his unzipped jacket flopped open to reveal a union button, someone yelled, "Get that union son of a bitch!" Beaten to the ground, Merriweather was kicked repeatedly, his assailants crying, "Kill him! Kick his brains out! Stomp his face in!" The union man lost consciousness. Mrs. Gelles and another woman ran up and grabbed him under the arms. "Oh, my God, Merriweather, come on!" implored Mrs. Gelles. The attackers ordered, "Run! Run!" Merriweather could not run. Collapsing, he rolled under a parked automobile and hid. His back was broken.

UAW volunteer Robert Dunham had salvaged some leaflets from the besieged women and, distributing them to passing motorists two blocks from the Rouge, noted a group of men pointing at him from across the street. Ducking into a nearby beer garden, Dunham telephoned the West Side Local. Assured that a car would pick him up, he returned to the sidewalk and felt relieved when a green Ford pulled to the curb. Three men got out and, as Dunham greeted them as friends, they beat him unconscious. He spent three weeks in the hospital, vomiting blood all the while. He was unable to work for months.

A UAW group approached Gate Five and faced about 30 men who raced toward them shouting, "Here the bastards come! Go get them!" One member of the union party was a Negro, John Clemens. "You black bastard!" cried a Ford goon, seizing Clemens and tossing him around as if he were a sack of flour. "Hit him in the stomach! Hell, you can't hurt a nigger when you hit him over the head."

Reporters and photographers had notes seized and film plates confiscated. For all save the men of Ford Service, May 26 was a day of horror at the Rouge. Reuther, after his brutal beating, was remembered as having "a look of terror written upon his face."

John L. Lewis sent a telegram to Frankensteen: "Keep your poise. It is merely an instance." Frankensteen said: "If Mr. Ford thinks this will stop us, he's got another think coming. We'll go back there with enough men to lick him at his own game."

Within the week, *Time* magazine published a devastatingly accurate account of events at the overpass, featuring photos of the effective Ford Service technique, practiced on Frankensteen, of pulling the victim's coat over his head and pinning his arms in the process, so the body is defenseless against oncoming blows. Another picture showed Reuther, swollen-faced, trying to comfort a bloodied Frankensteen. "It looked very much," *Time* concluded, "as if that brutal beating might hurt Henry Ford as much as it hurt Richard Frankensteen." Henry R. Luce, often at odds with Ford, paid a price for that summation. All Ford Motor Company advertising was withdrawn from *Time, Life,* and *Fortune* for the next 70 weeks.

Ford and his lieutenants pretended innocence. Harry Bennett insisted no Ford Service employes nor plant police had been involved in violence of any kind. His men, he stated, had written instructions to permit the leaflet distribution without interference.

W. J. Cameron, the company spokesman on radio's "Ford Sunday Evening Hour," told a Detroit convention audience: "Henry

Ford has not rioted. His employes have not rioted. As a matter of cold fact, there never has been any labor disturbance of any sort in the Ford shops."

The public prosecutor and a municipal judge in Detroit took a different view, convening a one-man grand jury. Even in the city of Dearborn there were official demands that charges be preferred against half a dozen members of the police force. Most important, however, the recently created National Labor Relations Board acted quickly and cited the Ford Motor Company for alleged infringements of the rights of labor. After a month of hearings, during which some 150 witnesses gave more than 3,000 pages of testimony, the federal agency decided that, with insignificant exceptions, Ford was guilty as charged.

"The testimony concerning the events on the overpass," the board concluded, "establishes that the attack upon the union group was vicious and unnecessarily brutal, particularly in view of the fact that no resistance was offered by those attacked. Reuther and Frankensteen were singled out for particular attention and given terrific beatings. . . ."

Reuther was the first union witness at the NLRB hearings, where he was the target of dogged baiting by Ford's counsel, Louis J. Colombo, Sr. Persistently tossing out unsupported innuendo, Colombo tried to exploit Reuther's period of employment in the Soviet Union by suggesting it was evidence of sinister ties with conspiratorial Communism:

> *Q. You went to Russia?*
> A. That is correct.
>
> *Q. . . . You and your brother were in Russia?*
> A. Well, I have already told you that. We worked there.
>
> *Q. You both worked in factories in Russia?*
> A. That is correct.
>
> *Q. And you went over there to study their system of government, didn't you?*
> A. I studied their system the same as I studied the system of Germany, Italy, and Japan.

Q. I am not talking about that.

A. You asked me why I went there.

Q. One of the purposes of going there was to study the Soviet system of government?

A. The purpose—

Q. Please answer the question. Was it?

A. We went into Russia to study conditions there the same as we did in Germany.

Q. The Russian system of government?

A. No, we didn't. We went there to study conditions.

Q. What conditions: political conditions and economic conditions?

A. Social and economic conditions.

Q. In other words, the Russian system—the political, the social, and the economic conditions under the Soviet Union, is that not right?

A. We went there to study, as I said before, the social conditions of Russia as we did in other countries.

Q. Under the Soviet system?

A. Naturally, it would be under the Soviet system.

Q. You also studied the method which they used to start riots—?

A. I never saw any riots started in Russia.

Q. . . . . All right. Did you study the Russian method of revolution?

A. I didn't. I worked there in a factory as a technician.

Q. Are you a Communist?

A. I am not, never have been.

Q. You never have been a Communist and you are not a Communist now?

A. That is correct.

Q. Do you have any respect for private property?
A. I do.

Q. Do you respect private property?
A. I do.

Q. Are you a member of the CIO?
A. I am.

Q. And the UAW?
A. I am.

Q. How many Communists belong to the CIO?
A. I am in no position to tell you that.

Q. How many Communists are there in the UAW?
A. I can't answer that either.

Colombo asked about the UAW Ladies Auxiliary and the Emergency Brigade of the West Side Local:

Q. Any Communists among them?
A. I do not know that.

Q. Wives and sweethearts of Communists?
A. I couldn't state that. I said I didn't know whether they were Communists.

Q. Any single women among them?
A. There were.

As the NLRB piled up evidence against Ford, Reuther was planning a second leaflet distribution at the Rouge—to make it clear the UAW had not been frightened off by the company's musclemen, and to put a Reuther imprint on the Ford organizing drive that was so important, politically, within the union.

On the day fixed for the repeat demonstration, August 11, 1937, the UAW Executive Board was meeting in Milwaukee. Reuther, Wyndham Mortimer, and Ed Hall were absent; they were in Detroit. Frankensteen, guarding his position as director of the Ford drive, argued that another demonstration might alienate more Rouge workers than it would impress. He won adoption of an ultimatum to the absentees that they return at once to the Board meeting or stand suspended. The threat was effective. Reuther and the others returned to Milwaukee.

Then came a battle of words, the opening public shots in a bitter factional struggle that was to threaten the very existence of the UAW in the months ahead. Homer Martin argued in a public statement that the suspension threat was necessary because of the "insolent and disruptive attitude and action" of Reuther, Mortimer, and Hall. More pointedly, he added, "Walter Reuther is not, nor has he been, chairman of the Ford Organizing Committee, and as a member of that committee it was not necessary that he be in Detroit. . . ."

At 3:00 A.M. the next morning Reuther, Mortimer, and Hall countered with a joint statement of their own in which they contended that Martin's words reflected "an emotional outburst rather than sober thought." Claiming they had gone to Detroit with Martin's full knowledge and consent, they said: "Every automobile worker will regret such emotional outbursts on the part of their leaders, as the only people who benefit by publicizing individual differences and factionalism are the employers. We prefer that all differences in our organization be ironed out on the floor of our international convention and not on the front pages of the daily press."

With Reuther absent, about 1,000 union members and sympathizers returned on schedule to the gates of Henry Ford's fortress and handed out leaflets during the afternoon change of shifts without a semblance of disorder. This did not mean Ford was opening his gates to organized labor. Persisting fear inside the Rouge seemed evident. Reported the Associated Press: "Many of the Ford workers, particularly those entering the plant, displayed a marked reluctance to accept the newspapers. Those who did take them either discarded the papers or stuffed them in their pockets before entering the plant. Employes leaving the plant accepted the papers much more freely."

In an editorial *The New York Times* said: "It may be a sad commentary on the state of affairs in the United States that a presentation of arguments for and against unionism, made at the gates of a manufacturing plant, should be treated as rather important news merely because it did not produce violence. Nevertheless, the fact that nobody got hurt may show that the pressure of public opinion is having its effect."

· Public opinion had no effect on the officials of the city of Dearborn, which remained a company town subservient to the wishes of Ford's leaders. In its own rejoinder to Reuther's second demonstration, the City Council adopted an ordinance prohibiting the distribution of literature in "congested areas." In the next few months nearly a thousand UAW people were arrested for violations, effectively curbing handbill distribution at the Rouge.

Although the immediate outcome was inconclusive, with the union failing to achieve its organizing goal, Henry Ford never again dared unmuzzle the goon squads of his Service Department in a public situation. Because of the power of public opinion the UAW was the winner on points at "The Battle of the Overpass." It was one of the classic confrontations in labor history, and the leaders of the union forces, Reuther and Frankensteen, emerged in heroic roles. The attention they received for their beatings, however, only strengthened their rivalry for power within the United Auto Workers. Each saw himself as the heir to Homer Martin's throne.

CHAPTER NINE

The Leaping Parson

SOME CALLED HIM "THE LEAPING PARSON," BECAUSE OF HIS BACK-
ground as athlete and preacher. He was christened Warren Homer
Martin but had dropped the first name long before becoming president of the United Auto Workers. One of the more bizarre figures
to gain prominence in the labor movement, Martin in 1937 sat on
an uneasy throne, challenged by a host of subordinates, Walter
Reuther included, who considered themselves better fitted to be
lord of auto labor's still-shaky manor. In truth, Martin was a man
of many limitations.

Born in Marion, Illinois, a coal mining town in a region with
a deserved reputation for frequent and violent labor disputes, Martin initially had no thought of associating with trade unionism.
Sports and a fundamentalist zeal for spreading the word of God
were his preoccupations. After study at the Baptist Theological
Seminary in Kansas City, he was ordained at the age of 19. When
he was 22 Martin won the national hop, step, and jump champion-
ship and thus became the Leaping Parson. Named to the 1924
Olympic team, he was not able to make the trip to the games and
with that his athletic career ended.

The Depression found Martin preaching in Leeds, Missouri, near
Kansas City. It was not a well-to-do parish. Many of its members
were auto workers with uncertain incomes. Quite appropriately,
Martin took an interest in the men who made cars and began
demanding reforms in the plants. Some of the influential folk in
the congregation thought the pastor out of line and, in 1934, invited him to leave the pulpit. Finding a job in the Chevrolet plant
in Kansas City, he joined the UAW.

Martin's revivalist skill at convincing audiences of workers that
they, as union members, would be doing the will of the Lord
pushed him into prominence as a UAW leader. Although this was
one of his few qualifications for leadership, it was vitally important
in the years when the union was struggling to get a footing. It was

not deemed remarkable, therefore, that the AFL, upon chartering the federal locals of auto workers in 1935, reached out to Homer Martin and, by naming him international vice-president, gave him a national pulpit. A year later, on the eve of the UAW's great breakthrough at Flint, Martin had moved into the presidency and, at that point, his limitations became more apparent.

Frank Winn recalls Martin summoning him to draft a telegram to all General Motors locals, before Flint, ordering them to go on strike at seven o'clock the next morning. Aware of the union's weaknesses, Winn asked Martin if he possibly could be serious. "I'm really not going to do it," was the reply. "I'm going to get them all on the telephone tomorrow morning before seven o'clock and tell them not to go on strike. I'm just trying to scare General Motors." Aghast at Martin's concept of intelligent strategy, Winn and other UAW aides transmitted word of Martin's folly to John L. Lewis, who squelched the maneuver.

As an administrator, the UAW president was almost totally inadequate. Merlin Bishop, then the union's national education director, recalls that when Martin would leave Detroit on business, UAW men along his route who coveted the education job would persuade him to fire Bishop. "When he came back," the victim remembers, "I'd have to get Walter Reuther and the Education Committee to parade into his office to get me reestablished. What the hell, I was fired five times in six months!"

Trouble within the UAW high command boiled up in April of 1937, almost immediately after the Flint triumph. Sensing threats to his $3,000-a-year job, Martin broke up the leadership of Flint Local 156, now the largest in the union and studded with men known nationally because of their sit-down successes. He demoted Robert Travis and ordered the transfer of Roy Reuther to another city. Victor Reuther, then director of organization for Indiana, was downgraded and Winn was fired as publicity director.

Following the sit-downs there was an epidemic of unauthorized wildcat strikes, 170 in five months at General Motors, or an average of more than one a day. The walkouts partly resulted from failure of the auto companies to fully accept the UAW and handle grievances promptly and effectively. The workers "didn't have much patience if they were frustrated at this first level," says Winn, "and they found out that stopping work was the quickest way to get action. There were plently of foremen resentful or bullheaded enough . . . to provide the frustration."

Martin did not know how to handle the situation. He vacillated. After General Motors proposed a new contract clause requiring the company to "forthwith discharge" anyone stopping production before exhausting grievance procedures, Martin responded that "we are prepared to cooperate and assist your position." UAW militants were outraged and Martin withdrew his offer to cooperate on firings.

The UAW's 1937 convention at Milwaukee was the public stage upon which Martin and his opponents battled for authority. The Martin faction, with Richard T. Frankensteen as principal lieutenant, was called the Progressive Caucus and was, in effect, a political party within the union. The Progressives claimed majority support among top UAW leaders, most of whom were not averse to centralization of power. Also giving Martin their allegiance were many of the more conservative secondary leaders.

Walter Reuther was a leader of the opposition party, the Unity Caucus, which was an alliance of Socialists, Communists, and nonpolitical but otherwise militant trade unionists. As of 1937 Wyndham Mortimer, the UAW's first vice-president, was considered the most powerful individual in the Unity group.

The two caucuses fought an unceasing war that consumed much of the energies of union officers. "There have been few occasions in the annals of American labor on which fratricidal strife reached an equal pitch of bitterness and fury," concluded labor historian Walter Galenson. To Walter Reuther and many others, the internal struggle was a tragic and unhappy distraction from the work that had to be done, yet something that had to be dealt with as reflecting the inevitable contest in a new and democratic union to establish a sound and stable leadership.

Initially, the in-house bickering did not inhibit UAW growth. Richard T. Leonard, an Auto Workers pioneer, recalls Board member Tracy Doll remarking, "If we don't cut out this damn factionalism, we'll wake up tomorrow morning with another million members."

Preparations for the Milwaukee convention began weeks beforehand. Martin chartered new locals calculated to favor his cause. And more than a month before the opening gavel, the two factions held pre-convention meetings to plot divergent strategy on issues and personalities.

The Unity party met in Toledo with Mortimer the chief. Frequently quoted in union circles as saying. "I'd rather be red than pink," Mortimer had gone to work in the coal fields at age 12 for thirteen hours a day and joined the UAW while employed at the White Motor Company plant in Cleveland. Others prominent at the Unity meeting included Ed Hall, Robert Travis, Walter Reuther, and Emil Mazey, just ousted by Martin as chief organizer of the Briggs local. Their slogan: "Unity for the Auto Workers."

On that same summer weekend, Martin gathered his Progressives in South Bend, proposing that Mortimer be replaced by Frankensteen as first vice-president and that Hall be dropped, too, from the list of officers. The Unity Caucus dispatched Reuther to South Bend to argue for what he pictured as a peace program: disband the political parties, make Frankensteen a vice-president, and re-elect Mortimer and Hall. The Progressives booed him from the meeting hall.

More than 1,000 delegates attended the Milwaukee convention, many of those from Detroit traveling by chartered train. One coach passenger, a Communist, thought it a good idea to enliven the journey by leading group singing of the "Internationale." A wiser Unity-ite interrupted the songfest.

Opening day was August 23 and, upon his arrival at the meeting, Martin was acclaimed for 90 minutes by delegates snake-dancing and singing in the aisles. Raised on sturdy shoulders, the UAW president was carried to the platform. Even members of the Unity Caucus, having endorsed him for another term since they lacked the votes to do otherwise, joined in the ovation.

Secretary-Treasurer George F. Addes gave the delegates something else to cheer about. Membership since the 1936 convention had grown to 375,000 from 30,000 and the UAW had $428,799.99 in its treasury, an increase of more than $400,000 in just fifteen months.

To help promote, if not impose, harmony, John L. Lewis and a crew of CIO aides went to Milwaukee. One of the Lewis agents, Ora Gassaway, told the convention: "The reason you haven't got more contracts in the automobile industry is because you have too damn many other things to do that are irrelevant and derogatory to your best interests. General Motors representatives are here waiting to see how wide the breach grows and Walter Chrysler has a representative here reporting every day."

One of the first resolutions to reach the delegates was a Unity-backed proposal to abolish pre-convention caucuses, such as those just held in Toledo and South Bend. Victor Reuther took the floor to argue there was no reason for "selfish cliques holding meetings prior to the convention." Frankensteen, speaking for the Progressives, said such sessions were necessary to prepare union programs. If the two warring factions abandoned the practice, he contended, they would be at a disadvantage because "certain powers outside of this organization would continue to get together for their own secret sessions." He meant the Communist members of the UAW. The issue was pigeonholed.

The Martin forces then tried to reduce the voting strength of big local unions like Walter Reuther's West Side Local. Martin's plan was to give disproportionate voting strength at conventions to the smallest locals and to cut back the votes of the larger ones. Since most of the bigger new locals in Michigan were allied with the Unity Caucus, his motive was transparent. After Reuther argued against the "undemocratic" scheme, the plan was voted down by a substantial margin.

Unity forces got another lift when it came the turn of John L. Lewis to address the gathering. He called on the delegates to stand by their elected officers, a source of comfort to the Unity faction, which regarded his words as a veiled endorsement of Mortimer and Hall.

Aided by Gassaway, David Dubinsky, CIO Director John Brophy, and others, Lewis politicked in the back rooms of the convention to make certain his views prevailed.

The five top UAW officers, Mortimer and Hall included, were reelected. Two additional vice-presidents were named: Frankensteen and R. J. Thomas, out of the Chrysler plants. In addition the Executive Board was increased from twelve members to seventeen. But the Unity Caucus was required to make major concessions: Conventions henceforth were to be held every second year, postponing the next opportunity to challenge Martin. And the union constitution was revised to concentrate additional power in the hands of the president.

"I am convinced that this arrangement is not a victory for either side," Dubinsky told the convention. "It is a victory for the Auto Workers Union." To dramatize the enforced harmony of the moment, election of officers was followed by an ostentatious demonstration during which delegates removed distinctive caucus badges from their shirts and threw them onto the floor.

Next day, however, the two factions seemed prepared to do physical battle with each other over a postponed credentials fight. Walter Reuther noted with alarm that delegates had removed heavy oak arms from the folding chairs in the hall, planning to use them as weapons. The depth of intramural distrust was underlined by the fact that Reuther and his Unity Caucus allies had installed their own public address system so Martin could not silence them. Reuther, intending to argue the Unity position on the credentials dispute, abandoned the idea upon assessing the situation. "It was just an invitation to disaster," he recalled. "I got up there and I looked around and said to myself, 'My God, if I make the speech I came up here to make, the blood is going to be running in the streets.' So I made a unity plea. It didn't influence Martin and my guys were sore at me for folding up."

At the first post-convention meeting of the Executive Board, Martin ousted one member of the Unity camp on technical grounds and substituted one of his supporters, giving himself a clear two-to-one edge in Board balloting. More important, he flouted the convention decision to abolish the ranking of vice-presidents, announcing that Frankensteen would have the title, nowhere sanctioned, of "assistant president."

Martin also charged publicly that Communist Party leaders had been active in Unity Caucus affairs at the convention. Clay Fountain, then a Communist, later reported attending a number of CP meetings in Milwaukee at which party representatives "gave out orders for the conduct of Party members on the floor."

Although he was not a Communist, Walter Reuther was collaborating with the UAW's CP faction, convinced that Martin was a greater immediate evil and that, with the eventual elimination of Martin, he could readily overwhelm the Communist elements. Dubinsky years later recalled entering a Milwaukee hotel room, just vacated, and picking up scraps of memoranda listing convention delegates deemed deserving of Communist support in whatever moves they might make on the floor. According to Dubinsky, Reuther's name was on the list.

During the convention a Michigan delegate, John Anderson, rose to complain about speakers he thought were taking up too much time. A Scotsman from Glasgow, Anderson was leader of Local 155 with jurisdiction in the tool and die shops. In 1932 he had been the Communist Party candidate for governor of Michigan. Martin displayed scant patience with Anderson's complaint. "Brother Anderson," he said, "I am going to answer you in your own kind. Go down to your committee and get Nat Ganley and some of the rest of the obstructionists, who have been absolutely hindering the work of these committees." Ganley was Communist Party "whip" in the UAW. Walter Reuther rose to speak. "Let's all settle down to earth now," he urged. "Let's try to be intelligent. Let's control our emotions." He went on to defend Ganley and accuse Martin of being "very unfair."

Louis Stark, labor reporter for *The New York Times,* believed at one point—he later changed his mind—that Reuther was a part of the CP operation. Writing some three months after Milwaukee, he stated that the leadership of Reuther's West Side Local "adheres to the Communist Party 'line.' " Further, he saw Reuther participating in a calculated campaign, "directed from the New York head-quarters of the Communist Party," to discredit Martin. Stark acknowledged that "unwittingly caught up in the campaign" were UAW men who opposed Martin on trade union grounds alone and without political motivation.

For his part, Reuther was trying to counter Martin's tendency to label all his opponents as Communists. Picturing Martin as playing into the hands of management, Reuther wrote in the Ternstedt *Flash:*

> Many years ago in this country when the bosses wanted to keep the workers from forming a strong union, they tried starting scares of various kinds. . . . So now the bosses are trying a new stunt. They are raising a new scare; the red scare. They pay stools to go whispering around that so-and-so, usually a militant union leader, is a red. They think that will turn other workers against him. What the bosses really mean, however, is not that he is really a red; they mean . . . he is a loyal dependable union man . . . and is not afraid of the boss. So let's all be careful that we don't play the bosses' game.

Inside the Socialist Party, there were those who criticized Reuther for being too close to the Communists. For the moment, however, he deemed the alliance to be expedient. He did not want a Martin-engineered return to conservative AFL-style unionism.

During this period Martin came under the influence of Jay Lovestone who, until 1929, had been general secretary of the Communist Party in the United States. In May of that year Lovestone journeyed to Moscow for a meeting of the presidium of the Communist International and, because his views of the strengths and weaknesses of the American party differed from those of Stalin and his Soviet party puppets, Lovestone and his colleagues from America were accused from the podium of being right deviators, unprincipled opportunists, gross intriguers, and slanderers of the Russian Communist Party. Dedicated to his own conception of Communism, Lovestone declined to repent and was ousted as head of the U.S. Communist Party.

Bereft of his old base, Lovestone fashioned a splinter movement he called the Communist Party (Opposition). Later he changed the designation to the Independent Communist Labor League and, still later, decided it was best to drop the word "Communist" from the title of his independent revolutionary movement.

As Lovestone's influence increased, Martin became more strident in his attacks on UAW Communists allied with Moscow and, at the same time, talked more and more like a trade union conservative. Much as the Reutherites and the CP were organizing against Martin, the Lovestone faction began organizing for Martin. Lovestoneite Francis Henson was hired as top assistant to the UAW president. Also installed on the headquarters payroll were research director William Munger, Eve Stone as head of the women's auxiliary, John Tate as publicity man, and Irving Brown as an international organizer. Lester Washburn, an Executive Board member, was a Lovestone man.

A few weeks after the Milwaukee convention Martin persuaded the Board to transfer Robert Travis from Flint to Muncie, Indiana, and four days later, in another blow aimed at the Unity camp, announced the firing of ten organizers for "economy reasons." These included Victor Reuther and Melvin Bishop. Earlier, Victor had balked at a proposed transfer to the farming community of Adrian, Michigan, far removed from any UAW power center. He was dismissed after rejecting an alternative Martin suggestion that he work in a small town in upstate New York. He took a new job as education director of the West Side Local.

Passions aroused by the latest Martin purge were reflected in a bizarre drama enacted at the Eddystone Hotel, where the union president maintained a suite. Dan Gallagher of the West Side Local led nearly 40 union members to the Eddystone on the morning of September 30, 1937, for the purpose of complaining directly to Martin about the firings. When there was no response to their knocks at Martin's fourth floor quarters, the delegation began kicking and beating on the door. Martin appeared in shirtsleeves and leveled a revolver at Gallagher.

"Get that gun out of my belly, Homer!" cried the representative of Reuther's local. "That's a hell of a way to greet a union man!"

"I mean business," said Martin. "What's all this noise?"

"We just want to know when you are going to see us," Gallagher replied.

"I'm in conference," Martin announced. "It is important. I'll see you at the first opportunity."

The union president slammed the door shut and the startled delegation went to the lobby to wait, accompanied by a couple of labor reporters who had happened on them. The newsmen telephoned Martin and got this explanation for his behavior: "I've been threatened, and when somebody knocked on the door I thought it might be someone trying to get me." He expressed fear of company-hired goons. As for Gallagher's committee, he found them "irresponsible demonstrators directed by someone trying to embarrass the union." He meant the president of Gallagher's local, Walter Reuther.

The Gallagher group maintained a siege in the Eddystone lobby for seven hours. Reuther appeared in mid-afternoon and, taking two members of the Gallagher committee with him, rode the elevator to the fifth floor and walked down one flight to Martin's suite. By this time the UAW chief had induced the hotel management to suspend elevator service to his floor. Martin admitted the trio and agreed to hear their grievances at UAW headquarters. The meeting, once held, accomplished nothing. Reporters outside heard little except shouts and yells and, at one point, "the ominous sound of falling chairs." Reuther termed the whole episode "a spontaneous reaction of the men in the shops against the policy of the international in the recent discharge of organizers."

Where Detroit politics was concerned, the UAW displayed a degree of cohesion quite lacking in its intramural affairs. Because Franklin D. Roosevelt had carried the city over Alf Landon by 200,000 votes in 1936, the UAW and the CIO were emboldened to believe they might achieve control of the local government in the 1937 nonpartisan municipal elections. A major union goal was to get enough leverage at City Hall to force the removal of Police Commissioner Heinrich Pickert, who was hostile to organized labor. The UAW determined to field its own candidates—the Labor

Slate—for the Common Council. These included Walter Reuther, Frankensteen, R. J. Thomas, and Maurice Sugar, the UAW attorney closely linked with the union's Communist faction. Running in a field of 66 candidates, every member of the Labor Slate won nomination in the October 6 primary. Reuther ranked fourteenth in number of votes among the eighteen nominated for nine Council seats. He launched his general election campaign with a statement to the voters:

> As an automobile worker, as a union official, as a member of the Socialist Party, and as a patriotic citizen of Detroit, I pledge myself to the service of all the people of the city. I shall try to make Detroit a healthful and hopeful community to live and work in, not just a happy hunting ground for Wall Street profiteers.

The UAW, ignoring charges by the Chamber of Commerce, the conservative press, and some civic leaders that it was threatening traditional nonpartisan government, mounted a major effort on behalf of its Council candidates and the man it had endorsed for mayor. *The New York Times* estimated that the union made a $60,000 investment in its pioneering political action effort. The *Times* also spoke wonderingly about the massive organizational campaign mounted by the Auto Workers:

> An elaborate card index system has been installed in the offices of the Political Action Committee of the UAW.
> There, in steel filing cabinets, are the names of 125,000 union members, classified by ward and precinct. . . .
> Making the list was an expensive and tedious job for the union, but it is considered a permanent investment, because the union is in politics to stay. Forty-three girls worked night and day for two weeks, poring over precinct polling lists and matching membership cards to compile this card index.

Governor Frank Murphy returned the day before the general election from a White Sulphur Springs holiday timed to keep him out of the state during the climactic days of the campaign. Bowing to union pressure, he summoned two of the UAW candidates,

Sugar and Frankensteen, and was photographed wishing them well. The *Times* reported that both men seemed certain to be elected and Reuther "appeared to have an even chance to win."

A record 425,000 votes were cast but, except for its contribution toward swelling the total, the United Auto Workers had no cause for self-congratulation. Perhaps it was backlash. Whatever the reasons, the union candidate for mayor lost by more than 100,000 votes. The entire UAW slate for Common Council was defeated. Sugar topped the union ticket with 145,342 votes yet still fell more than 23,000 shy of victory. Reuther again ran fourteenth in the field of eighteen, getting 126,323 votes. It proved to be his first and last campaign for public office.

Although Reuther had proclaimed himself a Socialist during the campaign, his ties to the SP were rather fragile by 1937. His preoccupation was trade unionism, not ideological politics, and, to the extent that politics interested him, he backed Democrats like Roosevelt and Murphy. Winn has recalled Reuther's loose attachment to Socialism during the period:

> The Socialists who were active in the union, including myself, and a number of others, looked upon him as a leader generally of our point of view. However, during that period of 1936 and 1937, I can remember Walter's being present at only one Socialist Party meeting. That, as I can recall, was not a business meeting of the Party but a more or less educational, informative meeting to hear some speaker or other. . . . Walter himself was too thoroughly tied up and immersed in union activities to pay attention to the activities of the Socialist Party. . . .

Victor Reuther was asked why he and Walter gradually lost interest in the Socialist Party after returning from their global travels. His reply:

> I don't think it was so much the overseas experience that brought with it a disillusionment. I think it was the feeling that you really can't do anything significant in the political field unless you've got some kind of organized base to operate from. And the trade union movement offered far greater possibilities

for social gains, for legislative improvement, than did the vehicle of a political party. Of course, we were disenchanted with
what the two old parties were. And before Roosevelt came
on, anyone who was a wage earner in the United States had
good reason to be disenchanted. But Roosevelt sparked new
hope and new faith and we openly campaigned for Roosevelt
and have very consistently supported Democratic candidates
in all the years since. . . . Why should one waste his life with
a third party in a country where traditionally third parties have
only been little splinter groups?

Although Reuther was the ally of the Communists in the anti-
Martin battle at the time, his ties with the CP did not go beyond
that, much as the Communists would have wished it otherwise.
Louis Budenz tried to recruit Reuther for the Party, suggesting the
Communists in return would support him for the UAW presidency.
The attempt went for naught. Victor also was approached, with
the same result, by William W. Weinstone, a member of the Com-
munist central executive committee who had been assigned by Earl
Browder to build a CP apparatus within the UAW.

In his running battle with Martin, Reuther in late 1937 and early
1938 excoriated the UAW president for not working out a new
agreement with General Motors. When Pontiac workers staged a
six-day sit-down in November 1937, protesting against a proposal
that would have eroded past union gains, Reuther and Mortimer
sought Executive Board sanction for the strike. Martin blamed the
sit-down on "professional provocateurs" and, making a personal
appeal, got the workers back on the job. When the old GM agreement was renewed in March 1938, along with a supplementary
document that chipped away at the grievance machinery, Reuther
used his Local 174 newspaper, the West Side *Conveyor,* to denounce the package. Martin retaliated with an order suspending
all local union publications but Reuther, firmly entrenched in his
local, ignored the edict. Walter won reelection as president of the
West Side Local by an impressive 2,785-to-636 vote, while Roy
lost a bid for the presidency of the Flint local to a Progressive
Caucus candidate, 7,540 to 4,080.

Early in 1938 the marriage of convenience between the Reuther brothers and the Communists came to an end. At first there merely was a cooling of mutual ardor for the alliance, the CP moving away from its United Front position and the brothers becoming increasingly hostile toward Communist attempts to make Moscow's foreign policy positions the official line of the Unity Caucus. Still, the final break came with such suddenness that even UAW insiders were stunned.

The occasion was the founding convention of the Michigan CIO Council in Lansing on April 23-24. As was customary, the Unity-ites met in advance to agree on a slate of officers. With the con-currence of the Communists, Victor Reuther was endorsed for secretary-treasurer, a job he wanted because it would make him the CIO's chief lobbyist in Michigan. The endorsement seemed to as-sure his election.

On the second morning of the convention a passerby beckoned Frankensteen away from a breakfast meeting he was having with Richard T. Leonard, president of DeSoto Local 227 and a non-political trade unionist. When Frankensteen returned to the table, he said, "You know who that was? Well, that's Gebert. You're going to be the secretary." Although Leonard already was in the race as Martin's candidate, this development astounded him. B. K. (Bill) Gebert, who was not an auto worker, was a principal Com-munist Party agent for penetration of the UAW. Leonard had as-sumed Gebert was firmly fixed in his support of Victor Reuther. He did not know that Frankensteen, as a leader of Martin's Pro-gressives, was maneuvering to split the Unity Caucus and block the Reuther forces from expanding their influence into statewide CIO affairs.

On the convention floor Frankensteen rose to seek a recess, say-ing he needed time to caucus on a plan to "unify" the meeting. Sensing trouble, Walter Reuther invaded Frankensteen's off-the-floor caucus and found him conferring with, among others, Com-munists Gebert, Weinstone, Ganley, and Anderson.

"What are you bastards doing?" he exploded. "Do you realize

you're going to destroy the Unity Caucus, the only force that can save this union from a disastrous split?"

"We know what we're doing," Weinstone told him.

"Brother," retorted Reuther, "count me on the other side in every fight."

Victor was defeated by Leonard.

CHAPTER TEN

Letter from Gorki

THE PROMINENCE OF THE REUTHER BROTHERS WAS SUCH BY THE spring of 1938 that one could begin to judge them by the enemies they had made during their first two years in the labor movement. Foes were most numerous among Communists on the political left, reactionary Detroit business elements on the right, and among actual or potential rivals for power in the United Auto Workers, a category that knew no political bounds. As controversial figures in a time and city marked by recurrent violence, the brothers were not unmindful that their adversaries might strike out at them in varied and ugly ways.

Unknown to Walter and May Reuther, their second-floor apartment at 13233 LaSalle Boulevard came under close surveillance late in March 1938. A couple of weeks later, on April 9, the Reuthers planned to go to Victor's home to help celebrate the 25th birthday of Victor's wife, Sophie. But Walter came down with a heavy spring cold that, at the last minute, prompted Victor, Sophie, and Roy and their friends to gather at the LaSalle Boulevard place for the party. Telephoning a Chinese restaurant in the neighborhood, Walter ordered delivery of enough chop suey for everyone. When there was a subsequent knock on the apartment door, it was assumed the food had arrived. To the astonishment of the party-goers, two thugs marched in, one leveling a revolver and the other brandishing a blackjack.

Pointing at Walter, the man with the gun commanded, "Come on, we want you." To the Reuthers and their friends, it seemed ominously like the prelude to a one-way gangland "ride."

While the gunman blocked the doorway, the man with the blackjack advanced on Walter. One of the party guests, Al King, inched toward the kitchen and, finding an open window, leaped to the street to summon help. He barely missed striking a concrete incinerator. Sophie Reuther picked up a jar of pickles and heaved it at the invaders.

Jumping into a corner as the blackjack swung his way, Walter grasped a floor lamp and swung back. Once within grappling distance, he dropped the lamp and wrestled away the blackjack, tossing it to Roy.

"Let's plug him here," the gunman suggested to his cohort.

"If you do," Roy countered, "you'll never get out alive."

A noisy crowd was gathering in the street in response to King's shouts. Abruptly, the assailants, who had not expected to crash a well-populated party in any case, fled. Except for a few bruises, Walter was not hurt. By his later account, police arrived an hour and 15 minutes after the attack "and when they got there, we were afraid to let them in."

A few days later an anonymous telephone caller promised Walter the names of the thugs upon delivery of $5,000 in cash in a Detroit bar. Agreeing to meet the informant, Reuther took the precaution of peopling the saloon with huskies from the West Side Local before making an appearance. By virtue of his foresightedness, he got the names he wanted without charge. Arrested as the assailants were Willard Holt, a former Ford Serviceman, and Edward Percelli. They persuaded a jury that Walter had hired them to fake an assault for publicity purposes and were acquitted. Twenty years later Reuther told a Senate committee:

> . . . The night the Ford gangsters broke into my home, and I was told this, there was a deal between the City Hall, the police department, and Harry Bennett, to have Bennett's gangsters bump me off and drop me in the Detroit River.

Reuther testified further that after the invasion of his home, Victor got a dinner invitation from one of the invading duo, who told him, "Well, look, I was just hired to do that job. It was nothing personal. And, I would like to take you out now because we have been told we have got to live with you fellows now."

The incident prompted Walter and Victor to get gun permits as a precaution, although Victor says, "I do not recall that Walter really actually carried the gun on his person."

The next attack on the Reuthers was verbal, coming from witnesses at the first hearings of a Special Committee on Un-American Activities of the House of Representatives, soon to be popularized as the Dies Committee after its most well-known chairman, Democratic Congressman Martin Dies of Texas. One of the initial witnesses in August of 1938 was John P. Frey, an AFL official who burdened the record with some fact, a considerable number of half-truths, and a variety of misstatements, all calculated to picture Walter Reuther as a servant of the Communist Party. Reuther was described, for example, as a close associate of Jay Lovestone, his intraunion foe, and as a participant in caucus meetings to which only highest level Communists were admitted. Ironically, the testimony followed by four months the rupture of the working alliance between the Reuther brothers and the UAW's Communist bloc. Frey, however, was by no means the only witness to link the Reuthers and Communism. J. B. Matthews, a onetime Communist who later became a key aide to Senator Joseph McCarthy (in whose behalf, before committing suicide, he alleged that the Protestant clergy was honeycombed with Communists), testified:

> The night that Walter and Victor Reuther sailed for Russia, many years ago, I had dinner with them and saw them off and had some contact with them while they were in Russia and subsequent to their return. I do not know what their exact political connections are at the present time. I only know that their ideology, if I may be permitted to use the word here, is Communist.

Fred W. Frahn, Detroit's superintendent of police, asserted that Walter Reuther "is not a Communist, but he associates with Communists at all times, and they work together." Ralph Knox, former president of Local 212 and a Reuther opponent in the UAW's factional fight, found Walter "very radical, harebrained." Clyde Morrow, who said he was a former Communist now associated with an American Legion Americanization Committee in Detroit, declared that Reuther's West Side Local "is what I would call an old soldiers' home for discharged Communist Party members whom Martin has fired." Herman Luhrs, chairman of a joint Americanization Committee of the six American Legion posts in Flint, took aim at Roy and Victor Reuther. His committee, he related, made quite an exhaustive check on them because "the whole town was beginning to get suspicious of these two men, owing to their active part in the [sit-down] strike at the time." He testified that Roy had substituted for Walter at a Flint rally in May 1938, and "stood at a Communist salute, singing the Russian 'Internationale.' "

The Committee spent considerable time hearing witnesses describe an alleged Communist plot, with various of the Reuthers among the participants, to defraud the city of Detroit. John D. McGillis, a local Knights of Columbus official, asserted that Walter, Victor, and Sophie Reuther received city-paid medical attention in 1937 after signing Board of Health cards stating they were indigents. He said they were examined by Dr. Eugene M. Shafarman, who, according to his testimony, gave physical examinations to recruits for the Spanish Loyalist army. A similar account came from Sgt. Harry Mikuliak of the Detroit Police Rackets Squad, popularly known as the "Red Squad." Testifying that many Detroit Communists made it a practice to sign false affidavits that they could not afford medical care, Mikuliak stated that, among other things, he specialized in investigations of "labor riots, agitators."

Walter Reuther did not rebut the testimony of McGillis and Mikuliak, and he surely was acquainted with Shafarman, the physician who treated him on the day of the brutal Rouge beatings of 1937. In his appearance before the NLRB panel more than a year earlier, however, Reuther stated that his choice of Shafarman was accidental: "We tried several doctors' offices along Vernor Highway, but the doctors were out, and we finally succeeded in finding a doctor in on Vernor Highway; I don't recall the doctor's name, I think it is Reed."

As hearings continued over many months, with the great mass of testimony unrelated to the Reuthers, Walter did respond to a claim by one witness, William McCuistion, once a Communist and leader of the National Maritime Union, that he had heard Reuther discussed as a Communist "among Party circles." In a telegram to the Committee, Walter declared, "I am not and never have been a member of the Communist Party nor a supporter of its policies nor subject to its control or influence in any way."

Perhaps the greatest hurt done the Reuthers by the Committee came at the outset of the hearings, when the panel placed in its record one version of a letter said to have been written from the Soviet Union in January 1934 by Victor Reuther over the signatures, "Vic and Wal." The letter was addressed to Mr. and Mrs. Melvin Bishop, he a fellow Socialist and brother of their recent Detroit apartment mate, Merlin Bishop. Both the AFL's Frey and the American Legion's Luhrs cited the letter in testimony.

It is Merlin Bishop's recollection that the controversial letter was published first in a Socialist newspaper three or four years before the Dies Committee hearings began. In one form or another, and there would appear to be at least half a dozen versions, it has reappeared in print periodically ever since. The Flint Alliance used it as anti-UAW propaganda during the 1937 sit-downs and one version, read into the record of the NLRB hearings on the Battle of the Overpass by Ford's counsel, Louis Colombo, Sr., had appeared earlier in the *Detroit Saturday Night,* a weekly. Here is one of the more lengthy versions, as published in a quite unfriendly biography, *Walter Reuther, the Autocrat of the Bargaining Table,* by Eldorous L. Dayton:

> Dear Mel and Glad:
>
> Your letter of December 5 arrived here last week from Germany and was read with more than usual interest by Wal and I. It seemed ages since we had heard from you, so you might well imagine with what joy we welcomed news from Detroit. It is precisely because you are equally anxious, I know, to receive word from the "worker's fatherland" that I am taking this opportunity to answer you.
>
> What you have written concerning the strikes and the general labor unrest in Detroit plus what we have learned from other sources of the rising discontent of the American workers, makes us long for the moment to be back with you in the front lines of the struggle; however, the daily inspiration that is ours as we work side by side with our Russian workers in our factory, the thought that what we are building will be for the benefit and

enjoyment of the working class, not only of Russia, but for the entire world, is the compensation we receive for our temporary absence from the struggle in the United States. And let no one tell you that the workers of the Union of Soviet Socialist Republics are not on the road to security, enlightenment, and happiness.

Mel, you know Wal and I were always strong for the Soviet Union. You know we were always ready to defend it against the lies of the reactionaries. But let me tell you, now that we are here seeing all the great construction, watching a backward peasantry being transformed into an enlightened, democratic, cultured people, now that we have already experienced the thrill, the satisfaction of participating in a genuine proletarian democracy, we are more than just sympathetic toward our country, we are ready to fight for it and its ideals. And why not? Here the workers, through their militant leadership, the proletarian dictatorship, have not sold out to the owning class like the S.P. in Germany and like the Labor Party in England. Here they have against all odds, against famine, against internal strife and civil war, against sabotage, against capitalist invasion and isolation, our comrades here have maintained power, they have won over the masses, they have transformed the "dark masses" of Russia into energetic, enlightened workers. They have laid the economic foundation for socialism, for a classless society. Mel, if you could be with us for just one day in our shop meeting and watch the workers as they offer suggestions and constructive criticism of production in the shop. Here are no bosses to drive fear into the workers. No one to drive them in mad speedups. Here the workers are in control. Even the shop superintendent has no more right in these meetings than any other worker. I have witnessed many times already when the superintendent spoke too long, the workers in the hall decided he had already consumed enough time and the floor was given to a lathe hand who told of his problems and offered suggestions. Imagine this at Ford or Briggs. This is what the outside world calls the "ruthless dictatorship" in Russia. I tell you, Mel, in all the countries we have thus far been in, we have never found such genuine proletarian democracy. It is unpolished and crude, rough and rude, but proletarian workers' democracy in every respect. The workers in England have more culture and polish when they speak at their meetings but they have no power. I prefer the latter.

In our factory, which is the largest and most modern in Europe, and we have seen them all, there are no pictures of Fords and Rockefellers, of Roosevelts and Mellon. No such parasites, but rather huge pictures of Lenin, * * * etc., greet the workers' eyes on every side. Red banners with slogans "Workers of the World Unite," are draped across the craneways. Little red flags fly from the tops of the presses, drill presses, lathe kells, etc. Such a sight you have never seen before. Women and men work side by side—the women with their red cloth about their heads, 5 days per week (our week here is 6 days long). At noon we all eat in a large factory restaurant where wholesome plain food is served. A workers' band furnishes music to us from an adjoining room while we have dinner. For the remainder of our 1-hour lunch period we adjourn to the "red" corner recreation, where workers play games, read papers and magazines or technical books, or merely sit, smoke and chat. Such a fine spirit of comradeship you have never before witnessed in your life. Superintendent leaders and ordinary workers are all alike. If you saw our superintendent as he walks through the shop greeting workers with, "Hello, comrade," you could not distinguish him from any other worker.

The interesting thing, Mel, is that 3 years ago this place here was a vast prairie, a waste land, and the thousands of workers here who are building complicated dies and other tools were at that time peasants who had never before even seen an industry let alone worked in one. And by mere brute determination, but the determination to build a workers' country second to none in the world, urged on by the spirit of the revolution, they have constructed this marvelous auto factory which is today turning out modern cars for the Soviet Union. Through the bitter Russian winters of 45° below they have toiled with their bare hands, digging foundations, erecting structures; they have with their own brute strength pulled the huge presses into place and set them up for operation. What they have here they have sacrificed and suffered for; that is why they are not so ready to turn it all over again to the capitalists. That is why today they still have comrades of the "red army" on guard at the factory at all times to prevent counter-revolutionaryists [sic] from carrying out their sabotage.

About a 20-minute walk from the factory an entirely new Socialist city has grown up in these 3 years. Here over 50,000 of the factory workers live in fine, new modern, apartment buildings. Large hospitals, schools, libraries, and clubs have sprung up here, and all for the use of those who work, for without a worker's card one cannot make use of all these modern facilities. Three nights ago we were invited to the clubhouse in Sosgow (Socialist city) to attend an evening of enjoyment given by the workers of the die shop. Imagine, all the workers with whom we daily work came together that evening for a fine banquet, a stage performance, a concert, speeches, and a big dance. A division of the "red army" was also present as guests. In all my life, Mel, I have never seen anything so inspiring. Mel, once a fellow has seen what is possible where workers gain power, he no longer fights just for an ideal, he fights for something which is real, something tangible. Imagine, Mel, Henry Ford throwing a big party for his slaves. Here the party was no gift of charity from someone above for we own the factory, we held the meeting, and decided to have the party, and it was paid for from the surplus earnings of our department. What our department does is typical of the social activities which are being fostered throughout the entire factory and the entire Soviet Union.

Mel, we are witnessing and experiencing great things in the U.S.S.R. We are seeing the most backward nation in the world being rapidly transformed into the most modern and scientific with new concepts and new social ideals coming into force. We are watching daily socialism being taken down from the books on the shelves and put into actual application. Who could not be inspired by such events?

And now my letter is getting long and still I have said little, for there is so much to say and so little time in which to do it. We have written Merlin and Coach rather lengthy letters and have requested they forward them to you to save duplicity of material.

I believe there is little in this letter which they have not already received so there will be no need of your forwarding this to them.

A word about your letter. * * *

Keep your eye on the S.P. It is being affiliated to the Second International, I am not so certain it is "drifting" in the right direction, certainly not in the light of recent events.

Let us know definitely what is happening to the Y.P.S.L. and also the "Social Problems" Club at C.C.C. * * *

Carry on the fight for a Soviet America.

VIC AND WAL

After reading aloud a considerably shorter version at the NLRB hearings, Ford's counsel Colombo asked Walter Reuther if he had written the letter.

A. . . . I did not.

Q. You did not write it?
A. That is correct.

Q. Well, does that letter express your true sentiments?
A. It does not.

Q. Those are not your sentiments at all?
A. Not as expressed here.

Before the Dies Committee, witness Luhrs displayed his expertise as Americanization chairman by identifying the "S.P." referred to in the letter as "an organization in Germany." As for the "Social Problems" Club, he testified it was an organization operating in camps of the Civilian Conservation Corps. Obviously, S.P. meant the Socialist Party and the "C.C.C." mentioned in connection with the Social Problems Club was a misspelled abbreviation of City College of Detroit. Luhrs correctly identified "Coach" as Roy Reuther.

Victor Reuther readily acknowledges that he wrote to Melvin Bishop from the Soviet Union, but adds:

> I'm sure of one thing: that none of the reputed letters is written in the style which is the way in which I expressed myself

then or subsequently. I'm sure that I wrote some letters that were quite enthusiastic about things we were experiencing; it was a fascinating period to be there. But to imply that letters were written back calling for the establishment of a Soviet America is not only nonsense, it's childish. I think that young as we were, we had enough brains then to know that even if we had held such beliefs, it would have been rather stupid to put it in a letter and send it back. I don't think we were quite that stupid.

Hostile employers, rival unions, opponents within the United Auto Workers, and right-wing organizations and pamphleteers repeatedly cited the "Vic and Wal" letter for years thereafter. The anti-Reuther forces at the 1941 UAW convention circulated one version, which Melvin Bishop insisted was authentic. A number of unions, including the International Association of Machinists, employed it against the Auto Workers in bargaining agent elections. When the *Saturday Evening Post* reprinted excerpts a decade after the first Dies Committee hearings, it added a footnote:

> Both of the Reuthers concede that Victor wrote a personal letter to the Bishops at about the date noted, describing with approval the strivings of the Russian workers for economic improvement. Walter says it was a "burst of adolescent enthusiasm" and adds that whoever gave currency to the circulated version distorted the original and made additions to it, including the closing phrase.

Howe and Widick, in their biography of Reuther and his union, concluded that "anyone who was familiar with the socialist movement of the thirties knows that the Reuther brothers were merely the victims of a then prevalent uncritical enthusiasm for the Stalin regime."

Certainly the picture given of Soviet factory life in the letter does not differ markedly from Victor Reuther's recollections years later. Nor is the tone out of line with Walter Reuther's initial impressions, as expressed in his letter published at the time in the Moscow *Daily News*: "I have always pictured the Soviet Union as a beehive of social and industrial activity, but it was not until I arrived that I realized that even in my most imaginative moments, I had underestimated the scope of socialist construction."

Of course, all variants of "THE letter" cannot be accurate in all respects. Without question, some people have added to or subtracted from the original to suit their own purposes. A number of close associates of the brothers insist, however, that, in its essentials, the letter in whatever form is genuine. One summed up the reaction of many when confronted with the multiple versions, which differ principally in length, with a word or two changed here and there: "Damn it, I do know there was a letter and it was an authentic letter. . . ." As part of the Reuther folklore, it even has been suggested that May Wolf, when not yet imagining she would become Mrs. Walter Reuther, typed the first copy of the letter received by Melvin and Gladys Bishop, so it could be published in the Socialist press as a firsthand account of conditions in the Soviet Union.

Billie Sunday Farnum, a charter member of the UAW's Pontiac local who later became a Congressman from Michigan and a deputy chairman of the Democratic National Committee, recalls:

> In every election that I've even known in the union—not only for the top spots but in all these other things that were going on, it would come up. There were people who would rise up and say: "Look, he worked in Russia. Victor worked in Russia. This is the letter he wrote to Mel Bishop." And they would always spread these letters out. . . . Local election after local election.

During the 1958 Congressional election campaign, Edward A. Rumely's Committee for Constitutional Government, an organization hardly known for liberal tendencies, purchased a full-page advertisement in the *Wall Street Journal* that repeated the line, "Carry on the fight for a Soviet America."

Uncomfortably aware that Walter Reuther's close identification, by then, with the Democratic Party would be a 1958 campaign issue, the brothers planned a careful counterattack, with the collaboration of the UAW's Washington attorney, Joseph L. Rauh, Jr.

An exchange of correspondence, with great care given to each word, was arranged between Hubert H. Humphrey, then a Senator, and Chairman John L. McClellan of the Senate's Select Committee on Improper Activities in the Labor or Management Field. Humphrey started it off:

> I have received a number of letters and personal inquiries from Congressional friends and others concerning a pro-Soviet letter which Walter and Victor Reuther are alleged to have written from Russia some 24 years ago. Apparently, despite their long and distinguished anti-Communist records, the "letter" continues to be widely circulated in a number of different versions by hate groups and fanatics.
>
> I have known the Reuther brothers personally for many years and have long admired their untiring work in defeating the Communists in the trade union movement at home and abroad. . . . I would like to be in a position to answer inquiries and to help clear up the matter of this ancient "letter". . . .

Replying ten days later, McClellan, a Southern Democrat known for his probity, replied:

> . . . During the staff investigation of the United Automobile Workers Union in preparation for public hearings, information was received concerning a letter which Victor Reuther is alleged to have written to one Melvin Bishop of Detroit when he and Walter Reuther were working in Russia in 1934.
>
> As you may recall, this purported letter previously had been given considerable publicity. I, therefore, instructed the staff to locate and interview Mr. Bishop. They did, and reported to me they doubted Mr. Bishop's story about it. I then had them bring Mr. Bishop to my office, where I interviewed him at some length. I too was skeptical of his story but I directed the staff to pursue every clew and lead they had for those to whom Mr. Bishop had referred as having knowledge of the facts.
>
> We discovered there were several versions of the letter. An exhibit in the possession of our Committee indicates that three different versions of it have been previously placed in the *Congressional Record*.
>
> As a matter of precaution, and to preclude anyone's charging

the Committee with not having looked into it, I placed Mr. Bishop under oath and took his testimony in executive session. He admitted that he has not seen this letter for over twenty years, and his story concerning his disposition of it is completely contradicted by reliable information the Committee has obtained.

I think it is significant that, with the established unreliability of Mr. Bishop and the fact that the existence and text of the letter were so questionable, no member of the Committee saw fit to ask Mr. Reuther any questions about it when he testified before the Committee in public hearings.

There the matter rests, seeming more remote and less important year by year. Whatever the enthusiasms and attachments of Walter Reuther in January of 1934, they became submerged in good measure, it would seem, by the political and economic realities he faced.

CHAPTER ELEVEN

Martin's Fall

IN THE RAGING FACTIONAL FIGHT WITHIN THE UNITED AUTO WORK-
ers, the split between the Reuthers and the Communist Party group
complicated an already-tangled situation. Tactically, the two elements still had to make common cause against Martin, even as they
tried to outmaneuver each other. Allies came and went. Richard T.
Frankensteen, Martin's chief lieutenant for a year, moved into the
Unity camp after the Communists suggested they could help make
him the unifying figure in a drive to end UAW factionalism. No
Communist, Frankensteen simply thought that by changing his
allegiances, he could promote his own political standing in the
union. Martin retaliated by stripping him of his status as "assistant
president."

With a climactic struggle for control of the UAW approaching,
a mimeographed "Confidential Report of the Socialist Party on the
Inner Situation in the Auto Union," issued from SP offices in Chicago in June 1938, stated: "Many of the leading comrades are
either very busy or very tired. Walter Reuther has been ill. Others
are preparing for summer relaxation."

The battleground at this point was the UAW Executive Board.
In early June the Unity faction thought it had caught the Martin
forces off guard by producing a majority at a Board meeting.
Reuther and his Unity allies intended to take up matters opposed
by the Progressives but Martin and his followers withdrew, preventing a quorum.

Reconvening the Board in Washington on June 13, Martin announced he was suspending Frankensteen, Ed Hall, Wyndham
Mortimer, George F. Addes, and Walter N. Wells. Accusing them
of insurrection, he ordered the five men to appear for trial before
an emergency meeting of the Board.

When Martin took this drastic course, Walter Reuther and five
other Board members stalked out in protest. Reuther said the
former preacher had "declared war" and was dividing the union.

Traveling to Washington, he appealed for intervention by John L. Lewis. "The rank and file is sick and tired of the fight of the top leadership," said Reuther, claiming to speak for 200,000 UAW members.

As Martin moved ahead with trial plans, Frankensteen, Mortimer, Hall, and Wells responded: "Charges against us are so vague, indefinite and loose we hardly know whether we are accused of taking candy from orphans or robbing the United States Treasury."

The trial was set to begin on Monday, June 25, at UAW headquarters, but partisans of each side staged a free-for-all there. Even Addes found himself trading blows with a foe and, *The New York Times* reported, "blood flowed freely." R. J. Thomas, regarded as a Martin ally, told the milling group: "We will not get anywhere if we have gangs in the office here. This fight is not helpful to the international." Walter Reuther then added his own appeal for order. Martin's reaction: it was all a "typical Communist demonstration."

The next day Martin stationed 150 guards in the headquarters lobby and the trial opened with the defendants facing Martin and, with right arms outstretched in the Nazi salute, crying "Heil Hitler!"

In their defense, the suspended officers cited correspondence exchanged among Martin, Lovestone, and others, letters unveiled as a sensational "exclusive" in the *Daily Worker.* It subsequently developed they had been stolen from the Manhattan apartment of one of Lovestone's friends before the trial began. Lovestone charged that the break-in had been carried out by "Stalinist agents, under the direction of special experts of the Russian G.P.U." He found it "not significant that the central organ of the Communist Party, the *Daily Worker,* took a one-day jump on the entire press of the country in the publication. . . ."

The correspondence, skillfully exploited by Communists and others in the anti-Martin camp, was used as evidence that Martin himself was in league with a Communist—Lovestone—and that he was preparing to sell out his union to the Ford Motor Company, still the only major auto producer without a union contract. Said the *Daily Worker* in a sweeping introduction to its exposé: "Sensational documentary evidence was produced today showing that

Homer Martin, president of the Auto Workers Union, and Jay Lovestone have been working in collaboration with the representatives of a large motor company against the CIO." The newspaper asserted, "These letters, some of which bear the official UAW letterhead, tell the sordid tale of Lovestone's control over Martin and the use this American Leon Trotsky made of his power to organize factionalism in an effort to render asunder a mighty CIO body so that only his agents could direct its activities—activities that were to be directed to serve the auto barons."

While the letters did not prove all the *Daily Worker*'s charges, they indicated Lovestone was taking a direct, if not commanding, interest in Martin's activities and was receiving reports from his own agents at UAW headquarters.

On August 6 the bobtailed Executive Board, with Reuther and others continuing their boycott, concluded the trial. The defendants did not appear, claiming they had "unimpeachable evidence" that 150 Martin men had been mobilized to do them violence: "It is our understanding that we are to be brutally beaten and maimed, if not killed."

Frankensteen, Mortimer, and Hall were expelled from the Auto Workers Union. Addes had been expelled a few weeks earlier by the Martinites. Wells was suspended from his vice-presidency for three months, receiving a lesser penalty because, as Martin phrased it, he "never was identified with the so-called Communist conspiracy."

Walter Reuther went to New York to seek the support of David Dubinsky but could not induce the head of the Ladies' Garment Workers to withdraw support of Martin and Reuther came away "pretty discouraged."

On the night of August 10 Frankensteen's garage was bombed while he and attorney Maurice Sugar were conferring inside the house. No one was injured.

On August 20 Martin's foes met in Toledo, where Victor Reuther argued that the CIO should be given a large voice in deciding the UAW's future, but without going so far as installing a CIO official to run the union's affairs. The delegates felt otherwise and asked

Lewis to appoint an administrator. They also called for a special convention.

Walter Reuther was absent when the expelled officers went to Washington to convey the Toledo recommendations to Lewis. But he flew to the capital the next day to join the talks as an influential "neutral." Lewis proposed reinstatement of the officers and sent Sidney Hillman and "Uncle Phil" Murray to Detroit as mediators. Hillman and Murray held separate meetings with representatives of the opposing factions and, in Murray's words, found that "the boys were loud and rough and tough." Just how tough was demonstrated late one evening when an uninvited delegation, guns slung in arm-pit holsters, burst in upon the CIO emissaries. Hillman, lying on a bed, got up, pale and angry, and began pacing the room. The unexpected visitors were silent and finally Hillman spoke: "Guns, always guns! Why is it there are always guns in Detroit? Now you, please go away." The thugs departed without having announced their mission.

After about two weeks of patient labor, Hillman and Murray put together a shaky compromise that Martin and the Unity group accepted.

Hoping to recoup his personal standing, Martin launched direct negotiations with the Ford Motor Company. Suggesting publicly that Henry Ford did not know the true nature of conditions in his plants and would welcome the UAW once the facts were brought to his attention, Martin went to the Rouge for a conference with Ford and Harry Bennett.

Within the union, Martin suffered a setback as the Executive Board forced him to fire four Lovestoneites occupying key staff positions. These included Martin's assistant, Henson.

The infighting detracted from UAW efforts to secure the reelec-tion of Governor Frank Murphy, who was defeated as Republicans achieved significant victories nationally. Walter Reuther had pressed for all-out union support of the Democratic governor, but more doctrinaire Socialists preferred to back their own candidate. One account states that Reuther offered to cut his ties to the Socialist Party but was persuaded by Norman Thomas to delay the break until settlement of the Martin faction fight.

The battle came to a head early in 1939. On January 11 the Executive Board stripped Martin of the right to edit the UAW newspaper. He said the Board wanted a president "who cannot read, write, make a speech, broadcast on the radio or walk." He said "they want a mummy, a dummy and a flummy."

Martin's dealings with Harry Bennett now became a critical issue. Bennett told the press that he had had "a number of meetings" with Martin in the past three months but that, inasmuch as the Ford Motor Company felt it "has been fair and just" toward its employes, "there is no intention of changing the policy of the company on labor." Anti-Martin members of the Executive Board complained they had been "kept in the dark" regarding the sessions with Bennett. The Board scheduled a meeting to hear allegations that Martin had entered into secret negotiations on a "sweetheart" agreement with Ford. Boycotting the session, the union president said: "There are three or four Communists who are going to appear before the Board on the Ford matter. Let the Board hear their comrades."

On January 17, with Martin absent, the Board voted without dissent to convene a special convention in Cleveland on March 20 to elect new officers. Three days later Martin removed UAW records to his Eddystone Hotel suite, sent strong-arm squads to seize union headquarters, and announced the suspension of fifteen Board members, including Walter Reuther. The remaining members, he said, would make plans for a rival special convention in Detroit.

When Martin tried to address members of the Chevrolet Gear and Axle Local, his toughs were "laid out three deep on the sidewalk" by Unity Caucus huskies. Each faction resorted freely to alley fighting tactics. Use of "pool cues, blackjacks and ball bearings inserted in gloves" was not uncommon. *The New York Times* found that "guards armed with short clubs were in evidence" at Martin-occupied headquarters, and that every large UAW local had posted burly sentries to protect records against any invasion attempts.

Typical of the battles that erupted was one at a meeting of Plymouth Local 51 in the auditorium of Detroit's Cass Technical High School. Local leader Leo La Motte, a Board member ousted by

Martin, tried to speak from atop a table on the stage while an arch rival, F. J. (Pat) McCartney, who had accused the local leadership of Communist leanings, waved an American flag. Fist fights broke out and more than a score of union men were injured.

When a Detroit *News* reporter went to UAW headquarters and was escorted by armed guards to a press room where newsmen were kept under surveillance by Martin agents, he loudly proclaimed he would not accept such treatment and, if assigned in the future to the union headquarters, would carry a gun. A Martin bodyguard, weighing some 300 pounds and nicknamed Tiny, picked up the reporter and held him upside down by the ankles until he retracted his statements.

On January 23 Reuther and other Board members suspended by Martin named R. J. Thomas acting president. Thomas then announced, to cheers, that Reuther's West Side Local had paid $13,000 in dues to Treasurer Addes. Martin's reaction: "I cannot understand why the other fellows did not elect Earl Browder as president."

Next day in Washington, Hillman and Murray met with Thomas, Frankensteen, Reuther, Mortimer, Hall, and others. The CIO troubleshooters announced "complete support and recognition" of the anti-Martin officers and accused the former preacher of "direct and flagrant violation" of the union constitution: "His activities can only lend strength to the enemies of labor and to the reactionary employers. . . . The CIO supports fully and completely the position of the international Executive Board."

Martin declared his independence from the CIO and flew to New York to confer with Dubinsky, who also had just left the CIO. Dubinsky helped arrange financing for Martin on the theory he might lead the UAW back into the AFL.

With each faction claiming the allegiance of the membership and responsibility for contracts, Thomas wrote all affected auto makers: "The international Executive Board has emphatically reaffirmed the position of this union to scrupulously carry out its contractual obligations." General Motors replied that it would no longer negotiate nationally with either UAW faction "until their position and authority have been clarified."

Trying to regain the initiative, Martin asked the courts to bar his foes from claiming to represent the Auto Workers union. He alleged a conspiracy to deliver the UAW to the CIO and the Communist Party, further claiming that the plot, as he saw it, originated with Mortimer, Hall, Addes, and Walter Reuther.

The rank and file of the union remained confused and divided in its loyalties, as was shown when 4,000 members, turning out to hear Frankensteen, clashed in about a hundred fist fights. According to the Associated Press, Frankensteen pulled a pistol on a Martin partisan at one point, threatening to shoot him on the spot.

(Almost unnoticed in the pre-convention jockeying was a February 27 decision by the Supreme Court of the United States depriving the UAW, and all other unions, of the sit-down weapon that had brought it from infancy to instant adolescence. Acting on a case originating in the steel industry, a Court majority declared: "The strike was illegal in its inception and prosecution. . . . It was an illegal seizure of buildings in order to prevent their use by the employer in a lawful manner.")

Walter Reuther was available to succeed Martin as president of the UAW-CIO, but not at the cost of making a deal with the Communist Party. In a March 3 Detroit radio speech sponsored by the West Side Local, he described Local 174 as middle-of-the-road. Trying to carve out middle-ground support, he said: "The West Side Local agrees completely with the position of the CIO in condemning the factional activities of both the Communist Party and the Lovestone Communists. Local 174 has served notice that it will not tolerate the interference of any outside political group."

Martin's convention began in Detroit the next day, with 400 delegates participating. Cheered as he assailed "the dictatorship of John L. Lewis," Martin claimed the support of 200,000 UAW members. *The New York Times* quoted "close observers" as believing he had only 60,000 adherents while his opposition had an estimated 140,000.

Advance caucusing and secret conferences preceded the anti-Martin convention. The Communist faction drew up a slate headed by Addes and Frankensteen that promised to be strongest in terms of delegate support. One Communist goal, retaining vice-presidencies for Mortimer and Hall, was threatened by the Constitution Committee, which wanted only one vice-president, arguing that that would damp down factional infighting.

Some three weeks before the convention, Walter Reuther led 300 of his followers into a caucus that endorsed the single vice-presidency plan. The Reutherites proposed that R. J. Thomas be elected president and that Addes retain the secretary-treasurership. They would have called for dumping Addes, but his position was impregnable. The Reuther caucus did not choose a vice-presidential nominee.

Early in the convention Reuther was recognized for a five-minute speech in which he bitterly assailed Frankensteen, accusing his rival of mismanaging the Ford organizing drive and turning it into "a political football." Reuther suggested Frankensteen and his allies were using the Ford drive as a vehicle for political advancement in the union. "Give it to them, kid!" shouted an approving delegate. Another demanded that Reuther be silenced because he had exceeded his time limit. Faced with a "We want Reuther!" chant, the convention voted to suspend the rules and hear him out. Interrupted by frequent applause, Reuther went on to report, in scornful tones, that Frankensteen had tried to put the Detroit Symphony on a thirteen-week national radio hookup at UAW expense, to demonstrate that the union offered culture rivaling that of the popular "Ford Sunday Evening Hour." Reuther scoffed, "That was not the way to organize Ford's, with a symphony orchestra costing $86,000." His plan was to conduct an "educational program" combining anti-Ford stickers, pamphlets, and posters with nationwide picketing of Ford dealers. Such tactics, he said, could lead to organization of the company in six months. Acknowledging that he had been quite blunt in his attack on Frankensteen, Reuther said he had spoken frankly because it was the proper time to let off steam and clear the way for a united UAW: "Let's don't swallow hard here and then go out and cuss one another in the beer gardens like we have done for a few months."

Replying to what he termed Reuther's half truths, Frankensteen was booed at first but began claiming applause as he warmed to his subject. "Now, if Brother Reuther has something that was so wrong," he argued, "why did he wait six months to bring it before the convention, instead of making it at the last convention?" And he wondered why the West Side Local, although it geographically embraced the Rouge and its workers, had contributed a mere $4,000 to the Ford drive. As for the symphony, it would play soothing ballads in between anti-Ford speeches by men like Lewis, Hillman, and Murray. Frankensteen blamed Martin for failure of the Ford organizing effort and complained that only $43,000 had been spent in the attempt.

Frankensteen wanted the UAW presidency and thought he had the votes to get it. He even hoped he would have the support of George Addes. In fact, Addes wanted the job for himself, although he did not openly campaign for it, and his prospects seemed reasonably bright since he was the union's most powerful officeholder. Born in LaCrosse, Wisconsin, in 1910, of Syrian parentage, the wavy-haired, dark-browed Addes became a key leader of Auto-Lite Local 12 in Toledo during a 1934 strike. He had been the UAW's secretary-treasurer from the beginning.

Reuther, as another presidential possibility, realized that an Addes-Frankensteen slate probably could top him in delegate strength but, for a time, he toyed with pushing a proposal that might have enhanced his chances. He felt that, since Martin had succeeded in corralling dues payments from Flint, Pontiac, Lansing, and most cities with General Motors plants, he would be the gainer if convention balloting was limited to locals paying dues to the anti-Martin UAW. In his assessment, most of the Addes-Frankensteen strength lay in "paper votes, because they did not represent any real substantial membership payment." But Reuther ultimately agreed to give full voting rights to all locals in order to avoid a new union split. In any case, John L. Lewis was a more formidable obstacle to Reuther's ambitions than any voting arrangement. The CIO chieftain had a strong distaste for people he called "Socialist ideologues" and had vowed that Reuther never would be president of the UAW so long as he was president of the CIO.

CIO representatives concluded that many UAW members would

be alienated by the selection of any highly controversial figure as president. They also were determined to avoid any candidate who would give the Communist Party a major voice in union affairs, a blow to Addes' hopes since he was closely associated with the far left.

Reuther went to Hillman to argue that R. J. Thomas was the most widely acceptable candidate. Together they worked out a deal and, in return for pledging that his caucus would support Thomas, Reuther got an agreement that he would be made national director of the union's General Motors Department. The Communist bloc had hoped to reserve the GM assignment for Ed Hall.

Roland Jay Thomas, 38, amiable, earthy, red-faced and a husky 240 pounds, was known for his love of poker and chewing tobacco. He always carried Mail Pouch in his pocket. Born in East Palestine, Ohio, the son of a railroad worker and one of seven children, Thomas had aspired to the ministry and attended Wooster College with eventual ordination in mind. He became a tobacco chewer there because smoking was prohibited. Dropping out of college in 1923, he went to Detroit and got a job as a metal finisher at the Fisher Body Plant. He moved to Chrysler as an electric welder in 1929 and, with the emergence of the UAW, became president of the Chrysler local. An old line unionist, he cared nothing about ideology. As he put it in his raspy, high-pitched voice: "I don't know much about the class struggle. I'm interested in wages, hours and working conditions."

With Thomas elected with ease, the convention moved on to the selection of Board members. Facing each other in an eleven-man field for four Board positions allotted the Detroit area were Reuther and Frankensteen. Their close rivalry was reflected by the voting: Frankensteen, 657; Reuther, 652; Richard T. Leonard, 574, and Leo La Motte, 557. Ed Hall and Wyndham Mortimer were without union offices for the first time since the founding of the UAW.

On April 17 Homer Martin went to the Washington office of William Green to accept an offer of an AFL charter for his splinter union. Said John Brophy: "He now becomes the No. 1 problem child of the AFL as he was to the CIO." Michael Widman, a

Lewis troubleshooter sent to Detroit to get the bungled Ford organizing drive back on the track, pronounced a gentle epitaph for Martin's eccentric career as a trade union leader: "I just think he didn't know all the things he should know to be president of a growing union. With inexperience in the ranks as well as at the top—this makes for real growing pains."

CHAPTER TWELVE

Renaissance

SCHISM IN THE UNITED AUTO WORKERS LEFT THE THREE-YEAR-OLD union in shattered condition, its survival threatened by Homer Martin's link-up with the American Federation of Labor. Despite the show of unity at the Cleveland convention, there was no moratorium on factionalism among Martin's foes. And dues-paying membership had been cut sharply by the former preacher's pullout. Taking advantage of the split, General Motors announced early in 1939 that it was suspending collective bargaining at the national level on the theory that it did not know which organization represented its employes. But GM continued to talk to the UAW-CIO in plants where there was no challenge from Homer Martin's forces. In eleven factories where both groups claimed majorities, however, the corporation refused to talk at all.

This appeared to leave the UAW-CIO leadership with two rugged alternatives: use economic strength to force GM to the bargaining table on a national basis, with all the hazards that a long strike would entail, or submit to lengthy delays involved in arranging plant-by-plant elections under the auspices of the National Labor Relations Board.

As new head of the union's GM Department, Walter Reuther had another plan in mind: call a strike of skilled tool and die workers, a relatively small but well-organized group, to delay retooling for GM's 1940 models. This would allow the bulk of production workers to stay on the job making 1939 cars until the model run was completed. If laid off at that point, they could collect unemployment benefits. From the union's standpoint, the plan made a lot of economic sense because most production workers had exhausted their savings during the 1938 recession and could not afford a lengthy strike.

Homer Martin moved first, calling strikes at General Motors plants in Flint and Saginaw. His offensive failed when workers loyal to the UAW-CIO ignored his AFL picket lines and stayed on the job. The way now was clear for Reuther to test his strategy.

Negotiations came first, of course, with Reuther urging that the union seek a guaranteed annual wage for auto workers. He cited government statistics which showed that the industry's most skilled craftsmen had averaged less than six months' employment a year during the preceding five years. In 1939 the proposal was visionary indeed. The union settled for a simpler set of demands: a ten-cent hourly wage increase, a standard apprentice plan, the union label on parts, time-and-a-half for Saturday work, and double-time for Sundays and holidays. The package was not terribly ambitious. The unstated, underlying issue, however, was a survival demand for tacit recognition of the UAW-CIO over its AFL rival. That was what mattered most.

The Reuther idea for besting General Motors represented a bold gamble, full of risks for a union sundered by turmoil and uncertain about its future existence. Only 8 percent of the workers in plants organized by the UAW-CIO were paying dues at the time the strike began. The treasury was nearly empty and General Motors was complaining that not even the United States Post Office Department knew where to deliver a letter addressed simply to "United Auto Workers" in Detroit. GM broke off negotiations on the tool-die demands, refusing to meet until "somebody can tell us who the UAW is." For the UAW-CIO, everything now depended on whether Reuther's rather ingenious strategy would succeed in convincing the most powerful of auto manufacturers that it had best cast its lot with the CIO.

Final strike plans were made at a Fourth of July meeting of the Executive Board. Reuther had worked methodically to line up support for his tactic among the rank and file and he reported that strike votes were approved by nine out of ten workers involved.

Reuther explained his "strategy strike" this way: "A strike in tool and die, maintenance and engineering is opportune now because GM has been rushing to complete a great program on 1940 tools and dies, jigs and fixtures. A victory for the skilled men will establish the UAW-CIO as a bargaining agent nationally. . . . The watchwords of the GM workers are solidarity and discipline— power under control." He reminded production workers their turn would come later, when the union decided the time was ripe.

The tool and die strike hit five key plants in Detroit and Pontiac early in July 1939. Included was the largest tool-die shop in the world, Fisher 23 in Detroit. Violence flared at Fisher Body in Pontiac, followed by a battle in Cleveland and two near-riots in Detroit. When state police responded to the Pontiac outbreak, they found about 1,000 pickets massed at the factory gate to keep production workers from entering. Roy Reuther, the UAW-CIO man in charge, ingenuously explained that the pickets were only "protecting themselves." Assemblages thereafter were limited to 40 men. In Cleveland former Treasury agent Eliot Ness directed police in his new role as city safety director when violence broke out. Tear gas, clubs, and rocks were used as weapons as police fought with thousands of pickets. Mayor Harold Burton, later to become an Associate Justice of the Supreme Court, promised to maintain "law and order."

Retaliating, General Motors canceled a plan for interest-free loans to laid-off workers in plants affected by the walkouts. Walter Reuther called this "nothing but an attempt to blackmail the workers into submission, . . . vindictiveness and pettiness that one would hardly expect from the third richest corporation." William S. Knudsen, GM's president, shot back that the strike involved the "power and prestige" of union leaders rather than the welfare of the workers. He also complained it was not fair of the UAW-CIO "to embarrass the corporation at a critical time."

Unchastened, Reuther urged UAW-CIO members employed in smaller tool and die shops in the Detroit area to boycott General Motors' work. When they did, he exulted: "This puts GM completely behind the eight ball." The union's strike bulletin reported: "GM is squirming. The heat is on and the solid ranks of the UAW-CIO will keep GM's seat hot, or hotter, as long as needed to bring GM to decent terms."

Time focused national attention on the Reuther strategy, saying it was "not unlike amputating one finger at a time to cripple a hand." A few men at a time, the magazine declared, "were exerting pressure as menacing as a general walkout would be, while those still working are drawing pay." Reuther, alluding to sales gains by Ford and Chrysler, reminded the employer that "until GM gets these plants in operation, it cannot make a single 1940 car."

The effectiveness of the tool-die strike offered a sharp contrast to the dreary outcome of the walkouts called a month earlier by Homer Martin's organization. Grudgingly, General Motors agreed to begin negotiations. As Reuther explained later: "The first contracts we had were really like shotgun marriages. The parties were most reluctant to get together."

At the negotiating table Reuther sat opposite Charles E. Wilson, then rising rapidly in the GM hierarchy, and they began developing a rapport that later would be reflected in historic bargaining breakthroughs for the union. At the moment the mood was bitter and relieved only infrequently by any sign of humor. One night, while Reuther listened, Wilson unfolded a new proposal and began developing a series of variations, eight in all. An observer recalls the scene: "It got to be about midnight, and Walter pushed his chair back and laughed like hell, and he says: 'I'm going to offer a recess until morning. I damned near took that last position of yours and it's not as good as the first one you offered.'"

In another exchange GM's Knudsen wagged a finger at the UAW-CIO negotiator and said, "Now, see here, Reuther, we don't want any commissars in America!" Reuther, barely four years away from his experience with the Soviet system at the Gorki auto works, replied: "We auto workers don't want commissars any more than you do. . . . But what you and other powerful leaders of American industry do about helping make democracy work for the average man will determine whether we get commissars or not."

Reuther prepared a radio address denouncing the du Ponts, controlling stockholders in the auto corporation, but Detroit's Station WJR forced him to remove personal attacks from his manuscript. Reuther's original text accused the du Ponts of blocking a settlement and concluded, "This family, grown wealthy and powerful from its mercenary sale of munitions and from the misery of widows and orphans of soldiers, pulls the strings in General Motors."

Economic pressure—not oratory—was having the greatest impact on GM. A strike involving 7,000 workers in, by now, a dozen tool and die shops had virtually halted tooling on the 1940 car. Besides, the strategy allowed the union to mask its weakness at major plants by permitting laid-off workers to receive jobless benefits they could not have collected as strikers.

The strike was settled four weeks after it began. GM agreed to recognize the UAW-CIO as exclusive bargaining agent for tool and die makers in 42 plants, raised their minimum pay, and improved overtime provisions. The agreement was a signal achievement for Reuther and his union, demonstrating a revival of CIO strength in the struggle with Martin's auto union. Louis Stark of *The New York Times* wrote that General Motors "bitterly fought every inch of the way" to the ultimate agreement. The significance of the settlement, he concluded, was that GM, "for the first time since the split in the union, departed from an attitude of neutrality" and favored the CIO faction in a written contract. In return, the corporation received a no-strike agreement during the 1940 model year. Reuther said the most important GM concession was its agreement to raise wages in more than one plant. The 1937 settlement that ended the sit-down strikes did not even include a wage clause. Dropping his demand for a ten-cent pay raise across the board, Reuther gained from GM a formula that he said would bring "substantial" wage increases to the thousands of workers who had struck.

The outcome lifted union morale and spurred renewed organizing efforts. As Reuther later phrased it, "That was the beginning of the whole renaissance of our union."

For whatever reason, the UAW-CIO began sweeping federal bargaining rights elections at Packard, Motor Products Corporation, Briggs Body, Chrysler, and, on April 17, 1940, General Motors. Before the GM balloting, CIO leaders John L. Lewis, Sidney Hillman, and Philip Murray addressed mass rallies in the Detroit area. The UAW-CIO carried 48 GM plants with more than 120,000 workers while the AFL rival prevailed in but 5 plants with 5,600 employes.

A beaten man, Homer Martin resigned nine days later as president of the UAW-AFL, asserting, "I leave the labor movement, temporarily at least, with the knowledge that I have always served the interests of labor honestly and to the best of my ability." A short time later he began receiving lucrative contracts from the Ford Motor Company as a "manufacturer's agent." Harry H. Bennett, the company executive who dealt with labor matters and who helped earn Ford's reputation as a foremost enemy of auto unionism, said Henry Ford directed him to "help Homer" after the AFL's defeat. Martin was handed Ford orders for supplies and was provided by the company with a completely furnished home.

The union at this point zeroed in on Ford—little realizing that the boss's wife would help clinch its eventual victory. With every other major auto producer under contract by mid-1940, the UAW-CIO had achieved a measure of stability, claiming a dues-paying membership of 290,000 and contracts at 647 factories. Internal rivalries remained so strong, however, that the leadership had to ask the parent CIO for a man to direct the Ford organizing drive rather than assign the plum to one of its own ambitious young men.

Reuther could have staked a claim on the basis of his five years as a Ford worker. "I saw Harry Bennett and his gangsters running that company," he had recalled. "I worked in the B Building back before the Depression when they were driving fellows in the skilled trades department, not only on the production lines."

John L. Lewis, as CIO president, picked an old friend from the United Mine Workers, Michael Widman, to direct the Ford campaign, which was backed by a $100,000 fund. When Widman arrived in Detroit in October 1940, he found only 150 UAW members in the enormous work force of 89,000 at the principal Ford bastion, the River Rouge plant. But the Ford drive got a quick boost when a justice of the peace in Dearborn, Lila Neuenfelt, struck down as unconstitutional a town ordinance forbidding the distribution of handbills. When her ruling was upheld, a major obstacle to unionization was removed. And even before the court decision, Widman directed 25 sturdy-lunged organizers to march past the Rouge gates shouting, "Join the union," to circumvent the longstanding ban on circulation of leaflets.

UAW organizers insisted that the Ford Motor Company, once Detroit's high-wage employer, now lagged behind General Motors and Chrysler in pay scales, sometimes by more than ten cents an hour. And Ford's techniques for controlling its employes were challenged by the aggressive union. When worker John Gallo was fired in 1940 for smiling on the job, the union objected and a state labor referee ordered him reinstated. Ken Bannon, who later became director of the UAW's Ford Department, remembers how an organizer was locked in a tool cage from Friday night until Monday morning as punishment for his activities. Because of the company's calculated Balkanization of the work force, union strategists had to sponsor radio broadcasts in nearly 30 languages to get their message across. UAW speakers often told of a tough Ford executive who encountered a workman seated on nail keg, splicing wires, in violation of a plant rule against sitting down. The executive kicked the keg, the wire-splicer fell, then bounced up and knocked his tormentor to the floor with one punch. "You're fired!" roared the Ford official. "The hell I am," countered the other man. "I work for the telephone company."

In Dallas, Ford terrorism was no joke. Union adherents at the company's big Texas plant became targets for a strong-arm squad. When CIO organizers were tarred and feathered, Ford said it was a manifestation of the "spontaneous" reaction of loyal anti-union employes. A trial examiner for the NLRB thought otherwise, ruling that a series of 30 beatings was Ford's fault. The company, he concluded, used "the most brutal, vicious and conscienceless thugs in its employ" to discourage union sentiment through liberal resort to blackjacks, leaded hoses, and rubber-coated electric wires as instruments of persuasion.

Ford defended its notorious Service Department at the Rouge in proceedings before the NLRB:

> In a plant employing upwards of 85,000 men, . . . it is necessary to maintain a police and investigating force to unearth

and discover and prevent attempts to steal, actual thefts, and other criminal acts and forms of illegal and unlawful conspiracies. . . . It is only the dishonest citizen who objects to a police force, and it is only the dishonest employes or one with subversive intentions who has reason to fear such an investigating body and who tries to destroy it by false charges and by calling it names such as "spies."

The union drive was having an impact, even inside the family circle of Henry Ford. Henry's son Edsel favored bargaining with the UAW-CIO, arguing that the union's radio campaign was hurting the company. Henry Ford disagreed and the two men had long, heated arguments over the issue. Mike Widman, reporting to John L. Lewis late in 1940, predicted success: "I've got him. No doubt in my mind." Lewis replied, "I'm sure glad to hear you say that." But rejoicing would have been premature, for just 24 hours after Franklin D. Roosevelt's election to an unprecedented third term, Ford scored a coup. The War Department awarded the company a $122 million contract for aircraft engines despite CIO protests against the choice of a non-union manufacturer.

The UAW circulated thousands of copies of Upton Sinclair's satirical novel about Henry Ford, *The Flivver King,* to help its campaign. And CIO attorneys persuaded the Supreme Court to order the reinstatement of 22 workers fired for wearing union buttons.

Communists were active, too, notably Bill McKie, a Rouge tool and die maker who had been at the Overpass with Reuther and Frankensteen and who had chaired many organizing meetings. The Party had its own network of activists in the gigantic plant. But Ford's oppressive methods probably were the greatest spur to the unionization effort. "The people with whom I worked were treated pretty much as dogs," recalls Ken Bannon. ". . . The older you got the worse the treatment was."

Early in 1941 the UAW began to step up pressure on Ford. On February 27 the union filed notice of its intention to strike, but without announcing a date. Ford was ordered by the NLRB to rehire 1,000 workers laid off since the start of the organizing drive. In late March union men stopped work briefly in Ford's pressed steel plant, and several thousand workers halted an assembly line in another factory.

The climax came on April Fool's Day of 1941, when Harry Bennett abruptly ended a meeting with a UAW grievance committee by firing each and every committee member. The reaction in the Rouge was virtually instantaneous: "Strike!" Widman and other union leaders were stunned, although strike sentiment had been building among the UAW activists. Bannon explains:

> On the afternoon before, Mike Widman would not authorize this thing. . . . We decided amongst ourselves we were going to do it anyway. The reason they would not authorize it was that . . . we only had about 30 percent of the people signed up. They were damned apprehensive about whether we could hold this thing. . . . We who worked in the plant knew that these people would do the right thing at the point they could have a secret ballot.

Federal conciliator James Dewey arranged a meeting between company and UAW officials a few hours after the sit-in began. Joined by Walter Reuther and four others, Widman drove to the Rouge gate where Reuther had been beaten nearly four years earlier. Special guards stopped the car, checked with the Ford hierarchy, and brusquely informed the unionists, "They will not meet with you—get off our property." After this rebuff the UAW Executive Board voted unanimously to sanction the strike. Evacuation of the Rouge began. Bannon recalls leading about 10,000 workers out of the Motor Building to an all-night rally in back of the local union headquarters, once a schoolhouse.

While Reuther and other UAW leaders gave pep talks to strikers, Bannon and others improvised a barricade of automobiles to stop traffic on highways leading to the Ford plant. Bricks were stacked nearby to discourage any strikebreakers who might try to reach the Rouge on foot. "We had hundreds of cars," Bannon remembers. "There was no way you could get through." The militancy of Ford workers was "like seeing men who had been half dead come to life," said one union officer.

Later, when the UAW dismantled the auto barricade after receiving assurances the company would not attempt to operate the sprawling plant, union men equipped with nightsticks and whistles directed traffic around the Rouge. Bennett wired the White House to protest against a "Communistic demonstration of violence and terrorism."

The day after the strike began, a brief flareup of violence with racial overtones threatened to crack the union's solidarity. Henry Ford had hired a higher percentage of Negro workers than any other Detroit manufacturer, employing more than 9,000 of them in the production foundry alone. Virtually all the Negroes left the plant when the strike was called but about 200 out of 300 workers who remained in the Rouge were blacks. Some of them had been recruited by Bennett's Service Department to serve as the cadre for a strikebreaking force. The UAW leadership tried to defuse the potentially explosive situation. Walter White, then the executive secretary of the National Association for the Advancement of Colored People, and other Negro leaders were enlisted to join the union's picket line and appeal to the blacks to leave the plant. Some did but most of the 200 stayed. White encountered one nonstriking Negro with a weapon made of tool steel, sharpened to a knife point. "He told me in exceedingly profane and biological language what he thought of unions in general and me in particular," White recounted. "He said that Ford was the only place in Detroit where he had been able to find a job to support himself and his family and the union had not done a blankety-blank thing to break down employment discrimination in other Detroit plants." UAW activists argued that most Negro workers were more strongly pro-union than whites at Ford. A number of blacks were organizers.

Several hundred anti-union employes, most of them Negroes, attacked the picket line from inside the Rouge with ball bats, clubs, crude pikestaffs, and fists, temporarily breaking the UAW ranks. Reported *The New York Times*: "Iron bars were used freely in the rioting. . . . Scores were hurt as the heavy forged iron shafts were thrown at pickets by nearly 200 Negroes who made sorties from Gate No. Four on Miller Road." A union spokesman said 150 unionists were treated for injuries. Thousands of UAW supporters raced into the breach and beat back a second assault. The attacks were regarded by union leaders as a Ford attempt to provoke a racial split inside the labor organization.

Racial tensions were fanned further when Ford tried to initiate a back-to-work movement in Detroit's Negro community. Homer Martin, depicting himself as an AFL organizer, told an audience of blacks to "march back in a body." Walter White and others countered his advice and the union ran ads in Detroit newspapers declaring that Negroes and whites would get the same pay and have equal standing under a UAW contract.

Ford officials eventually came to fear a race riot and they arranged for a peaceful withdrawal of Negroes from the Rouge.

With that explosive issue resolved, Michigan's Republican governor, Murray D. Van Wagoner, proposed a settlement to both sides that encompassed an expedited NLRB election. His formula was accepted. The balloting, on May 21, 1941, was a crushing blow to Henry Ford. The UAW won worker approval over its AFL rival by a margin of 51,886 votes to 20,354. And together the two unions polled more than 97 percent of the ballots cast, despite the Ford company's resolute anti-union stance. Said R. J. Thomas: "Fordism has been repudiated by the men who know it best—by the Ford workers." Harry Bennett snapped, "It's a great victory for the Communist Party, Governor Van Wagoner, and the National Labor Relations Board."

Charles E. Sorensen, one of Henry Ford's closest associates and most valued production expert, said later that the auto magnate, then in his seventies, never was the same after the votes were counted. In despair, Sorensen reported, Ford talked about closing down the company and allowing the union to take it over. Yet, in a surprise turnabout, Henry Ford agreed to sign the best contract the UAW had yet obtained. It not only included pay raises of up to 30 cents an hour and other benefits worth $52 million a year, but the erstwhile arch-enemy of unionism also consented to dues check-off and a requirement that every Ford worker must join the UAW to keep his job. Sorensen asserted that the dramatic shift resulted from pressure applied by Mrs. Henry Ford. She threatened to walk out of the family home if Ford closed the plant, according to Sorensen, and the master of mass production industry capitulated, later telling a colleague: "I'm sure she was right. The whole thing was not worth the trouble it would make. I'm glad that I did see it her way. Don't ever discredit the power of a woman."

Reuther had another version of the settlement.

"We got a union shop in Ford for different reasons," he recalled years later. "Harry Bennett thought he could take the union over from the inside with his service department. If everybody had to belong, then we wouldn't be able to screen out the guys who shouldn't belong and he'd take it over. And when we made him put his service department into uniform and wouldn't take them into the union, his little plot collapsed. But that's why he gave us the union shop—there was no philanthropy involved."

Whatever the case, the abrupt capitulation to organized labor's demands came only after heavy pressure on Ford from the federal government and the courts, as well as the UAW. In the 1936-1941 period, for example, the Supreme Court upheld NLRB findings that Ford had discharged illegally 2,566 workers and owed them back pay of two million dollars. And the government was beginning to have second thoughts about granting major military contracts to an employer who, until then, had ignored federal collective bargaining requirements.

But most of all, the victory belonged to the new auto union that had persisted in its organizing attempts despite the physical brutality and economic pressures that for so many years had seemed to be a way of life at Ford's.

Overwhelmed by their success, Ford workers pulled 84 wildcat strikes in the first two months under their generous new contract. In truth, there were many old scores to settle. Yet with all that, Harry Bennett, long the symbol of iron-fisted oppression, had to be persuaded not to let workers elect their own foremen. His turnabout was such that UAW leaders were astounded. When Richard T. Leonard, head of the union's new Ford Department, complained that the manager of a small plant in Ypsilanti was refusing to meet with officers of the local there, Bennett dispatched an emissary who informed the manager, in front of a UAW delegation, "Look, the little guy says we play ball with this crowd." Taking a stack of unresolved grievances to Bennett's office, Leonard was amazed when the Ford official divided them into two even piles and declared, "We win these, you win those." Leonard hastened to accept the unorthodox arrangement, convinced he had fared better than would have been the case under normal procedures.

The UAW-CIO was on its way.

CHAPTER THIRTEEN

Prelude to War

IN JULY OF 1940 WALTER REUTHER JOURNEYED TO CHICAGO TO attend his first national political convention, the nominating session at which the Democrats chose Franklin D. Roosevelt for an unprecedented third term. With Hitler's legions already in possession of Paris and a militaristic Japan expanding at the expense of China, global crisis weighted the scales in F.D.R.'s favor, over vocal minority opposition.

To organized labor, Roosevelt was the runaway favorite on the strength of his record as an eloquent advocate of social welfare and collective bargaining. Kingpins of CIO unions met in Chicago in advance of the Democratic convention to add their weight to the draft-Roosevelt movement. An exception was John L. Lewis who, having pointedly failed to publicly endorse the President, kept in touch from his Washington office.

The United Auto Workers were as active in the New Deal cause as any of the CIO affiliates. On July 10 the UAW Executive Board met in the convention city to formalize its support with a resolution urging the President to seek a third term and demanding a draft should he demur. The policy statement read: "President Roosevelt has been the greatest friend of labor ever to hold the office of President of the United States. The record of social legislation enacted during his eight years in office, including the Social Security Act, with its unemployment compensation and its old-age pensions, tower high as monumental achievements for all our people." The Republicans already having nominated the able and energetic Wendell Willkie as their candidate, the UAW declared that neither the nominee nor the platform of the GOP merited labor's support. Reuther was entirely in agreement.

Although supporting F.D.R., brothers Roy and Victor had remained active in the Socialist Party until 1940, drifting away at that point because the SP responded to the war in Europe by affirming a pacifist, neutralist position. To the three Reuthers,

Hitler represented a real and present danger to the United States which made aid to embattled Britain imperative.

Inside labor's ranks, and especially within the UAW, the fact that Hitler had enlisted Joseph Stalin as an ally and collaborator in the two-front assault against Poland was having a profoundly divisive effect. When the Auto Workers met in convention in St. Louis in August 1940, the gulf between men of Walter Reuther's persuasion and the Communist-lining unionists was evident in acrimonious floor debate. Except for the Nazi-Soviet alliance, the UAW might have been expected to endorse Roosevelt's reelection without dissent. However, when delegates were offered a resolution pledging "unswerving support and allegiance" to F.D.R. and the New Deal, Wyndham Mortimer took to his feet and, obliquely noting that Lewis had yet to declare himself, said the proposed endorsement would represent "a direct kick in the face to the greatest labor leader this country or any other nation has produced." Nat Ganley, a faithful servant of the Communist Party, came closer to the truth in explaining his opposition to the pro-Roosevelt resolution. The President's policies were shoving the United States ever closer to war, he said, without mentioning that any such involvement would be on the anti-Nazi and, at that point, anti-Communist side of the conflict.

Walter Reuther rose to argue that the invocation of Lewis' name was a smokescreen to "conceal other reasons." Waving a copy of the 1939 convention transcript, he continued:

> Brother Chairman, I wish I had time to go through this book of proceedings of the last convention, and review the beautiful resolutions that Brother Nat Ganley introduced, praising Roosevelt, because those were the days of collective security and the People's Front. That is no more; there has been a deal between Stalin and Hitler, and therefore People's Front and collective security have been put in the ash can once and for all.

In sharp contrast to the boos Mortimer and Ganley had received, Reuther drew prolonged cheers. The Communist position on the resolution drew but 30 votes out of 550.

After easily winning on this issue, the Reuthers and their allies were more determined than before to further embarrass the UAW's vocal Communist element with yet another policy statement: "Resolved: That this convention . . . vigorously condemns the brutal dictatorships, and wars of aggression of the totalitarian governments of Germany, Italy, Russia and Japan." R. J. Thomas and George F. Addes lined up behind the proposition. Ganley, as a leader of the opposition, argued that he was "convinced that Russia cannot be classified as a totalitarian dictatorship," which earned him fresh catcalls. Another Communist wheelhorse, John Anderson, charged that Victor Reuther was the chief promoter of the resolution and, in that connection, cited the "Vic and Wal" letter from the Soviet Union. As a member of the Resolutions Committee, Victor retorted that the proposed policy statement was needed to "clear the air" and make the UAW's position abundantly clear to the thousands of aircraft and other defense workers it was attempting to enlist. The Resolutions Committee did not link the Soviet Union with Germany, he argued, but rather the Soviet Union did: "Russia saw fit to make that alliance with Germany and it is that alliance which the Committee condemns." Only about twenty delegates voted against the resolution, which prompted Louis Stark to write in *The New York Times:* "It marked the first clear-cut defeat of the left-wing and Communist-supported group in the union on a question which linked Russia to the dictatorships. At previous conventions, the leftists had usually been able to sidetrack attacks on subversive forces or to whittle these down to compromises."

The political strength of the Communist faction in the UAW clearly was at its lowest ebb since the union's founding. Even so, the convention delegates tossed one bone to the leftists. Instead of barring Communists, Nazis, and Fascists from membership, as was proposed, they were content to disqualify from union office members of organizations "declared illegal by the government of the United States through constitutional procedures." In a sense, in view of the voting on other proposals, this was more a victory for civil libertarians than for the Communist Party.

In balloting for the Executive Board, Reuther and his partners gained enough ground to permit them to insist, a few days later, on the dismissal of known Communists from the UAW staff. Half a dozen were fired, including Robert Travis.

Reuther's stonewall stance against the union's left wing won him persistent attacks from Communist and Trotskyite publications. These organs became so critical of his leadership of the General Motors Department that the Executive Board felt it necessary to give him a unanimous vote of confidence.

During the autumn months Reuther and his brothers did whatever they could to advance the Roosevelt campaign. They, and others in the UAW hierarchy, not to mention the rank and file, were angered and dismayed, if not surprised, when John L. Lewis addressed a nationwide radio audience of millions just eleven days before the election, to declare: "The present concentration of power in the office of the President of the United States has never before been equaled. . . . America needs no superman. . . . I recommend the election of Wendell Willkie."

On the night of the well-publicized broadcast Reuther convened the Executive Council of the West Side Local to hear Lewis, and then listen to a report on the Ford organizing drive from Michael Widman, a member of the Lewis staff. When the CIO chief voiced his endorsement of Willkie, declaring he would resign as president of the labor federation should Roosevelt win a third term, a husky hammerman from the Timken unit of the West Side Local grabbed a metal folding chair and smashed the radio. An embarrassed Widman left quietly, without giving his report.

To counter Lewis, the UAW invited to Detroit 700 local union officers who forthwith voted to invite F.D.R. to a union-sponsored mass meeting "so he can learn for himself how the automobile workers feel about him." The response was an invitation from the President to Thomas, Reuther, and Frankensteen to meet with him for lunch at Hunter College, in which setting he expressed appreciation for their support but gave his regrets on the contemplated mass meeting. Three days later Reuther delivered a thirteen-city radio reply to Lewis, declaring that "the personal spite or the hatred of one man will not switch labor's votes from Mr. Roosevelt. . . . The issue is wholly and simply: Roosevelt or reaction! American labor will take Roosevelt!"

Although Willkie collected more votes than any presidential candidate in any previous election, Roosevelt included, the incumbent received even more—a New Deal victory that left questions about the future career of John L. Lewis. In mid-November the CIO convened in Atlantic City and awaited word from Lewis on whether indeed he would step down after five years as the guiding light, often the guiding genius, of America's first federation of industrial unions. Redeeming his pledge, John L. went the way of a loner back to where he started, to the United Mine Workers. His hands-off attitude toward the war in Europe, however, found support among the CIO delegates. Whereas the AFL was on record as sympathizing with Britain and warning of a Hitler threat to America, the CIO's national defense resolution confined itself to demands for improved wages and enforcement of labor laws. A disinterested observer might have been pardoned for suspecting that labor's conservative element had become liberal, and vice versa.

Walter Reuther was in the front ranks of a losing battle to strengthen and broaden the CIO policy pronouncement. ". . . Just this week," he told the convention, "the warmongers of Europe—Hitler, Stalin, and Mussolini—are planning how they are going to carve up the rest of the world." He said he favored all possible aid to Britain short of sending foot soldiers to Europe. He termed the war a struggle between democracy on the one hand and totalitarians of right and left on the other. Michael Quill of the Transport Workers Union saw no threat to the United States from developments in Europe and declared that real national defense rested upon strong labor unions. The Quill position prevailed.

With the advent, in advance of war, of a national defense program, which meant distribution of lucrative contracts to dozens of major corporations, with subcontracts parceled out to hundreds, labor troubles spread. Union organizers, handicapped since the 1937 recession, began signing up many thousands of workers recruited for aircraft and shipyard jobs. A renewal of prosperity inspired increasingly ambitious union demands, which led in turn to an upward curve on the "strike" graph.

As head of the GM Department, Walter Reuther faced the problem, early in 1941, of trying to wrest significant contract gains from the world's biggest auto producer while fearing a work stoppage that could adversely affect the defense effort he enthusiastically supported. On behalf of the UAW, Reuther sought a ten-cent hourly wage increase, the union shop, and assorted fringe benefits. Unable to settle their differences, company and union notified the federal government on April 11 of a possible strike by 165,000 workers in 76 plants which handled, apart from civilian orders, $600 million of defense contracts. If a strike developed, Reuther said, the union would not call out men engaged in defense work. GM President C. E. Wilson interpreted that to mean a "half-strike" and added, "As far as I know, there has never been a half-strike called." He contended it would be impossible to separate defense production workers from all others.

The union twice postponed strike deadlines, once at the behest of state authorities and again at the urging of the National Defense Mediation Board, which won corporation agreement that any settlement would be retroactive. When GM offered $15 million in wage hikes compared to a union demand for $50 million, Reuther declared that "although General Motors earns the largest profits in the nation, it has taken the most backward position."

Just minutes before a third strike deadline in May, the federal government engineered a compromise: the union would get its ten cents an hour but must abandon the union shop demand. "The agreement," exclaimed Reuther, "represents the greatest victory won by General Motors workers since the first contract was signed in 1937." He termed it the largest wage increase ever won in the auto industry. Editorially, *The New York Times* did not share his enthusiasm: "What now effectively prevents workers from demanding, say, twice as much as they expect to get, have their dispute referred to mediation, have at least half their demands granted, and in a short time begin the same process over again?" As it developed, the wage increase made bigger consumers of GM workers and did not deter the corporation from earning bigger-than-ever profits.

If the General Motors dispute was settled without a strike, the record elsewhere was sometimes quite different, to the displeasure of many voters. The Gallup Poll reported early in 1941: "In place of the strike, the public wants to see a law compelling employers and unions to submit their differences to a federal board of conciliation. The vote favoring this method of settlement is more than 9 to 1."

One of the most bitter and bloody strikes of the period was against the Allis-Chalmers Manufacturing Company in West Allis, Wisconsin, a Milwaukee suburb. It was complicated by sometimes-intertwined conflicts of ideology. The company president, Max D. Babb, was a union hater and, in foreign policy, an isolationist. Heading the UAW local, No. 248, was a militant, Harold Christoffel, who was closely identified with the Communist Party. It was an instance in which neither Babb nor Christoffel had any ideological attachment to the defense program, for which Allis-Chalmers had more than $40 million of contracts. The result was a 76-day strike culminating in three days of rioting, during which scores were injured and the governor of Wisconsin, Julius Heil, was stoned. The defense program was among the casualties, particularly the Navy's destroyer program so essential for protection of the seaways against Nazi submarines. Destroyer production was delayed several months for lack of turbines on order from Allis-Chalmers. Louis Budenz, as an apostate Communist, subsequently claimed the CP high command had ordered the strike to help cripple defense preparations. The UAW chiefs, Walter Reuther among them, sided with the strikers because of the union-busting record of the employer. Reuther labeled Babb "one of the most vicious reactionary employers in the country."

When a local Auto Workers' union struck North American Aviation in the summer of 1941, however, Reuther and most other UAW officials were agreed in denouncing it as Communist-inspired.

North American held $300 million of contracts for military aircraft and produced about ten planes a day, a fifth of all military output. With Britain battling alone against Hitler's aerial blitz, the planes were needed urgently. That happened not to be a matter of concern among the UAW's top men on the Pacific Coast, where the company was located. The union's regional director, Lewis H. Michener, Jr., was a willing collaborator of the strike's principal instigator, Wyndham Mortimer, who represented the UAW Aircraft Division in the West. Mortimer, according to *The New York Times,* was said to have been a Communist Party worker in Cleveland under the name of "Baker." The president of the North American local was Elmer Freitag, who had registered as a Communist in a 1938 local election in Los Angeles.

In March 1941 the Auto Workers won a bargaining election at North American by a margin of 70 votes out of 7,016, the loser being the AFL International Association of Machinists. Inasmuch as North American workers were paid 50 cents an hour, compared with a defense industry standard of 75 cents, the UAW followed up its slender victory by demanding a 75-cent rate from the aircraft producer. When the company balked, the union threatened to strike on June 5.

Frankensteen, as director of the Aircraft Division, and West Coast officials of the union were called to Washington by the Defense Mediation Board. Responding to a federal appeal, the union agreed to postpone a strike pending mediation and won assurances that the eventual settlement would be retroactive. Although the UAW leadership in Detroit now assumed the dispute would be resolved along lines of the GM mediation, Michener, Mortimer, and Freitag ordained otherwise, ordering a wildcat strike for June 5 despite the contrary assurances they had given officials in Washington. Setting up powerful picket lines that fought off police, they shut down the big plant.

Following a Cabinet meeting two days later, President Roosevelt announced that unless the workers voted within 24 hours to return to work, he would direct the Army to seize the plant.

Frankensteen flew to California to make a back-to-work appeal.

Speaking first from a local radio station, he declared that "the infamous agitation, the vicious maneuvering of the Communist Party is apparent." He said, "The irresponsible, inexperienced, and impulsive action of local leaders in violating their own agreement will find no support from myself or our organization." He told the workers that if they did not follow UAW policy they would be suspended.

The Aircraft Division director then addressed a mass meeting of workers in a harvested bean field near the plant. The improvised platform on which he stood was ringed with tall huskies who blocked his view of the strikers and interrupted his every pronouncement with boos and catcalls. His appeal went largely unheard and the workers shouted approval of the strike. "Your action today," cried Frankensteen, "has made one man the happiest in the world; that is Hitler!" Waving banners that featured caricatures of Frankensteen's face attached to the bodies of rats, skunks, and snakes, the crowd threatened to become a lynch mob. As Emil Mazey recalled later: "I had the rather dubious privilege of driving Frankensteen to the famous bean field meeting, and that was no picnic. Brother Frankensteen and myself, and every one of us was escorted out of the bean field by a squad; otherwise we would still be out there—planted."

Calling a meeting of his West Coast staff, Frankensteen asked if anyone present opposed his anti-strike position. Mortimer squinted his eyes and declared, "My position is with the rank and file." Retorted Frankensteen: "It sure is. You just joined them." The summary dismissal of Mortimer ended his career in the leadership of the UAW he had helped establish.

The day after the bean field meeting, President Roosevelt, without peacetime precedent, used 2,500 troops of the regular Army to seize the North American plant. Production was resumed the following day with shifts virtually at full strength. An eventual settlement brought pay scales up to industry standards.

A few days after the seizure of North American, Plymouth Local 51, a Communist Party power center in Detroit, submitted a resolution urging the Wayne County CIO Council to denounce the European war as an imperialist adventure that did not warrant United States assistance to Britain. Before the Council could act, Hitler's armies, on June 22, 1941, invaded the Soviet Union. Local 51 immediately presented a substitute resolution appealing for all possible aid to the victims of Nazi aggression. Abandoned was the CP slogan, "The Yanks are not coming."

To anti-Communists like the Reuther brothers, the overnight flip-flop provided a relished opportunity and ample ammunition for months of agitation against CP tactics and motives. Said Victor, "We just used that to beat them over the head to show how slavish they were."

In an instant, Communists shifted from issuance of indiscriminate strike calls to dogged opposition to all strikes. The once-idolized isolationist, John L. Lewis, became in CP eyes an appeaser of the Nazis and Fascists. Sidney Hillman, long excoriated for his strenuous efforts to avert defense strikes, became a workers' hero. F.D.R. was back in the Party's good graces.

The national effort to fashion in a hurry an effective defense establishment where none had existed before created a personal problem of sorts for Walter Reuther. At the age of 33 and in excellent physical condition, Reuther registered for the military draft in 1940 and was classified 1-A, subject to immediate induction. In filling out his draft questionnaire, Reuther did not ask for deferment but listed two dependents, his aging mother and his wife, the latter employed as his confidential secretary at $1,000 a year.

When it seemed apparent Reuther was destined for early induction, R. J. Thomas as UAW president appealed for an occupational deferment for him, arguing that Reuther was making essential contributions to the defense program as head of the General Motors Department and member of the Defense Advisory Commission's subcommittee on training in industry. Philip Murray, who had succeeded Lewis as CIO president, joined Thomas in making the appeal. Said Thomas, "Murray and I are insisting that Reuther file his appeal because of his indispensable services to national defense and to stable relations in a vital defense industry." Selective

Service, deciding Reuther had not fully answered all questions about dependents, sent him a new questionnaire. This time he listed only his wife as a dependent. An appeals board subsequently reclassified him 3-A, ruling that May Reuther was dependent on him because she would lose her job if he were drafted. The board declined to grant an occupational deferment, saying it was able to rule on the dependency question without having to decide on Reuther's essentiality in his job.

The UAW's Communists were quick to assail the draft ruling. With Reuther seizing every opportunity to harass the CP faction at the union convention in 1941, John Anderson retaliated. During debate on an anti-Communist resolution backed by the Reuther brothers, Anderson declared:

> The "Royal Family" that sponsored this resolution has in its ranks a man that would sooner face cameras than bullets. Let me make this point clear. I say that our union has got the right to ask for deferment for our key men. If industry has that right, our union has that right. But this man was not deferred because of that. He was deferred because he told the government of the United States his wife was depending on him. He hid behind the skirts of his wife, and every man in this hall knows that.

Rising to Reuther's defense, R. J. Thomas replied that he, not Reuther, had told the draft board Mrs. Reuther would be removed from the union payroll should her husband be inducted. Reuther then spoke in his own behalf:

> It just so happens that I never at any time requested the appeal board or the draft board for a deferment. The only requests were made . . . by Brother Thomas and Brother Philip Murray. It just so happens they gave me the deferment for dependency rather than for occupational reasons because . . . they are compelled to give you the type of deferment that will give you the lowest classification. . . .
>
> Brother Murray and Brother Thomas asked me if I was willing to use my case as a test case; I agreed to be a guinea pig. . . .
>
> Brother Thomas and Brother Murray were very much worried about what was going to happen to many of the CIO unions,

a large part of the top leadership of which was in the draft age, and they felt if the draft would take our key people throughout the whole union it would tend to undermine the status and strength of the union.

. . . I think it is damned dirty and damned unfair when people inside of our own union, who know Brothers Murray and Thomas asked for this deferment, play politics with it. . . .

That Reuther should be the target of enemies within and without the UAW was inevitable because of his increasing power and prominence. Assessing the hierarchy of the Auto Workers in 1941, *Fortune* said, "It becomes immediately apparent that the two most important men in the union are Walter Reuther . . . and George F. Addes." The magazine concluded that only the "cautious centrist politics" of R. J. Thomas and the "opportunist juggling" of Richard T. Frankensteen kept UAW cleavages from becoming unbridgeable.

There were two principal issues at the 1941 convention in Buffalo's Memorial Auditorium: Communism and Walter Reuther. Contributing to the development of both issues was Reuther himself, who was determined first to strike hard at union Communists, then mount a major effort to end the long tenure of Secretary-Treasurer Addes. About half the Executive Board was on his side and his West Side Local went into the convention with the single largest bloc of delegate votes, 180.

Apart from Reuther, the key figure in the approaching donnybrook was the swarthy Addes, a devout Roman Catholic who collaborated with the UAW Communists more closely and consistently than any of the other major officeholders. Victor Reuther found Addes "a tireless worker and the kind of guy who had real appeal for factory workers; he didn't appear to be an ideologue but clearly his appointments deferred to these kind of people. . . ." To Leonard Woodcock, Addes "had in association with him some very bright guys and had the intellectual services of the Party apparatus, which in those days at least was no mean thing." Frankensteen felt Addes had one great flaw: "He was vindictive and never forgave a person who was against him; in a factional union he ostracized people and lacked flexibility."

For a year in advance of the Buffalo meeting, Walter Reuther and the ever-flexible Frankensteen had achieved a close collaboration despite their many and deep differences in the non-too-distant past. They went to Buffalo in apparent agreement on a common program. In fact they drove there together with their wives, detouring south from Detroit to enjoy a pre-convention holiday in the Great Smokies. At Berea College Reuther bought carved wooden napkin rings for the Frankensteen children. (At a mountain cookout each of the travelers was allotted one steak, with an extra to be divided by the men. When the time came to share the fifth steak, the meat was gone and a pair of animal eyes glittered at the picnickers from the dark woods.)

In making common cause, Reuther and Frankensteen hoped to dominate the convention and strengthen their individual positions of leadership. It was their intention to promote an anti-Communist resolution, punish Lewis Michener for his role in the North American strike, and support each other for UAW vice-presidencies. Reuther also felt he had Frankensteen's commitment to join in a move to replace Addes with a Reuther ally, director Richard T. Leonard of the Ford Department.

The Communist issue was one of the first to arise on the convention floor as the Reuther brothers and Frankensteen argued against seating ten Allis-Chalmers delegates led by Harold Christoffel. Walter Reuther contended that the procedures used to select the delegation represented "the worst kind of strong-arm political racketeering in this union." Defending Christoffel's delegates, Addes said Reuther opposed them because he thought they were Stalinists. When Frankensteen rose to accuse Christoffel of using Hitler-Stalin tactics, delegates from the West Coast and Allis-Chalmers waved small American flags. Frankensteen jibed back that it was the first time they had been known to wave an American flag instead of the red banner of Communism.

The convention sent a special panel to West Allis to supervise a new election of delegates. It returned to report that Christoffel had assailed Thomas, Reuther, Leonard, and Frankensteen as "a bunch of phoneys, rats, and Hillmanites," and had called the convention delegates "a bunch of bastards." A nettled Leonard shouted,

"If this convention is not willing to defend me as not being a bastard, then I will call Harold Christoffel out in the hall and I will accept the challenge." A delegate from Flint decried the fact that the convention "must listen to an international Executive Board member invite someone out into the hall for a common brawl." Another, from Detroit Packard, said he felt certain Leonard's bravado was inspired by the fact that Christoffel had been released from a hospital only recently. Despairing of the bitter debate, R. J. Thomas intoned from the chair: "We are not here revising the Constitution of the United States. We don't have . . . Reuther on trial. I am not even on trial now. Let's try and stick to the issues." The Christoffel group ultimately was seated, prompting *The New York Times* to report "a distinct victory for the Communist group in the union."

At this point the Reuther-Frankensteen alliance began to unravel. On the third day of the convention Louis Stark of the *Times* reported: "Mr. Frankensteen has been drawn away from his colleague, Mr. Reuther, by CIO officials who have informed him that the CIO wants Mr. Addes to remain in office." Another factor behind the developing schism: Allan S. Haywood, a CIO regional director, had persuaded Frankensteen there was no necessity to share vice-presidencies with Reuther—that he could have the office alone.

The breach became very apparent next day when the convention acted on the status of Lewis Michener, the 33-year-old West Coast regional director who had been copper miner, ranch hand, logger, door-to-door salesman, Ford worker, and, in the early 1930's, convicted bootlegger. The Credentials Committee proposed that the West Coast region be put under an administratorship, without imposing a personal penalty on Michener. Victor Reuther was plainspoken in his opposition: "The committee has not made one suggestion or recommendation as far as penalties for that individual who dared to tell Phil Murray, R. J. Thomas, and the director of aviation, in so many words, to go to hell. Why?" Victor insisted Michener be barred from the Executive Board for a one-year period. Frankensteen now hedged: "I agree with what has been said; there has been Communist domination on that West Coast situation. . . . Brother Michener made bad mistakes on this situation, but I do not think it is the thing to do to go out and crucify him because he made those mistakes." Walter Reuther argued that Michener had permitted the UAW to be used by groups who serve interests not in this country but interests beyond the shores of our country." He held Michener responsible for the North American strike, saying the regional director had "jeopardized the entire labor movement of America, because at that very time the enemies of organized labor on Capitol Hill in Washington were working out the most vicious anti-labor legislation in the history of America. Brother Michener gave the most vicious reactionary forces of this country a club to use upon us. . . ."

Replying, Michener said:

> If Walter Reuther, Sidney Hillman or anyone else who subscribes to the principles of the OPM [Office of Production Management], the so-called friends of labor, think for a moment that Richard Frankensteen and I are going to engage in a death struggle on the floor of this convention and ignore the welfare of the workers while Walter Reuther sits back there gleefully as a spectator and laughs and smirks at what he apparently considers his high-handed maneuvering, I want to state here and now he is going to be mistaken.

Wyndham Mortimer was on hand to make a swan song defense of his West Coast ally but, for his pains, succeeded mostly in gaining wider currency for the allegation that he, Mortimer, was a Communist. When delegate Roy Speth accused him of just that, Mortimer replied: "I am sick and tired of these people that talk about Communism every time they want to hide some dirty work. I don't think Brother Speth knows the difference between Communism and rheumatism." Frankensteen, retaining his distaste for Mortimer, jumped into the argument: "If Mortimer is not a Communist—and I don't know that he is—but if he isn't, he is sure as hell cheating them out of dues, because he certainly follows their line."

The Reuther brothers won the first round, over the opposition of

Thomas, Frankensteen, and, operating backstage, Allan Haywood. The report was returned to the Credentials Committee, which produced a substitute, barring Michener from reelection as a regional director. It was approved on a roll call vote of 1,558 to 1,460. Michener was placed on the national CIO payroll and won back his regional directorship in 1942.

Many years later, testifying in the federal trial of Harry Bridges on perjury charges, Michener admitted: "In 1941 I was carrying out the Communist Party line." There were the following exchanges during the proceeding:

Q. Did there come a time, sir, when you joined the Communist Party?

A. Yes, sir. . . .

Q. When and where was that?
A. That was in Los Angeles, California, late in 1938.

Q. Did you become an active member of the Party?
A. I did. . . .

Q. When if ever did you leave the Communist Party?
A. I left the Communist Party in 1944. . . .

Q. Did you join in your own name?
A. . . . I was advised to use the name of Lewis Herbert.

Q. Did you tell lies to people while you were a Communist? Lies, of course, that you were ordered to tell by some top leaders?

A. Well, the only outstanding lie that I could think of that I told the people, I denied my membership in the Communist Party.

Q. When did you do that?

A. On several occasions. Various trade unionists accused me of being a member of the Party and I denied it.

The most bitter convention clash was yet to come, over an anti-Communist amendment to the UAW constitution that was pushed by Victor Reuther, who was chairman of the Constitution Committee. Its text:

No member or supporter of any organization whose loyalty is
to a foreign government or who supports organizations which
approve of totalitarian forms of government, shall be eligible to
hold elective or appointive office in the international union or
any subdivision thereof. The regular trial procedure provided
for in this constitution shall be observed in this regard.

"This union of ours, as well as our nation, is at the crossroads,"
Victor told the delegates. "We cannot preserve democracy in the
CIO or in our nation as long as there are those within our ranks
who would use the strength which the CIO gives them as leaders
to advocate a policy which would lead to dictatorship and totalitarian rule and the destruction of free, democratic trade unionism."

James Lindahl of Detroit Packard Local 190 insisted Communism was not the issue: "The real question is whether or not the
Socialist Party in the person and voice of Walter Reuther and
Victor Reuther and the rest of the Reuther family is going to have
a privileged minority position in this union. That is the issue, my
friends." Lindahl proposed an amendment that would bar Socialists
from union office, a maneuver seen by the Reuthers as an attempt
to defeat the entire proposition.

Addes backed up Lindahl and, trying to rebut Victor's argument that there were no free trade unions in the Soviet Union,
declared: "The only regrettable part about this whole thing, so far
as I am concerned, is that Brother Reuther did not tell me in 1936,
1937, and 1938 what he told this convention tonight. The fact
of the matter is, delegates, he told me the opposite in his convincing manner. And I just about believed him. . . ." Then, lest anyone
mistake his alliance with the Communists as anything more than
that, Addes vowed, "I am not, nor have I ever been, a member of
any minority political party, and I am too old to start joining these
minority political parties."

Melvin Bishop, to whom the "Vic and Wal" letter from Russia
had been addressed, already was on record at the convention as
taking the Addes-CP side:

... When I hear people talking about influences coming from
other countries and when I hear Brother Reuther—Victor

Reuther in particular—talk about influences of the Communist
Party and Stalin in Russia, I would just like to state that Brother
Victor Reuther is the only person in this union who has ever
tried to influence me concerning the Communist situation in
Russia. I have in my possession a letter which he signed with
the salutation of "carry on the fight for a Soviet America,"
which is written from Russia.

Victor's response:

> I am aware, as I speak to you tonight, that the floor of this
> convention has been flooded once again with the same scandal
> sheet that was passed out at the gates of many factories through-
> out this country, a reproduction of a phoney letter that the
> Flint workers themselves know first appeared in Flint during
> the sit-down strike, and was used in an effort to discredit those
> of us who were active in Flint at that time, those of us who were
> active in the Battle of Bulls' Run, to discredit us as agitators,
> as agents of a foreign government. That letter is not new to
> the Automobile Workers. It has been booted around in every
> convention. It has been used by every stool pigeon and every
> corporation in the country that has sought to discredit the lead-
> ership of our union.

John Anderson was the avowed Communist in the debate. "I
have no apology to make for my beliefs," he said at one point.
"You never saw a Communist walk through a picket line." Now,
in attacking the Reuthers, he became vitriolic:

> I want to know if it is a crime for a working-class party when
> the leaders of this union, including the Reuthers, come for ad-
> vice to Communist leaders and accept that advice, and on pre-
> vious convention floors have spoken over microphones and
> taken applause for policies that were worked out in my house
> with Walter Reuther—and I defy them to deny that, and if I
> am wrong, let them prefer charges, and by God I will provide
> the proof. . . .
> The "Royal Family" came into the first convention as left
> wingers, the last convention as middle-of-the-roaders, and this
> convention as right wingers, and if they follow the policy of the
> Socialists in Germany as pronounced at the last meeting of the

Reichstag, they will come into a future convention as full-blooded Fascists.

"I want to say," said Walter, "that personally I am getting damn sick, and I think this convention is getting damn sick, of talking about Walter Reuther. I think we came here to do a job for the membership, but certain people will stoop to any level in order to try a smear campaign."

Emil Mazey, a Reuther partisan, was more colorful in his response to the Addes-CP line, prompting one delegate to remonstrate, "When a speaker gets up and mixes his conversation with an amazing reservoir of profanity, when our delegates' wives and precious little children are in these galleries, my point is he should be ruled out of order." Addes, occupying the chair at the moment, agreed.

In the end, an equally strong substitute for the Reuther amendment was adopted by a lopsided vote, and with the support of the brothers.

The Reuthers were thwarted, however, when they sought their principal objective: election of Leonard over Addes for secretary-treasurer. With Allan Haywood backing Addes on behalf of the CIO, Thomas threw his weight into the balance, arguing that retention of Addes would avert another disastrous factional split. Frankensteen joined the Addes camp, too. Until the CIO moved, Walter Reuther felt certain he had the votes to beat Addes. And he wanted to act in 1941 because he was not certain he could muster as large an anti-Addes vote again. Even so, Leonard made a respectable showing, bowing to Addes by a vote of 1,759 to 1,307.

Walter Reuther subsequently was reelected to the Executive Board, but just barely. At one point, a tabulating error made it appear that Reuther had been defeated. Leonard Woodcock went into the streets to find his friend, who had not bothered to stay around for the vote, and break the bad news. He found Walter and May Reuther emerging from a movie theater and relayed the erroneous report. Walter was philosophical, but May, thinking immediately of the future, suggested a comeback route: "Why don't you go to work in the Rouge and become president of Local 600?"

When all votes were counted, Reuther and his allies had picked up a couple of seats on the Executive Board. Walter, as a Board member, also received a pay raise of $500, to $3,000 a year. While he had not lobbied for the additional money, believing strongly in small salaries for union officials, he at least had cause for satisfaction on other grounds. *Business Week* offered this assessment of the convention: "The faction led by Walter Reuther of Detroit had put its program through almost to the letter."

Frankensteen, recalling the events years later, stated that in Buffalo in 1941 Reuther "pretty near finished me politically." By virtue of his own vacillation, Frankensteen emerged estranged from the Reuther camp and not quite trusted by his new left-wing allies.

A few months later, on December 7, 1941, Walter Reuther was driven from Detroit to New York City by Edward Levinson, then the union's chief publicist. As chairman of the UAW Housing Committee, Reuther was to report to the Executive Board on that panel's activities and plans. The car had no radio, and newsboys waving "Extras" brought them their first word of the Japanese attack on Pearl Harbor.

"Well, Eddie," said Reuther, "this means we'll have to rewrite the report. We'd better go and wash up and I'll see you in the room in twenty minutes." Reuther also told Levinson the Board would have to adopt a no-strike pledge, which it did. The UAW was the first union to take such a step.

CHAPTER FOURTEEN

500 Planes a Day

A YEAR BEFORE PEARL HARBOR, WALTER REUTHER PUT FORWARD an imaginative and controversial proposal to mobilize the vast resources of the automobile industry for military production. He hoped that after months of foot-dragging, Washington and Detroit would respond to the Japanese attack by putting into effect the "Reuther Plan" to turn auto plants into aircraft factories.

The plan had its genesis on a summer morning in 1940 as Reuther drove by the site of a Packard aircraft engine plant being built with generous federal support. He noted that concrete foundation footings were just being poured, a discouraging reminder that it might take another year and a half before Packard produced its first engine. Meeting in Washington with Sidney Hillman of the Office of Production Management, Reuther told his former labor colleague: "This doesn't make sense. Hitler isn't going to wait 18 months." Remembering that the Soviet auto plant in Gorki had been tooled simultaneously for civilian and military production, he suggested that idle capacity in Detroit's existing factories could be converted to weapons output. With Hillman's enthusiastic approval, he promised to develop the idea.

Recruiting Ben Blackwood, a top tool and die man at General Motors, as his assistant, Reuther directed a survey of the auto industry's production base. Shop chairmen and local UAW officials gathered detailed statistics on idle machines, unused floor space, and available skilled labor. Working closely with Blackwood, Reuther concluded that virtually all idle space and machinery could be converted quickly to aircraft production. When about 25 technicians from union ranks met in November 1940 to debate the merits of the Reuther plan, only two opposed it, one because he saw no reason why the Auto Workers "should help the bosses run their plants more efficiently."

Seeking maximum public impact, Reuther suggested the plan be taken directly to Franklin D. Roosevelt by R. J. Thomas. "I've got an idea I think is exciting," he told Thomas. "You're the president of the union and I think it would be fine if you submitted this." Unwilling to risk his prestige on an untested idea, and suspicious that Reuther might be trying to gain personal advantage at his expense, Thomas was emphatic: "Screw you. You're not going to make a horse's ass out of me." Union men, he declared, should "stick to their knitting."

Reuther next went to Philip Murray, who told him, "I don't know a damn thing about this but if you say it makes sense, I'm agreeable." Murray met F.D.R. for lunch at the White House two days before Christmas, 1940, and unfolded Reuther's plan. The President expressed interest and promised to take it up with his defense production advisors, notably William S. Knudsen, Hillman's partner in operating the OPM. Headline writers and editorialists responded quickly, if not always with approval, because the proposal centered around an attention-getting slogan: in six months, if Reuther's thinking was correct, the auto industry could begin turning out "500 planes a day," or the staggering total of at least 150,000 a year. Asserted Reuther:

"England's battles, it used to be said, were won on the playing fields of Eton. This plan is put forward in the belief that America's can be won on the assembly lines of Detroit."

With help from UAW publicist Levinson and journalist I. F. Stone, Reuther put his ideas in writing. He and Murray filled hundreds of requests from inquiring industrialists and citizens for a "500 Planes A Day" pamphlet detailing the proposal:

> Time, every moment of it precious, its tragic periods ticked off by bombs falling upon London and the Midlands, will not permit us to wait until new mass production factories for aircraft and aircraft engines finally swing into action late in 1942. Emergency requires short-cut solutions. This plan is labor's answer to a crisis.
>
> Mr. William S. Knudsen says that airplane production is 30 percent behind schedule. It will continue to be behind schedule so long as we continue to rely on the expansion of existing aircraft plants, and on the construction of new plants. Expansion

of existing aircraft plants means the expansion of plants utilizing the slow and costly methods of an industry geared to hand-tooled, custom-made production. . . .

New plants, when finally erected, must be filled with new machinery and this new machinery largely duplicates machinery already available in our automobile plants. The machine industry is overtaxed. The emergency of war cannot be met in the normal time necessary to construct new plants and equip them with the required production machinery.

We propose, instead of building entirely new machines, to make the tools required to adapt existing automotive machinery to aircraft manufacture.

We propose to transform the entire unused capacity of the automotive industry into one huge plane production unit.

. . . A careful survey will show that the automobile industry as a whole is not using more than 50 percent of its maximum potential capacity if that capacity were properly coordinated and operated to the fullest degree.

Reuther went on to list a number of plants that could be used in the undertaking, citing one he claimed could make all needed drop forgings for 500 aircraft engines a day and still produce enough forgings to manufacture a million Chevrolets a year. In like vein, he cited body and parts plants that could be used to manufacture wings and fuselages, saying: "Proof of this is provided by the tentative plans being made by the automotive industry at the suggestion of Mr. Knudsen to manufacture parts of wings and fuselages for large bombers." The labor leader also pointed to Detroit's large manpower pool, including thousands of skilled mechanics and tool and die experts. Conversion to the production of a mass-produced, all-metal pursuit ship should take no more than six months, he estimated.

To Detroit's captains of industry, the most controversial aspect of the Reuther plan was the suggestion that organized labor be given an active role in economic planning. If adopted as an emergency measure, such a practice could survive in peacetime, serving as a wedge for broadened UAW bargaining claims in an area from which labor traditionally had been excluded. Yet the idea presented potential pitfalls for the union, too. Should the UAW become closely involved with management in emergency production planning, its role as a free bargaining agent could be inhibited. Here is the core of Reuther's production planning suggestion:

> We propose that the President of the United States appoint an aviation production board of nine members, three representing the government, three representing management, and three representing labor. We propose that this board be given full authority to organize and supervise the mass production of airplanes in the automobile and automotive parts industry.
>
> The first task of the board would be to organize a staff of production and tooling engineers and assign them to make a plant-by-plant survey of the industry to determine the capacity of each plant and the extent to which it is being utilized. The next task of the board would be to break down a blueprint of the type of plane chosen for mass production into its constituent parts and allocate the various parts of the engine, wings, and fuselage among the different automotive plants in accordance with their unused capacity and the kind of work to which that unused capacity is being adapted. . . .
>
> The production board should have power to allocate the tooling and designing necessary among the various tool and die shops in accordance with their capacity and their specialized qualifications. . . .

Predictably, the aircraft industry was not happy about the Reuther blueprint for turning over the lion's share of aircraft output to the auto makers. Speaking as president of the Aeronautical Chamber of Commerce, Colonel John H. Jouett said: "These aircraft manufacturers have made lifetime studies of aircraft production. They would be the first to adopt mass-production methods wherever possible. Manufacturers of aircraft in other countries—France, England, Germany—who have had vast industrial experience have been unable, either during preparation for war or during wartime, to establish mass-production methods as we know them in the automotive industry."

But the Reuther plan was gaining momentum, gathering substantial support from those in and out of government who felt industrialists preferred to conduct business as usual and avoid radical innovations at a time when the United States was not directly involved in war. Demanding a hearing for the labor leader's ideas were such influential columnists as Walter Lippmann, Dorothy Thompson, Ernest K. Lindley, and Raymond Clapper.

Almost overnight Reuther became a national figure. Roosevelt invited him to the White House for a conference and the UAW official spoke out for his plan on nationwide radio hookups and before such opinion-molding forums as Washington's National Press Club. His partisans were impressed because "500 Planes A Day" embraced vast technical knowledge as well as a generous measure of idealism—a combination Reuther would rely upon many times in the years ahead.

Industry intensified its counterattack, John Jouett telling the National Press Club the plan was impractical:

> . . . At $50,000 each, 500 planes a day would cost $25,000-000 a day. Carrying this through to the absurd, at 300 working days a year there would be required an appropriation of seven and a half billion dollars—all spent on one model, as compared to the total of about one billion provided for all types this year.
>
> . . . At 500 planes a day, that means 4,000 machine guns a day. In other words, in 2½ days such a program would eat up the present annual production of machine guns in the United States. The rest of the plane production would have to sit idle until guns could be provided.

Jouett's figures were based on hand-crafting of planes rather than mass production. In a letter to *The New York Times* Reuther replied: "If Chevrolet Motor Car Company had to build 6,000 cars a day by the same methods that are now being used to build planes, the total manpower and floor space of the entire automobile industry would not be adequate to turn out its present production." He added that his plan could be adapted for medium and heavy bombers, too. "If these latter types are built rather than pursuit ships, the daily production would be scaled down in proportion to the increased amount of work required on each plane.

Nevertheless, our program could build many more bombers, large or small, than are now being built or are contemplated, and in much shorter time."

The Automobile Manufacturers Association was restrained in its initial reaction to the Reuther plan, wiring Roosevelt that it would "respond in full measure to every call for service that comes to it from our government's Office of Production Management, regardless of sacrifices that may be involved."

The public, George Gallup found, was not pleased with the rate of warplane production, 58 percent registering disapproval while only 28 percent approved.

In both its news and editorial columns *The New York Times* raised doubts about the Reuther proposal, but never more scornfully than in the following editorial: "A woman who had a typewriter and a sewing machine in her home would not think it simple to 'adapt' the typewriter for sewing or the sewing machine for writing letters; yet these machines are no more specialized than the great bulk of machine tools. . . . No miracle is to be expected from any all-embracing 'plan' or slogan, however attractive it may look in a headline."

Reuther was elated, however, when Roosevelt told a press conference that the "500 planes" idea had been turned over to his new Defense Council and would represent a major contribution if it could be exploited. In six months, Reuther predicted, the United States could put "ten planes into the air for Hitler's one."

Late in 1940 Chairman Jerome Frank of the Securities and Exchange Commission brought together Reuther and some leading figures of the New Deal for a Sunday morning breakfast at the Cosmos Club in Washington. For several hours Reuther discussed his proposal with Tommy Corcoran, Paul V. McNutt, Leon Henderson, Harry Dexter White, and others. A War Department labor advisor who was there concluded, "It probably can be done, but who the hell will pay attention to a squirt of a labor leader?" White was so impressed he arranged for Reuther to meet that afternoon with Secretary of the Treasury Henry Morgenthau. The Treasury chief agreed to urge that F.D.R. insist on a full hearing for the plan but suggested: "There is only one thing wrong with the program. It comes from the 'wrong' source."

On New Year's Day of 1941 the Associated Press reported from Washington that "defense experts who declined to be quoted by name" had concluded with reluctance that Reuther's recommendations were impractical and must be rejected. Their objections: problems in geting enough machine tools, new or old; impossibility of acquiring sufficient aluminum products; lack of armament for the number of planes envisioned; the fact that auto plants already were being assigned major defense tasks, including the production of thousands of aircraft engines.

Reuther pressed ahead, undeterred by the anonymous critics. On January 3 he returned to Washington to meet with Robert A. Lovett, special assistant to the Secretary of War. Two weeks later, using an Air Corps plane made available by Undersecretary of War Robert P. Patterson, he visited two large aircraft factories to check out some of his ideas.

On March 1 Reuther discussed his proposal with the one man who could swing more weight behind it than anyone else in the capital, William S. Knudsen. Reuther and Knudsen had met before, across the General Motors bargaining table. The earlier encounters had given rise to a report that Knudsen once surprised Reuther by expressing a wish that the labor leader were selling used cars for GM. "*Used* cars?" asked Reuther. "Yes, *used* cars," Knudsen is said to have responded. "Anybody can sell *new* cars."

Few men in the auto industry cared to challenge Knudsen's credentials as a production genius. As director general of OPM, he gave Senate testimony against creation of a new agency to set priorities for materials. "I'm against it," he declared. "It just won't work." Pressed to explain why, he shot back, "Gentlemen, where I come from, when I say a thing won't work—*it don't work.*"

With Sidney Hillman sitting in on the conference, Reuther proposed they tour an auto plant together and see for themselves what could be done to shift to plane production. Knudsen said he doubted he had authority even to take the labor leader into any plant. Angry, Reuther issued a public statement: "Mr. Knudsen and I met previously, on opposite sides of the table. I thought on this matter of national defense we might sit on the same side. I was mistaken."

A few weeks later, with civilian auto production increasing, advocates of the Reuther plan seized upon official figures showing that, in one month, the Army Air Corps had taken delivery of only two Flying Fortresses, the principal bomber of the period. Wayne Coy, who had an emergency management job, sent Roosevelt a memo calling attention to the scant output and suggesting use of auto plants for the purpose. F.D.R.'s troubleshooter, Harry Hopkins, intercepted the memo and summoned Coy to accuse him of trying to feed the President false information. Surely, said Hopkins, more than two bombers had been produced. Coy rechecked and discovered that only one bomber had been delivered during the month. A second, finished early the following month, had been added to fatten the figure. To Reuther this was further evidence that his plan was needed immediately.

Although his belief in the plan remained unshaken, the UAW official had to concede it had been shelved. To the union's 1941 convention he said, "If industry had put its best foot forward and proposed the plan, it might have been adopted, but people in Washington were afraid to fight and push it through because they knew organized industry stood solidly against this proposition."

Pearl Harbor changed the outlook. Addressing the Union for Democratic Action in New York City on December 13, Reuther returned to the offensive. Industry, he declared, was trying to prevent recognition of labor as a full partner in the war effort out of fear that labor would do "such a good job that it would convince the world it should continue after the war." And he came up with a new proposal: GM, Ford, and Chrysler should pool their facilities for making 30-ton tanks and use a single set of tools and dies instead of three. "In that way," he said, "we can tool up for production in half the time now estimated for the tooling period, and once we are in production we can turn out three times as many tanks as are contemplated under present schedules."

Reuther was being listened to with new respect. Called to Washington to testify before a House Committee investigating production mobilization, he could afford to crow a little: "The thing that we pointed out a year ago was that the machine tool industry was overtaxed, not because of the defense effort, but because of the fact that new plants were going up and the machine tool industry was being called on to duplicate machinery that was going to be idle in our own industry." He advocated vigorous federal direction of the economy:

> You can't expect due process of law to finally jar a screw machine out of one plant and into another. You have got to have an agency which can say, "O.K. If we need so much transmission capacity, we are going to use that capacity; no matter where it is, who owns the machines, or where they may be standing, we are going to get that capacity together on an industry-wide basis." If we have this overall agency, we can get this work done in half the time.

Appearing with Sidney Hillman at a joint news conference, Knudsen was asked if industry now thought it could convert more rapidly than when the Reuther plan was first presented. "Of course," was his answer, "there's nothing else to do." Then, edging close to the heart of the Reuther proposal, Knudsen told industry: "Conversion is tool-making. Take all these machines you have and see if there isn't some way to utilize them."

Historian Bruce Catton, then a publicist for federal war agencies, felt from his vantage point that the Reuther plan suddenly came close to being adopted soon after Pearl Harbor. "For about 24 hours the plan hung in the balance," he wrote, "not because the labor people had converted anybody but simple because nobody else had anything whatever to offer." He believed the plan ultimately was dismissed anew, "not because it had been carefully studied and found to be unworkable, but because it fell outside of the established points of reference." He saw Reuther in the role of the child in the fairy tale "who tactlessly pointed out that the emperor was naked."

Government recognition came belatedly to Reuther, if not his plan. He was made chairman of the union component of an industry-labor advisory committee assigned to spur conversion of the auto industry, and the War Department sent him on a fact-finding tour of auto plants, to reexamine much the same ground covered in his rejected proposal. He was invited to share his thinking with Donald Nelson, chairman of a new War Production Board and successor to Knudsen as the government's top conversion official. Nelson was impressed, telling an associate: "He's quite a fellow. . . . Three-fourths of the dollar-a-year men around this place are scared to death of that little fellow. And, you know, they ought to be scared of him—because he's smarter than they are."

With conversion layoffs in the auto industry approaching 400,-000, Reuther found it tragic that the world's most productive industry should be "blacked out at a time when, to a very large extent, victory or defeat in the struggle that lies ahead will be determined by our ability to mobilize our maximum productive capacity." Talking to delegates from GM plants, he scoffed at sudden industry complaints that government was responsible for failure to convert sooner. He said:

> They had Mr. Knudsen down there, surrounded by hundreds of dollar-a-year men, who spent all of their time looking around to see how they could protect their own individual interests— how they could maintain the status quo and superimpose a defense economy on the existing economy. And so when they say the government was responsible, they are merely saying that the dollar-a-year men from industry, who were running the government, were representing industry instead of the needs of the nation.

Charles E. Wilson, president of General Motors and symbolic leader of the industry, challenged Reuther to meet him in face-to-face debate on the Reuther plan. The labor leader welcomed the contest and the resulting national attention for his ideas.

The two men met in the auditorium of the General Motors Building on March 31, 1942, Wilson, 51 and white-maned, was flanked by three GM executives. Reuther, his hair flame red at 34, had his own advisors: brother Victor, Ben Blackwood, and an organizer for the CIO's Designing Engineers Union. The moderator, at a $400 fee paid by the corporation, was George V. Denny, Jr., chairman of America's Town Meeting of the Air, then radio's most popular discussion program. Questions were posed by 56 newspaper and magazine writers. Cross-questioning was by the two principals, Reuther addressing "Mr. Wilson" and the General Motors president referring to "Walter."

The debate became an endurance contest, Reuther and Wilson talking for six hours and filling a 157-page transcript. Each began in fighting fettle:

REUTHER: The Reuther plan is just as sound today as when it was originated. There is still tremendous waste, inefficiency, and duplication. The automotive industry is still interested primarily in profit. . . .

WILSON: When the plan was published, industry did not reply because an analysis showed clearly it was proposed for political and publicity purposes. I am doubly sure today that industry's appraisal was correct. It's a guns-and-butter plan and not a conversion plan. . . .

A measure of good-natured harmony emerged at the conclusion of the debate:

REUTHER: If we can rise above our partisan considerations and go down the line arm in arm, uniting in effort and will, working together, sweating together, we can win together. Democracy will be safe in America only if we can perfect this teamwork.

WILSON: I think that I can truthfully say that the whole General Motors organization, workmen and management alike, are dedicated to the single purpose of producing more tanks, airplanes, Army trucks, engines, guns, and ammunition to help win this war.

The labor leader and the industrialist rose from their places, grinned, shook hands, and, with arms draped around each other's shoulders, walked beneath a poster that read: "PLEASE KEEP THE BOMBS AWAY." Then they made their only joint statement: "That's our job and we'll do it." Citing the finale, the Detroit *News* editorialized: "If we were judging the debate, we would call it a draw between the two contestants, but on grounds of the above agreement and the handshake that went with it, a victory for both of them, and for America."

Despite industry's coolness, key elements of the Reuther plan were put into practice by the auto makers within the year. Testifying before a Senate committee in 1943, K. T. Keller, president of the Chrysler Corporation, was proud to state that 89 percent of Chrysler's machine tools had been converted to war production and could be converted back to civilian chores. Philip Graham, one of Reuther's Washington friends, concluded that this meant the labor leader had been 89 percent right all along.

In 1945, with the war ending, *Fortune* paid a belated tribute: "Reuther was on the right track. Compared with many industrialists who sat back and hugged profits and . . . the aimless agencies of Washington, the redheaded labor leader exhibited atomic spirit of action. He never let up."

1933—Walter at a youth hostel in the Swiss Alps during his trip around the world with Victor. *Courtesy of Victor Reuther*

Childhood photograph of Walter Philip Reuther. *AFL-CIO News*

1934—Victor and Walter cycling through a Russian village outside Gorki near the automobile factory, *Avtozavod,* where they worked. *Courtesy of Victor Reuther*

1934—Walter (foreground) and Victor (right, standing) are shown with Italian, Finnish, Polish and Russian workers in the Gorki auto plant. This photograph was first published by the Moscow *Daily News* in 1935. *Wide World*

1935—Walter (3rd from left) and Victor (right) near Peiping, China, with Chinese students and a professor from Yenching University. *Courtesy of Victor Reuther*

1937—Before the Battle of the Overpass, May 26, union organizers are confronted by "Ford Service" bullies who thwarted distribution of leaflets urging workers to join the UAW. Walter Reuther is flanked on the left by Robert Kanter and on the right by Richard Frankensteen. *Press Associates, Inc.*

1937—Battle-scarred Reuther and Frankensteen after the assault.
Wide World

1937—Roy, Victor, and Walter at the UAW convention at Milwaukee. *Courtesy of Victor Reuther*

1942—In wartime Washington on January 5, Reuther and R. J. Thomas of the UAW conferred with Sidney Hillman and William S. Knudsen of the Office of Production Management and Charles E. Wilson, president of General Motors. Reuther was then a UAW vice-president and Thomas was president. *Wide World*

1943—At Camp Atterberry, Indiana, Walter Reuther is given a sampling of the basic training experiences of an enlisted man. Detroit *News; War Dept. Photo*

1949—Walter at a reunion with auto workers at the Renault plant in Paris following the formation in London of the International Conference of Free Trade Unions.

1949—CIO president Philip Murray receives jovial welcome from Walter Reuther at UAW convention in Cleveland. *Wide World*

1952—Walter Reuther poses with CIO secretary-treasurer James B. Carey and executive vice-president Allan S. Haywood, left, after Reuther's election to the CIO presidency.

1952—President Harry S Truman meets with Walter Reuther at the White House.

1952—Veterans of the Flint sit-down strike display 25-year-old newspaper announcing settlement with General Motors. *AFL-CIO News*

1953—President Eisenhower greets a group of CIO leaders (from left, Jacob Potofsky, Allan S. Haywood, Walter Reuther, the President, David J. McDonald, James B. Carey).

1955—George Meany and Walter Reuther together wield the gavel at opening of the first convention of newly merged AFL-CIO. *AFL-CIO News*

CHAPTER FIFTEEN

The War Years

WALTER REUTHER'S "ATOMIC SPIRIT" NEVER FLAGGED DURING THE years of World War II. He was a troubleshooter for the Army, an increasingly influential spokesman for his union, and a battler for the Reuther Caucus within the UAW. At one point, however, his career as a labor leader came close to being sidetracked by a job offer from Franklin D. Roosevelt.

"We had a million ideas in those days," Reuther said of his win-the-war efforts. "I was just churning and spinning off ideas. Some of them made a lot of sense and some of them didn't go very far."

As Americans began saving tin cans and metal scrap of all kinds, Reuther conceived a plan to spur the collection of scrap iron: "I was going to launch this big national drive. I had it all figured out. The dramatic opening thing was to take down that iron fence around the White House." This was one idea that did not go far at all. But it was typical of Reuther's flare for the attention-getting gimmick, of his ability to combine idealism and action.

Officially Reuther was a member of the Labor-Management Policy Committee of the War Manpower Commission. Unofficially he was much more, serving without title as a key advisor to Sidney Hillman and Undersecretary of War Robert P. Patterson on production problems of the metalworking industries. Among others with whom he consulted frequently were the President and Mrs. Roosevelt, Secretary of the Interior Harold L. Ickes, and his Undersecretary, Abe Fortas.

Not all of Reuther's associates in the UAW were pleased with his activities outside the union. Some complained that "he began to spend all his time with committees in the capital." Others were dismayed he was getting so much public attention when he held no higher UAW office than that of director of the General Motors Department.

In some respects, the wartime Reuther was a gadfly. He did seem to have a million ideas, and he did not keep quiet about them. Two and a half months after Pearl Harbor, he proposed that American labor be armed and trained to fight, just in case the country should be invaded: "American workingmen, maintenance men, and construction workers at Guam dropped their tools and seized guns to fight by the side of the Marines. The workers of our cities, and the women, if necessary, would be ready to do the same."

For all the Reuther ideas that were vetoed, many others were adopted and represented significant contributions to war production. In 1942, for example, Reuther challenged the aircraft industry's practice of grinding all engine gears. True, ground gears were more accurate than the shaved gears used in cars and trucks. But the auto industry lacked the gear-grinding equipment needed to fulfill its engine contracts, and the machine tool industry had a two-year backlog of orders for such items. At Reuther's urging, Patterson summoned Air Corps generals and production experts from the aircraft engine manufacturers so the labor leader could present a case for shaved gears. "It was a rough, rough session," Reuther recalled. "They demolished me." Patterson decided, "We're just stuck," but his volunteer advisor did not give up easily. Returning a few days later, Reuther persuaded Patterson to ship two finished engines from the Pratt & Whitney plant to the Ford factory in Dearborn, which had a contract to produce duplicates. At Ford's, Reuther arranged to replace most of the ground gears in one engine with the shaved gears the company was able to produce in quantity. The two engines then were sent to Wright Field in Dayton for block and flight testing. The Air Corps was not told one had been altered. Testing proved that, except in the smallest sizes where utmost precision was essential, shaved gears were more than adequate. Engine production was increased dramatically as a result.

Bringing another problem to Reuther, Patterson reported the auto industry was making M-4 tanks faster than the arsenals could equip them with 75 millimeter guns. Reuther and Ben Blackwood, still serving as technical advisor, went to the Imperial Arsenal near Philadelphia to look around and seek ideas. Neither had any notion how the guns were produced. They learned that the bores of the gun barrels were machined to within a minute fraction of their final size, then were honed to perfection in an operation requiring eight to ten hours' work on each gun. Back in their hotel room Reuther said, "Damn it, Benny, there must be a better way to do that. How do *we* do that kind of thing?" They agreed to try the auto industry practice of "broaching." The gun barrel first was drilled with a hydraulic bore and then a broach, equipped with successively larger rings of sawlike teeth, was pulled through the barrel to make it perfectly smooth. Broaching took about one minute per gun. Another bottleneck was broken.

Involvements like these gave Reuther a satisfying sense of direct participation in the war effort. He could not afford, however, to neglect the GM workers who were his UAW constituency.

Early in 1942 Reuther led the union into negotiations with GM that reached an impasse over the issue of double pay for Sunday work. The corporation argued that it made sense to discourage Sunday work in peacetime but that double pay should be dropped as the plants prepared for wartime production seven days a week.

At Reuther's invitation, GM's C. E. Wilson spent nearly two hours making a case for his views, and answering questions, at a February meeting of UAW leaders from 90 General Motors plants. The union delegates appreciated the fact that the corporation president's appearance at one of their conferences was without precedent, but they did not accept his arguments. GM could afford double pay for Sunday work, they insisted, as Reuther pointed to profits per employe of $1,366 in the first nine months of 1941 compared with $983 in the same period a year earlier. Wilson said the UAW demand represented "business as usual for the union." Reuther countered: "Mr. Wilson and three other top executives of General Motors are drawing salaries and bonuses of $6,644,437 a year. Maybe these things ought to be brought up when Mr. Wilson talks of sacrifices and business as usual."

In late March the government called for an end to all premium pay except time-and-a-half for overtime work. The CIO endorsed the proposition, giving Reuther and the Executive Board little choice but to reverse the UAW's position. To make the turnabout more palatable to the rank and file, the leadership convened a special convention in Detroit to formalize the no-strike pledge, accept the government's recommendation on premium pay, and approve an "Equality of Sacrifice" program. The delegates ratified the package, although a vocal and sizable minority voted against giving up Sunday pay.

The union advertised its "Equality of Sacrifice" plan in major newspapers under a heading, "NO LUXURIES IN WARTIME—NO WAR MILLIONAIRES." A key proposal was for a $25,000 annual ceiling on individual incomes, an idea Eleanor Roosevelt heralded in her "My Day" column as "a constructive suggestion showing that someone is doing some thinking." Less than three weeks later F.D.R. sent Congress an economic program that included a $25,000 income lid. As R. J. Thomas remarked later, "Congress paid no more attention to that part of the President's program than to an individual who would go to church and burp."

The War Labor Board eventually arranged a GM-UAW settlement, the union winning a four-cent hourly wage increase and a maintenance of membership clause. It had asked for twelve and a half cents and the union shop. Reuther put a $69 million price tag on the agreement.

As UAW delegates gathered in Chicago August 3 for the union's annual convention, they represented, for the first time, a million signed-up members. With wartime employment rolls swelling, the Auto Workers were organizing dozens of aircraft and other defense plants as thousands of laborers migrated to Michigan.

At the top, the UAW leadership was settled and tranquil for the first time since 1936. Thomas, Reuther, Addes, and Frankensteen were collaborating in unaccustomed harmony. In the ranks, however, there was disquiet. The very fact that no UAW member had to fear unemployment made for impatience with the leadership's patriotic restraint. Grumbling over the loss of Sunday pay continued, and there was widespread discontent over the War Labor Board's "Little Steel" formula, limiting wage increases to 15 percent of the pay rates of January 1, 1941, regardless of subsequent increases in living costs.

The wartime emergency prompted unusual alliances at the convention. When Victor Reuther urged union support for a second front in Europe to relieve Nazi pressure on the Soviets, then under siege at Stalingrad, Communist Nat Ganley seconded the resolution.

Walter Reuther roused the delegates with an impassioned attack on the slow pace of war production and "the chaos and confusion and waste and nonsense going on in Washington." He offered an illustration of what he regarded as bureaucratic bungling. The Manpower Commission panel on which he served had been told the sugar beet crop in the South might go unharvested because of a shortage of agricultural workers; meanwhile, 80,000 needle trades workers in New York City were unemployed. He went on:

> We went to the Quartermaster General's office and we said, "What about the pants business? Don't you need pants for the Army that will give these needle trades workers jobs?" And the Army told us they had placed a contract for 70,000,000 pairs of pants. . . . We learned that they had put 60,000,000 of the 70,000,000 pairs into the southern industry and only 10,000,-000 pairs in New York City where 90 percent of the industry is located. We asked why and they said they saved about three cents a pair on each pair going South. We checked further and we found that in order to meet contract demands on 60,000,000 pairs of pants, the clothing industry in the South had to build new plants. . . . They had to equip them with new machinery which had to be made in the machine tool industry. And then those expanded clothing industries of the South absorbed the agricultral workers who normally would have harvested the beet sugar crop. And they are making the pants while the pants workers of New York City are walking the streets.

Reuther argued that such situations could not be corrected "until such time as we get an overall agency with the power of responsibility to direct the allocation of machinery, the allocation of materials, and the allocation of manpower. . . ." He was equally blunt in dealing with management shortcomings:

> . . . To date, we are losing the war. There can be no mistake about that. We are losing the war because men in high places

charged with the responsibility of operating these plants seem
to have the idea that you can win the war with press releases,
with publicity and ballyhoo.

In the Willow Run plant a month or two ago they built the
first plane there. They had the newspaper men out, the newsreel
people and they took pictures of the first plane being flown
away—a plane that was fabricated everyplace and assembled
in Willow Run, and the whole world believes that Willow Run
is turning out bombers every hour. It will be months before they
produce bombers in Willow Run.

In Pontiac Fisher Body they made one gun, and they came
out with front page publicity, saying that the Pontiac Fisher
Body was five months ahead of schedule—and they had only
made one gun.

That is going on in the whole war effort. They are putting
on a lot of chocolate coating and America believes we are going
along in high gear when we are just crawling along. . . .

Delegates shouted approval of Reuther-backed resolutions demanding a "supreme economic council" with labor participation
and a new system of allocating strategic materials.

George F. Addes was nominated without opposition for another
term as secretary-treasurer. In a seconding speech, Reuther sought
to bury the factional hatchet: "There is one fight that we have got
and that job is against Hitler, so, as I say, let's vote Brother Addes
in unanimously. Let's support the officers of this union, back Philip
Murray and President Roosevelt, and knock hell out of Hitler!"

The convention, with leadership backing, created two vice-presidencies, these going to Reuther and Frankensteen. In seconding
Reuther's nomination, Addes asserted, if a bit hesitantly, "I have
watched Brother Reuther work, and I have reached the conclusion
that Brother Reuther is an able leader, an energetic leader, one
whom I have become convinced in the last year is desirous of
establishing, along with others of us, unity within this great organization."

Many delegates were restive when confronted with the closed
ranks at the top. Lacking a clear focal point to dramatize displeasure, they shot down a series of "establishment" recommenda-

tions. The jeering and haggling over insignificant matters prompted R. J. Thomas to shout, "What do they have—Lewis money or what!" Delegates refused to increase dues by 50 cents a month and higher salaries proposed for officers were pared. "Pay them like bosses," said one convention goer, "and they begin to think like bosses."

On the Sunday pay question the UAW hierarchy had to give ground when faced with rank and file anger. Just a month earlier, 20,000 employes of a Curtiss aviation plant in Buffalo had voted for the AFL Machinists over the Auto Workers because the AFL union had not surrendered premium pay. The convention, setting a deadline, resolved to revoke voluntary suspension of Sunday, Saturday, and holiday pay unless all unions made the same sacrifice. On August 28 President Roosevelt met with Thomas, Addes, Reuther, and Frankensteen to hear their arguments that unless premium pay was banned everywhere, firms offering premiums could lure away UAW workers and disrupt the war effort. On September 9 Roosevelt signed an executive order prohibiting all premium pay except time-and-a-half for hours worked past 40.

By the fall of 1942 Walter, Victor, and Roy Reuther were engaged in one or another aspect of war mobilization activities. The able, gregarious Roy, drafted in mid-year, was released early in September at the request of the War Production Board, which hired him as a field representative. Victor was assistant coordinator of the union's Defense Employment Division.

Because of his prominence, Walter was heard from most often, writing two articles in four months, for example, for *The New York Times Magazine,* one on "Labor's Place in the War Pattern." In it he made a case for new grievance machinery, saying that since labor had agreed to forego its right to strike, it at least could demand prompt settlement of grievances:

> Labor's proper course under the circumstances should be insistence that the National War Labor Board create a series of courts manned by impartial umpires. These might be geographic or industry-wide in their scope. Obviously the hundreds of grievances which arise in a single area or in a large corporation

within a week cannot be handled by the War Labor Board in Washington. They should be turned over to industrial arbiters who would have the obligation of rendering a decision within two or three weeks at the outside.

On October 1 Reuther was in Washington attending a War Manpower Commission meeting when he was informed that Ferdinand Eberstadt, materials chief of the War Production Board, wanted to see him. Eberstadt asked the UAW leader to become his deputy and, when Reuther asked if this simply was a move to give token recognition to the labor movement, replied: "No, I want you; I don't want the labor movement." Reuther said he felt he was making a meaningful contribution in the production field, which he knew best, but he promised to consider the offer. Next day he refused it.

Within an hour after rejecting the proposal, Reuther received a note from Charles E. Wilson of General Electric, Eberstadt's WPB counterpart in the production area, requesting an immediate meeting. Meeting "Electric Charlie" during the lunch hour, Reuther was told: "I'm glad you turned down Eberstadt. When he and I were going over a list of top people we were going to ask to be our deputies, you were on both lists." Reuther was equally firm in turning down Wilson's proposal.

Roosevelt then entered the picture. He was impressed because hindsight had convinced him Reuther's "500 planes" plan of two years earlier demonstrated that labor was capable of executing a creative role in the war effort that could go well beyond the obvious area of labor-management cooperation. At a periodic meeting of his "Victory Committee," composed of half a dozen representatives of the CIO and AFL, F.D.R. outlined a plan to create a special agency that would give labor broad involvement. He suggested Reuther would be the ideal choice to head it. The AFL's William Green objected: "Why, Reuther's just a kid!" The idea was vetoed.

Subsequently there was discussion of Reuther's being given an Army commission to serve as a special Roosevelt aide on production problems. This time the CIO intervened, telling F.D.R. that

Reuther was needed in the labor movement. Reuther, who probably would have taken either assignment if approached directly by the commander-in-chief, continued to make his contributions and suggestions from outside government.

At Reuther's urging, the United Auto Workers established a permanent base in Washington early in 1943. It set up a twelve-man office there to keep a close watch on legislative developments affecting labor and to deal with federal agencies. Heading the operation was Donald E. Montgomery, who had been the Agriculture Department's consumer counsel.

Collaborating closely with Montgomery, Walter and Victor Reuther began working out of the new office much of the time. Walter helped establish an "army" of UAW price watchers to check up on observance of price ceilings and rationing regulations. Reuther soon thereafter wired Fred M. Vinson, Director of Economic Stabilization, to accuse War Food Administrator Chester Davis of "obstructing and delaying" a Roosevelt program to roll back food prices. Reuther charged that Davis was encouraging trade groups to resist price controls and demanded an investigation. Davis resigned within ten days.

In January 1943 Reuther urged establishment of a guaranteed 40-hour week in the auto industry, to be increased to 48 hours within 60 days. He said several auto makers were hoarding labor, working thousands less than 40 hours while hiring hundreds to relieve "labor shortages." Within three weeks Roosevelt ordered a 48-hour week for 32 labor shortage areas, including Detroit. This meant a 30 percent pay hike at time-and-a-half for those who had been working 40 hours.

Came spring and Reuther was dramatizing the UAW's home front role by taking 250 local union officials to Camp Atterbury, Indiana, for three days of training as foot soldiers. "What most of the boys are looking forward to," he said, "is a chance to operate some of the tanks, jeeps, guns, and other equipment they have been building in the plants for the last year." Robert P. Patterson, who had approved the project, said the union men would be subject to military discipline. "They will have to keep pace with men who have been toughened by months of intensive training. It will provide an unparalleled opportunity to learn what the Army is like and what the Army needs."

"We left Detroit just as though we were going to be inducted into the Army," Reuther recalls. With the union footing the bill for transportation and Army chow, the contingent traveled aboard special coaches attached to a scheduled train. Joining men of the 83rd Division, the unionists were assigned in small groups to infantry companies and were issued uniforms and supplies, as would inductees. Reuther was surprised when he was handed a set of fatigues: "I thought a fatigue outfit was a kind of military lounging pajama." Then he was made to run a gauntlet of belt-swinging barracks mates.

The commanding general proposed that he and Reuther tour units performing a variety of drills: practicing with bayonets, running obstacle courses, crawling under machine gun fire, and swinging across streams on ropes. Reuther thought it sounded like a plush assignment—like being the general's aide. "That was my mistake," he says. "Every goddam place I got to, they insisted I go through the maneuver. Man, they put this 90-pound pack on my back and I had to climb hand over hand on a rope across a river. When I got in the middle they were throwing dynamite. The whole goddam river was coming up. And all these guys were watching me and I couldn't quit. . . . I'm telling you, by the end of the day I had blisters everywhere. I was beat." But the 35-year-old labor leader found strength for a heroic speech: "We will rededicate ourselves to the proposition that no American fighting man will ever want for fighting equipment as long as we have breath and brawn in our bodies."

A racially integrated group of Army sergeants paid a return visit to Detroit and its war plants. Their stay ended with a UAW-sponsored dance, the first integrated social function ever held in the old Book-Cadillac Hotel.

Elsewhere in Detroit, racial tensions were rising. More than 60,000 Negroes had migrated to the city between 1940 and 1942. Contributing to the unrest were a housing shortage, the reluctance of many employers to hire Negroes despite manpower shortages, and a wartime influx of Southern white workers whose attitudes ran counter to the tradition of tolerance that had been developed in the auto union. The Reuthers did what they could to promote racial harmony. Victor Reuther and George Romney, then with the industry's trade association, fought for desegregated housing. Walter expressed himself at an integrated rally in Cadillac Square, sponsored by the union and the National Association for the Advancement of Colored People. Addressing a crowd of more than 5,000, he said any white worker refusing to work beside a Negro could leave the plant because he did not belong there. No thinking American, he declared, would discriminate against a fellow citizen: "It is against the Constitution of the United States, against the constitution of the UAW, and it is against the best interests of the country in winning the war."

Pleas of this sort by Reuther were not always heeded. Early in June 1943, 25,000 workers in a Packard plant making engines for PT boats staged a wildcat strike to protest against promotions for three Negroes. The UAW hierarchy strongly opposed this and similar walkouts, with R. J. Thomas branding the strike leaders as members of the Ku Klux Klan.

The bloody Detroit race riots erupted that same month, yet, despite some trouble spots, Walter White of the NAACP found the union a force for reason: ". . . White union members fought against white mobbists to protect Negroes, and Negro unionists fought Negroes in protection of white fellow workers. There were two areas in Detroit during the riots where peace was maintained —in the plants which had been organized by the UAW-CIO and in the nonsegregated residential areas."

Reuther addressed the 270 Negro seniors of Northwestern High School that June while eight military policemen guarded the auditorium and 80 local police patrolled outside. "The most tragic thing I know," he said, "is that the same time you youths are graduating, soldiers in armored cars are patrolling the streets of Detroit with guns made here in the arsenal of democracy." After the ceremony Reuther watched from a school window as a white mob gathered across the street in Perrien Park. "We saw the hoodlums drifting through the police all through the park, and we all agreed that the cops were not even attempting to break up the mob that was forming," hc said. Just as the graduates were leaving in their caps and gowns, the mob moved to attack. Providentially, four truckloads of Army men arrived and prevented violence.

Inside the UAW the unprecedented wartime harmony among top leaders was ruptured in 1943, due largely to a Communist maneuver. On Ferbruary 25 Earl Browder, as Communist Party chairman, proposed in the *Daily Worker* that war production be put on a piecework basis, a system long used in the Soviet Union. With the United States serving as the wartime arms supplier of the Soviets, the CP favored any device that might spur output of war goods. "It is patriotic," wrote Browder, "to demand increased earnings based on increased production."

George F. Addes, renewing his close alliance with the UAW's Communist element, dutifully proposed that the Executive Board authorize piecework and other forms of "incentive pay." Frankensteen argued, as director of the Aviation Department, that he spoke for one of the lowest paid basic industries and that, because of wage ceilings, an incentive system would give him an opportunity to obtain greater total wages for his constituency.

Reuther, long opposed to the piecework system that had been virtually abandoned by auto makers because of worker resentment over its resulting speedup and other inequities, led the fight against the Addes proposal. The Executive Board went on record against incentive pay but authorized Frankensteen to sit on a War Production Board committee studying the idea. "As of today," said the Detroit *News,* "Reuther is the fair-haired boy of the rank and file." Browder responded with a speech attacking Reuther that subsequently was reprinted as a half-page advertisement in the *News.* Browder accused the labor leader of "wrecking" efforts to increase war production "by the use of the most unprincipled demagogy and lying propaganda."

The piecework battle was resumed in October 1943 at the UAW

convention in Buffalo. As chairman of the Resolutions Committee, Victor Reuther led a six-man majority that restated opposition to the introduction of piecework at plants where it was not already employed. A three-man minority wanted to leave the issue up to the locals. Nearly two-thirds of the delegates approved the Reuther position.

Capitalizing on this issue, the Reuther Caucus again made a bid to replace Addes with Richard T. Leonard. The vote quest was vitriolic. Copies of the "Vic and Wal" letter were circulated and rival groups of delegates caroused around the city singing campaign doggerel to the tune of "Reuben and Rachel." The pro-Reuther version was:

> *Who are the boys who take their orders*
> *Straight from the office of Joe Sta-leen?*
> *No one else but the gruesome twosome,*
> *George F. Addes and Frankensteen.*
>
> *Who are the boys that fight for piecework,*
> *To make the worker a machine?*
> *No one else but the gruesome twosome,*
> *George F. Addes and Frankensteen.*
>
> *When it comes to double-talking,*
> *Who is worse than Willie Green?*
> *No one else but the gruesome twosome,*
> *George F. Addes and Frankensteen.*
>
> *The Auto Workers have their sideshow.*
> *One is fat and one is lean.*
> *Who are they but the gruesome twosome,*
> *George F. Addes and Frankensteen.*

The Addes-Frankensteen camp distributed song sheets with rival lyrics:

> *You have given the workers nothing*
> *Except hot air and lots of steam,*
> *And when the votes have all been counted*
> *We'll still have Addes and Frankensteen!*

Leonard is your side-kick Reuther.
You two sure make a fine team.
But we want men who take a position
So we'll take Addes and Frankensteen!

When you were in Russia Reuther
You thought much of Joe Stalin.
While you were in Russia Reuther
Where was Addes and Frankensteen!

You have fought a dirty battle,
You've yelled RED, you've lied and schemed.
We know you by this time Reuther
So we'll take Addes and Frankensteen!

The Reuther forces narrowly lost the crucial election contest. The outcome was decided, in effect, by a bloc of Negro delegates, most of whom supported Addes because he favored creation of an Executive Board position to be reserved for a Negro. Reuther argued that this was an inverse form of Jim Crow and, in practice, would limit Negro membership on the Board. He carried the issue but Leonard lost the election, bowing to Addes by just 71 votes out of 7,425.

Reuther and Frankensteen then opposed each other for the first of the two vice-presidencies. Reuther won by 345 votes, the only time he ever topped Frankensteen in a head-to-head contest. Leonard challenged the loser for the second vice-presidency but Frankensteen prevailed by 253 votes. In the balloting for the Executive Board *The New York Times* calculated that the Reuther Caucus emerged with almost as much strength as the Addes faction. R. J. Thomas held enough votes on his own to swing the Board one way or the other. And although the UAW president often sided with Addes on issues and in convention elections, his enthusiasm for the secretary-treasurer was limited. On a wartime flight from Washington to Detroit, Reuther and Frankensteen awakened Thomas to tell him one engine of their DC-4 was in flames. "Good God!" exclaimed Thomas, "George Addes will be president!"

Wartime troubleshooting continued to be a part of Reuther's routine. With Eleanor Roosevelt and Harold Ickes, he even worked on a plan to raise the liner *Normandie,* which sank in New York harbor following a disastrous fire. The vessel ultimately was floated, without assistance from Reuther, but subsequently heeled over and sank anew.

"I saw Mrs. Roosevelt very frequently and I saw the President quite frequently," Reuther remembered. "Mrs. Roosevelt and I became really very, very close and warm friends." He called the First Lady "my secret weapon" because she had the President's ear. "Every time I had an idea, good or otherwise, I always talked to her."

At one White House meeting F.D.R. took both of Reuther's hands in his and declared, "Here's my young red-headed engineer." That was too much for R. J. Thomas, who snorted: "He's not an engineer! He's just a tool and die maker!"

In 1944 the UAW leadership had to contend with a wave of wildcat strikes as the rank and file lost patience with referral by management of even minor plant disputes to the slow-moving War Labor Board. Another factor was a cutback in war contracts as allied stockpiles of weapons increased. By mid-1944 some plants were operating at less than prewar levels.

Resentment boiled up at the union's convention in Grand Rapids. The 2,300 delegates were divided into four major caucuses, more than ever before. The key issue was the no-strike pledge. Caucusing, a hallmark of the Auto Workers, was so entrenched that, according to one story, the practice even spilled over into a co-operative nursery school sponsored by May Reuther and other UAW wives. When one mother asked the instructor how the youngsters were doing, she was told the girls would put their dolls in bed at the start of the day and announce: "You stay here, darling. Mother's got to go and caucus."

Feelings ran so high in Grand Rapids that fighting among the delegates became a problem. With leadership backing, the convention ordered an investigation of disorderly conduct in and out of the meeting hall. Brawling was said to imperil community good will. Referring to a slugfest in the lobby of the headquarters hotel, R. J. Thomas said that if delegates did not behave, "we won't get anybody ever to invite us anywhere." Addes spoke of the smashing of hotel furniture and other depredations and lamented that "no organization has the reputation for destructiveness we have."

The four major factions at Grand Rapids were the Addes-Frankensteen group, the Reuther Caucus, the Thomas element, and a new Rank and File Caucus dedicated to repeal of the no-strike pledge. Rank and Filers felt management was taking advantage of the pledge, particularly in plants producing civilian goods. Since most members of the new rebel faction normally would have been in Walter Reuther's camp, the four-way convention split posed a threat to his political survival.

Philip Murray called on the delegates to retain the no-strike pledge, as did Roosevelt in a written message of greeting: "We are winning the war but the needs of our soldiers, sailors and Marines are as great as ever. To supply the demands for the weapons and materials of war calls for continued production so that the battles may end and lives be spared. I know the American workers will cooperate. . . ."

The first test came on the Rank and File proposal for outright repeal of the pledge. During five hours of debate, Thomas was blocked by the delegates from speaking more than five minutes despite his position as UAW president. If the vote went against the pledge, he announced, he would not continue in office: "I will not preside over the dismemberment of this union." He was jeered. Immediate repeal was rejected on a 6,617 to 3,750 roll call. Although the Rank and File position did not prevail, the show of strength by the new caucus was considered remarkable.

Aiming at a compromise, the Reuthers put forward a resolution that would reaffirm the pledge for the present but allow it to lapse in plants wholly engaged in civilian production once Germany was defeated. Frankensteen termed it "a complete assault on the intelligence of the delegates," arguing that any management seeking to avoid strikes could "keep a little war work in their plants while they were making their conversion." Thomas and Addes lined up with Frankensteen and the Reuther resolution was beaten decisively.

Next up for a vote was a proposal supported by virtually all top UAW figures except Reuther. It reaffirmed the no-strike pledge with but one qualification: "New conditions may affect our no-strike pledge after the defeat of Germany." When that day came, it stated, the Executive Board and the CIO would "review and decide a further policy . . . for the balance of the war to drive Japan to unconditional surrender." But even this policy was rejected, 5,233 against and 4,989 in favor.

At this point a Rank and File spokesman asked if defeat of all three proposals meant the UAW lacked a policy on wartime strikes. If so, each local could decide its own course. Taken aback, the leadership closed ranks, if only briefly, to find a way out of their dilemma. Reuther and Thomas came up with a plan for the convention to reaffirm the pledge, subject to membership ratification in a mail referendum. The strategy worked and the pledge ultimately was upheld.

At Grand Rapids, for the first time in five years, Thomas had nominal opposition for the presidency but easily won reelection by a nine to one margin. Addes was not opposed.

Richard Leonard, the periodic Reuther Caucus candidate for secretary-treasurer, had a new goal this time: to get himself elected to one of the two vice-presidencies. Leonard's entry into the race sent a chill through the Reuther camp. The thinking of many was that Leonard would split the vote of the Reuther Caucus in a three-way contest for the first vice-presidency and assure the election of Frankensteen. Then, it was feared, the Addes-Frankensteen forces would back Leonard for the second vice-presidency, giving him a fighting chance to defeat Reuther.

Leonard had appeared at the customary pre-convention meeting of the Reuther Caucus and, making known his ambition for a vice-presidency, declared he would not follow the normal practice of putting his candidacy to a vote by the Caucus, which he contended had been stacked by Reuther. In an adroit maneuver, Reuther forced Leonard's hand by suggesting there be no formal Caucus choice. Instead, Reuther proposed that the issue be decided by the convention vote for first vice-president. If Leonard topped him in the contest with Frankensteen, he would not run on the second roll call. If Leonard ran third in the three-way race, he would be expected to follow the same course. Correctly anticipating that Reuther would come out on top under such an arrangement, Leonard bolted the Caucus.

On the first convention roll call Frankensteen won easily, polling more than his two opponents combined. The results: Frankensteen, 5,444; Reuther, 4,528; Leonard, 385.

Although Leonard's poor showing encouraged Reuther's following, the Addes-Frankensteen faction showed Sidney Hillman its head count for the second vote, a tally that indicated Reuther would be defeated. Hillman, who had left government service, hurried to Leonard with a sermon: "You know, in the Amalgamated when we have one job open and more than one person is after that job, we don't have elections." Leonard's reply: "Sidney, this is the Auto Workers."

At the behest of Philip Murray, who feared a Reuther defeat would split the union, Allan Haywood called a meeting of the top leadership between the two votes. "Haywood begged us to work it out," said Reuther, but neither side was willing to budge. Having studied the first roll call results, Reuther now was confident of victory. He had learned that significant numbers of pro-Reuther votes from politically divided locals had gone to Frankensteen in return for pledges of support for Reuther on the second ballot. And he felt "there were a lot of guys in the opposition that just wouldn't have any part of them dumping me because, while I was in the opposition, they knew goddam well I was in there battling for this union and for them."

In the early morning hours of September 16, Reuther was declared the winner. The vote: Reuther, 6,176; Leonard, 3,477; John McGill, a Rank and File candidate from Flint, 364. Reuther received 732 more votes running against Leonard and McGill than had Frankensteen in opposing Reuther and Leonard.

Years later, Reuther's 1944 opponents remained convinced they could have prevailed. Leonard attributes his defeat to CIO intervention, saying he knew he was beaten when Communist Pat Touhey came to him before the second vote and announced, "We hate this little redhead sonofabitch but we hate Hitler worse." Yet the roll call indicates top UAW Communists voted against Reuther. For his part, Frankensteen insists Reuther was "thoroughly beaten" until "I kept Walter in this union" by swinging some vitally needed votes from aircraft locals to Reuther. Again, the roll call raises questions about the validity of Frankensteen's claim.

Years later, Reuther said he was certain he would have defeated Frankensteen on the first ballot if some of his backers had not traded votes with the opposition.

In the Auto Workers, the rumbling from old battles can echo for decades.

Whatever the uncertainties at Grand Rapids, Walter Reuther remained the most imaginative and, to the public at large, best known of the UAW leaders, devoting much of his energy and talent to the formulation and promotion of postwar conversion plans.

As early as May 1943 Reuther had reported that General Motors already had set aside $48 million for the postwar rehabilitation of machinery. He called for an equally large "security fund" to protect regular employes, including those returning from military service.

A year later he was pushing a sixteen-point conversion program that he said was "capable of infinite elaboration." It included a postwar pool of manpower and machines cutting across corporate lines, a 30-hour work week, government operation of monopolistic industries as "yardsticks," fixing of "normal" sales prices, and, initially, civilian production in compliance with quotas based on social needs deemed most urgent.

Reuther urged creation of a Peace Production Board (PPB) representing labor, management, consumers, agriculture, and government. Arguing that business leadership could not be relied upon to oversee a smooth conversion, he proposed that the Board allocate manpower, materials, and tools to meet social priorities. Labor also would be given a voice in industry councils that would assist the PPB in developing practical conversion plans for each industry.

With *The New York Times* Forum as his platform, Reuther declared that because of wartime advances in technology, it would be possible to create with a 30-hour week as much wealth as had been generated in the prewar period with a 40-hour week. "Work in itself is not an end," he said. "It's the means to an end. The end is a more abundant life, to be able to conquer the job of feeding and clothing ourselves in as little time as possible, so that as civilized men we can enjoy the finer things—culture and education. That is the struggle. . . ." The labor leader debated his 30-hour week idea with Eric Johnston, president of the Chamber of Commerce of the United States, and industrialist Henry J. Kaiser. Johnston countered that "if you carry Mr. Reuther's proposal to its absurd conclusion, no one should work at all and then everyone would be rich." Kaiser thought many people would want material goods obtainable only through increased production and, anyway, he said, "Most of us will want to work more than 30 hours a week."

Reuther also used the *Times* Forum to advocate two other ideas: use of government-owned aircraft plants to mass produce low-cost housing, which he said must become "America's No. 1 postwar industry"; and creation of a "strategic job reserve" to put the unemployed to work on such public projects as hospitals, schools, recreation centers, flood control and power development, highways, airports, and waterways.

As the UAW's director of aviation, Frankensteen favored conversion of bomber and other plants to the mass production of light planes selling for under $1,000. He predicted sales could reach a million planes a year. Insistent that housing was more socially desirable, Reuther elaborated on his plan in *The New York Times Magazine,* adding as another goal the manufacture of railroad rolling stock.

Reuther also kept working on ideas with military applications. George Edwards, a veteran of the Kelsey-Hayes sit-down strike, was overseas with the Army and, Reuther said, "was sort of my battlefield consultant." After Edwards urged the invention of a portable foxhole, Reuther collaborated with Robert P. Patterson on plans for a very light armorplate shield to be used in storming beaches and other exposed areas. The war ended before it could be developed.

With the return of peace, rank and file discontent with the UAW leadership reached a high point. There were demands for special meetings at which union officials could be called to account for their "do-nothing" record. Matt Hammond, head of the Detroit Tool and Die Local, spoke for many: "Our international officers have failed us to the extent that at least they could have fought and kept fighting for our economic demands. Instead they sat back and let everything drift along." Responding to such criticism, R. J. Thomas promised uncompromising postwar militancy:

"We will authorize strikes in every plant where a present grievance continues to exist. Employers in the automobile industry simply haven't accepted the union."

CHAPTER SIXTEEN

On Strike at GM

EVEN BEFORE THE END OF WORLD WAR II, WALTER REUTHER BE-
gan intensive preparations for the first round of peacetime negotiations. Working with Donald Montgomery of the Auto Workers'
staff in Washington, he wanted to revolutionize the traditional trade
union approach to the bargaining table, an approach that subordi-
nated questions of broad social significance to the bread-and-butter
issues that had been taken up with predictable regularity for many
years. With bold disregard for his nominal superior in the union,
Reuther filed a voluminous economic brief with federal manpower
and price control agencies on June 30, 1945. The document foreshadowed a titanic struggle with General Motors Corporation in
the months to follow. His union rivals were reluctant to see Reuther
set the postwar bargaining pace in the impending battle with GM,
but they felt compelled to give him a green light.

Although his arguments were lengthy, the heart of the Reuther
brief was uncomplicated: "Labor contends that the economic facts
of life prove that wages can be increased without increasing prices.
Increased production must be supported by increased consumption,
and increased consumption will be possible only through increased
wages. . . ."

But even as organized labor yearned to expand its influence in
the postwar world, many businessmen hoped to reassert their traditional domination of the work force in the mass production industries. Ira Mosher, then president of the National Association of
Manufacturers, met secretly in New York with executives from
leading steel, motor, electrical, and food-processing firms to forge
a united front against a rising tide of union demands.

Labor had an excellent case for substantial wage increases. The
U.S. Bureau of Labor Statistics found that living costs had gone up
by 30 percent since January 1941, and union economists argued
45 percent was a more accurate measure. In either case, it was clear
that inflation had far outstripped wage increases, which had been

limited to a 15 percent advance by the "Little Steel" formula in effect throughout the war. Moreover, take-home pay was cut sharply in the months before V-J Day by reduction or abolition of high-wage overtime. When Japan surrendered, President Harry S Truman issued an executive order to permit wage increases provided they would not result in higher prices.

This was precisely what Reuther had been waiting for. Two days after Truman acted, the United Auto Workers vice-president demanded that General Motors raise wages by 30 percent without charging more for GM cars, trucks, and other products. In fact, the union leader said, the company simultaneously could grant the pay demand, reduce car prices, and increase profits. Federal officials had expressed similar views. William H. Davis, as director of economic stabilization, had declared that industry could raise wages as much as 40 to 50 percent in the postwar years without boosting prices.

The reaction from General Motors was quite different. There was no reply at all for six weeks and then GM president C. E. Wilson rejected the demands as unreasonable, adding: "We shall resist the monopolistic power of your union to force this 30 percent increase in basic wages. . . . Automobiles would shortly cost 30 percent more to produce."

At that time the average pay for a GM worker was $1.12 an hour. The union proposal would raise it to $1.45 an hour, or $58 a week on a 40-hour basis. According to the UAW's calculations, this would maintain the wartime scale, including overtime, for a standard work week in the postwar era. Before the war, in 1940, GM workers averaged less than $35 a week.

To Reuther, his demand embraced an entirely new concept of collective bargaining, and one he regarded as socially responsible. As he explained it: "We condemn the discredited policy of old-line labor leadership which pretends to promote the interests of the workers by conspiring with management, as in the coal industry, to exact higher prices for consumers. . . . We shall realize and hold on to our gains only by making progress with the community, not at the expense of the community."

A union aide later underlined another bargaining breakthrough: "We were prepared to prove that what we were demanding could be paid without the necessity of price increases, or if we couldn't prove that, to scale our demands down to what the facts indicated."

Writing for a national audience in *The New York Times Magazine,* Reuther argued for strengthened buying power for the mass of Americans to keep the economy strong. At a time when many respected economists foresaw an enormous peacetime bust, and obviously in agreement that the outlook was not sanguine, he wrote: "We are gambling on the effect of a combination of pent-up demand for civilian goods and a backlog of savings to prevent a tailspin into deflation. This 'coming in on a wing and a prayer' economics rests upon too many unwarranted assumptions."

The *Times Magazine* article was part of a shrewdly calculated public relations buildup for the showdown with General Motors. There were other examples. A month later, Reuther debated George Romney, then general manager of the Automobile Manufacturers Association, on the popular "Town Meeting of the Air" radio program. The union assembled a massive document outlining the GM demands, sent it to all UAW locals, and urged them to publicize it. Copies were mailed to important newspaper columnists, radio commentators, members of Congress, and federal officials. "The success of a strike—if it becomes necessary to strike—will, in large part, depend upon public opinion," Reuther told officials of GM locals across the country. In itself, the bid for public support of the Auto Workers' bargaining goals marked another departure from tradition. Unions heretofore had been interested almost solely in the reaction of their memberships.

Within the UAW Executive Board, Reuther won support for a "one-at-a-time" strike strategy. He based his thinking on the sharp competition among the major auto producers at a time when consumers were ready to scramble for almost any car they could get in the immediate postwar market. A strike directed only against General Motors, Reuther argued, would put the corporation under heavy pressure to settle so it could share in the bonanza assured by the unprecedented demand for new cars that had been unavailable at any price since early 1942.

When negotiations with GM opened on October 19, Reuther again played to the public by inviting the press into the bargaining conference room. General Motors officials refused to spar in front of reporters so Reuther hired a public stenographer and released transcripts of the talks to the newsmen. GM countered by publishing full-page newspaper ads early in October to denounce the UAW's demands and by sending letters to the homes of all production workers to warn that any strike called by the union "may be a long one."

The principal antagonists presented a sharp contrast in bargaining style, age, and manner. On the company side of the table was the 55-year-old Charles E. Wilson, white-haired and blunt-spoken champion of conservatism. On the UAW side was the "radical" Reuther, then 38, earning $7,000 a year in comparison to Wilson's $459,000 salary, to which were added generous bonuses.

Reuther's 76-page brief contained a 14-page section devoted to a "multiple correlation analysis" of GM's profit picture. At one point it stated: "The basic equation employed is——Profits equal Automotive Sales Plus Other Sales Plus Other Income Minus (Labor Cost plus Materials Cost plus Selling, General and Administration costs plus Depreciation and Amortization plus Taxes, other than U.S. Income and Excess Profits Taxes plus other costs)." In contrast, Wilson's proposed solution for any postwar slump was typically simple, and most appealing to manufacturers everywhere: extend the basic working week to 44 hours without payment of overtime premiums.

It was inevitable that bad feelings would surface in this first major peacetime confrontation between labor and management. Less than a week after bargaining began, a GM negotiator compared Reuther to a skunk for reporting details of the talks to newspapermen. Harry Coen, assistant personnel director, showed GM's attitude in a tirade against the red-topped iconoclast: "Why don't you get down to your size . . . and talk about the money you would like to have for your people and let the labor statesmanship go to hell for a while? It is none of your damn business what the OPA does about prices!" Of course Reuther was much concerned about OPA actions, having decided from the outset that he was nego-

tiating for consumers as well as wage earners. Later this exchange
took place:

REUTHER: Unless we get a more realistic distribution of
America's wealth, we don't get enough to keep this machinery
going.

COEN: There it is again. You can't talk about this thing
without exposing your socialistic desires.

REUTHER: If fighting for equal and equitable distribution
of the wealth of this country is socialistic, I stand guilty of being a
Socialist.

COEN: I think you are convicted.

REUTHER: I plead guilty.

Reuther whipped up strike sentiment, declaring that "the reactionaries are hell-bent to destroy the gains we have made in the
last years." He got strong backing in a strike vote conducted by
the National Labor Relations Board, with 70,853 workers favoring
a walkout to enforce UAW demands and only 12,438 against.

In the midst of the negotiations, President Truman issued a new
wage-price policy that would permit pay increases reflecting the
rise in living costs since 1941 and, quite at variance with the
Reuther philosophy, allow higher prices on the basis of such wage
boosts. In an address to the nation on October 30, 1945, the President gave moral support, however, to the Auto Workers' cause,
saying: "I wonder how many of you know that many war workers
have already had to take, or will soon have to take, a cut in their
wartime pay by one-quarter or more. Think of what such a decrease
in your own income would mean to you and your families. . . .
Unless checked, the annual wage and salary bill in private industry
will shrink by over $20 billion. . . . The corner grocer is going to
feel it, as well as the department store, the railroads, the theaters
and the gas stations, and all the farmers of the nation. It is a sure
road to wide unemployment." Reuther immediately wired con-
gratulations to Truman and contended anew that GM would not
have to raise prices even if it granted a 30 percent pay increase.
The next day Secretary of Commerce Henry A. Wallace partly

bolstered UAW arguments by issuing a report that said auto pay-rolls could be raised 25 percent over two years without a price increase. The Automobile Manufacturers Association quickly protested Wallace's calculations.

In November 1945 Truman summoned 36 leading labor and management spokesmen to a summit conference in Washington to discuss mounting industrial strife. Three weeks later the meeting broke up without producing any recommendations from the conferees, an ill omen for the nation.

General Motors on November 7 made its first offer to the Auto Workers: a 10 percent wage increase. It was spurned immediately by Reuther as a "bribe" aimed at undermining union militancy without providing adequate protection against inflation already recorded. He presented a surprise counterproposal to arbitrate the pay demands with two unusual conditions: first, GM would furnish its books, records, and other documents to the members of an arbitration board to aid in an "intelligent and factual solution," and secondly, the corporation would agree not to raise prices on the basis of any resulting wage increase. The thrust of Reuther's argument was that the arbitrators could make a dispassionate and knowledgeable decision on the kind of wage increase that would be noninflationary. He demanded a reply within 24 hours.

When General Motors did not meet his deadline, Reuther on November 21 called a strike of 175,000 GM workers in 95 plants without waiting longer for an answer. Two days later the reply he anticipated was received. H. W. Anderson, GM's vice president for labor relations, wrote the union leader: "This was not an offer of arbitration but a demand for abdication." The company did not intend to turn over management responsibilities to arbitrators, Anderson stated.

The strike itself was remarkably nonviolent. In contrast to its prewar practice, GM did not attempt to operate the plants, and union picketing was conducted mainly for publicity and morale-building purposes. It was largely a verbal war this time, almost as if Reuther had been given the choice of weapons.

One of his first actions was to appoint a "citizens' committee" to investigate the union claim that GM could raise wages but not prices and still increase its profits. The committee, carefully selected to provide a sympathetic forum of well-known Americans, included a Protestant cleric, a St. Louis banker, the national president of the Parent-Teachers Association, and Walter White, the NAACP's executive secretary.

In a dramatic move at the outset of the committee's inquiry, Reuther offered to reduce wage demands from 30 percent to one percent if GM would hold the line on prices and open its books to show any "hidden profits." GM's brusque rejection of the proposition seemed unreasonable to some members of the "citizens' committee." Walter White said he was "amazed at the ineptitude of the corporation from the standpoint of public relations." It was not surprising that the committee's report supported the union's view that GM's ability to pay without resort to higher prices should be considered in a settlement. The panel also found that Reuther's proposal "has lifted the whole matter of collective bargaining to a new high level by insisting that the advancement of labor's interest shall not be made at the expense of the public."

Inside the labor movement, however, Reuther's position was not universally applauded. UAW president R. J. Thomas, who referred disparagingly to his younger rival as "The Comet," received from an aide an analysis sharply critical of the union brief for a 30 percent pay demand: "It contains a lot of irrelevancies—such as the current value of a GM share purchased so many years ago—which may appeal to the readers of *PM* but which will buy us nothing in negotiation or arbitration."

Philip Murray, president of the Steelworkers and the CIO, chided Reuther privately for his concern with prices as well as wages but publicly backed the UAW demands. Under Murray's prodding, Reuther asked Thomas and George F. Addes to take a bigger role in the bargaining.

John L. Lewis, the coal union chief, offered a plague-on-both-your-houses appraisal of GM and the UAW, saying, "The dishonesty of the company is equalled only by the stupidity of that labor organization."

But Thomas, Murray, and Lewis were old-line trade unionists and obviously were not quite prepared to come to grips with the Reuther vision of postwar bargaining. And still other factors were at play, as Walter White subsequently outlined in a retrospective view of the internal strains within the house of labor:

> Reuther was then emerging as the most vocal and implacable enemy of Communism in the trade union movement generally and in the UAW in particular. Pitted against him was a small but powerful coalition which sought control of the union either because of political beliefs, personal ambitions, or honest disagreement with Reuther's opinions and tactics. It was obvious that some of the members of this opposing faction would gladly have seen the negotiations fail rather than see Reuther, with his anti-Communist views, emerge victor and thereby become a more powerful figure in American affairs.

The UAW eventually found it necessary to issue a press release to assure the rank and file that all decisions of the strike strategy committee had been unanimous. It said company officials were circulating "sly rumors that the strike is ineffective and untimely."

Two weeks before Christmas General Motors took a get-tough attitude, canceling its old agreement with the Auto Workers and declaring its hostility toward union security clauses in any future contracts. Responding, Reuther told the corporation it faced "the damndest fight you ever saw."

Confronted with a deadlock, Truman first asked the GM strikers to return to work and thus remove a "major obstacle holding up our reconversion program." When the union spurned this appeal, Truman named a three-man fact-finding board to investigate the dispute and make settlement recommendations. The chairman was Lloyd Garrison, a University of Wisconsin professor, with Walter P. Stacy and Milton S. Eisenhower as members.

At first UAW officials voiced misgivings about the fact-finding process but Reuther soon realized it would provide him with an unparalleled opportunity to put his case before the public. If GM refused to take part, he reasoned, it would be put in the position of defying the President. The overriding issue was whether the corporation would discuss the relationship between wages, prices, and profits with the UAW to show why it could not raise pay without increasing prices.

When the presidential panel assembled for its first hearing in Washington, the GM representatives did not even take their seats. Instead they stood at their assigned table while their special counsel asked the chairman if "ability to pay" was a matter under investigation. At that moment, a telegram from Truman was delivered to Garrison and, somewhat flustered, he read it to the parties. Truman went on record as favoring a study of the relationship between wages and prices. GM's delegation promptly walked out of the hearing room and the UAW began presenting its case to the board without rebuttal from management. The corporation insisted that prices and profits were not proper matters for the board to consider. The real issue, according to GM, was whether industry would remain free or become "socialized."

Liberals saw the contest in different terms. A *New Republic* writer described Reuther's appearance before the fact-finders as if he were a Lochinvar from the West:

> Your first impression is of youth. He has brownish-red hair, almost pitch-black eyes. His voice is high and loud, he is speaking easily and excitedly. . . . His eyes are narrow, like a plainsman's. He is self-confident, young and sure of himself. . . . This is a new kind of strike, a new kind of leader. Reuther is emphasizing again and again the concept that workers have got to have high pay to buy the goods they produce. . . . What he implies is that this isn't a strike; it's a crusade.

Eventually the presidential board issued its recommendations: a 19.5-cents-an-hour pay increase without a boost in prices. The auto union accepted the proposal, feeling it had won a major principle even if the wage recommendation fell short of its demand. General Motors balked, claiming the panel's findings were based on an "unsound principle" that a rich company should pay higher wages than a less profitable one.

As the strike dragged on, Reuther moved in many ways to

mobilize national support for his cause. He established a Citizens' Committee to Aid Families of GM Strikers, sponsored by such prominent figures as Eleanor Roosevelt, Henry R. Luce, Harold E. Stassen, and Wayne Morse. A union attorney in Washington, using political influence, obtained an extraordinary Treasury Department ruling that donations could be regarded as charitable contributions for income tax purposes. CIO officials took the UAW story into meetings of Rotarians and Kiwanians from coast to coast, telling what the strike meant in terms of community buying power. Reuther fired off suggestions to the field on how to enlist war veterans in the strike: "It is extremely important that special efforts be made to have veterans in prominent positions on the picket line. . . . Ask the veterans to wear their service uniforms. . . . Special picket banners should be prepared. . . . 'I did not fight over there to protect GM's billions over here,' etc." He also sent letters to retail merchants that started off by asking, "How many of the du Ponts do you have among your customers?" In mid-December the UAW sold buttons inscribed with this bit of Reutherese: "We fight today for a better tomorrow. I gave to win higher wages—no price increase." Donating his own pay to the strike fund, Reuther counseled union officers on how to help strikers get onto welfare rolls. Urging that wives be added to picket lines and rally turnouts, he observed boyishly, "Women can frequently make a swell contribution to the life of the party."

Despite the frenetic activity, R. J. Thomas was not happy about the fund-raising drive, declaring: "All we have been able to gather from within our union . . . amounted to something like $300,000, . . . less than 50 cents a members for those who were on strike. You can't win strikes that way."

More important, wage settlements elsewhere were eroding Reuther's bargaining position. In January 1946 his rivals in the UAW settled with Ford for an 18-cent hourly raise and won 18.5 cents an hour from Chrysler, without a strike in either case. A frustrated Reuther urged that Truman put pressure on General Motors to accept the fact-finding board's 19.5-cent recommendation, telling the President the company was "in open revolt against the American government . . . in a conspiracy to destroy organized labor." But the best GM would do was renew its last offer of 13.5 cents an hour.

By late January the GM crisis was but one of many major industrial disputes. Steel, packinghouse, and electrical plants were shut down by more than 1,650,000 strikers. As Reuther saw it, General Motors was spearheading a drive of "Wall Street financial operators, who control vast sections of American industry," to crush labor unions. GM officials, however, were encouraged by a report from their New York office that Philip Murray had "jumped all over Walter Reuther and told him to get cracking on more money for his men and to stop trying to be a labor statesman."

A telling blow came in early February when the CIO United Electrical Workers, bargaining secretly with GM, accepted an 18.5-cent hourly pay increase for its 30,000 members. Reuther was outraged both at the company and the union. Since UE leaders were aligned closely with the Communist Party, he sensed a left-wing plot to undercut his leadership in the UAW. GM, he charged, had cooperated in hopes that a settlement with the relatively small UE group would force the much larger UAW to accept the same terms. When Reuther formally was offered the one-year contract the UE accepted, he stalked out of the conference room spitting fire. "I won't be made a damn fool of forever," he raged. "The President's offer of 19.5 cents was a compromise of our demand and I will be God damned if I will compromise a compromise. We are not going to take less than this and this is all horseshit about going back to work!"

A few days later Phil Murray and the Steelworkers settled a four-week strike with an identical 18.5-cent hourly pay raise and Reuther's hopes of getting more from GM were shattered. Later that month, as it had promised beforehand, the federal government approved a $5-a-ton increase in steel prices, continuing the wage-price spiral that Reuther had so strongly opposed. Old-line trade unionism had won over the social engineering of the UAW's bright young man. Reuther now was faced with a truculent GM and a take-it-or-leave-it offer of 18.5 cents.

The head of the General Motors Department also was beginning to feel some pressure from the rank and file. A welder at Cadillac who had joined the auto union in 1935 wrote to R. J. Thomas in late February: "For God's sake, shut up Walter Reuther and get us back to work. . . . Most of my savings are gone—and all of my patience—and there are a lot more in the same shape. For real gains, the strike is lost. . . . The quicker we cut the loss until another try, the better."

Reuther tried a final appeal to Truman through Chester Bowles, director of economic stabilization at this point, in hopes that GM negotiations might be shifted to the White House to back up the recommendation of the presidential board. Truman refused to go to bat for Reuther. Secretary of Labor Lewis Schwellenbach told the President in a Cabinet meeting that the UAW official was making it difficult to get a settlement and was trying to force Truman to use his prestige in backing UAW demands. Schwellenbach said Reuther was able to start strikes but had not shown any ability to settle them and was using the GM walkout to further his ambitions to become president of the Auto Workers.

When the Rubber Workers also accepted an 18.5-cent package, General Motors alleged that political differences within the UAW were blocking a strike settlement. Reuther's demand for a price freeze obviously had become unattainable some weeks earlier and only a penny an hour separated the two sides in the closing weeks of the dispute.

Finally, after 113 days, an agreement was reached at a session attended by Phil Murray and Charles E. Wilson. Reuther was not even present. The Auto Workers got 18.5 cents an hour but contended that other concessions, including checkoff of union dues and improved seniority clauses, were the equivalent of the extra penny recommended by the Truman panel. GM did not argue the point.

For Walter Reuther, the outcome fell far short of the specific objectives he had sought in his anti-inflation crusade. By August 1946 the auto companies were allowed no fewer than three rounds of price increases and Congress junked the wartime system of price ceilings before the year was out. Reuther's unorthodox demands drew scorn from president Thomas, a bread-and-butter unionist who loudly asserted the GM strike was "called six weeks too early and ended a month too late." Conservatives saw in Reuther a threat to free enterprise and a potential "czar of labor" because of his pioneering efforts to prevent price increases, long the private preserve of management, while seeking higher pay scales.

Reuther's supporters claimed, however, that his leadership of the 113-day struggle against a corporate colossus marked an historic turning point, demonstrating that industry could not crush the CIO unions and return to prewar "normalcy." His bargaining goals were ahead of their times, they said, and foreshadowed later precedent-setting agreements with General Motors containing the cost-of-living escalator clause and annual pay raises tied to productivity gains. It seems evident that the bitterness of the 1945-1946 strike led GM management into a reappraisal of its relationship with the UAW and produced a higher level of collective bargaining in later years.

"The fact that we did not win the battle against price increases does not change the fact that we were right in principle and that we took a socially responsible position," says one of Reuther's strike aides. "The position we took at that time set a direction of policy and a course of action which has unquestionably brought tremendous benefits to UAW members and which many people think has benefited American society as a whole."

CHAPTER SEVENTEEN

Battle on the Boardwalk

IN THE WANING DAYS OF THE LONG STRIKE AGAINST GENERAL Motors, Walter Reuther decided to challenge R. J. Thomas for the presidency of the UAW. The older man, in the eyes of the 38-year-old Reuther, was a caretaker, a compromise choice who had been adequate for wartime leadership but lacked the vision and drive that would be required in the postwar era. Thomas, the roly-poly extrovert who loved chewing tobacco and late-night poker games, lacked Reuther's single-minded dedication to his job.

Equally important, Reuther's principal followers felt that Thomas was increasingly willing to accept guidance from hard-core Communists and party liners in the union. The Reutherites urged an immediate challenge to Thomas, theorizing that the Communist element would become more deeply entrenched through patronage appointments to the UAW staff. If Reuther did not act immediately, his lieutenants contended, Secretary-Treasurer George F. Addes eventually would displace Thomas in the top job. Pressure on Reuther to run for the presidency had been building since 1939, when he considered making the race but bowed out in the interests of intraunion harmony. In 1946 he was persuaded by his supporters that they could elect him with votes to spare.

Thomas had a certain appeal to the rank and file and claimed strong UAW political allies as well as the blessings of the CIO and its respected president, Philip Murray. In most unions, Thomas could have staved off rivals for power without great difficulty. The UAW, however, had a tradition of hard-fought contests for leadership that made dissent respectable.

One of Reuther's first moves was to try to neutralize Addes by promising to support him for reelection as secretary-treasurer if he would refrain from endorsing Thomas. Although Addes showed interest in Reuther's overtures, he finally rebuffed the ambitious redhead and threw his considerable strength to Thomas.

Maneuvering at the top was only part of the battle, however.

The real struggle took place on and near the Boardwalk at Atlantic City in late March of 1946. At that time of year Atlantic City resembled more an icy ghost town than a popular resort, with bone-chilling ocean breezes blowing over an empty beach. From one standpoint, reasonable prices, it was tailored to the requirements of the UAW treasury, depleted by the 113-day GM strike. Addes, in fact, reported the union was running a deficit of $98,000 a month and had assets of only $800,000. The financial pinch had been aggravated by a sharp decline in dues-paying membership from a wartime peak of 1,242,569 early in 1945 to 539,575 by the end of the same year.

Along the Boardwalk, Reuther and Thomas backers invaded hotels and taprooms in their enthusiastic campaigns to sway uncommitted delegates. Rival groups came to blows in the Chelsea Hotel lobby and two bands of Reuther supporters, each mistaking the identity of the other, clashed briefly at the Ambassador. The fist swinging was part of the boisterous behavior associated with UAW conventioneers in those days: they dropped water-filled bags from hotel windows, tossed firecrackers, and smashed furniture. The troubled manager of the Ambassador wrote the union that $500,000 had just been spent on redecorating and pleaded, "We hope that it will be possible for you to bring to the attention of your delegates the necessity for cooperating with the hotel management in respecting the personal property of the hotel during the duration of your stay here." Addes, in a display of unconscious humor, warned the convention that dropping bags of water from upper floors of hotels could be fatal to a "delegate or a human being."

In his own campaign, Reuther stressed that a Thomas victory would increase the power of the Communist elements in the UAW. Those familiar with left-wing politics judged the number of Communists in the union to be relatively small, probably fewer than 500 in a national membership of a half million or more. However, the Communists often were strategically placed and, responding to Party discipline, were able to influence non-Communist leaders, such as Thomas, by hard work and force of argument. To Reuther, they were menacing not because of their political beliefs but simply because the Party was the chosen instrument of a totalitarian regime, the Soviet Union, and would put the UAW's interests second to the Kremlin's wishes.

"Against Outside Interference" was the slogan the Reuther Caucus used against Communist opponents. This stand drew the candidate support from such varied sources as the Association of Catholic Trade Unionists, anti-Stalinist radicals, Socialists, and many others who shunned all ideology. In meeting after meeting Reuther recalled how the Communists tried to impose piecework and incentive pay during World War II, supported a labor draft law, and undercut the UAW in the GM strike by making a secret deal with the corporation on behalf of the Communist-dominated United Electrical Workers. On the convention floor Reuther's followers heckled Communist speakers by making loud quacking noises. The harassment may have stemmed from the old trade union adage on how to tell a Communist: "If he walks like a duck and quacks like a duck, he must be a duck." Some of the quacks, however, were directed specifically at Communist Nat Ganley, whose high-pitched nasal voice and Brooklyn accent made him sound remarkably like Donald Duck.

Fighting back, Thomas accused Reuther of plotting to take the UAW back into the hated AFL and assailed his leadership of the GM strike. Aiming ridicule at intellectuals in the challenger's camp, Thomas complained, "These guys are always clustered so thickly around Reuther there isn't room to talk to him." The blunt-spoken UAW president sneered at his opponent's "fancy economics," prompting one observer to remark that Thomas "found more meaning and pleasure in a straight flush than in a chart on industrial productivity."

The lean, ascetic Reuther presented quite a contrast, physically and intellectually, to his opponent. In fact Reuther's aversion to traditional masculine pastimes was considered by some at the time to be a distinct liability. Labor writer Edwin A. Lahey gave this appraisal:

> Most labor men are pretty good drinkers, and make friends and keep them in barrooms during convention time. If Reuther was ever in a gin mill, the incident has been overlooked in re-

corded history. Union politicians—even the supposed "high-
brows" in the clothing unions in New York—play poker and
shoot craps. If Reuther even knows that the opposite sides of
the dice total seven, he must have picked up the information in a
study of permutations and combinations.

   Reuther has none of the charm of fallible men who go
through life committing indiscretions and deviating from the
path of moral righteousness. He lacks human warmth.

Frank Winn, a close friend of more than 30 years' standing,
insisted Reuther's abstention from liquor and tobacco never damaged his popularity with the rank and file. "He is not pious or
self-righteous. . . . Walter is a demanding taskmaster but in his
relations with other people, whether personal or business, he is
not pompous nor austere nor cold." Winn is convinced Reuther
always had greater rapport than Thomas with most UAW members.

As the convention opened, Thomas was counting on a strong
assist from Philip Murray, president not only of the CIO but of
the mighty Steelworkers' union. It was Murray and Sidney Hillman
who had tapped Thomas for the presidency in 1939 during the
UAW schism, and Murray's antipathy for Reuther was evident
even during the strike against General Motors. There were sharp
personality differences between the gentle Murray, who inspired
near-reverence among his admirers, and the hard-driving Reuther.
James B. Carey, then one of the few Reuther fans in the CIO
hierarchy, remembers the predominant feeling: "Murray was very
much for Thomas. . . . There were some who thought Reuther
was too much like a machine; he had a plan; he would liquidate
his enemies, and so forth, in the course of which he would tear the
organization apart."

Reuther was aware of Murray's influence with the delegates
and did his best to offset it. When the CIO president came to
Atlantic City to address the convention, Thomas named an escort
committee to bring Murray from his hotel to the big meeting hall.
Although Reuther was left off the prestigious delegation, he was
on the scene anyway when Murray entered the hotel lobby to meet
his escorts. Richard Frankensteen, in charge, bluntly rebuffed the

redhead. Pointing to Reuther, he told the CIO chief, "Walter—he's not a member of this committee." Richard T. Leonard, another escort, recalls Reuther's persistence:

> Walking down the Boardwalk, I was alongside Phil and I was getting my heels kicked by Walter trying to get up alongside Phil. As we hit in back of the Convention Hall, Walter had Phil by the left arm and he walked right up the steps with Phil, you know, onto the platform. And I overheard the conversation. I guess Phil wasn't sure if Walter was a candidate at that point. I think Phil probably was trying to prevail upon him not to be a candidate. And I remember Walter saying, "Well, damn it, Phil, I'm going to run!" And so he did.

Greeted by an ovation, Murray refrained from any direct endorsement in his speech. But in his soft Scottish burr he hailed Thomas for "very extraordinary and unusual services" in helping to establish the World Federation of Trade Unions. In a much-quoted line, he referred to R. J. as "this great big guy for whom I have such a distinct fondness." Murray also denied as "preposterous" the rumors that he and the Steelworkers had not backed the GM strike—a denial apparently aimed at Reuther's privately held view that the steel union had sabotaged, in effect, the "wage increase without price increase" line advocated by the UAW. Long after the convention was over, Reuther told his followers in Detroit, "The torch we lit during the General Motors strike was not picked up by the Steelworkers. . . ."

Thomas' forces naturally interpreted Murray's "fondness" as all-out support for their candidate. This theme was emphasized at evening caucuses conducted by Thomas for fence-sitting delegates.

Although Reuther's leadership of the GM strike was a major issue, it never was discussed extensively in the formal convention sessions. But Leo Fenster, a delegate from Cleveland Local 45 and no friend of the challenger, referred to continuing strikes at local GM plants by thousands of UAW members, then asked how it was possible "for us to go out first so far in advance and stay out last so far in the future, getting no more than the other locals and the other unions." Reuther, who knew that his oratorical skills could best Thomas, demanded, a closed-door debate on the GM strike with his antagonist. A delegate from Dodge Local 3 voiced the Reuther line: "Let us have a night session in this hall, with the press and the public excluded, so that we don't have to pull any punches and so that the two candidates can give us their points of view in no uncertain terms." Thomas wisely refused to debate and Addes, who was presiding, helpfully discovered a convention rule requiring approval by two-thirds of the delegates before a closed session could be held. The Reuther-backed proposal fell just a few votes short of adoption, a good omen for the challenger. The Thomas camp called the debate idea "a new low in union politics."

David Dubinsky, the powerful head of the International Ladies' Garment Workers' Union, also became an issue. Thomas accused Dubinsky of contributing several thousand dollars to the GM strike fund as part of a plot to bring the UAW back into the AFL, and recalled Dubinsky's financial support for the discredited Homer Martin. Years later Dubinsky acknowledged a pro-Reuther intervention. He had authorized ILGWU Vice-President Charles S. (Sacha) Zimmerman, a leading Lovestoneite, to pledge funds to pro-Reuther locals so they could send delegates to Atlantic City for the showdown with Thomas. Dubinsky's role was motivated by his strong anti-Communism rather than AFL chauvinism, however.

Even sex was employed in the contest. Clay Fountain, who was then on Reuther's staff, reported that Communist leaders tried every trick they could devise to influence the outcome. "Not the least . . . was the importation of glamorous female comrades who worked the swing shift in hotel rooms at night to convert delegates to the Thomas cause," Fountain wrote. "Some of these babes got taken in by smarter and lustier delegates on our side, who pretended they wanted to be converted—both for the joy of it and for the practical purpose of wasting the time of the CP Mata Haris."

The CIO hierarchy, with the evident blessing of Murray, joined forces with the anti-Reuther coalition. Hillman, Allan Haywood, and other federation officials arrived in Atlantic City to try and swing the election. The atmosphere was tense. When the contestants met shortly before the vote, a still-confident Reuther offered to shake hands but Thomas declined. "Tommy, if you're not big enough to lose, you're not big enough to win," huffed Reuther.

Edward J. Cote of the West Side Local nominated Reuther as a "man who consistently translates the will of the workers into action." A hush fell over the cavernous hall as the balloting began. First to vote was a delegate from UAW Local No. 1, representing employes of the Buchanan Steel Products Corporation at Buchanan, Michigan. His lone vote went to Reuther. The roll call continued, local by local, for several hours. The rules allowed vote-splitting among delegates, down to three decimal places, so the scorekeeping grew complex. Each vote represented approximately 100 dues-paying members. Dozens of people were hunched over tally sheets, calculating furiously to keep a running total. Cheers rang out from Reuther and Thomas forces whenever an unusually large bundle of votes was delivered to their champions. Twice during the long count, fist fights broke out on the convention floor, temporarily disrupting the roll call. The reading clerk droned on with his list of locals—Plymouth, Pontiac, Studebaker, Curtiss-Wright, Allis-Chalmers, North American—testament to the UAW's strength in industrial America.

Abruptly, as the voting neared a close, a commotion arose on the platform. Loyal supporters around Reuther hoisted him to their shoulders and began shouting hoarsely with joy—a cry of triumph. Many in the hall assumed Reuther now was assured of victory no matter how the rest of the votes were cast. They did not suspect at the time it was a ploy, devised by Brendan Sexton of Local 50, to try and stampede doubtful delegates who had not yet declared their sympathies. Even today, UAW men differ about whether it changed the results. Leonard Woodcock, who was scorekeeper for the Reuther Caucus, is convinced Sexton's maneuver had no practical effect. "It didn't change a single vote that was cast afterward," he says. "The only change it made was the manner in which the pro-Reuther delegates cast their votes—jubilantly—and the others, the Thomas votes, with a sort of grimness." Others insist the ploy clinched Reuther's victory.

Just before the balloting ended, Thomas conceded defeat with tears in his eyes. "It was a good race," he told Reuther, who replied, "We will work together, R. J."

At 4:00 P.M. on March 27, 1946, the UAW had a new president. Reuther had received 4,444.839 votes compared to 4,320.451 for Thomas—a margin of just 124.388. When the outcome was announced by Addes, the packed hall roared an ovation. Reuther's wife May was at his side as he promised to work for unity and uphold the CIO tradition in the union's top office:

> Like other officers of this union, too many times have I gone home feeling that I represented only half of the union and someone else represented the other half. I want to say to George Addes . . . that I extend my hand to him and together we will stand united.
>
> We have had a bitter contest . . . [but] I am going to make every possible effort to see to it that the fight on top is stopped and the fight in the local unions is stopped. I stand here humble. . . . Let us go home motivated by the same spirit that motivated us back in 1936 and 1937 when the only thing you could get for belonging to a union was a cracked head.

Crushed by his defeat, Thomas left the stage muttering, "Maybe I didn't do a good enough job, but believe me I tried." In the wings, Reuther already was conducting his first presidential press conference.

The margin of victory was so slim that almost any large Reuther local could claim credit. Brendan Sexton's Local 50, which represented the thousands who had worked at Ford's Willow Run bomber plant during the war, cast a solid 132 votes for Reuther, for example. This was possible even though only a few hundred men remained on the Willow Run payroll at the time of the UAW convention, because of the past dues payments and good-standing membership of 4,000 when voting strength was determined. Just as solidly for Thomas were some other large locals whose swollen wartime memberships had evaporated by convention time.

Years later a former UAW official claimed the Reuther Caucus had a victory margin of 1,250 votes going into the convention, before the CIO forces began their pro-Thomas efforts. Even so, the outcome was cause for celebration and Reuther's followers filled the bars of Atlantic City to toast their hero. The winner made a great display of downing a glass of beer and puffing awkwardly on a cigar.

Reuther soon discovered, however, to his shock and dismay, that he had won a purely personal victory. Other leading candidates on his ticket, with one exception, went down to defeat. Thomas was elected first vice-president and one of his leading supporters, Dick Leonard, won the second vice-presidency. Thomas-Addes followers captured a top-heavy majority of Executive Board seats, successfully isolating Reuther in the presidency. One of the few victories scored by the Reuther Caucus was the election to the Board of Emil Mazey from Detroit's East Side. Mazey, still in the Army and stationed in the Pacific at convention time, did not even know he was a candidate. The mixed results indicated Reuther would reign but not rule. Perhaps the delegates felt the need to put a check on their eager young president, or did not fully appreciate the bitterness and deep distrust between the rival camps that was certain to engender continued disruptive factionalism.

One potential Reuther challenger, Richard Frankensteen, bowed out of the Auto Workers hierarchy at Atlantic City, but he did so on his own. Frankensteen a few months earlier had lost a hotly contested campaign for mayor of Detroit during which he had pledged that, win or lose, he would not seek another term as UAW vice-president. Had he made the race, it is possible he would have been defeated by the Reuther Caucus. Frankensteen had been publicly ridiculed for taking a Florida vacation, following his mayoral campaign, while union colleagues were picketing GM plants in snowy Detroit.

Assessing the convention results, Walter Reuther was aware of the necessity for a duel to the finish with his foes, at least those

in the Communist bloc. A few days after his election he vowed
to isolate the "10 percent who are more loyal to outside interests
than to the union," including the leadership of several Detroit
locals he labeled as members of "the left wing." Following this
tacit declaration of war, Reuther's first term in the UAW presidency was marked by a tumultuous struggle for supremacy that
turned union brother against brother in one of the labor movement's sharpest internal battles.

CHAPTER EIGHTEEN

Purge

WALTER REUTHER DISCOVERED HOW DIFFICULT IT CAN BE TO meet a payroll when he took office as president of the United Auto Workers. The UAW treasury was bare—in far worse condition than the back-dated convention report of Secretary-Treasurer Addes had indicated—and union officials faced payless paydays in the absence of prompt action to replenish the general fund. As one of his first official acts, Reuther flew to New York City, hat in hand, seeking a loan to keep the union solvent. Sidney Hillman's Amalgamated Clothing Workers, one of the founding unions of the CIO, advanced $250,000.

"We started from zero—or less than zero—and things were kind of lean," recalls Jack Conway, a youthful auto plant veteran lured away from sociology studies at the University of Chicago to become, at that time, Reuther's principal assistant. "We had to make some kind of accommodation in order to live and fight another day. And that's exactly what we did."

A second unpleasant surprise for the new president was the vigorous early use by his union opponents of their "mechanical majority" on the UAW Executive Board. Less than a month after the convention election, and on the first major test of strength, the Board split fourteen to seven along factional lines in approving a policy statement that, among other things, was designed to limit Reuther's attacks on Communist Party members and their sympathizers within the union. Soon thereafter, votes were forced on resolutions that Reuther and his allies did not even see in advance or get an opportunity to debate. According to Reuther aides, some of the official pronouncements were drafted by Detroit leaders of the Communist Party. Fighting back, Reuther publicly vowed not to appoint any known Communist to union office.

As the months passed, hopes for peaceful coexistence between the rival factions were dashed by the solidarity of the Thomas-Addes-Leonard forces and the endless wrangling at each Executive

Board meeting. Doing his best to ignore the hostile Board majority, Reuther tried to act independently. "The next year and a half was a nightmare for the UAW," declared one observer. "The faction fight raged with a complete lack of restraint."

The ever-resourceful Reuther, however, found ways to negotiate from strength with his union foes. A study of the bylaws, for example, showed that checks drawn on the UAW account required the president's signature. When Reuther demanded control of financial records in the hands of Addes and, predictably, was turned down by the Executive Board, he advised the union's bank that no Auto Workers check was valid until he verified the check number by telephone. Then he threatened to stop signing paychecks for Board members unless he was given access to the records he wanted. His opponents relented because, as Reuther put it, "Those fellows hated my guts but they loved their paychecks."

In another bargain, struck with R. J. Thomas, two key appointments for Reuther men were nailed down. In return for a Reuther pledge to name him director of the UAW's Competitive Shops Department, which would give the former president power to assemble a large staff of organizers who would owe him their jobs and their political loyalty, Thomas supported Victor Reuther to head the union's Education Department. He gave similar backing to the less controversial Frank Winn as head of the Publicity Department. Victor Reuther and Winn were to become important leaders in Walter's 1947 drive for reelection.

A Communist-led strike against Wisconsin plants of Allis-Chalmers, launched soon after Reuther's elevation to the presidency, provided him with another opportunity. The walkout, poorly organized and violent, was widely attributed to the Party's new emphasis on radicalism under its postwar chairman, William Z. Foster. Accompanied by the veteran CIO official John Brophy, Reuther went to Milwaukee to take over the negotiations. When a settlement appeared imminent, the Thomas-Addes forces accused Reuther of trying to make a secret deal with management and torpedoed any chance of an accord. Although the strike dragged on for nearly a year, it enabled Reuther to depict his unhappy

Milwaukee experience as dramatic evidence of the way Stalinism could harm the interests of American workers. His union opponents countered with accusations that the UAW president lacked militancy. They made Allis-Chalmers a rallying cry for their team in the factional struggle.

Outside the union the fight for supremacy continued in Middle West conventions of CIO state bodies, with each UAW faction attempting to advance its candidates for state or regional offices in the parent federation. The Michigan CIO convention, an important battleground, was controlled by Reutherites even though delegates from Phil Murray's Steelworkers lined up with the Thomas-Addes group. This victory in the auto industry's heartland, plus similar triumphs in Wisconsin, Illinois, Indiana, and Ohio, proved that Reuther's cause was gaining widespread backing. Murray, closely observing developments from his headquarters in Pittsburgh and Washington, could not help but be impressed.

At UAW headquarters in Detroit, even the typists took sides, as became evident after Reuther brought in his own "shadow cabinet" to fill key subordinate staff positions where he lacked the power to oust Thomas-Addes loyalists. Nat Weinberg, who had been at Brookwood Labor College with Roy Reuther in the 1930's, was hired for research work. Weinberg's nominal boss, James Wishart, saw him only long enough to say hello and never gave him an assignment. "I had no clerical or stenographic help," Weinberg recalls. "If I had something I wanted typed for Walter, I would walk around the headquarters building and find some girl who had a few minutes free and who was on Walter's side of the internal fight."

The rejuvenated Education Department, under brother Victor, spearheaded the Reuther campaign for rank and file support. The UAW used a CIO resort area school in Port Huron, Michigan, and established a leadership training base. Among Victor's helpers was Mrs. Mildred Jeffrey, who became Democratic National Committeewoman from Michigan two decades later. At the time, Mrs. Jeffrey and others were concentrating on lining up votes for Walter Reuther.

Public speaking, parliamentary law, and similar subjects useful to union activists were taught to officers of various locals. Students were selected for their potential value in the anticipated convention showdown. With the aid of an intelligent and youthful staff, Victor's department provided unprecedented aid to UAW locals, which bore dividends in the form of loyalty to the Reuther program. "It was tremendously important," states Conway.

Late in 1946 the union sponsored a massive educational conference in Cleveland that became a "junior convention." Reutherites and their opponents worked to enlist converts between appearances by such speakers as Eleanor Roosevelt and Walter White, the principal Negro spokesman of the era. White recalled the occasion in his autobiography:

> There was an undercurrent of tension and caucusing. . . . No quadrennial convention to select a Presidential candidate by any of the political parties was ever more steeped in political maneuvers than the Cleveland meeting. Buttonholing proceeded feverishly.

Addressing the audience of 1,200, White struck a blow for Reuther by warning that factional quarrels "to satisfy personal ambitions or grudges could mean destruction of the union." Victor Reuther later wrote White that the speech had "helped to turn the tide against the attempts of the Communists to capture the meeting."

In addition to convening this and other union-wide meetings, Reuther called caucus after caucus of shop stewards and local officials in Detroit to explain how Communist Party tactics undercut UAW bargaining strength. He did not have to name those he considered responsible for sponsoring or tolerating such tactics. The message was spreading.

Philip Murray, speaking at a banquet in Reuther's honor, referred to the union's "eternal, internal difficulties." The CIO president, for all his hardly covert 1946 efforts in behalf of Thomas, was warming up to Reuther—perhaps as a matter of simple expediency—and accepted his invitation to a UAW Executive Board meeting, at which Murray complained that the factional feud had "sunk to a level of complete moral degeneracy." If not exactly a pro-Reuther declaration, it indicated that Murray at least would not takes sides against him in the convention battle ahead. Moreover, Murray's growing antagonism toward Stalinism was made evident at the 1946 CIO convention when he sponsored a resolution declaring that the delegates "resent and reject" efforts by the Communist Party to interfere in CIO affairs.

Reuther's opposition was not idle, however. When the Auto Workers' president complained that Thomas was attacking him in the "reactionary anti-labor press," Thomas replied that Reuther often did the same: "He is like a guy delivering a lecture on temperance to himself in the middle of his second bottle of whiskey. . . . Reuther wants unity of applause for Walter, Victor, and Roy Reuther and, by God, anybody who doesn't go along with that program is a disrupter." Later in 1947 former UAW leader Wyndham Mortimer volunteered his own anti-Reuther strategy in a letter to Thomas: "That redhead is not going to be licked by our staying on the defensive. He doesn't hesitate to pin the red tag on you, so why in hell should we hesitate to pin the Homer Martin tag on him? If this bastard isn't a stool pigeon, I never saw one." Privately, Thomas agreed with Mortimer's assessment, saying, "Everything that comes into our hands proves it more every day."

Despite the intensity of intraunion feelings, Reuther did not welcome testimony before the House Committee on Un-American Activities by Michigan's Republican governor, Kim Sigler, who charged that Thomas, Addes, and Richard Leonard were "Communist captives." Reuther issued a press release denouncing Sigler for mounting an attack on the UAW and organized labor. "The reactionaries of the country have launched a red-hunt whose ultimate victims are intended to be, not Communists, but all effective labor leaders and labor unions," he asserted. At least some of his supporters did not agree. The Association of Catholic Trade Unionists, for example, lauded Sigler for "exposing a lot of Communist monkey business."

Throughout 1947 Reuther and Thomas fired nasty memos at each other concerning union duties and policy until "R. J." loosed a final salvo: "Frankly I believe that our time could be much better used . . . than in composing long inter-office memoranda. . . . Your personal ambitions and political calculations have so largely drawn you away from action on basic issues."

Auto negotiations inevitably were adversely affected by the squabble. Reuther, aided by economists Weinberg and Don Montgomery, prepared a brief to justify a 23.5-cent hourly wage increase for the second round of postwar bargaining. Thomas, however, was able to delay public release of the document. Meantime, the Communist-lining United Electrical Workers again beat the UAW to the punch in General Motors, settling for an increase of 11.5 cents an hour and six paid holidays a year. The package was said to be worth 15 cents an hour and became a pattern-setting agreement in the auto industry. Clay Fountain, then a Reuther publicist, was convinced "the Commies had used the UE-CIO to prevent Reuther from getting the credit for winning a raise that would set the pattern for 1947." Reuther was boiling mad, and showed it, at bargaining sessions with GM. Tactically, however, he had little choice but to accept a carbon copy of the UE settlement. The UAW, barely back on its feet from the grueling 1945-1946 GM strike and ripped by factionalism, lacked both the strength and the stomach for another confrontation. General Motors was well aware of the union's weaknesses and, when the Auto Workers went along with the UE pattern, it was scored as "no gain" for Reuther in the factional contest.

Almost simultaneously, however, the Reuther forces nullified a potential political plus for opponent Leonard during bargaining on pensions at Ford. Leonard urged ratification of a contributory pension plan proposed by the company but Ford workers agreed with the Reutherites and voted down the proposal in favor of the pay increase already negotiated with General Motors and Chrysler.

Ironically, Reuther's enemies managed to hand him a winning issue through a maneuver supposedly engineered to ensure his defeat. Meeting secretly in the spring of 1947, UAW leaders opposed to Reuther concluded a merger pact with a small CIO union known as the Farm Equipment Workers, or FE in labor's shorthand. This 35,000-member organization, under strong Communist Party influence, had jousted with the Auto Workers in the past over rival claims concerning jurisdiction in tractor and farm machinery plants. The Thomas-Addes-Leonard group agreed that merger would end these difficulties and provide the FE with far greater bargaining power. What made unification the more attractive to anti-Reuther forces, however, was a stipulation that the FE would have 500 votes at the coming UAW convention, votes that were expected to be cast almost solidly for the Thomas-Addes-Leonard slate.

To the stunned surprise of Reuther and his associates, the merger agreement—already semi-sealed without the approval of the Auto Workers president—was brought up at an Executive Board meeting in June 1947. Frantically, Reuther's men tried to delay action but the "mechanical majority" rammed through a favorable resolution. Jack Livingston, a Reuther lieutenant, managed to attach an important proviso: the merger would be conditional on approval by a rank and file referendum to be conducted during the following month. The Thomas-Addes coalition accepted the amendment, partly because they believed they would face no difficulty in soliciting a favorable vote for "labor unity" and also because they believed a referendum would nail down the merger beyond challenge.

To Reuther, the development presented a crisis and a challenge. Success for the merger plan almost surely would topple him from office. But the referendum gave him a grand opportunity to carry his own campaign to the grassroots—and he leaped at the chance. Squads of his supporters crisscrossed the country, down to the Gulf of Mexico and north into Canada. They argued that the FE merger plan was a trick to get 500 anti-Reuther votes into the convention and claimed it would set up a privileged class of autonomous members in violation of the UAW tradition of democratic industrial unionism.

"We beat their ears off and, in the process, converted a lot of the leadership to our point of view," Conway recalls. "They [the opposition] made a very serious tactical error." Even a pro-Addes observer acknowledged that Reuther "licked the pants off" George F. Addes in a Detroit debate on the question. The outcome was a major upset victory for the Reuther forces. The merger proposal was defeated by a vote of 3,653.56 to 1,719.92—a margin of better than two to one.

The setback only intensified the determination of Reuther's opposition. Attacks on the UAW president became more personal and, in a few cases, vicious. His adversaries circulated a letter purportedly written by the Reverend Gerald L. K. Smith, an anti-Semite on the far right of the political spectrum, applauding Reuther's "excellent job" in curbing the influence of Thomas, Addes, and Sidney Hillman. Smith was said to have cautioned his followers that "any public statement complimentary to him by one of our known leaders might limit his sensational usefulness." Reuther reacted by filing a libel suit against the publisher and author of the broadside. At about the same time, a comic book entitled "The Bosses' Boy" was distributed in auto plants. Depicted here as a puppet of the auto makers and big business, Reuther responded with a cry of "distortion, fabrication, and forgery." During the heat of the pre-convention campaign, the anti-Reuther Executive Board majority even declared that the union-denounced Labor-Management Relations Act of 1947 should be renamed the "Taft-Hartley-Reuther Act"—unparalleled ridicule of the head of their own union. Incredibly, the late radio commentator and columnist Drew Pearson aired a rumor that Reuther was being boomed to run for Vice-President of the United States on a ticket headed by conservative Republican Robert A. Taft. The story whistled through the shops before Reuther's denials could overtake it. "From late July until early October," said Clay Fountain, "the Commies threw everything but their hammer and sickle at Walter."

When not busy issuing denials, Reuther let fly with his own charges against his opponents. He accused rival UAW officials of wasting $500,000 in a Cleveland organizing drive. His supporters alleged that the opposition had padded the payrolls of Executive

Board members in return for their political backing. Reuther accused an old antagonist, John L. Lewis, of pouring money into the Thomas-Addes caucus to help defeat him. And the embattled UAW chief secretly arranged to send a sizzling indictment of his opponents to every member of the union, doing the final editing by telephone as the Executive Board met in Buffalo.

Stung by the surprise appeal to the rank and file, the opposition authorized Addes, Thomas, and Leonard to print and mail an equally sensational rebuttal. The anti-Reuther majority also deprived the Auto Workers president of his traditional authority to appoint members of convention committees.

Neither side missed an opportunity. When Reuther appeared before the membership in Flint, Thomas showed up and engaged him in debate and mutual insult for nearly four hours. Angrily, Reuther confronted his adversary backstage afterwards: "I had this meeting scheduled to present my side and you had to louse it up with this debate!"

Jack Conway, along with caucus chairman Ken Bannon and others, assembled a "powerhouse" to back a Reuther slate. Meeting late in October, the caucus decided it had enough strength to capture all four top offices in the union, an unprecedented goal for the Reutherites. Once the preliminary headcount was made, Reuther flew to Pittsburgh to tell Murray about the plan. The CIO chief urged him not to oppose Addes, the officeholder with the longest tenure, but the UAW leader was adamant. He also bluntly told Murray to stay out of the union's internal struggle and not throw his support to the other side as he had done in 1946. Murray acquiesced.

The election of convention delegates in one unit of Ford Local 600 illustrated the determination of the Reutherites. The local leadership, friendly to the Thomas-Addes bloc, kept the polls open only two hours on a Sunday to discourage voting. When Reuther backers still won nine of the ten contests, the leadership set aside the results on a technicality. In the second election pro-Reuther delegates won all ten seats by a margin of three to one.

In vain did Thomas charge that Reuther wanted to "run the

great auto union as a one-man show, surrounded by a crew of faithful lieutenants and yes-men."

Preoccupation with the factional fight was universal in the weeks before the convention, prompting one UAW leader to complain, "Every local union in the Detroit area has been so busy playing politics that whether our workers won a strike or starved to death did not mean a damn thing." For Reuther the survival of the UAW itself was at stake in the 1947 contest, as he asserted, "We cannot continue to function as a union while bitterly divided into factional groups." Also at issue, of course, was the extent to which the Communist Party would be permitted to influence Auto Workers' affairs.

By the time Reuther rapped his gavel to open the convention in Atlantic City, his opponents were demoralized and the Reutherites were in full control of the proceedings. Reuther won an early victory as the delegates rejected a proposal to instruct UAW officers to ignore non-Communist oaths required under the newly adopted Taft-Hartley Act. Instead, the convention supported his position: comply with the law under protest, challenge the oath in the courts and seek its repeal.

In his opening speech Reuther ridiculed the Republican-controlled 80th Congress, accused large corporations of profit-gouging at the expense of workers, and called for establishment of a union-sponsored daily newspaper "so that our people can read the facts instead of the propaganda of the employers." Philip Murray appeared and recalled a mutual aid pledge he and Reuther had made following the union's 1946 convention, saying:

> I took his good little right hand in mine and I patted his red locks. 'Walter,' I said, 'I am going to support you.' He said, 'Phil, I am going to support you.' And he did, and I did.

With Murray leaping aboard the bandwagon, Reuther's opponents decided not to run a major candidate against him. Two token challengers garnered only 399 votes between them while the triumphant president polled 5,593. Most Thomas-Addes supporters, accounting for 1,219 votes, simply abstained.

In the race for secretary-treasurer, the Reuther steamroller was so strong that even the durable George Addes was soundly defeated by Emil Mazey, the 34-year-old Socialist who had led the organizing drive at the Detroit Briggs plant in the 1930's. Mazey, a Reuther stalwart, polled only 760 votes less than the UAW president. Two relatively conservative candidates for vice-president on the Reuther slate—John W. Livingston of St. Louis and Richard Gosser of Toledo—also won handily.

In region-by-region elections for members of the Executive Board, the Reuther Caucus scored overwhelming successes, sweeping 18 of 22 contests. It was a massive vote of confidence for the young redhead who, during the preceeding 18 months, had been outvoted and isolated in the Auto Workers' hierarchy. Downing a shot of whiskey and puffing a token cigar to fulfill a campaign promise, Reuther jokingly declared a ban on all-night card games at Executive Board meetings. The next day he struck a more serious note:

> We are the vanguard in America in that great crusade to build a better world. We are the architects of the future and we are going to fashion the weapons with which we will work and fight and build.

He also was ready with a slogan to symbolize the new regime: "Teamwork in the leadership and solidarity in the ranks."

Delegates voted Reuther a $1,000 pay increase, raising his salary to $10,000 a year. Executive Board members were given an even bigger boost, from $5,000 to $6,500 a year, and top pay for UAW organizers was raised to $100 a week. Some delegates wanted to increase the president's pay to $12,000 a year, but Reuther, proud to be the lowest paid head of any major union in the country, objected.

The convention outcome was widely reported as a "swing to the right" in the UAW because of the left-wing, right-wing labels that had been applied to the rival factions. James Wechsler, a liberal journalist, writing in *Harper's* about "Labor's Bright Young Man," emphasized, however, that Reuther was hardly a "full-blooded Tory who spent his evenings at the Union League Club." Philip Taft, a labor historian, hailed the election results as "a sign of the union's coming of age, . . . a good day for the free world." Taft said the Reuther landslide had placed the UAW "solidly in the anti-Communist camp" under a leader who could keep a tight rein on the Stalinists who had exercised influence out of all proportion to their numbers in the auto union. A rank-and-filer from Buffalo put it this way: "There was a combination in them days that was more what you would call the left element. And these were one of the things that Walter cured up."

Once armed with a mandate, Reuther lost little time in using it. He dismissed more than 100 UAW staff members who were Communists or followed the Party's line. Defeated opponents scattered. George Addes left the union to open a nightclub. R. J. Thomas took a minor staff job with the parent CIO. Dick Leonard returned to a factory job, hoping to build a new political base, but soon left for a CIO post in the Southwest.

On the UAW's top staff, general counsel Maurice Sugar was among the first to be ousted because of his pro-Communist stance. Don Montgomery regained his top assignment in Washington and Nat Weinberg became research director, each replacing allies of the convention losers. Ken Bannon, who had directed the Reuther Caucus, was named head of the Ford Department and Harvey Kitzman, an ally in Milwaukee, was appointed director of the Agricultural Implements Division. In the ensuing months two anti-Reuther members of the Executive Board stepped down into lesser-paying staff jobs rather than risk defeat by Reuther-backed opponents at the next convention.

The victory also helped the union on the bargaining front as union officials enjoyed a respite from internal quarrels and could devote their full energies to contesting with the auto manufacturers. One of Reuther's first post-convention visitors, surprisingly, was Henry Ford II, who called at union headquarters to size up the man beaten by Ford goons a decade earlier. "Ford merely dropped by for a talk," explained Reuther. "Our chat was very satisfactory and very pleasant all around."

In the CIO, Reuther's success encouraged anti-Communist forces to insist on a clean break with affiliated unions that were following the Kremlin's propaganda line. Reuther's concern about Communist influences within the CIO was traced by Blair Moody, a Washington columnist for the Detroit *News,* to the spring of 1946 when Reuther began talking about a coalition of the auto, steel, and clothing unions to check the "creeping spread of power" by Communist-dominated affiliates. The battle was not won immediately, however, and in 1948 Reuther still was making speeches against Party-lining labor officials he described as "colonial agents of a foreign government, using the trade union movement as a base." He referred to Communists as "the phoney left, the corrupt left, and the morally degenerate left."

Early in 1948, long before the CIO was ready to act, Reuther announced that the UAW would admit rank and file members of Communist-dominated unions who were seeking a democratic labor organization. His action brought charges of raiding from the United Electrical Workers.

On the Communist issue, Phil Murray long had followed a policy of "tolerance" that caused Reuther, along with others, to grow increasingly impatient with the CIO chieftain. Gradually reversing direction, Murray removed a Communist-line leader from the CIO Executive Council at one meeting and later invited Secretary of State George C. Marshall to a CIO convention despite left-wing opposition to the United States recovery program for postwar Europe. Influential members of Murray's own union, the Steelworkers, argued for expulsion of Communist-leaning unions and the ouster of Lee Pressman, CIO general counsel and a major figure in the organization. Alarmed at reports of Pressman's discussion of CIO affairs at Communist headquarters, Murray fired him and engaged a liberal Chicago attorney, Arthur J. Goldberg, to take his place. With Reuther's strong backing, Murray eventually moved against eleven unions accused of espousing Communist doctrine and defying CIO policy. The drive reflected the view Reuther expressed following his 1947 triumph:

> Exposure, not repression, must be our goal. We must get the Communists out of the political back alleys and walk them up Main Street in the full light of informed opinion.

At the 1949 convention of the CIO, the United Electrical Workers and the Farm Equipment Workers were expelled outright, and machinery was established to bring charges of Communist domination against nine other unions. The nine were banished from the federation the following year.

On the world stage, Reuther joined with other CIO leaders in November 1949 to establish the International Confederation of Free Trade Unions (ICFTU) after the CIO quit the Communist-dominated World Federation of Trade Unions.

Early in 1952 the UAW successfully challenged top officers of Ford Local 600, accusing them of being under Communist Party influence and thus weakening the bargaining power of the 80,000-member organization at the River Rouge plant where Reuther had worked twenty years earlier. By the end of 1952 Reuther could say of Communists in his union, "There are very few of them left and we've done a pretty good job of learning how to get rid of them." His effective efforts did not escape notice in Moscow, where the trade union newspaper *Trud* charged that the onetime hero of Soviet labor in Gorki had become a "traitor and a strikebreaker" and a darling of the U.S. Chamber of Commerce. The UAW, declared *Trud,* had been placed under an "anti-democratic regime." Reuther considered the source and felt complimented.

CHAPTER NINETEEN

Shotguns and Dynamite

TWO UNSIGNED LETTERS, EACH THREATENING WALTER REUTHER with bodily harm, arrived at the UAW president's office in mid-April of 1948. One took exception to Reuther's successful battle against the union's Communist block. The other disagreed sharply with a Reuther effort to promote racial integration of bowling tournaments. Neither letter persuaded the Auto Workers' leader that he should take precautions against possible violence.

On April 20 Reuther spent the afternoon at an Executive Board meeting in the Book-Cadillac Hotel, telephoning wife May to put his dinner on the back burner because the conference would run into the evening. The session broke up about 8:30 P.M., and Reuther and his chief assistant, Jack Conway, drove to UAW headquarters. After attending to some chores there, the union president took the wheel of his seven-year-old Chevrolet sedan and drove alone to the family home at 20101 Appoline Street on the northwestern outskirts of Detroit. The Reuthers had bought their six-room brick and frame bungalow for $7,800 in 1941 and had paid off the mortgage in the summer of 1945.

The middle-class dwelling occupied a corner lot and, normally, Reuther would park on the side street, entering the house through the kitchen door after walking across the back yard. This night, arriving home at 9:40 P.M., he altered his routine and, for no particular reason, parked on Appoline Street and entered through the front door.

Shedding his coat, Reuther ate a dish of warmed-over stew at the kitchen breakfast bar, then went to the refrigerator to get a bowl of preserved peaches. As he turned, bowl in hand, to reply to a casual remark by May, the quiet of the neighborhood was shattered as Double O buckshot from a 12-gauge gun smashed through the kitchen window. Four pellets ripped into Reuther's right arm and a fifth plowed through his chest from right to left. Had he not turned, the full force of the blast would have struck him in the chest. As it happened, most of the buckshot passed by him to perforate a cupboard and kitchen ventilator. Had he entered the house from the rear, he would have walked into the muzzle of the weapon.

Four alarmed neighbors raced to windows in time to see a man run to a late-model Ford sedan, red or maroon, parked on Chippewa Avenue around the corner from the Reuther home. Someone apparently was waiting behind the wheel because the vehicle sped away as soon as the running man reached it.

Another neighbor, Richard W. Ruen, sprang from his bed upon hearing the shot and, throwing a coat over his pajamas, ran across an alley to the Reuther house. Seeing the UAW president lying on the kitchen floor, he raced down the street and summoned a physician, Dr. Angelo V. Lenzi, who, finding Reuther conscious and in great pain, administered morphine and stanched the bleeding.

"Those bastards had to shoot me in the back," muttered Reuther. "They couldn't come out in the open and fight."

Lenzi placed the shattered right arm in a splint as the victim insisted, "Doc, don't let them cut off my arm." Said Lenzi later: "I decided Reuther would have a better chance to save his arm if we could get a splint on quickly, before he was transported to the hospital. The arm was hanging at such a crazy angle."

As police gathered, Reuther was taken to New Grace Hospital where he was given three pints of whole blood and one of plasma while undergoing two and a half hours of surgery. Later his upper body was placed in a plaster cast and his right arm put in traction. Electric shocks were administered to the arm to prevent it from stiffening. Even with sedatives, Reuther slept but two hours in 24.

Two detectives guarded the hospital room around the clock and four were stationed at the Appoline Street home to protect the family and control the throngs of sightseers who congregated there. The two Reuther daughters, Linda Mae, 5, and Elizabeth Ann, 9 months, had slept through the shooting. Linda was told her father had fallen against the kitchen window and "cut his arm."

Solid clues to the identity of the assailant were few. One empty shotgun shell was found two blocks away along the escape route but it proved nothing. Police Inspector Joseph V. Krug determined that the gunman had held the barrel of his weapon about two feet from the window. Krug surmised he was short or had fired from a stooping position. "Reuther was about seven feet from the window," he reported. "If he hadn't turned just when he did, the charge would have blown his chest out."

The police department made a great show of zeal. The office of Commissioner Harry S. Toy ordered a search of "every garage in the city"—an impossible undertaking—for a car matching the description of the getaway vehicle. Moreover, Toy's staff directed that "everybody who had any personal animosity" toward Reuther be taken into custody and questioned. The dragnet was to cover "Communists or anyone in industry or a union." One of the first to appear voluntarily for questioning was George F. Addes. He was absolved of any complicity in the shooting.

Said Gus Scholle, president of the Michigan CIO Council, "I believe Communists are behind this." Many shared his suspicion.

At New Grace Hospital hundred of flowers and basketsful of telegrams and letters arrived for Reuther. Mother Anna Reuther came from Wheeling and gently suggested her son could make a safer living writing books or working at his tool and die trade. "No," Walter told her, "I'm all tied up in this thing, all involved. I must do it." Returning home from the hospital in May, he wrote in the UAW newspaper:

> The momentum and power of our new kind of labor movement cannot be stopped and thrown back by slugs from a shotgun. The social and economic democracy for which we struggle is a practical vision that cannot be clouded or killed by assaults on one man. . . .

The principal concerns of the UAW leadership were to find Reuther's assailant and provide adequate protection for the union president and members of his family. Jack Conway was made responsible for arranging protection.

Exposed on two sides, the Appoline Street home was seen as

an immediate security problem. And with popcorn vendors cater-
ing to the crowds of curious outside, the Reuthers worried about
the impact on their children, particularly 5-year-old Linda, who
asked, "Daddy, why can't they leave us alone? Why can't I be
like other kids?"

After a few months the family moved into a two-story house
on Longfellow Street, closer to union headquarters. The new home
was in the middle of the block. The UAW installed bulletproof
glass in the ground floor windows, put a fence around the back
yard, set up floodlights, and acquired two watchdogs for the property.

Drawing heavily on professional advice from George F. Boos,
then head of the Detroit field office of the U. S. Secret Service,
Conway provided the Reuther brothers and their families with a
protective program patterned on methods used to guard Presidents
of the United States. The union purchased a $12,000 bulletproof
Packard sedan, which Walter Reuther used reluctantly and briefly.
At least two armed men normally accompanied him wherever he
went. Bodyguards took Linda to and from school. Others were
posted around the homes of the three brothers. More than 40
gun permits were issued to the UAW. Said Walter Reuther years
later:

> It's the kind of thing that one tries to forget. It's not a very
> pleasant thing to live with—to know that people are trying to
> eliminate you. It's not a nice thing. And so you try not to think
> about it. You try to put it out of your mind and live as normal
> a life as you can, even though you know you can't. I think the
> greatest price that one pays for fighting for the things you be-
> lieve in is that, in the process of acquiring a certain public
> prominence, you lose what I think is the most precious thing,
> and that's a sense of privacy.

Reuther's recovery was complicated and prolonged. As a result
of blood transfusions, he ultimately contracted both hepatitis and
malaria. More disturbing was the seemingly irreparable damage
to the radial nerve controlling use of his right hand. Dr. Barnes
Woodhall, a specialist in nerve surgery, told Reuther he must

decide on a position in which the hand would be permanently fixed. The patient replied that no decision was required, that he intended to have a working hand and would not agree to have it immobilized. "I admire your spirit," said the doctor, "but your medical judgment is very bad."

Reuther went to the Duke University Medical Center where, on election day of 1948, Dr. Woodhall probed for five hours in a desperate effort to piece together tiny shreds of the radial nerve. The shotgun victim was informed he had one chance in a million of regaining the use of the hand.

Returning to Detroit, Reuther began making twice-daily hospital visits for whirlpool bath treatments. About eighteen months after the surgery, he was in the bath when he realized he could move his right thumb about a sixteenth of an inch. He let out a yell of triumph. "I knew I'd made it," he recounted. At home he exercised the withered arm by squeezing a hard rubber ball for several hours at a time. Gaining greater freedom of movement, he took up woodworking with the hope of speeding his recovery. By the spring of 1949 Walter was well enough to resume a full schedule of union activity.

Enemies of the family soon struck again, however. On the evening of May 22, thirteen months after Walter's shooting, Victor Reuther was relaxing in the living room of his home when he became the target of another shotgun blast. In the recent past something had been happening in the neighborhood at night to cause repeated barking by a small cocker spaniel belonging to Victor and his wife Sophie. After two visits by a police officer who had relayed anonymous complaints, the couple had given the dog away.

On this particular evening Victor was reading a newspaper and Sophie was mending when a shotgun was fired through the living room window. The blast caught the bespectacled Victor in the face, throat, and right shoulder. As his shattered glasses and a dental bridge flew across the room, Victor rose from his chair, then collapsed to the floor. His wife called police and ran screaming into the street. At Henry Ford Hospital a surgeon removed Victor's right eye.

There were more clues to this second shooting. A double-barreled shotgun and two empty shells were found in the shrubbery outside. There was one clear heel print in the mud beneath the window.

Walter Reuther hastened to the hospital to comfort his brother: "Remember, Vic, how you held my hand a year ago. Now I'm holding yours. Keep fighting, Vic, keep fighting." Replied the brother, "Look after the kids and Sophie." In a formal statement, Walter said: "The same people who paid to have me shot paid to have my brother shot and for the same reason. They could be die-hard elements among employers, or they could be Communist or fascist agents."

Anna Reuther came again from Wheeling and joined in a family council in the living room of Walter's new Longfellow Street home. Those assembled feared brother Roy would be the next target but Anna no longer was advising a retreat from the labor movement. She told the family:

> I've been thinking about this and, you know, mothers in the whole history of the world have to wrestle with this problem of losing their sons. Too many mothers have lost their sons in wars. I haven't lost any of my sons in wars. But you boys have made a decision—made a decision to give your time and your energy to the labor movement. That's what you believe in, and if you believe in it, as I know you do, you must be prepared to give your life for it.

Walter Reuther later said that "I came out of that meeting feeling like I could lift a mountain with one hand."

Eight months later, on December 20, 1949, reporter Jack Pickering of the Detroit *Times* received an anonymous phone tip: "You did me a favor once. I want to tell you a story. You know the building at Milwaukee and Cass? Dynamite has been planted in the building. It was planted when the big guy was in the office." Alerting police, Pickering summoned a photographer and joined officers in a futile hour-long search of UAW headquarters. Shortly before midnight, however, a watchman found a rain-soaked cardboard carton outside a seldom-used basement entrance. Wrapped in red and green Christmas paper and tied with cheap ribbon, it contained 39 dynamite sticks taped together. Police decided the fuses had sputtered out because of the rain and poor workmanship on the part of the bomb-maker. The union added another $25,000 to a reward fund that now approached $250,000.

The Reuthers became more security conscious than ever, with Walter and May seeking still another home in a rural setting. They found what they wanted near Rochester, Michigan—a small summer cottage on a trout stream 35 miles northwest of Detroit. Originally intended as a weekend and summertime retreat, the property became the family's permanent home in 1952 after Reuther had spent long and painful hours winterizing it and expanding the original redwood and glass structure. Still struggling to get full use of his right hand, he would saw and hammer until his eyes filled with tears, then dunk the stiffened hand in a bucket of hot water. After stretching the fingers, he would return to his labors. "I got a good house and a good hand—all for the same money," he declared.

The Auto Workers built a ten-foot-high steel fence around the four-acre site and set up a gatehouse for security guards at the entrance. The house itself was circled by streams, a circumstance that once prompted Reuther to joke, "I'm the only union leader who lives behind a moat."

From the start there had been reason to suspect underworld involvement in the shooting of Walter Reuther. Three weeks after the attempt on his life, two Detroit hoodlums, Pete Lucido and Sam Scroy, vanished. Their abandoned auto was found in Toledo. Investigators began picking up gossip that the two men had known something about the shooting and were thinking of making a claim on the reward money when they disappeared.

Not long thereafter, police arrested a Carl Bolton and four other men in connection with a burglary in Pontiac, Michigan. Two of the men said Bolton, a former vice-president of UAW Local 400, was implicated in the shooting. However, Bolton was in prison at the time Victor was gunned down and a jury acquitted him of assault on Walter.

Because of moves by the Reuthers against the Communist-dominated United Electrical Workers Union and the Farm Equipment Workers, many suspected Communist involvement in the shootings. It was known, too, that the UAW's left wing, the Reuther opposition, had mutually profitable links with underworld figures who dominated illegal gambling in the auto factories, an operation grossing perhaps $20 million a year. Because of the freedom of movement accorded local union stewards and shop committeemen, they made ideal collectors and runners for the crime syndicate. The Reuthers realized this and were trying to stop betting in the plants. Moreover, the national UAW leadership could not forget that the underworld and anti-union employers in Detroit had formed alliances long before Harry Bennett's activities at the Rouge became a matter for public inquiry.

One employer with a labor relations record that the union felt left much to be desired was the Briggs Manufacturing Company. As the Reuther camp cast about for clues to the shootings, attention reverted to a series of brutal beatings of union men at Briggs that coincided with a power struggle between followers of Emil Mazey and Melvin Bishop, the latter an unsuccessful Reuther Caucus candidate for UAW vice-president in 1946 and recipient of the "Vic and Wal" letter from the Soviet Union.

Bishop had been elected UAW regional director for Detroit's East Side, which encompassed the Briggs plant, in the autumn of 1941. With Mazey soon to return from Army service, Bishop faced a potential challenge to his job. Beginning in May of 1945, leading Mazey partisans were struck down in a series of assaults that led some to suspect the underworld might have taken Bishop's side in an intra-union rivalry. Although the still-absent Mazey defeated Bishop for the East Side directorship at the 1946 convention, the beatings continued for another three months. Ken Morris, then recording secretary of the Briggs Local, was the final victim. A lead pipe and hat found at the scene of the Morris slugging later vanished from a police department property room.

Recalling events of the period, Jack Conway related that "by accident, Emil Mazey was fingering Mel Bishop's telephone finder pad and he hit the 'P' and the thing popped up and here's this private phone number of Santo Perrone." Sometimes known as "The Shark" and "The Enforcer," Perrone was a former convict suspected of having intimate ties with the Mafia.

Late in 1946 Judge George B. Murphy of the Wayne County Circuit Court began sitting as a one-man grand jury to investigate the Briggs beatings. Witnesses were questioned by Ralph Garber, an assistant prosecuting attorney, and much of the investigatory work was done by police detective Albert DeLamielleure. One witness testified his wife had been beaten by hoodlum types after being interviewed, supposedly in confidence, by DeLamielleure.

Judge Murphy quickly turned his attention to Santo Perrone, who was represented at the hearings by Louis J. Colombo, Sr., the man who had been the Ford Motor Company's counsel at the 1937 hearings on the Rouge beatings of Reuther and other UAW activists. Perrone, born in Alcamo, Sicily, in 1895, immigrated to the United States in 1912 and eight years later had his first brush with the law. He became a naturalized citizen in 1922.

Perrone and his brother Gaspar were coremakers at the Detroit-Michigan Stove Works when, in 1934, the Mechanics' Educational Society of America struck the company. Santo and Gaspar were enlisted by John A. Fry, president of the Stove Works, to recruit strikebreakers, many of them tough Sicilians who knew how to use their fists on a picket line. The strike was broken and the fortunes of the Perrone brothers took a remarkable upward turn. Gaspar by "verbal agreement" took over operation of the Stove Works Foundry, providing the labor force and getting paid for each core or mold on a piecework basis. He was not required to put any capital into the enterprise and all materials as well as tools were provided by the Stove Works. Santo fared at least as well. Although he could neither read nor write, had little money and no business experience, he received from Fry a contract to haul scrap away from the plant. He paid nothing for the scrap yet by the time Judge Murphy questioned him, Perrone estimated he was netting $4,000 a month from its sale.

The Perrones suffered a temporary reverse in 1936 when, convicted of liquor law violations, they were sentenced to six years in Leavenworth federal prison. Santo, however, continued to collect regularly for the scrap haulage: "My wife was taking care of it."

With the Perrones away, the CIO stepped in and organized the Stove Works. Fry, who was serving as Detroit's deputy police commissioner in charge of traffic even while running the company, joined with Frank Martel of the AFL to urge parole for the brothers. Released after serving 29 months, Santo and Gaspar returned to the Stove Works and the CIO local quickly evaporated.

There was one known link between the Stove Works and Briggs, and Judge Murphy explored it: Fry and Dean Robinson, son-in-law of founder Walter O. Briggs and labor relations director of the Briggs company until becoming president in 1945, were longtime friends. Robinson was asked, "Did you ever discuss labor troubles with John Fry?" The Briggs president acknowledged, "I have in a general way, from time to time," but denied they had ever discussed the union-busting talents of the Perrones.

The one-man grand jury turned his attention to a second scrap haulage contract, this one between the Briggs firm and Carl Renda, son-in-law of Santo Perrone. The contract was awarded to the 28-year-old Renda on April 7, 1945, some seven weeks prior to the first of the Briggs beatings. A graduate of Albion College, Renda had no experience in scrap hauling, owned no trucks, had no yard for sorting and processing the metals he was hired to collect. His most recent employment, working with lathe-making cutters, had earned him $1.65 an hour. He testified that the scrap contract with Briggs—the actual work was subcontracted to professionals— earned him $53,000 in 1946 and $101,000 in 1947. He further disclosed that his father had been shot to death in the Wayne County Jail and that an uncle Jim was a professional gambler in Windsor, Ontario, just across the Detroit River.

Before the grand jury and at later Detroit hearing of the Senate Crime Investigating Committee, an effort was made to determine how and why the contract was given to Renda. George N. Lilygren, an assistant Briggs comptroller in charge of salvage department finances at the time the contract was awarded, testified he complained about the arrangement to W. J. Cleary, director of purchases.

Q. Is it not a fact that Mr. Cleary told you he had orders from Robinson . . . and there was nothing he could do about it?

A. That was my understanding, yes.

Q. . . . and you had an opinion as to what the cause of that was, did you not?

A. . . . I had an opinion there was some relief from labor troubles. We had a considerable amount of wildcat strikes there during that period of time.

Robinson swore Cleary had been wholly responsible for the Renda contract. Cleary could not be questioned; he had died. But another witness, metal dealer Max W. Temchin, echoed part of Lilygren's testimony:

A. The whole tie-up seems to work.

Q. Well, what indication have you that it works?

A. Well, the only indication I have is that Briggs has less strikes. See, it's evident Briggs haven't had any trouble at all in the last year or so that wasn't settled in a day.

The grand jury learned that Briggs lost 1,600,000 man-hours of labor in 1945 due to unauthorized work stoppages, compared with 600,000 man-hours in 1946. George W. Herbert, who had left his position as general supervisor of salvage at Briggs after Renda was retained, aired another provocative line of thought:

> We also have a certain amount of belief that the higher ups in the union are in with the Renda Company. . . . I believe from information I could gather at the time, the higher ups in the union are receiving part of this money Renda Company is receiving.

Herbert testified that although at the end of the war people were lining up in stores to purchase scarce cigarettes, Renda would drive to the plant with his auto loaded with cartons "and these stewards, committeemen, and different ones of the union would come there and receive their ration of cigarettes, free of charge." Herbert said he complained to his superiors "and they raked me over the coals for putting my nose in other people's business.

Another witness, Nathan Silverstine, had been manufacturing manager of all Briggs plants and, like Herbert and Lilygren, had left the company's employ subsequent to the Renda arrangement. He elaborated on Herbert's theory:

Q. But the opinion has been expressed to you that there is a connection between the salvage and the beatings that may have occurred at the Briggs?

A. Yes; and also expressed to me it is a battle between some guy on the take, up on the inside, and the union fight also.

Q. Explain that a little more.

A. . . . A union official or union head, vice-president in charge of some part of the union, who might be in line there.

Q. You mean, there would be a payoff between Renda and Company or Perrone and some union official?

A. There must be.

The grand jury probe led neither to solution of the Renda contract mystery nor to apprehension of those responsible for the beatings of Mazey partisans.

The UAW brought Melvin Bishop, who had become head of its Skilled Trades Department, before a trial board which exonerated him of any complicity in the beatings. Bishop, however, was dismissed from the UAW staff on December 14, 1947, shortly after Walter Reuther won solid control of the union's Executive Board, and later became an organizer for the Teamsters Union.

A few weeks earlier, on November 21, Bishop and Santo Perrone had been arrested by a state policeman near Comins, Michigan, on a charge of illegal deer hunting. The owner of a hunting preserve caught them "shining" deer with a spotlight, then shooting at them as they stood transfixed in the glare. Perrone, who owned a nearby hunting lodge, professed not to know Bishop. Said the arresting officer, Walter Sokol: "They were not strangers. I know that." Perrone and Bishop pleaded innocent before a justice of the peace, were found guilty and fined $50 each plus court costs. Confiscated were a portable spotlight and a 16-gauge shotgun. More than three years later Bishop refused to discuss his acquaintance with Perrone when questioned by Detroit police, and declined to take a lie detector test.

By 1949, following the shooting of Victor Reuther, the UAW was thoroughly dissatisfied with the investigation of the two shootings by Detroit police, an inquiry supervised by the same Albert DeLamielleure, now a detective sergeant, who had worked with the one-man grand jury. The union retained two sleuths on its own: Colonel Heber Blankenhorn, who had been chief investigator for the LaFollette Senate Civil Liberties Committee, and Ralph Winstead. Said Mazey later: "The first thing DeLamielleure told them was for Blankenhorn to go to Europe to look for some Communists who may have attempted to shoot Walter Reuther and he told Winstead to go to Mexico. We had reason to think that he had done this because he did not want a solution to the shooting."

Late in 1949 the Detroit *News* offered the UAW its "Secret Witness" plan, designed to ensure the anonymity of informants while preserving their claims to any cash rewards. The *News* shortly thereafter received a letter bearing a code signature: "Would You Please Make A Quiet Investigation of Clarence Jacobs Regarding The Walter Reuther Shooting." Two days later the newspaper received a more detailed communication suggesting the inquiry should center at a service station at the corner of East Jefferson Boulevard and Canton Street—that Jacobs and the owner of the station were closely associated. The *News* turned over the letters to DeLamielleure, who had no difficulty determining that the station owner was Santo Perrone. The Detroit-Michigan Stove Works was directly across the street.

Almost simultaneously, the U.S. Immigration and Naturalization Service took an interest in the Stove Works. Receiving a tip that 60 smuggled aliens would be found there, district chief James Butterfield raided the plant on January 9, 1950, and arrested 20 Sicilians. Said Butterfield: "The thread of suspicion of a smuggling ring has kept our investigators busy. But there is no proof. No one has talked. Of course, we have found smuggled aliens working in other Detroit plants. But we made our biggest haul at the Stove Works." The plant was conveniently located for traffic in aliens, on the bank of the Detroit River which afforded easy access by boat to the Canadian shore in Windsor. It was also handy for the type of rum-running activities that had sent the Perrone brothers to Leavenworth.

With no discernible progress being made in unraveling the mystery of the Reuther shootings, the special Senate Crime Investigating Committee, under the chairmanship of Estes Kefauver, began hearings in Detroit on February 8, 1951. The second witness, Governor G. Mennen Williams, appealed for legislation that would permit a governor to seek assistance from the Federal Bureau of Investigation "in the solution of crimes which appear to him to be beyond the scope of any single city or state police agency." Williams said that in the case of the Reuther shootings, "there was ample reason to suspect that these crimes had their origin in a wide conspiracy."

The Committee retraced much of the ground covered by the 1946-1947 grand jury, and Fry of the Stove Works again was asked about his relationship with Dean Robinson of Briggs:

> *Q. He is a good friend of yours, isn't he?*
> A. Yes, for a long time.
> *Q. . . . Did you ever discuss with him your labor troubles?*
> A. No. Maybe informally at some time or another, but we never had any discussion.
> *Q. You never suggested to him, did you, that the pattern of dealing with members of the Perrone family had solved your problems and that he would do well to take on another member of the family?*
> A. Certainly not.

Santo Perrone was summoned to testify about his affluence—he had two Cadillacs and a Ford—and his ties, if any, with Melvin Bishop. Perrone denied knowing Bishop and, after his memory of the deer hunting arrest had been refreshed, said: ". . . I was arrested with a few guys. I don't know their names. I can't remember their names."

In the summer of 1951 there was a fresh development. The new police commissioner, George F. Boos of the Secret Service, took an interest in the Canton Bar at 6925 East Jefferson Boulevard. Boos said police suspected secret ownership of the bar by Albert DeLamielleure of the Special Investigation Squad and noted the tavern was two doors away from Santo Perrone's Esso Station. Declared Boos: "We have received reports that the Reuther shootings were hatched in that bar. We are looking into that angle very critically." The commissioner said the Canton Bar ostensibly had been purchased October 3, 1949, by DeLamielleure's brother-in-law, Gaston Willems. He added that the detective's wife Mary had been assistant manager since that time and apparently was the only one there permitted to cash checks. A month later a police trial board found that DeLamielleure indeed had a hidden ownership in the tavern and ordered him demoted to general service bureau detective. The state Liquor Control Commission subsequently ordered him to sell the bar.

In June 1951 the UAW counterattacked Perrone and the Stove Works, mounting an organizing drive directed by another tough Italian, Angelo Bommarito. As Perrone watched from his service station, union men began distributing handbills in front of the plant. By autumn the Auto Workers had won representation rights through an NLRB election and a two-year contract was negotiated.

Perrone faced more serious personal problems. Because of the unfavorable publicity generated by the Kefauver Committee hearings, he was forced to give up his lucrative scrap haulage contract with Fry. Simultaneously, he faced trial on charges of bribing Stove Work employes to resist unionization. Four others charged with him included Harry (Poppa Dee) Johnson and another Perrone son-in-law, Agostino (Tino) Orlando. The defendants pleaded guilty, were fined $1,000 each, and were placed on probation for two years. All were released early from probation, it being decided that they had responded to supervision and therefore it was "doubtful that they are in need of further rehabilitation."

With the statute of limitations about to expire on the Walter Reuther shooting, investigators for the Auto Workers stepped up a private search for one Donald Joseph Ritchie, a Canadian ex-convict and nephew of the Clarence Jacobs named in the "Secret Witness" letters. Receiving a tip in the summer of 1953 that Ritchie was in the Windsor area, the UAW dispatched investigator Sam Henderson—himself once questioned by police about the Walter Reuther shooting—to Canada.

Henderson later testified he first contacted Ritchie on November 18 in a Canadian jail and quoted him as saying, "I know what you want, but see me when I get out." At a subsequent meeting Ritchie promised to cooperate but expressed dissatisfaction with the union's reward offer. He told Henderson he feared he would be murdered should he provide information and demanded $25,000 for his common-law wife, an attractive brunette known as Betty White and Elizabeth Ritchie, so she could be provided for should anything happen to him.

A Windsor attorney was enlisted by the UAW to help with financial arrangements and, by his account, security precautions were elaborate: "I met an official [of the union] one place and then was taken to another. We went into a building and left by another door and drove around several blocks. At the hotel [where negotiations were completed] we got off on one floor and then walked down two or three flights of stairs." With the knowledge of Gerald K. O'Brien, the Wayne County prosecutor, the attorney was handed a UAW check in the amount of $25,000 and instructions to make an initial payment of $5,000 in $100 Canadian bills to Betty White once Ritchie was in Detroit and had told his story. The check was marked for the purchase of property in Canada, a deception later explained by Mazey who had become secretary-treasurer: "I took this precaution because the underworld in my opinion had contacts inside my union. The only way I could protect the life of Ritchie and the only way I could try to bring a solution to this matter was to make certain that nobody outside of a few of us, nobody had any knowledge as to what the transaction was."

At 6:00 A.M. on the last day of 1953, Henderson brought Ritchie and Prosecutor O'Brien together in Detroit. Six days later O'Brien announced "solution" of the Walter Reuther shooting and said warrants had been issued for the arrest of Santo Perrone, Carl Renda, Peter M. Lombardo, and Clarence Jacobs, Ritchie's uncle, who listed his occupation in Windsor as barber. Convicted in Detroit in 1928 of smuggling aliens into the United States, Jacobs was deported to Canada but returned to the Motor City illegally in 1940. Arrested in 1948 on an illegal entry charge, he was freed pending trial on a $5,000 bond posted by Santo Perrone. Jacobs forfeited the bond, fleeing to Canada.

Ritchie signed the following statement made public by O'Brien:

> I was in the car the night Walter Reuther was shot. For about four or five years I had been working for Santo (Sam) Perrone. I made about $400 or $500 a week.
>
> In the occupation, I was—well, it just wasn't what people would call work.
>
> Clarence Jacobs approached me for this particular job. He told me I would get five grand.
>
> I was approached about five days before it happened and asked if I wanted to go. This conversation took place in Perrone's gas station. Perrone asked me several days before the shooting if I was going on the job. I said I was.
>
> I didn't ask a lot of questions. These people don't talk things over very much.
>
> All I knew was that Perrone had once said: "We'll have to get that guy out of the way." Did he mean Reuther? Yeah.
>
> The night of the shooting I was picked up in the gas station. The car was a red Mercury. I don't know who it belonged to.
>
> I sat on the back seat. Jacobs drove and Peter Lombardo was in the front seat with Jacobs.
>
> I was there in case there was trouble. If anything happened, I was to drive the car away.
>
> Jacobs did the shooting. He was the only one who got out of the car. I don't know how long he was gone. It's hard to remember time.
>
> I heard the report of the gun. Then Jacobs got back in the car and said: "Well, I knocked the bastard down." We took off in a hurry.
>
> After the job they dropped me back at the Helen Bar, about 200 feet from the gas station. I don't know what they did with

the car. I heard later it was demolished and junked. I haven't
any idea what happened to the gun.

I had some drinks at the bar and then went and saw Carl
Renda. Why? I always went in to see Renda. He said, "I have
something for you."

He got a bundle of cash and handed it to me.

I went downtown and met a girl. I stayed with her until four
in the morning. Then I took a taxi to Windsor. I didn't count
the money until I got to Canada. It was exactly five grand.

Ritchie, then 33, was housed under police guard in Detroit hotels
as a material witness. On January 8, 1954, he was in a three-room
suite at the Statler, guarded by detectives Wayne Glisman and
William K. Krupka. Announcing that he wanted to take a shower,
Ritchie stepped into a bathroom between two of the rooms and
turned on the water. An hour later, his guards investigated and
discovered he was gone.

Soon thereafter a man identifying himself as Ritchie telephoned
police reporter Ken McCormick of the Detroit *Free Press* and said
he was in Canada, that his account of the Reuther shooting was a
lie, and that he would resist extradition. At the request of police,
the *Free Press* reported only that a key witness was missing, then
took up the hunt on its own. It soon learned that a man answering
Ritchie's description had deposited $3,500 in a Chatham, Ontario,
bank on January 8 and later purchased a 1952 Dodge sedan for
$1,400 cash. A young woman was with him.

Said a disconsolate Prosecutor O'Brien, once word of Ritchie's
flight was disclosed: "I felt—and I still feel—we have the solution.
. . . We have a lot of evidence along the same lines, but he is the
case."

In nearly six years since the shooting of Walter Reuther, nearly
500 men and women had been detained by police and questioned.
Some were prosecuted on other charges but, apart from the abortive Carl Bolton case, none for the maiming of the UAW leader.

On the evening of January 12, 1954, while authorities on each
side of the border were hunting for the missing witness, off-duty
reporter Dennis Harvey of the Hamilton *Spectator* walked into an

all-night restaurant to find three men, all laughing, at the counter. One turned to the newcomer and announced, "These fellows won't believe I'm Ritchie." Harvey asked for positive identification, satisfied himself, and, with Ritchie's permission, telephoned police. The fugitive's common-law wife had been picked up elsewhere in Ontario, which apparently occasioned Ritchie's act of self-revelation. Neither was in custody for long, however. The extradition case against the witness collapsed, partly because of differences in the criminal statutes of the United States and Canada. Ritchie left a Canadian court laughing: "I conned the [union] officials into giving me $25,000. Who wouldn't give a story for $25,000?" Of course, his flight from the custody of Detroit police was fortuitous. There detectives Glisman and Krupka were found to have neglected their duty as Ritchie's guards and were ordered to forfeit 30 days' pay each.

On April 15 in Lansing, Governor Williams signed UAW-promoted legislation extending from six to ten years the statute of limitations in cases of assault with intent to commit murder, allowing the search for Walter Reuther's attacker to continue.

The union, however, quickly found itself on the defensive. Carl Renda sued the Auto Workers, five of its officers, and a state police lieutenant for $5,200,000, alleging he had been the victim of "malicious prosecution." In December 1957, shortly before he was to testify in the Renda case, an important witness for the UAW vanished. He was Ralph Winstead, who had been investigating the Reuther shooting for eight years. Winstead's body, frozen and clad in fisherman's garb, was recovered a few days later from Lake St. Clair. The coroner's verdict: accidental death.

A Michigan Circuit Court found for Renda and awarded him $400,000 damages. Filing a brief that weighed more than thirteen pounds, the UAW won an order for a new trial from the Michigan Supreme Court. In 1963, a full fifteen years after Walter Reuther was shot, the Auto Workers reluctantly handed Renda a check for $12,500 in an out-of-court settlement.

Several of the principal figures in the prolonged investigation of the Reuther Case came again to public attention, although the inquiry itself languished. Santo Perrone switched on the ignition in his car on January 19, 1964, exploding a bomb that ripped off his right leg. Refusing to cooperate with police, he exploded, "I'll take care of the bastard who did this!" Donald Ritchie was convicted of perjury by an Ontario jury, which held he lied in a deposition given during the Renda damage suit against the UAW. Detective DeLamielleure left the Detroit police force and, according to Senate testimony by Mazey, became a Teamster business agent.

John Doe warrants issued as a holding action by potential prosecutors of Walter Reuther's assailants expired on April 20, 1968. The statute of limitations ran out that day and even should those responsible ever be found, they will remain forever immune to prosecution.

More than two decades after the shooting Reuther voiced his feeling about this most painful chapter in his often-troubled career:

> I, in effect, as a part of one's own peace of mind, sort of intellectually decided that why should I try to be a Sherlock Holmes and try to solve this crime, and get myself so deeply emotionally involved that I'm doing *that* rather than doing the things I want to do.
>
> . . . Now, obviously, no human being could avoid having his own little reflections and his little speculations about these things. And I've had mine. But I've not made it a major effort.
>
> I think that there's no question about it that there was a particular period in the history of the UAW when disposing of me by assassination or any other way happened to be a common denominator that a number of people could somehow share.
>
> I think that the Communist Party shared that, because in their judgment I was the only thing that stood between them and seizing the power of this union. They didn't think that anybody else could, in effect, coalesce the combination of forces in our union that could stop them. Therefore they would certainly like to see me eliminated.
>
> I think the underworld figured that I was the kind of person who would do everything that I could to try to keep them from

taking control of this union and using it for the rackets and everything else that they use unions for.

And I think that there were still a small group of diehard employers . . . who also were willing to work with the underworld and who, in effect, shared this same common denominator: that they could weaken the union if they get me out of the way.

Now I have been told, and this so far as I am concerned is only speculation, that there were several meetings at which these three elements had some contact with each other. I am in no position to tell you details because I don't know details. But I was told that.

Certainly there were some of the employers that were working with the gangsters. . . . There was this scrap iron deal which was a payoff mechanism. No question about that. It all ties together there somewhere.

CHAPTER TWENTY

Politics

BY THE LATE 1940's WALTER REUTHER WAS RANKED WITH WINSTON Churchill and Joseph Stalin in a widely published listing of the ten most influential men in the world. Historian Arthur M. Schlesinger, Jr., wrote in 1949 that "the extraordinarily able and intelligent leader of the United Auto Workers may well become in another decade the most powerful man in American politics." Even then, in the public consciousness, Reuther clearly was a major figure in the nation's political as well as economic life. To conservatives, his increasing influence with liberal political activists was cause for alarm, even fear. Despite all rumors and forecasts to the contrary, however, Reuther never interrupted his UAW career to seek public office nor did he organize the type of labor-oriented third party many envisioned following World War II.

"I was urged to run for the Senate and I was urged to run for the governorship of Michigan," he has said. "I think that had I wanted to be a politician, I could have competed successfully for either of those offices." By his account, he made a firm decision to forego officeholding in 1946 when he decided to seek the presidency of the Auto Workers. As he put it:

> I think I can communicate quite effectively with people—a whole lot better than some politicians who somehow get themselves elected. But I made a decision to work in the labor movement. I felt that's where I wanted to be. I felt that's where I could make the greatest contribution. Being associated with the leadership of an organization like the UAW gives me access to resources to do meaningful things. There are many things you can do in government, and there are many things in which you are restricted. . . . I do not believe that you can successfully have a political career and a trade union career at the same time. I think you have to make up your mind.

The last time any of the Reuther brothers sought public office was during World War II. Victor campaigned unsuccessfully for a seat on the Detroit school board and blamed his defeat on the schism between Reutherites and the Addes-Frankensteen forces. "Where we had counted on political support, it didn't materialize," he says.

The elections of 1942 were disastrous from the standpoint of organized labor, placing in Congress enough conservatives and reactionaries to ensure passage of legislation abhorrent to the unions. An example was the Smith-Connally War Labor Disputes Act, which became law over Franklin D. Roosevelt's veto in 1943. Although labor's no-strike pledge was being honored at the time, the Act imposed a 30-day cooling-off period before strikes could be called and empowered the President to seize struck plants. The CIO reacted by forming, under the chairmanship of Sidney Hillman, a Political Action Committee. Philip Murray explained the move in language that mirrored the thinking of the Reuther brothers:

> Labor has long recognized that the gains which it wins through economic action can be protected, implemented and extended only if it develops a progressive program of legislation and secures its enactment through effective participation in the political life of the nation. The elementary legislative safeguards for the protection of the health and safety of workers, such as Workmen's Compensation, maximum hours for women and minors, and safety and sanitary laws were all placed on the statute books through labor activity in the political arena. More recently, the broad program of social and labor legislation enacted in recent years was brought about largely because of the increasing participation of labor in the political life of the nation. . . .
>
> The deplorable record of the 78th Congress has brought sharply home to labor the dire results of its political apathy in 1942, and has made manifest the necessity of more effective intervention by its members in the political life of our nation.

The PAC recorded stunning initial victories. Martin Dies retired from Congress in the face of a surge in voter registration stimulated in his Texas district by labor's new political arm. Two other members of the House Committee on Un-American Activities, Joe

Starnes of Alabama and John Costello of California, were defeated in primary election contests. Opposed by the PAC, Representative Clare Boothe Luce fought back with tart phrases: "No foreign coup was ever so slickly devised as this political putsch. . . . What are the facts about PAC, this newly laid egg out of the Hillman hen by the red roosters? . . . If my head is to roll in a basket, at least it's a more American head than Sidney Hillman's." The target of her abuse responded, "I hope she carries her pretty head around for a long time—but not in Congress." Mrs. Luce was reelected.

In Wayne County the UAW and the CIO upset forecasts of a sharp 1944 drop in registered voters, because 100,000 or more workers had gone to war, and helped boost registrations to 800,000 —10 percent higher than the 1940 level. A longtime associate of Lyndon Johnson's found it not surprising that UAW leaders proved adept at partisan politics inasmuch as they were trained in the fierce union factionalism of the 1930's and 1940's. "In that union," he remarked, "you live politics 24 hours a day. If you go to sleep, you have to have somebody standing around who's keeping his eyes open."

A state PAC was established that year as a committee of the Michigan CIO Industrial Union Council. This group, with the support of a number of secondary UAW leaders, experimented in third-party politics with the Michigan Commonwealth Federation. Opposed by Walter Reuther and the UAW Executive Board, the MCF was a resounding failure at the polls.

Even so, as World War II ended, some influential union men, inspired by the British Labour Party's victory over war hero Churchill, thought the time opportune to establish such a party in the United States, perhaps under the leadership of Reuther. Indeed, from time to time the Reuther brothers flirted with third-party ideas. Writing in late 1945, Victor declared, "The time is now ripe for labor to divorce itself from the two old parties and resolve to build the base for an independent, indigenous, new national political party." None of the Reuthers ever implemented such theorizing, however, and all pointedly did not participate when A. Philip Randolph, Gus Scholle, and others toyed with establishing a People's Party in 1946.

Moreover, they by then had cut their final ties with the Socialist Party, Walter saying of its leader, Norman Thomas: "Norman is sincere, but the SP is too dogmatic; instead of from Marx, the American political concept must grow from American soil."

As his thinking developed in the postwar period, Walter Reuther spoke most often of a "political realignment." At one point he favored "a realignment of existing parties on the basis of issues. Roosevelt Democrats and Willkie Republicans belong in one party; Rankin Democrats and Clare Hoffman Republicans in another." He also wrote: "In Europe . . . labor parties are a natural political expression because there you have a highly fixed . . . class society. But America is a society in which social groups are in flux, in which you do not have this rigid class structure." He suggested labor unions combine forces with farmers and small businessmen to "do in America what needs doing."

On January 4, 1947, Reuther carried his search for a viable political-action instrument further, attending the founding meeting, at Washington's old Willard Hotel, of the liberal Americans for Democratic Action. Because the ADA charter expressly condemns Communism, it barred from its board a number of party-lining presidents of CIO unions, prompting Philip Murray to decree that if some were barred, none could participate. As a result, Reuther and some other CIO leaders bowed out of ADA for about eight months in 1947-1948. He returned to the fold at the organization's February 1948 convention, declaring, "I'm back where I belong and I don't intend to leave again."

Joseph L. Rauh, Jr., the Washington attorney and ADA activist and close Reuther associate for more than two decades, offered this assessment of the political odyssey of the UAW president:

> Reuther was really the independent in politics in the 1940's. When the ADA was formed . . . it really was his dish of tea because it was independent of the Democratic Party. . . . I think Walter was really attracted to the ADA because it wasn't part of the Democratic Party machinery. For many years he kept out of the Party machinery. He never used to go to a Jefferson-Jackson Day dinner. Now he goes and he's the hero. . . . There's

been a real shift from independence to [becoming] part of the
Democratic Party machinery.

At the time of ADA's founding, Michigan Democrats were in
disarray. Long a predominantly Republican state, Michigan had
no permanent Democratic organization until Murray Van Wagoner,
as state highway commissioner, built a patronage-based machine
in New Deal days and became governor. Due in good measure to
civil service reform, the Van Wagoner apparatus collapsed in 1942,
and political conservatives, known as the Old Guard, inherited the
Party's remains. Opposing this faction, with considerable futility,
were Reform Democrats and the Michigan Democratic Club. Early
in 1947, leaders of these dissident groups invited Gus Scholle, as
head of the state CIO Council, to join in discussions aimed at
combining liberal forces and seizing the Democratic Party machinery. Following a year of negotiations and bickering, the state
PAC, with Reuther approving, took the plunge in March of election
year 1948, issuing the following statement:

> Progressives and liberals within the Democratic Party have
> often been outnumbered by conservatives and reactionary ele-
> ments. The PAC is unanimous in its opinion that the best way
> of supporting liberalism within the Democratic Party, to con-
> form to national CIO policy, and to serve the best interests of
> Michigan labor, is to join the Democratic Party.
>
> It is our objective in adopting this policy to remold the Demo-
> cratic Party into a real liberal and progressive political party
> which can be subscribed to by members of the CIO and other
> liberals.
>
> We therefore advise CIO members to become active precinct,
> ward, county, and Congressional district workers and attempt
> to become delegates to Democratic conventions.

Leonard Woodcock, as one of Reuther's top aides, saw much
logic in the coalition from the standpoint of the UAW: "We didn't
make our people Democrats. Our people were naturally Democrats
and what we did was only possible because we were representing
the normal aspirations of an overwhelming number of our people."

Joining the new alliance were part of the AFL, the Brotherhood of Railway Trainmen, and major Polish and Negro political groups. ADA supported the move but did not become a part of the formal coalition. Standing with the Old Guard were the Teamsters Union and some Irish, Greek and Italian organizations in Detroit.

Very quickly the Scholle-Reuther forces and their allies learned a great deal about the politics of manipulation as practiced by the Teamsters' Jimmy Hoffa. Having long characterized Reuther and the UAW as "them squares from Milwaukee Avenue," then the street address of Auto Workers' headquarters, Hoffa rejoiced as, at a stormy meeting, he handpicked two of his lawyers to serve as Democratic national committeeman and state chairman. Strutting from the room, Hoffa boasted: "Some CIO punker wanted to throw me out. I told him to come ahead."

Nationally, Walter Reuther's influence on the political scene was greater than in his adopted state at that point. Even in presidential politics, his endorsement counted for a great deal in 1948. After Murray brought the UAW leader to a White House conference with Harry Truman, the President of the United States told the president of the CIO, "Phil, that young man is after your job." Smiling, Murray responded, "No, Mr. President, he's really after your job."

And so he was, but not for himself. Reuther believed it was tragic that a man of Truman's limitations, as he saw them, had succeeded by accident of death the towering Roosevelt, who had been Reuther's friend. He told the Detroit *News* that Truman was a man "with his heart in the right place but a man not adequate for the job he inherited." At least one associate thought Reuther "was always sort of patronizing toward Truman."

Reuther's objective was to find a liberal worthy of UAW support. Early in 1948, before he was shot, he and some of the top people at UAW headquarters met in the basement of Reuther's home on Appoline Street to discuss the forthcoming Democratic presidential nomination with Don Montgomery, the union's Washington representative. Montgomery reported that a good deal of

Party sentiment was building up behind General Dwight D. Eisenhower. Although Reuther saw merit in "Ike" as an alternative to Truman, he preferred New Dealer William O. Douglas, Associate Justice of the Supreme Court. When the ADA board met in early spring, Reuther made an eloquent extemporaneous appeal for support of Douglas. Majority sentiment, however, forced the UAW leader to go along with a resolution placing ADA on record as favoring Eisenhower "and/or" Douglas for the Democratic ticket.

Quite apart from the composition of the Democratic slate, Reuther had another political concern: the new Progressive Party led by Henry A. Wallace, former Vice-President and Cabinet officer. To James A. Wechsler of the New York *Post,* Reuther confided he was fearful "a lot of decent guys" in the UAW would vote for Wallace if the Democrats nominated Truman. Determined that Wallace be stopped, he put across an Executive Board resolution labeling the Wallace candidacy "a Communist Party maneuver."

At the same Board meeting the UAW declared that its "official political objective" was the formation of a political party that would welcome workers, farmers, small businessmen, professionals, and any others committed to gaining economic security without loss of freedoms, the qualification reflecting Reuther's adamant opposition to Marxism. Further, it was resolved that the party would not serve as mouthpiece for any other and would "advocate a program of full production and full employment based on democratic controls in every area of our economic life where the public interest is directly and vitally at stake." It was a radical statement envisioning not only a third party but, if the proposed organization could win the votes, peacetime federal controls over selected areas of the economy. Reuther backed the idea, not only because of the urgings of such colleagues as Emil Mazey but because he foresaw a Democratic defeat in November if Truman headed the ticket and anticipated the need for dramatic action to revitalize liberal forces for the next presidential contest in 1952. In an interview with the Detroit *Free Press,* Reuther talked about "paving the way for a genuine third-party movement next year so it could be a force in the 1952 election." He even offered a prospective slogan for the prospective party: "Not Back to the New Deal but Onward from the New Deal."

On July 10 Eisenhower announced he would reject the Democratic presidential nomination under any conditions, terms, or promises. With Reuther's boomlet for Douglas barely off the ground, Truman became the Party's nominee. The CIO promptly endorsed the President and the UAW dutifully took the same course, with Mazey and one regional director in opposition. Within the Auto Workers' hierarchy a calculated tactical decision was made to concentrate resources and energies "into those areas where we had the greatest chance of electing congressmen, senators, and governors, and not to put our limited resources into the presidential campaign, on the theory that we didn't have enough to make much difference anyway. . . ." That is how Jack Conway describes the decision, which was based on the widely held belief that Truman was certain to lose.

From labor's standpoint the 1948 election results represented a stunning success. In Michigan, shave cream heir G. Mennen Williams captured the governorship from incumbent Republican Kim Sigler. In Illinois, Adlai E. Stevenson was elected governor and Paul Douglas U.S. senator, each over a GOP incumbent. Democrat Estes Kefauver won in Tennessee's Senate contest, as did the mayor of Minneapolis, Hubert H. Humphrey, in Minnesota.

Reuther was under anesthesia in Durham, North Carolina, while the returns were coming in, because of the lengthy surgery to repair the radial nerve in his right arm. Conway arranged to get the results from a local radio station and, once the Truman-Thomas E. Dewey battle was decided near dawn the next day, hurried to the hospital to report to his boss, now sitting up in bed and eating a light breakfast.

"Well, how did the election go?" asked Reuther.

Conway replied that "as far as Congress is concerned, we did pretty well." He cited victories district by district.

"What about the Senate?"

The aide told Reuther about the triumphs of Douglas, Kefauver, Humphrey, and others.

"God, that's great! What about the governors?"

Conway went through the liturgy of Williams, Stevenson, and the rest, then added, "Incidentally, Truman got elected, too."

Without blinking, Reuther came back, "That just goes to show you what happens when you take the issues to the people!"

The Wallace party was dealt a death blow. In Michigan the Wallace total of 46,515 votes barely topped the number collected in 1932 by Norman Thomas. Less than three weeks before the balloting, the Progressive Party candidate had cited Walter Reuther as his "greatest single obstacle." Some observers believed that had Reuther lost his bid for the UAW presidency two years earlier, the Auto Workers might have endorsed Wallace and provided him with a sufficiently broad base of labor support to have ensured Dewey's election.

Suppressing his view that the Truman presidency was a tragic mistake, Reuther issued a statement from the Durham hospital declaring that "the President's victory dealt a staggering defeat to the forces of special privilege." He sized up the returns as "a mandate from the voters for their government to carry out that program of action to meet the everyday needs of the people."

There remained for Reuther one small post-election embarrassment. He had scheduled an "educational conference" for January 19, 1949—the day before the anticipated inauguration of Thomas E. Dewey—at which UAW delegates had been expected to take the initial steps toward formation of a new third party. After journeying to the White House in December 1948 to pledge complete cooperation in promoting the Truman legislative program, and silently eating a generous portion of humble pie, Reuther told reporters, "What happened on November 2 was an important step in bringing about the realignment of the farmers and the workers." This statement marked the end of any Reuther hope or desire to establish a new political party. The January conference became a debating session that accomplished nothing.

The next objective of Reuther and his allies in the Michigan CIO organization was to fend off a 1950 Hoffa attempt to seize complete control of the state Democratic Party. Seeking a voice in the distribution of federal patronage, Hoffa and the Teamsters formed the Truman Democratic Club of Michigan and submitted hundreds of petitions for precinct positions. Although many of the documents were regarded as fraudulent by the liberal coalition, the Wayne County election board and the county courts gave the liberals no satisfaction. The ultimate battleground thus became the district conventions that were to elect Party officers. The coalition assigned "bouncers" to the conventions in Wayne County that would name about 40 percent of all delegates to the state Democratic convention. One stated he was supplied six stalwart helpers, twenty clubs, and two pistols, but had need for none of them. In another district the liberal chairman wielded a toy baseball bat instead of a gavel. Out of the contests came a new folk song, "Blood on the Pavements," composed by an Old Guard delegate who was ejected from one convention. The outcome was a Hoffa rout, the liberals winning five of six district chairmanships and more than 750 out of 1,243 state convention delegates. All members of the state committee owed allegiance to the coalition. And on the board of the sympathetic but officially nonaligned PAC, the UAW held close to a two-to-one majority. Many of the Old Guard threw their support to Governor Williams, who was campaigning to become the first Democrat since 1912 to win reelection.

Initial results showed Williams a loser, but by a narrow margin. Recalling 1948 election irregularities in balloting for the state legislature, the coalition demanded a recount. Williams emerged the winner by 1,154 votes. Republicans insisted on a second recount. With the repeat canvass incomplete, the governor's lead grew to 4,119 votes, prompting the GOP to abandon the effort.

The state's next political crisis for Democrats came in 1951 when Republican Senator Arthur Vandenberg died of cancer. Reuther's candidate for appointment to the post was George Edwards, his old friend from Kelsey-Hayes sit-down days, who had been president of the Detroit city council and then lost a UAW-endorsed 1949 bid for mayor to AFL-backed Albert E. Cobo.

Blair Moody, Washington reporter for the Detroit *News*, had another candidate. Said Reuther:

> Blair Moody urged me to be the candidate to fill Vandenberg's spot and said, "You are the only person I would be willing to support and not seek it myself." I told Blair Moody that I appreciated his friendship. . . . We sat until four o'clock in the morning in my home . . . eating Swedish coffee cakes and drinking tea and coffee, where he was trying to persuade me . . . I could have had Vandenberg's spot.

Reuther also was convinced that, had he been willing to accept the appointment, no Michigan Republican during that period could have overcome the advantage he would have had as an incumbent at the next election. He said he rejected the proposition because he was unwilling to give up his union career. Governor Williams settled the matter by naming Moody to the vacancy.

In this period Reuther began earning perhaps more credit than was his due as a political power broker. He was establishing a position for the UAW that, some years later, inspired conservative writer Ralph de Toledano to label the Auto Workers the union "most powerful in political influence and most active in financial and ballot-casting support of Democratic administrations."

Although relatively free with counsel, Reuther did not concern himself directly with offices below the national level, even in Michigan. Said Leonard Woodcock: "Walter has not been involved in the state Party as such. For example, he's never been to a Democratic state convention. But his influence and his guidance are certainly felt." Despite that influence, Reuther was unable to persuade Governor Williams to abandon his support for Averell Harriman at the 1952 Democratic national convention. The labor leader's choice for the presidential nomination was Adlai Stevenson. Testifying later at a Senate hearing, Reuther said, "The only decision in which I have participated was the question of national candidates. I have not gone into the states in terms of gubernatorial candidates or the congressional candidates. That is a matter worked out in each state. . . ."

Reuther's attachment to Stevenson had a rather unusual beginning. The ADA felt the Illinois governor was avoiding a clear-cut stand in favor of a Truman proposal to establish a Fair Employment Practices Commission. Through the good offices of Willard Wirtz, a Stevenson law partner, Reuther and chairman Stanley Gwertz of the ADA executive committee got an appointment with the governor a few weeks before the nominating convention. Recalls Rauh: "The guy that really sent [Reuther] was Adlai Stevenson. . . . I saw Stanley later and he said neither he nor Walter were ever so impressed; greatest man they had ever talked to, and so forth. So I said, 'What's his position on FEPC?' And he said, 'Oh, my God, we forgot to ask!' "

Better remembered from 1952 is Reuther's role in discouraging the efforts of the then Vice-President, Alben W. Barkley, to gain the Democratic presidential nomination. The UAW chief was among several top labor leaders who had gone to Chicago for the Democratic convention, at which they collaborated closely in promoting platform planks favored by their organizations. Reuther was the principal CIO spokesman on the scene and George M. Harrison of the Railway Clerks performed the same function for the AFL. Although Reuther, Harrison, and their union colleagues were agreed on issues, they were not united in support of any single candidate. Moreover, union members serving as convention delegates—and their number was greater than ever before—were scattered in the camps of Stevenson, Harriman, and Kefauver, with the latter claiming the largest labor following.

It was at this point that Reuther and Harrison learned, in advance of a public announcement, that the 74-year-old Barkley planned to seek the nomination. They also were informed that the Vice-President was being encouraged by Senator Richard Russell of Georgia, Secretary of the Senate Leslie Biffle, and other conservatives whose views were in frequent conflict with those of organized labor. Two weeks earlier, the union leaders learned, Barkley had been invited to the White House and was told that, since Stevenson had not announced his candidacy, Truman would support his Vice-President if he were seriously seeking the nomination. The President also advised Barkley to solicit labor's backing.

Arriving in Chicago, Barkley attempted to dramatize his vigor by marching up Michigan Avenue at the head of a welcoming parade. One of his next moves was to invite the labor chiefs to join him and Mrs. Barkley for breakfast next morning in their Blackstone Hotel suite. Knowing what the Vice-President would ask of them, Reuther and his fellows caucused and agreed on a common response.

Among those at breakfast, in addition to Reuther and Harrison, were Joe Keenan of the AFL and Jack Kroll, head of the CIO Political Action Committee. The delegation was received graciously by the Barkleys and, during the meal, most of the time was devoted to inconsequential gossip, small talk, and the swapping of political anecdotes, a Barkley specialty.

Finally the Vice-President told them he would like to have the nomination and asked if they would endorse and support him. Although the union men had agreed on their reply, they had failed to select a spokesman. Reuther had rather expected that Harrison, as the senior labor leader present, would speak up. Harrison said nothing, however, nor did anyone else. The lengthening silence became embarrassing. Stepping into the void, Reuther said in effect:

"Mr. Vice-President, you know that we all have the greatest admiration and affection for you. That is why it is so painful for us to say what we feel we have to say. It is unfortunately true that it is sometimes necessary for us to hurt the people we love most."

He went on to list the reasons why he and the others felt they could not offer an endorsement: labor's own convention delegates were divided on the choice of a candidate; in all candor, they could not approve the auspices under which Barkley appeared to be seeking the nomination; finally, they felt he was too old to be subjected to the physical and emotional stresses that face a President.

Barkley accepted, seemingly without rancor, what Reuther had to say, then thanked his guests for coming.

Later the same day the Vice-President issued a statement withdrawing from the competition, saying he acted because the labor leaders had told him they would not support him. Most news accounts left the impression labor had exercised a veto on grounds of Barkley's age. In fact, the union representatives had not recommended Barkley's withdrawal, nor was the age factor the only one that had influenced their thinking. Nevertheless, various publications, columnists, and politicians denounced what they called the "arrogance" of labor in telling the Vice-President, through Reuther, that he could not be a candidate. In his *Memoirs*, Truman added a postscript:

> . . . in one essential respect Barkley failed to follow our suggestions to him. In meeting with the leaders of labor to enlist their support, we told him to be sure to see the leaders one at a time. Instead, he arranged a breakfast meeting with all 16 labor leaders at once. We knew that they would never commit themselves in a crowd, and all that came of this meeting with the labor leaders was a unanimous turndown. I am of the opinion that if Barkley had been advised by a manager skilled in dealing with labor this rejection would never have occurred and Barkley would have been the Democratic nominee.

A few weeks earlier Reuther had attended the Republican convention to testify before a platform subcommittee on foreign policy. Asked by Senator Richard Nixon if there were anything in the foreign policy of the Truman administration with which the CIO disagreed, the UAW president replied: "Senator Nixon, there are things in the foreign policy of the United States that we in the CIO disagree with, but in essence on its basic positions, we agree. We think that in some places the emphasis is wrong. We believe we need to do more on a positive basis in terms of Point Four, of helping people to help themselves. The essential difference between the CIO and the Republicans is that we criticize the Truman administration foreign policy for its deficiencies and the Republican Party criticizes it for its virtues. That is a fundamental distinction."

The 1952 election results were not to Reuther's liking. Stevenson conducted the most eloquent campaign ever, but Dwight D. Eisenhower's status as national hero determined the outcome. Reuther was philosophical about the Democratic setback, however, as he told the CIO convention a month later:

> This is no time to hang crepe in terms of the political outlook. We lost the election. It was disappointing but it was not disastrous. Look at the centers in which we had large CIO membership and you will find that in those centers our people came through with flying colors. I say that the great challenge ahead is to lift the level of political morality on the part of the politicians in Washington, but you cannot raise the level of political morality in Washington until you raise the level of political conscience on the part of the people back home. This is the job we must take on.
>
> We need to build. We need to organize. We need to educate on the political front, because the kind of labor movement that we are building cannot find the answers to the many complex social and economic problems solely at the bargaining table. Therefore let us determine not to do less but to do more on the political front.

CHAPTER TWENTY-ONE

Bargaining Pioneer

WALTER REUTHER ALWAYS TRIED TO SUBSTITUTE THE POWER OF reason for economic force in collective bargaining, but he usually found it necessary to combine the two, in varying amounts, in order to make gains for the union in major negotiations. Fortunately for Reuther and his constituency, the profitability of the auto corporations made it possible for the union leader to seek, and win, benefits that would have been out of the question in an industry with a large number of marginal employers. Reuther was fortunate also in having an enlightened antagonist, Charles E. Wilson, as chief executive of General Motors Corporation in the years immediately following World War II. Although Wilson developed a foot-in-mouth reputation as Secretary of Defense in the Eisenhower administration, he was as much a management pioneer in bargaining as was Reuther on the union side of the table. It was Wilson, in fact, who proposed the concepts of an annual wage increase and a cost-of-living escalator in auto negotiations. It was Wilson's thinking that made possible in 1950 a five-year contract, another industrial experiment in labor peace marred only by the spiraling inflation that accompanied the Korean War.

Even before World War II, Reuther and General Motors had broken new ground in the mass production industries by establishing an impartial "umpire" system to decide workers' complaints over job conditions and management disciplinary action. The result was a form of factory common law, based on interpretation of labor-management contracts, that helped avert plant-closing strikes because of individual grievance cases.

The turbulent GM strike of 1945-1946, however, had tested the Auto Workers' staying power and Reuther's leadership ability. Although Reuther eventually had been forced to accept a pattern established by other labor settlements—18.5 cents an hour—he felt there were hidden, long-range benefits from that bitter, 113-day shutdown of the nation's largest corporation.

During the strike Reuther had issued a warning: "The grim fact is that if free enterprise in America is to survive, . . . it must master the technique for providing full employment at a high standard of living, rising year by year to keep pace with the annual increase in technological efficiency." Later he said:

> That strike was about two questions. It was about the right of a worker to share—not as a matter of collective bargaining muscle but as a matter of right—to share in the fruits of advancing technology. The other issue was why should workers be victimized by inflationary forces, over which they have no control, which erode their real wage position.

Wilson, who was upset by the duration of the postwar strike and wanted to negotiate longer-term contracts, was quoted by Reuther as telling him: "You did not persuade us on those two basic principles during the strike. But when it was over, I began to realize that you were right, and that the two principles you had advanced were sound."

A close Wilson associate said the industrialist began contemplating a philosophy of wages, prices, and productivity as early as 1942. Louis G. Seaton, who was General Motors' chief negotiator for two decades, recounted that Wilson was hospitalized with a broken hip and had ample time also to consider methods of moving away from annual bargaining to a system of longer-range agreements. Seaton recalled: "Mr. Wilson rationalized that you ought to tie the protection of the buying power of an hour of work into it, but you also ought to enhance the buying power of an hour of work as the productivity of the country improved because that's the only way a worker can improve his standard of living."

The new ideas could not be introduced in wartime, when wages were controlled, and, by Seaton's account, the stormy bargaining climate in the immediate postwar period caused Wilson to delay further.

"In 1948 the climate was pretty good and it was Mr. Wilson's notion to make this proposal," Seaton related. Walter Reuther was not at the bargaining table to respond, having been seriously wounded in the April 20 assassination attempt, but his union colleagues quickly accepted.

At the heart of Wilson's offer were two major innovations in collective bargaining. The first was the "annual improvement factor," or the amount which management and the union agreed should be added to a worker's pay each year to represent his share of rising output per man-hour. In the 1948 agreement this provision called for a 2 percent wage increase, then amounting to three cents an hour, in each of the two years of the agreement. The other dramatic departure was a cost-of-living escalator formula to adjust a worker's pay up or down with price changes, as measured by the federal government's index of living costs. Under this provision, a quarterly pay raise of one cent an hour would take effect automatically for each rise of 1.14 points in the index issued by the Bureau of Labor Statistics. A decline of the same amount would result in a penny-an-hour pay cut. The contract provided for a maximum reduction of five cents an hour no matter how far the index might plummet.

Wilson proposed that the escalator clause remain in effect for five years but the UAW high command decided, after some hesitation, to agree only to a two-year trial. Reuther, then convalescing from his wounds, did not take part directly in the decision making but he had expressed skepticism about escalator clauses in the past. But the yearly increases and the floor under the escalator provided by the GM agreement reassured him.

The corporation, which had studied cost-of-living adjustments in Europe even before the UAW was organized, felt the escalator was a concession essential to winning union support for a two-year agreement. With a seller's market for new cars continuing, the giant of the auto industry wanted to avoid any threat of a work stoppage in 1949. Also, annual negotiations, GM had found, contributed to union-management tensions, as labor leaders began building support for a possible strike the following year almost as soon as the ink was dry on a new wage contract.

Little did GM realize that the escalator would prove to be a bonanza for the auto union's membership. Reuther calculated twenty years later that it had brought an additional $18,000 over that period to the pay envelope of a typical full-time year-round GM worker.

Over the years, the Auto Workers at times seemed to imply that the Union had wrestled the escalator clause from a reluctant management. As Seaton put it, however: "This was a General Motors proposal. After it got signed, it became a union proposal and we don't fight about it." Reuther, looking back on this pace-setting development, traced the concept to the UAW's postwar bargaining policies: "We planted the seeds in the '45–46 strike and we harvested the principles in the '48 agreement."

Wilson, appearing before the Rochester, New York, Chamber of Commerce shortly after the historic pact was signed, defended the departure from precedent, stressing the stability he hoped it would bring to GM plants. He also declared: "Union workmen as well as others can properly expect to participate in the prosperity of America. Benefits will accrue from these agreements not only to employes but to stockholders, dealers, and customers."

Reuther and Wilson had a special, trusting relationship. The red-headed militant and the white-haired millionaire frequently met privately, exchanging ideas and developing a warm friendship. They often talked on the telephone for a half hour or longer. Years afterward, Reuther said: "I've always thought that C. E. Wilson was really a very decent, genuine human being. The test of that is whether you can still act human after going through the GM corporation machine, and he passed that test."

Even while recovering from the shotgun blast that almost took his life, Reuther began setting a major new goal for his auto union —company-paid pensions. At that time, General Motors and other corporations were not willing to concede that they were required to bargain on retirement pay for their workers. Pensions, argued the captains of industry, were a managerial prerogative. Reuther, however, was determined to move on this front in the fall of 1949 against the Ford Motor Company.

Reuther went first to Ford with the pension issue for two reasons. First, in 1947, the company had offered its employes a pension plan, which was rejected in favor of an across-the-board wage increase. The 1947 proposal called for contributions by the workers and offered the union no voice in the operation of the plan.

Reuther's supporters opposed it on both grounds but, in the UAW's view two years later, the important thing was that Ford had shown a willingness to bargain about pensions when other manufacturers were insisting they could not negotiate on the issue. In addition, Reuther was developing a theory that Ford was the company from which to seek innovations in the social welfare area. Since the death of the original Henry Ford, who had fought the union so bitterly for many years, the firm's top management under grandson Henry Ford II had become far more flexible and imaginative in its dealings with the UAW.

Reuther began early to mobilize union and public support for his campaign, telling one audience that Wilson already was guaranteed a company-paid pension of $25,000 a year although his combined salary and bonus payments totaled $516,000 a year. "If you make $258 an hour, they give it to you," Reuther scoffed. "If you make $1.65 an hour, they say: 'You don't need it, you're not entitled to it, and we are not going to give it to you.'" Arguing against an industrial double standard, he said the employers were giving this message to the factory workers: "You cannot have security in your old age; that is reserved only for the blue bloods, the ones who were smart enough to pick the right grandfather before they were born. . . . If you live on the wrong side of the railroad tracks you are not entitled to it."

Perhaps the most effective phrase ever employed by Reuther was his description of men forced into a bleak retirement because they were "too old to work and too young to die." The catch phrase inspired Joe Glazer, the guitar-strumming education director of the United Rubber Workers, to write a song:

> *They put horses to pasture, they feed them on hay,*
> *Even machines get retired some day.*
> *The bosses get pensions when their days are through,*
> *Fat pensions for them, brother, nothing for you.*
> *. . . Who will take care of you,*
> *How'll you get by*
> *When you're too old to work and too young to die?*

"That was my slogan," Reuther recalled. "I used that for the first time, I think, at a mass meeting we had in Cass Technical High School. We weren't getting anywhere in Ford negotiations. We were in real trouble. . . . So we called a mass meeting of Ford workers 60 years or older, and we had 7,000 of them there."

Emotionally moved by the crowd of auto industry old-timers, Reuther pledged that he would not sign a new contract without a pension clause. Labor reporters immediately told him that he had put himself on the spot. "I don't think I'm out on a limb," Reuther replied with a wink. "I think I'm hanging on the last leaf on the last twig."

At that time the typical retired auto worker, unless he had purchased his own pension commercially, which was rarely the case, had to rely entirely on Social Security payments averaging $32 a *month,* or less than half what he might have earned in a *week* under wage agreements then in effect.

Under the threat of a strike, Ford agreed in October 1949 to pay the entire cost of pensions, putting $20 million a year into a special fund. The aim was to provide each Ford worker with 30 years' service a retirement income of $100 a month, including Social Security, at age 65—more than triple the previous typical retirement benefit.

But Reuther, with his 20–20 foresight, was just as concerned about another provision of the agreement that did not mean much at the time to anyone else except a few actuarial experts. He demanded that the Ford pensions be funded. That is, he wanted the corporation to put aside enough money each year to guarantee the payment of pensions to those workers who had earned them. This was in sharp contrast to the $100-a-month pensions negotiated by the United Mine Workers, for example, which were financed on a pay-as-workers-retire basis from royalties on union-mined coal. The soundness of Reuther's approach was demonstrated less than a decade later when the UMW retirement fund was forced to reduce pensions because revenues were insufficient to preserve the $100 payment.

The Auto Workers' leader demonstrated his devotion to the

principle when Chrysler Corporation refused to establish a funded pension plan but agreed to match the $100-a-month figure negotiated at Ford. To the average worker, the complexities of the UAW demand must have been baffling. Yet Reuther stuck to his principles even though the Steelworkers had accepted nonfunded pensions. A 104-day strike at Chrysler resulted, severely testing the union leadership's ability to communicate with the rank and file. Douglas Fraser, then assigned to the UAW's Chrysler Department, recalled the problem:

> We found out later . . . that the old mossbacks who ran the corporation thought that we would use this trust fund somehow to take over the corporation financially. . . . They offered to provide $100 a month and all we could say was that it wasn't actuarially sound. Even our negotiating committee didn't know what that meant when we started. I remember one mass meeting, about 85 days into the strike, after Chrysler offered to put $30 million into the bank as a sort of guarantee. Walter was explaining that this was a step in the right direction, when some guy screamed out from the back: "Yeah, Walter, but is it actuarially sound?" This meant to us that they finally were getting the message. We were bound and determined that if we told our fellows they were going to get $100 . . . there was going to be money there to guarantee it and pensions wouldn't be cut back after they retired. If you look at the history of the auto industry, there are a lot of casualties, and I'm sure this influenced Walter.

Developments since 1950 show clearly that Reuther was right on the funding principle. Most major pension plans now provide for such protection of pensioners, and federal legislation to make funding mandatory has drawn increasing support in Congress.

The UAW's pension drive, together with the similar breakthrough by the Steelworkers' union, helped indirectly to raise Social Security benefits for millions of Americans who did not belong to either union and, perhaps, never heard of the 1949–1950 negotiations. By linking private pensions with Social Security benefits to produce a total retirement income of $100 a month, the labor agreements softened traditional business opposition to higher Social Security payments. It suddenly became a matter of self-interest for major corporate employers to favor increased government-sponsored pensions in order to reduce their own outlays for the same purpose. While employers and their workers shared the cost of Social Security, negotiated pension agreements placed the full cost on the companies. Congress, which had not improved the Social Security Act since its passage in 1935, began increasing benefits periodically following the collective bargaining breakthrough.

Meanwhile, preparations were under way for the GM negotiations of 1950. As the corporation viewed it, the 1948 settlement had worked out well, with both labor and management reaping substantial benefits. The UAW was raising its sights, demanding a $125 monthly pension at the outset of bargaining, along with other wage-benefit increases.

Quietly, General Motors executives Harry Anderson and Lou Seaton began a series of private meetings with UAW negotiators Jack Livingston, Art Johnstone, and E. S. (Pat) Patterson. Another landmark agreement was taking shape in the auto industry, with Reuther keeping in close touch with his union lieutenants and approving their major moves. Seaton recalls: "We worked out the framework two weeks before the expiration of the contract. . . . Then Walter came into the situation." A chronological account kept by GM indicates that Reuther did not personally appear at the bargaining table until after the corporation made its proposal on May 15, 1950. A week later the union signed a new contract without a strike.

The agreement was for an unprecedented five-year term and continued the annual pay raise and cost-of-living features introduced in 1948 bargaining. It also provided for extension to GM of $125-a-month pensions, including Social Security payments, after 25 years' service. Finally, it granted a modified union shop, requiring new workers to join the UAW but allowing them to drop out following one year's membership. In return for its long-term generosity, General Motors felt it had assurances that the agreement could not be reopened for any reason until May 1955.

The length of the contract was, perhaps, its outstanding feature because, in Reuther's words: "It really indicated that the whole relationship between the UAW and the automotive industry had been put on a new and permanent and more responsible basis. The industry at that point had made a decision that the UAW is here to stay."

The 1950 contract embellished Reuther's already considerable reputation within the labor movement and in the nation at large, as an imaginative union leader who could win major gains without strife. *Fortune* summed up the UAW achievement: "In the year beginning June, 1950, his auto workers got about 24 cents added to their basic hourly rates; there was not a single strike of consequence in the industry. Most labor leaders are accustomed to puffing and heaving, and sometimes striking, for the pennies per hour they get for their men, but Walter Reuther makes it look easy."

The contract did not survive for five years, however. In July 1950—just two months after it was signed—the North Koreans invaded South Korea and U.S. forces were committed to a "police action" by President Harry S Truman. Within two years the war and its consequent economic dislocations sent prices soaring, shrinking the buying power of auto workers despite the favorable settlement. In the fall of 1952 Reuther moved to reopen auto contracts and seek additional wage increases. He urged that the "annual improvement factor" be raised from four cents an hour to a nickel for each year of the agreement, plus higher rates for skilled workers, and bigger pensions.

Reuther argued that labor agreements are "living documents" that should be revised to meet changed conditions—that they were not untouchable legal instruments. Jack Conway, then his top assistant, said later the UAW leadership was responding to rank and file unrest reflected in a rash of wildcat strikes: "The realities of the situation were such that we had to make that document come alive."

The corporations balked but Reuther had means of persuasion. Key plants were struck over local grievances that, in the past, would have been settled with the aid of Reuther's top staff. In the "living document" dispute of 1952–1953, the UAW president provided no aid or comfort to resisting managements. Production at GM and Ford was virtually halted by the UAW tactics and more than 100,000 auto workers were idled.

Three years after the five-year agreement was signed, General Motors agreed to raise pensions to a maximum $137.50 a month, including Social Security, to add 10 cents an hour to skilled trades-men's pay, to increase the annual productivity raise by one cent an hour, and to put 19 cents of the 24-cent hourly cost-of-living al-lowance into base wage rates. The pattern spread throughout the auto industry.

Defending the pressure he applied to reopen the five-year con-tracts, Reuther long afterwards argued:

> I think that one has a right to say that if you're selling a ton of coal, or a ton of steel, the contract that binds people to an exchange of goods does not have the same moral standing in a free society as a contract that relates to human beings. To equate the two is to say that labor is a commodity. There has to be a willingness . . . to recognize that if something happens which changes drastically the conditions of that relationship, there is a moral obligation to do something about it.

Reuther's "living document" theory was not universally popular. Many corporation executives denounced it as a violation of trust. David McDonald, who had become president of the Steelworkers late in 1952, expressed his disagreement with Reuther. "I knew this knife cuts both ways," he later wrote. "I could still remember vividly the misery and chaos caused by the coal companies in the 1920's when they abrogated signed contracts. I believe these contracts should be binding on both parties for the length of the agreement." McDonald felt so strongly on the matter that he went to New York City, where steel company executives were meeting, to make clear that he would not seek to invoke the "living document" concept to reopen steel labor agreements.

From the left, Reuther was criticized not for his unorthodox theory but on grounds that he was collaborating too closely with auto industry leaders to divert too much wartime steel from housing into automobiles. Early in 1952, in an unusual appearance before a group of congressional leaders, he had advocated larger steel allocations for car manufacturers. Top men at Ford and General Motors had urged Reuther's inclusion on a federal task force to frame recommendations on auto production and steel allocations.

Such problems soon were settled. The inauguration of President Dwight D. Eisenhower signaled an early end to the fighting in Korea and quick removal of wartime restrictions. Reuther looked forward to boom-year bargaining in 1955, hoping to transform into reality a vague dream he had nurtured for two decades: the guaranteed annual wage.

CHAPTER TWENTY-TWO

The Visionary

WALTER REUTHER'S INITIATIVES NEVER WERE CONFINED TO THE bargaining table but emerged in every type of forum and form, embracing virtually all of man's principal social and economic concerns. Indeed, old timers in the UAW relish a legend that the first copies of Reuther's 1940 warplane-production proposal came from the printer mistitled "500 Plans A Day." A writer once reported that Reuther even had a plan for licking his wounds. Before her death, he got together each year with Eleanor Roosevelt and exchanged clippings of the most hostile things critics had said about each other.

A continuing Reuther preoccupation since World War II was housing for the workingman and his family. Well into the 1950's he sought support for a peacetime version of the "500 Planes" program, urging use of idle war plants to produce prefabricated homes and modern rolling stock for the railroads. Less than a month after V-J Day he outlined his ideas in *The New York Times Magazine*:

> Government authorities similar to the Tennessee Valley Authority would be set up in housing and transportation, and under their jurisdiction a survey would be made of the $20,-000,000,000 in war facilities, the vast bulk of which is public property, financed by the War Bond investments of millions of Americans. Most of these plants have a high peacetime utility. They are ultra-modern and contain the most efficient machine tools and equipment. . . .

> After determination of the facilities adaptable to the program, these housing and railroad equipment authorities would place them in production either through direct operation, through lease to private manufacturers, or through lease to private workers' producer cooperatives. In each case the plant would be operated as part of the total program, and its management would conform to three standards: an equitable wage pattern, a good low-cost product, and protection of the government's investment.

> This program holds the promise of stimulating our whole

economy through the progressive introduction of the most modern rolling stock and the proportionate retirement of obsolete equipment. Use of roller and ball bearings, of aluminum, magnesium, and Diesel power will increase the payload (just as important in freight cars as in air transport) and will permit the radical scaling down of rail rates. As for housing, the same mass production miracles which have made us a nation on wheels can place a modern, durable, healthy home within the economic reach of the common man. . . . Government-owned war plants can be utilized in the mass production of complete homes, including all fixtures, complete bathroom, kitchen, garbage disposal, and air-conditioning units, electric dishwashers, and other appliances—all designed and constructed as integral parts of the house according to the latest standards of convenience and efficiency.

. . . the entire vicious circle of primitive methods and restrictive practices in the building industry can be broken.

. . . We have spent billions to destroy cities. Let us be lavish in the equally challenging and more creative assignment of building homes and rebuilding cities here in the United States, a victorious but poorly housed democracy.

Four years later Reuther appeared before the Senate Banking Committee and, speaking as chairman of the CIO National Housing Committee, introduced virtually the same plan, but confined to housing. He estimated that 21 million square feet of work space was unused in aircraft plants and that there were sufficient machine tools in federal stockpiles to permit production of 20 million homes in ten years. He called it a $120 billion program, a figure he arrived at by calculating that a two-bedroom house could be manufactured for $6,000 if mass production economies were realized.

Years before ghetto neighborhoods were burned during the racial strife of the 1960's, Reuther insisted, "We want the federal government to wipe out our slums, because the tax structure of the local community is not adequate to take care of the decay in the cores of our big metropolitan cities."

During a set of negotiations with General Motors, and while

awaiting a corporation decision that could have led to a strike, Reuther puzzled colleagues by writing page after page of script on a yellow pad. Asked if he were drafting a press release on the bargaining, he replied: "No, they're going to agree to what we want; don't worry about that. I'm writing a plan to rebuild the slums of America using the people who live in them."

An associate once remarked: "It's hard to guess where Walter's ideas come from. If you have an idea that is worth anything, you might as well give it to him because if you don't, he'll steal it from you." Asked for the source of his ideas, Reuther said: "I get them by reading and I get them by discussing problems with people who have problems. I have a habit—every time I read a newspaper I tear clippings out. . . . If there is a little . . . idea there that I think has some possibility, then I ask our research department or education department to dig into the matter more thoroughly and deeply and then give me a memo; and then I've got some ammunition. . . ."

One of Reuther's first moves as UAW president was to expand the research department and appoint a new director, Nat Weinberg. In a corporation, one writer speculated, Weinberg might be known as vice-president in charge of thinking. Here, in full, is Weinberg's autobiography: "Born in New York City in February 1914. Started working full time at the age of 14. First full-time job was on Wall Street—first as a runner, then as a board boy, then as an order and margin clerk in a branch office of a stock brokerage firm. Witnessed the crash of 1929 from inside a stock brokerage office. From 1930 to 1935 held a wide variety of jobs too numerous to mention here. Education from high school on was obtained at night, except for a few brief periods of working nights and attending classes in the daytime. Educational process was frequently interrupted by either other interests or fatigue. Finally got a B.A. from New York University in 1942." Weinberg ultimately became head of a new UAW Department of Special Projects and Economic Analysis.

Reuther sometimes is credited with having originated the Peace Corps concept. In any event, he broached the idea in a speech to educators in November 1956—nearly four years before John F.

Kennedy revived the proposition in a campaign talk. Said the UAW leader:

> I happen to believe—and my belief is based upon the fact that I have been around the world studying these problems, finding out why it is the Communists are able to forge poverty into power—that the more young Americans we send throughout the world as technical missionaries with slide rules, with medical kits, with textbooks, to fight Communism on a technical basis, the fewer young Americans we will need to send with guns and flame-throwers to fight Communism on the battlefields of the world. The kind of educational program I am thinking about would make it possible to enlist thousands of young Americans in the rewarding struggle to win the peace.

Health care was another Reuther cause of long standing. Addressing a UAW conference in Milwaukee in mid-1949, for example, he related health care deficiencies regarding a 28-year-old man he visited and encouraged during his own frequent hospital trips for whirlpool therapy. The patient had been paralyzed for nine years.

> . . . I came in one morning and he was just overcome with joy. He said to me, "I have been reborn this morning." I said, "What do you mean?" And he said to the nurse, "Pull this sheet back so I can show Mr. Reuther." And the nurse pulled the sheet back and he could wiggle his big toe, and he was just like a kid on Christmas morning, getting a new grip on life, with a whole new world opening up before him. Sometime later I came in to see him and he was crying. . . . He was broken-hearted, and I said to the nurse, "What's the matter, hasn't he been doing so well?" And she said, "He hasn't got any more money; he goes home tomorrow."
>
> I say there is something wrong in America when, if you happen to be born on the wrong side of the railroad tracks . . . and you lie on your back for nine years because you can't afford the treatment that medical science can give you, I say that is morally wrong. No nation that has an ounce of self-respect or human decency, no nation that can spend $400 billion for war,

can stand idly by and tolerate a continuation of that kind of double standard. . . .

What made this thing so ironic—and you begin to see what is wrong in America—the same week this happened the *Free Press* came out with a story about C. E. Wilson's bull. C. E. Wilson had a bull and the bull had a bad back. We are sorry about that. But what happened to C. E. Wilson's bull compared to this boy who was paralyzed for nine years? In the case of C. E. Wilson's bull, the General Electric Company sent a special 140,000-volt X-ray machine into Detroit on a special chartered airplane. It was picked up by a General Motors truck and taken out to C. E. Wilson's farm. The bull didn't even have to leave home to get medical care. Then when they got the 140,000-volt machine there they couldn't operate it because they didn't have enough power, so the Detroit Edison Company ran a special power line out to C. E. Wilson's farm.

Then medical specialists flew in from all over the country and they gave this bull the best medical care that modern medicine and science knows how to deliver. Now why? Why? I ask that simple, honest question. Why did C. E. Wilson's bull get the best of medical care while millions of these kids all over America are not getting that kind of care? It is because C. E. Wilson's bull cost $16,000, and you get boys and workers for free. . . .

Reuther did more than talk about health care. When dissatisfaction with Detroit's Blue Shield medical insurance became widespread, the union leader both talked and acted. He said: "Many of the benefits are hedged in by cash limits that leave the patient with large bills for services he thought were covered. Gross overcharges for doctors' services are commonplace. Contrary to basic precepts of modern medicine, few plans make any provision for preventive care or encourage early diagnosis of illness. . . . They overemphasize hospitalization and surgery. . . . At best they cover only about half of the average family's medical bill." As for action, Reuther sparked the establishment in 1956 of a Community Health Association to provide "economically sound, socially responsible" prepaid health services to any group in the Detroit area. Reuther, who become president of the CHA board, had been thinking earlier in terms of the Auto Workers operating its own hospital and health programs for members. He decided a community-oriented approach was more promising. UAW men are a minority of three on the fifteen-member board.

When asked to explain the general purpose of his busy schedule of speechmaking to a wide variety of audiences, Reuther had a one-word reply: "Education." He defined that as an attempt "to raise the level of understanding about the great problems that face the people of a free society so that out of that greater understanding you can get rational action." He went on:

> I think I can contribute more to the well-being of the membership of my union by trying to help America understand the broad problems because, as a union, we cannot solve our more limited problems in a vacuum. We can only solve these more limited problems as we try to get the whole of our society to intelligently and rationally find answers to the big problems, and if we can solve the big problems, the little problems somehow will fall into place. . . . I think that the future of human civilization lies in America trying to provide leadership in the solution of the great issues.

Victor Reuther has said that his brother, on the public platform, never appeared detached or simply to be making a speech, "because Walter himself has such a deep sense of mission, he regards the opportunity to speak as a challenge to him to persuade his listener of the rightness of his views." Walter Reuther believed the idea being conveyed by a speaker is only half the message, that the other half consists of projecting sincerity and a sense of purpose and belief.

Speaking in Chicago's Civic Opera House, with a broad orchestra pit between him and his listeners, Reuther had difficulty establishing a sense of intimate contact with the crowd. After half an hour a UAW member in the audience turned to a friend and remarked, "Walter ain't coming across too well tonight." The friend agreed but predicted, "He'll just keep talking until he does."

Reuther had a thin, high-pitched speaking voice that was not unpleasant but, one student of speech noted, "only shortly after beginning he reaches a plateau of vocal and emotional intensity and severity from which he gives his listener almost no relief until he has finished." Joe Walsh, former UAW public relations chief, agreed: "He reaches a level of almost stridency and he maintains it for an hour. It's almost as if he were beating you."

The Auto Workers' chieftain early abandoned the use of prepared texts. His explanation was that his delivered speeches bore such scant resemblance to the versions drafted by his speechwriters that "they had lost any incentive for preparing them." Using typing paper torn in half, Reuther wrote his own speech notes. All that appeared on each sheet were virtually indecipherable key words and phrases, each underlined.

Because his delivery was largely spontaneous, Reuther had a habit of returning to familiar and favorite themes in all his addresses, which prompted one professional observer to conclude that "he sometimes leaves the impression of trying to solve all of the world's problems in one speech." Reuther admitted, "I say almost the same things everywhere." Frank Winn offered a more precise analysis of "the speech":

> . . . It is an organic entity which, with the passage of time, gathers accretions and sloughs off vestigial matter. Thus a person hearing Walter make several speeches within a short period of time does feel he is hearing the same speech over and over again, or even if he hears him speak frequently over a longer period of time the changes are so gradual that he may not notice them. But if he hears him speak on one occasion and then a year or two or more years later, he will hear a different speech.

Occasionally a fresh Reuther proposal emerged in some form other than a speech or written policy statement. In June 1956, during an interview with the Detroit *News,* Reuther declared: "Autos should be priced like strawberries to avoid dips and peaks in production; if you want a car when demand is high, you'll have to pay a premium like you do for strawberries in February." Financial columnist Sylvia Porter surveyed brokers, businessmen, auto dealers, car owners, and auto manufacturers. "Every banker and broker I checked," she wrote, "applauded the basic idea although they admitted it would necessitate major adjustments in the industry." She quoted an anonymous businessman: "I can think of no other field in which the manufacturer is so completely dominant and so little guided by the standards of retail distribution. The times are catching up with the auto industry, forcing it to adopt modern merchandising methods." Several dealers thought the Reuther proposal would encourage off-season sales and cut their profits. A spokesman for General Motors stated, "If we all cut our prices at the same time, we'd risk violating the antitrust laws."

Smoothing out the humps and valleys in auto production was a natural enough Reuther goal. So, too, was coping with the advance of automation, from the workingman's standpoint. When automation became a matter of broad public concern in 1955, the president of the UAW was among the first to submit suggestions for meeting adjustment problems. To the Senate-House Committee on the Economic Report he declared: "One of the essentials of a strong and effective democracy is that we have leaders who attempt to anticipate situations which may arise and prepare in advance to deal with them. Too often in the past, nations have been surprised unnecessarily, by economic and social dislocations." Looking to the industry he knew best, Reuther outlined one example of automation's impact. In 1949, he said, it took six machines, representing a capital investment of $240,000, to machine 108 cylinder heads an hour at a direct labor cost of twenty cents per piece. He went on: "By 1954, however, those six machines had been replaced by a single automatic machine, representing an investment of only $230,000, for the same volume of production, and direct labor costs had been cut from twenty cents in 1949 to four cents a piece in 1954—a reduction of 80 percent in five years."

Sixteen months earlier Reuther had toured the Ford Motor Company's automated engine plant in Cleveland and had been asked if he favored curbs on the use of sophisticated machinery. "Nothing could be more wicked or foolish," he replied. "You can't stop technological progress and it would be silly to try it if you could." Before the Senate-House Committee, he spoke for the CIO:

> First of all, we fully realize that the potential benefits of automation are great, if properly handled. If only a fraction of what technologists promise for the future is true, within a very few years automation can and should make possible a four-day work week, longer vacation periods, opportunities for earlier retirement, as well as vast increases in our material standards of living.
>
> At the same time, automation can bring freedom from the monotonous drudgery of many jobs in which the worker today is no more than a servant of the machine. It can free workers from routine, repetitious tasks which the new machines can be taught to do, and can give to the workers who toil at those tasks the opportunity of developing higher skills.
>
> But in looking ahead to the many benefits which automation can produce, we must not overlook or minimize the many problems which will inevitably arise in making the adjustment to the new technology—problems for individual workers and individual companies, problems for entire communities and regions, problems for the economy as a whole.
>
> What should be done to help the worker who will be displaced from his job, or the worker who will find that his highly specialized skill has been taken over by a machine? What about the businessman who lacks sufficient capital to automate his plant, yet has to face the competition of firms whose resources enable them to build whole new automated factories? Will automation mean the creation of whole new communities in some areas, while others are turned into ghost towns? How can we increase the market for goods and services sufficiently, and quickly enough, to match greatly accelerated increases in productivity?
>
> Finding the answers to these questions, and many others like them, will not be an easy process, and certainly not an automatic one. . . .

Asserting that automation represents the Second Industrial Revolution, Reuther told Congress: "When the First Industrial Revolution took place, no effort was made to curb or control greedy, ruthless employers. Businessmen took advantage of unemployment to force workers to labor twelve and fourteen hours a day for a pittance so small that not only wives, but children scarcely out of infancy, had to enter the factories to contribute their mite to the family earnings. The benefits which we today can so readily recognize as the fruits of the First Industrial Revolution were achieved only after decades of privation, misery, and ruthless exploitation for millions of working people." Pleading for use of intelligent foresight to prevent a recurrence, he outlined potential human hardships:

> . . . Obviously, there will be problems for the workers who are displaced from their jobs by automation. This is not merely a problem of finding a new job. One point on which most of the writers on automation seem agreed is that, by its very nature, automation will tend to eliminate unskilled and semi-skilled jobs, while the new jobs it creates will be at a much higher level of skill. As one spokesman for the Ford Motor Company has put it: "The hand trucker of today replaced by a conveyor belt might become tomorrow's electronics engineer."
>
> That sounds very nice, but it immediately poses the problem: *How* does the hand trucker become an electronics engineer— or a skilled technician? If automation destroys unskilled jobs and creates skilled jobs, means must be found to train large numbers of unskilled workers in the needed skills.
>
> Another aspect of the same problem is that of the worker with a specialized skill who finds that his skill has been made valueless because of a machine that has taken over his job— such as the skilled machine operator displaced by a self-operating lathe. . . .

Reuther said programs for retraining such workers must also provide for replacement of lost wages during the training period because "they have to live and support their families" while acquiring new skills. Then he spoke of "older workers, not old enough for normal retirement, but too old to learn new skills or to adjust to the demands of the new technology." Early retirement could help, he said, adding, "I would strongly urge this Committee to con-

sider . . . the need for earlier Social Security payments to workers
who are forced into retirement before the age of 65 because technological changes have taken their jobs from them and their age
makes it impossible for them to find other work." He also spoke of
providing a mechanism for permitting young people of limited
means to delay their entry into the labor market while they acquired the education and training necessary to cope with the age
of automation. And he had a word on behalf of free enterprise
practitioners: "Automation may bring with it the danger that big
firms will grow even bigger, while small and medium-sized competitors are squeezed to the wall. The danger must be minimized
by government policies and actions to assist small business and
prevent trends toward monopoly."

Some years after his testimony, Reuther remarked, "You can
make automobiles, refrigerators, and TV sets by automation, but
you make consumers in the same old-fashioned way." He did not
realize that even the latter soon might change.

Education always had been a Reuther concern, perhaps because
of his own youthful struggle to learn while earning. Addressing
himself to the subject in 1956, he envisioned legislation that, within
a decade, was largely adopted:

> . . . I propose a five-year federal aid-to-education program in
> which the federal government would make available a sum equal
> to from 1½ to 2 percent of our gross national product. I pro-
> pose further that that amount of money would be used first to
> launch a comprehensive school construction program, to over-
> come at the earliest possible date the shortage of classrooms,
> to retire antiquated firetraps from use, and to take our children
> off swing shifts.
>
> Secondly, we ought to provide substantial salary increases for
> schoolteachers, to give them a salary commensurate with the
> training they have and the responsibilities they carry.
>
> It seems to me that the teachers of America ought to be just
> about fed up with being second-class economic citizens. . . .
>
> Thirdly, I believe we need a federal scholarship program on
> a competitive basis, so that we will not continue to lose almost

60 percent of our top high school students, who cannot go to college. This is a tremendous waste of human resources. The only way we can stop it is by a federal program of scholarships. I propose that if a young person is willing to sign up in one of these federal scholarship programs, that, after graduation, they would have the choice of enlisting in the teaching profession— or in some other fields where they are needed—for a period of one year longer than and in lieu of their military service. . . .

Finally, we need to do more about the gifted child. We do more for the child who doesn't make the grade, and we do less for the gifted child. . . . How many of these children do we have in America whose genius never had a chance to bloom? No one can know, but there must be many. How many Jonas Salks did we lose? How many Thomas Edisons? How many other people who have this special gift of genius? We never shall know.

Reuther estimated the annual cost of carrying out his ideas at between $6 billion and $8 billion a year. He commented, "It represents one week of the cost to the American taxpayers of World War II."

A theme common to many of the UAW chief's proposals was central planning. He told one union audience: "America must come to the sober realization that in the complex twentieth-century technological society it is dangerous and unrealistic to believe that the blind forces of the marketplace somehow are going to make everything come out just right, so that we can achieve full employment. . . . We in the labor movement must point out that America must free itself from the paralysis and prejudice which would have us believe that rational democratic planning is somehow subversive and un-American. . . . Every other democratic country in the world has some kind of a national planning agency whereby they look at the total needs of a society, and come up with a rational and responsible program that relates to the allocation of resources in meeting the national goals of that society."

Reuther expounded and expanded on such ideas at length. It is said he was brought a draft memo of six pages and, after declaring,

"It's too long," took a pencil to the document and transformed it into thirteen pages. Following a Mike Wallace television interview which he dominated, and after cornering his interrogator for an hour-long post-broadcast discussion, Reuther is reported to have remarked: "There was just one thing wrong with the program. The questions were too long."

At Auto Workers' conventions, labor reporters would set up a betting pool, each trying to predict the length of Reuther's principal address. Aware of this, the union president told one convention crowd:

"Now I have taken a lot of abuse and ribbing and a lot of good fun over the years about the length of my speeches and I want to tell some of the newer delegates, who are perhaps unfamiliar with my bad habits, that I am capable of making a short speech. But I find it so painful I do it only in extreme emergencies. I do not consider today such an emergency. So relax."

CHAPTER TWENTY-THREE

Road to Merger

WITHIN SIX MONTHS AFTER HIS 1946 VICTORY OVER R. J. THOMAS in the auto union, Walter Reuther felt it necessary to squelch rumors that he would challenge the revered Philip Murray for leadership of the CIO. Reuther angrily accused the Communists of spreading such talk in hopes of driving a wedge between him and Murray, then declared: "I wish to state emphatically and categorically that I would not run for the presidency of the CIO under any circumstances."

At that time, of course, Reuther was far too busy trying to consolidate his position in the UAW and purge his Communist-backed opponents to think about a CIO contest. Even had he been willing to run, his chances of defeating Murray would have been almost nil. The Scottish-born miner was looked upon with universal respect by others within the CIO, partly because of his pioneering role in the organization and partly because of his personal qualities.

"Murray had an extremely sweet disposition," said Thomas Harris, a lawyer who once worked at CIO headquarters. "Murray knew everybody in the building, knew them by their first names, knew their families, spent a lot of time on their purely personal matters. He was a kindly father figure."

The leader of the Congress of Industrial Organizations had another great strength. He commanded the unquestioned loyalty of the United Steelworkers of America, the largest and perhaps the most solvent union in the CIO, representing nearly one-fourth of its total membership. In addition, Murray was an older man, in his sixties, while Reuther then looked younger than his 39 years.

Nevertheless, Reuther's name remained high on the list of possible successors to Murray and even AFL president William Green paid the UAW leader a compliment early in 1948, saying: "If anyone can bring about a merger, Reuther is the man. We can get along with him better than anybody else in the CIO."

Reuther's strong anti-Communism undoubtedly appealed to

Green and other AFL officials who questioned the CIO's acceptance of far-left elements. Reuther had privately prodded Phil Murray to take decisive action against Communist-lining unions in the CIO. Receiving similar pressure from his own Steelworkers' advisors, Murray eventually agreed and the purge was completed in 1949–1950.

A series of developments in November 1952 opened the way for Reuther to lead the CIO and merge it with the AFL. The first was the victory of Dwight D. Eisenhower over Adlai E. Stevenson in the presidential election contest—a blow to the political hopes of organized labor that increased pressure for unity. Then, within a week, Murray died unexpectedly at the age of 66. His AFL counterpart, 82-year-old Bill Green, died twelve days later, opening the path for a new generation of labor leadership.

Almost immediately the CIO split into two hostile camps over the selection of a successor president. Out of respect for Murray's memory, a previously scheduled CIO convention was delayed for nearly two weeks, but political maneuvering began even before the funeral in Pittsburgh.

The contestants were Reuther, 45 by this time, well in control of his own union, a natural candidate for the position, and Allan S. Haywood, the 64-year-old executive vice-president of the CIO who had powerful backing from the Steelworkers and benefited from close identification with the Murray regime.

Haywood, an English-born coal miner, was a sentimental favorite. He was a likeable, gregarious trade unionist with many friends, particularly in the smaller CIO unions that looked to the CIO for guidance and financial aid. In fact, Michael Quill, the voluble Irishman who headed the Transport Workers Union, formed a "Small Businessman's Federation" to advance Haywood's candidacy.

Reuther was not idle. Shortly after Murray's death Reuther received the backing of the UAW Executive Board for the CIO presidency and virtually declared his candidacy to other CIO leaders who urged him to seek the post. Since Reuther had proposed Haywood for the executive vice-president's post, he hoped to have Haywood's backing in the presidential drive.

Arriving in Pittsburgh, Reuther met with fellow members of the CIO Executive Board to enlist their support. According to one account, he visited the hotel room of Joseph A. Beirne, head of the telephone workers' union, who had let it be known he might back Reuther if the teetotaling UAW president would unbend and take a drink once in a while. Reuther's first words to Beirne were, "Joe, I'm looking for a drink." He had two, then left.

David J. McDonald, who entered the labor movement by serving as a secretary to John L. Lewis in the turbulent 1930's, led the opposition to Reuther. The vain, silver-haired McDonald had just been elevated from secretary-treasurer to president of the Steelworkers on the death of Murray and was bitterly antagonistic toward his UAW rival. Years later, Reuther recalled the 1952 battle: "McDonald used Haywood to try to put a caretaker in charge of the CIO on the basis that at the next convention he [McDonald] would take over."

Reuther partisans argued that their man was young, vigorous, and far better qualified to be the chief public spokesman for the CIO than the rough-hewn Haywood. "Allan had such a thick Yorkshire accent it was very hard to understand him," said one CIO official.

Haywood's backers stressed his loyalty and dedication to the CIO, arguing that his full-time service at headquarters would be more valuable to the labor organization than Reuther's part-time commitment to the CIO on top of his Detroit duties as president of the Auto Workers.

Reuther's personality also became an issue. One of his supporters summed up the criticism: "He has a lot of features that put people off. He's single-minded, he's doctrinaire, he has very little capacity for small talk. Many people thought he was too pushy, overambitious. It reduced itself very largely to personalities. At that time in the CIO there were really no basic differences about issues . . . once the Communists had left."

So the lines were drawn tight when nearly 600 delegates arrived at the Atlantic City convention hall on a cold December day to decide the first contest for the presidency in the seventeen-year history of the CIO. In the bars and cocktail lounges, where Reuther might have seemed out of place, his UAW lieutenants buttonholed uncommitted delegates. Livingston, Pat Greathouse, and one of Walter's old adversaries, Dick Leonard, led this phase of the campaign.

A ruse helped swing the votes of the Oil Workers into line for Reuther. Livingston, aware that Oil Workers' president O. A. (Jack) Knight was solidly committed to Reuther but unsure of the rest of the delegation, asked the union's secretary-treasurer, Tom McCormick, about the split in the Oil Workers' ranks. McCormick pledged his word that there would be no split. When Knight refused to switch to Haywood, the small union came over to Reuther as a bloc. Livingston also arranged for a bombardment of pro-Reuther telegrams to United Rubber Workers delegates, which helped bring them into camp.

Other Reuther emissaries, such as Arthur J. Goldberg, worked on a higher level with the heads of undecided CIO unions. Goldberg was general counsel for the Steelworkers and the CIO at the time and commanded wide respect. He felt independent enough to split openly with the Steelworkers Executive Board, solidly behind Haywood, to work in Walter's behalf.

Gradually, Reuther attracted key votes. The Amalgamated Clothing Workers, the Textile Workers Union of America, and the Rubber Workers swung behind him. Caucusing went on incessantly, however, in the effort to shift votes or retain those already pledged. This produced one of the more ribald and enduring labor jokes:

> *Q. What is the difference between a caucus and a cactus?*
> A. A cactus has the pricks on the outside.

On the day of the vote the CIO Executive Board assembled for lunch with the signs pointing to a Reuther victory that afternoon. Dave McDonald, in a good-humored mood, made light of the rugged contest for the top office, telling Reuther, "At least we have come to like each other better." Bristling, Reuther brushed aside McDonald's overture, replying, "I would say that we have come to *know* each other better, Dave." That single remark, according to some observers, cost Reuther the traditional unanimous vote for convention winners.

In the cavernous convention hall the atmosphere was tense on the afternoon of December 4, 1952, as the CIO delegates met to choose their new leader. Jack Knight of the Oil Workers placed Reuther's name in nomination as "a fighting unionist, a great American, a man who believes in social progress, and a really swell fellow." Leading the opposition, McDonald made an extremely brief speech on behalf of his candidate—"Mister CIO himself, the strong, vigorous dynamo of leadership, Allan S. Haywood."

Emil Rieve, presiding over the election, asked the delegates to refrain from floor demonstrations in respect for the beloved Murray, an admonition that seemed more applicable to Haywood's emotional followers. Many Reuther backers were voting more with their heads that their hearts.

As the showdown neared, the CIO hierarchy discovered it had another problem—the taking of the roll call vote. Theoretically, each union was allocated votes on the basis of its paid-up membership. If the Steelworkers paid dues to the CIO on behalf of one million members, for example, the union was entitled to cast a million votes. The trouble was that many unions had been announcing inflated membership figures and the CIO itself claimed to represent far more than the 4,500,000 paid-up members it actually had. Acting in concert, the Haywood and Reuther forces agreed to increase the voting strength of all affiliates to reflect a total CIO membership claim of 5,700,000. This also helped to preserve the CIO's case for representation, along with the rival AFL, in federal government boards and world labor organizations.

Once the roll was called, the voting pattern became clear. Reuther had support from the bigger unions—except for McDonald's Steelworkers—and Haywood picked up nearly all of the smaller organizations. On the basis of membership-strength balloting, Reuther won by 3,078,181 to Haywood's 2,613,103—a close but decisive victory. Of the individual delegates, 373 were for Haywood and 180 backed Reuther but many of those in Haywood's corner were "one-lungers" who represented city bodies or small locals and added only a single vote to their candidate's total.

Haywood accepted his defeat with grace, declaring from the podium: "May I be the first to say, President Walter . . . We are going on from here." Then, as tears streamed from many faces, Haywood led the convention in a rousing labor song:

> *If the boss gets in the way,*
> *We're going to roll it over him . . .*
> *We will roll our union on!*

CIO secretary James B. Carey also tried to smooth over the deep split at the convention by introducing a gag resolution urging Reuther to smoke a cigar for every union that supported him and drink a glass of beer for each of the 3 million votes he received. "This resolution is adopted without the formality of a vote," ruled chairman Rieve. Reuther told the delegates, "I am compelled as a matter of physical necessity to say that the last resolution you adopted is beyond my capabilities."

Before presenting Walter to the convention for an inaugural address, Rieve publicly gave a Dutch-uncle lecture to the winner about the need to avoid one-man rule of the CIO. "I am not unmindful of the fact that he is a very capable young man," Rieve stated from the platform, "and I hope that he also possesses the humility and understanding and all of the other qualities that are needed for the leadership of our great institution. I am not going to say more. I have known Walter for many years and so have you." Considering an accolade he had given Haywood a few moments earlier, Rieve's remarks about Reuther were remarkably devoid of affection or sentiment.

In accepting his new office, Walter displayed the long-distance oratory that had become his trademark in the labor movement, speaking for nearly two hours. "I stand before you humble in the face of the tremendous responsibilities which you have placed in my care," he began. "No man can take Phil Murray's place." Reuther's main theme was a plea for CIO unity coupled with attacks on prosperous employers: "Our enemies have been watching the proceedings of this convention from the cocktail bars of the Union League clubs and millionaires' clubs all over America. Reading the stories in the press of the division in the CIO has filled their hearts with hope, filled their minds with designs to take us on if we are divided, drive us back and rob us of our hard-won social and economic gains. I say . . . that the fat men on the plush cushions are wrong. We are going to go out of here united to carry on this struggle until we win."

In a less flamboyant manner, in Washington, George Meany was elevated to the presidency of the American Federation of Labor by a vote of its Executive Board. For a dozen years Meany had been the strong Number Two man behind the aging Bill Green. Blunt, forceful, and eager for labor unity, the 58-year-old Meany carefully appraised the divisions within the CIO and Reuther's narrow victory.

Reunification of the AFL and CIO had been talked about almost since the split took place in 1935 but little had been done to bring it about. Green had contented himself with telling the CIO to "Come back to the House of Labor," as if the breakaway group were a prodigal son, and the CIO refused that invitation.

Meany and Reuther, however, were not bound by the rhetoric of the past and they both decided to make another try at merger. Five years earlier, after John L. Lewis left the AFL and the CIO had moved to expel Communist-led unions, Reuther had been encouraged about the prospects of reconciliation. "Now that the AFL has lost its 'eyebrows' and the CIO has taken a step against Communists, the possibility of unity is there," Reuther had told a board meeting of Americans for Democratic Action in the spring of 1948.

Within 48 hours of his election, Reuther met Meany at a dinner given by the International Confederation of Free Trade Unions and each pledged to work toward merger. Reuther was sidelined temporarily in December while his gall bladder was removed but he and Meany met early in 1953, over a lunch of grapefruit and sandwiches, in Reuther's suite at the Statler Hotel in Washington. They agreed to revive a moribund Joint AFL-CIO Unity Committee as a first step.

While these negotiations were continuing, Reuther also had to establish himself as president of the badly split CIO and take up Murray's mantle. He remained on the UAW payroll at $11,250 a year, refusing any additional compensation from the CIO, and quickly demonstrated that he would be a stickler on financial matters. A CIO attorney recalls having lunch with Reuther and two others, including the UAW president's bodyguard, at a Washington hotel early in 1953. Murray, who was paid $40,000 a year as head of the Steelworkers, traditionally picked up the tab on such occasions but Reuther had a different practice. "To my astonishment," said the attorney, "when the lunch was over and Walter got the check, he got out his pencil and started figuring out what each man owed—not even a quarter of it, but exactly what each man had eaten and what his fair proportion of the tip would be and so forth. Including the bodyguard."

In an effort to mend fences with unions that had opposed him at the convention, Reuther traveled widely to CIO union meetings. At the Woodworkers' convention in Vancouver, for example, he accepted a commission as commodore in the union's "navy"—vessels employed to reach remote logging camps—and was photographed in a snappy nautical outfit.

At CIO headquarters Reuther was equally serious about ordering a front panel for the receptionist's desk to shield the comely girl's legs from the stares of male visitors. Relating one of his rare off-color stories, he said the episode reminded him of a sermon in which evangelist Billy Sunday began by saying, "Ladies of the congregation, please cross your legs." There was a rustling movement and the preacher continued: "Now that the gateways to hell have been closed—."

Reuther flew often between his base in Detroit and his CIO office on Jackson Place, across from Dwight D. Eisenhower's White House. He was so busy, however, that many CIO staff members rarely saw him. CIO news editor Henry C. Fleisher once flew with Reuther to Detroit, just to have an airborne conference. Fleisher returned to Washington on the next plane going back to the capital.

Reuther risked some of his new eminence to attack Senator Joseph R. McCarthy, the Wisconsin Republican then riding a crest of national popularity for headline-grabbing investigations of alleged Communists in government. Traveling in Europe on business in the summer of 1953, Reuther said: "McCarthy employs immoral methods and plays Communism's game . . . [He] has done more to reinforce Communism than any other American."

Dual responsibility, to the United Auto Workers and the CIO, almost required a dual personality, as one labor official analyzed the situation: "Running a big union is a very different job than running a federation. Unions have to be run, really, with a pretty firm hand. The president of it has to be the unquestioned Number One man. . . . But this type of experience is not so ideal when you move in and try to run a federation . . . of autonomous unions." A former CIO staff man once remarked: "Within the UAW he's the boss but he didn't recognize that on a federation level there are equals. A president of a small union that may be no bigger than one of his UAW locals is a damned important guy within a federation."

In the fall of 1953 Walter summoned Victor Reuther home from a job as CIO representative in Europe to help run the CIO's Washington office. Others, including Robert Oliver and Paul Sifton, also acted as Reuther's Washington spokesmen on CIO matters in that period. "You never know who his lieutenant is," became a typical complaint at CIO headquarters. The CIO under Reuther's direction was an "administrative shambles," said one veteran of that era. Reuther's non-stop working habits and demands on the staff were a jolt to many who had worked under the more relaxed Murray administration.

Reuther's major problem, however, was political—the reluctance of David McDonald and the Steelworkers to give him their cooperation. Moreover, McDonald was threatening to bolt the CIO and form a new labor group with John L. Lewis of the Mine Workers and Dave Beck of the Teamsters. Reuther recalled: "McDonald was much disappointed, very uncooperative and troublesome. He did have a meeting with Lewis and Beck. They were discussing things but Dave McDonald could not have done anything about it because of his membership." Rank and file Steelworkers favored the alliance with the CIO.

The CIO was so torn that Meany's efforts to reach a merger agreement were viewed skeptically by A. H. (Abe) Raskin, then the labor reporter for *The New York Times.* "Why bother?" Raskin asked Meany. "Why not wait and pick up the pieces?" Meany replied that it would be better for the labor movement to have a merger of equals than a settlement imposed on the weaker side.

McDonald's restiveness clearly contributed to Reuther's desire to speed merger talks with Meany's AFL. Progress was rapid on a no-raiding agreement that reduced the competition for bargaining rights where an AFL or CIO union already was recognized and had negotiated a contract. A subcommittee chaired by Reuther and Meany had reported that interunion raiding was largely a waste of time, money, and effort. Their study showed that in 1,246 bargaining-rights elections in two years, the net shift of members from one federation to another was about 7,000. The no-raid agreement was announced June 2, 1953, and a year later a dinner was held to celebrate acceptance of the pact by 65 of 110 AFL unions and 29 of 32 CIO unions. The Steelworkers balked, however, and continued to talk about withdrawal until McDonald issued a surprising call for immediate unity at his union's convention in September 1954.

Because of his own sense of rectitude, Reuther repeatedly insisted on the ouster of "known racketeers" from the AFL, along with other demands, before he would agree to consolidation. An irritated Meany dispatched a stern letter to Reuther arguing that continued talk about corruption constituted "sniping" that might jeopardize the prospective merger.

Arthur Goldberg, the ubiquitous labor lawyer, decided to put a merger plan on paper for presentation to Meany and his colleagues at the next meeting of the AFL Executive Council in Miami Beach in February 1955.

The AFL had been meeting under the Florida sun each winter

for decades, but the glitter and luxury of Miami Beach were alien to Reuther's values. The CIO chieftain attended anyway but rejected all forms of conspicuous consumption. Jim Carey tells how Reuther scorned a large suite in the Monte Carlo hotel and allowed Carey to use it instead. When newspapermen came looking for Reuther, the impish Carey told them: "He's down the hall in the linen closet squeezing orange juice." Actually, Reuther and his bodyguard occupied a single room, barely large enough for two beds.

The contrasting styles of Reuther and Meany were dramatized at one of the preliminary meetings on the merger. Reuther made a lengthy statement of principles to the somewhat bored labor audience. Then Meany, brusque as ever, used four sentences to sum up the problem: "We can go after unity the long way or the short way. The short way is to merge into one trade union center which will protect the integrity of all affiliates. The long way is to solve all of our problems before merging. Which will it be?"

Merger was assured when Meany accepted Goldberg's plan "hook, line, and sinker," as one participant phrased it. In view of its larger membership, the AFL had always felt certain of getting the top office in the new federation but many had expected the Number Two job to go to a CIO man, probably Reuther. Goldberg's CIO proposal provided, however, that both the president and secretary-treasurer, the top assignments, would be filled by the AFL. The CIO would select only the director of organization.

Meany believed Reuther did not want to give up the presidency of the Auto Workers and approved of the Goldberg plan because he would not permit any other CIO man to outrank him in the new federation. Reuther later referred to the concession on the second-place job as proof that the CIO was not interested in patronage but rather in organizing the millions of non-union workers in the country.

Jack Livingston, Reuther's old UAW colleague, was named organizing director of the AFL-CIO at a salary higher than that of the Auto Workers' president. Nominally, Reuther became simply one of 27 vice-presidents, although clearly he was first among equals in that category. At that time, in the spring of 1955, he was far more widely known than Meany.

The merger agreement also provided for a "little CIO" in the form of an Industrial Union Department of the combined labor movement, with Reuther as its principal officer. At first, only old CIO unions were expected to join, but applications were submitted by several AFL unions—including the Teamsters, who apparently planned to grab control of the Department if they could. Meany put a stop to any takeover bid by acting as a one-man credentials committee for the IUD's founding convention. He limited each union's affiliation and representation to its industrial-type membership—a level far below the total strength of most AFL organizations. Even so, enrollments gave the Department a membership of more than 7 million—including a relatively small number of Teamsters—and annual dues income of $1.7 million. The Teamsters, along with the building trades unions, were fearful Reuther would use the Department as a power base to promote his pet causes.

When merger became final in December 1955, Meany and Reuther joined hands to swing a giant gavel opening the founding AFL-CIO convention. Pledging $1.5 million to aid an organizing drive, Reuther set a goal of doubling the membership, to 30 million, in the next decade.

His three-year tenure as president of the CIO had been, in many ways, a disappointment to Reuther. He never received the esteem accorded his predecessor by CIO colleagues, and he was plagued by McDonald's hostility as well. One labor scholar held that the very growth of industrial unionism had diminished the importance of the office. "When the national unions began to stand on their own," wrote Jack Barbash, "the tutelage of the CIO diminished. Walter Reuther's accession . . . marked the end of the period of CIO protectorship."

With the formation of the AFL-CIO, Reuther had every reason to expect that he would be in line to succeed George Meany, after a reasonable interval, and thus enhance his influence within the labor movement and in the conduct of national affairs.

CHAPTER TWENTY-FOUR

The Annual Wage

IN THE EARLIEST DAYS OF AUTO UNIONISM IN DETROIT, A CHIEF complaint was the long layoffs each year during model changeovers. While hourly wages were fairly high, the yearly income of auto workers was relatively low. And fear of layoffs—or of not being rehired when production resumed—was shared by each individual employed in the factories.

President Roosevelt showed his concern for this problem in a campaign speech in Detroit in October 1936 that Walter Reuther could have used as a text two decades later. Speaking of auto workers who had brought their grievances to the White House in 1934, F.D.R. reported: "One of them, a former Marine who had served through battle after battle in France, told me he was a machinist and that his pay was $1.25 an hour or $10 a day. I told him I thought that was a pretty good wage scale, and his reply was this: 'Yes, Mr. President, it is a good hourly rate and a good daily rate but last year I worked only 68 days.' In other words, the total income of himself, his wife, and his children was $680 for a year. On this yearly pay total he had lost the home on which he had paid down hundreds of dollars." Roosevelt offered a solution: "I stressed the need of spreading the work more evenly through the year. . . . It is my belief that the manufacturers of automobiles . . . must, by planning, do far more than they have done to date to increase the yearly earnings of those who work for them."

That was advanced thinking in 1936, even as campaign oratory. In that mid-depression year the United Auto Workers Union was in its infancy, struggling for recognition, and, as Walter Reuther later put it, the annual wage was only a "vague dream." He and others first had to build a strong union, end factional in-fighting, raise wages, win pensions, and achieve stability in labor-management relations before a guaranteed wage could become a serious demand.

As early as 1945, however, Reuther had banged the drums for

his visionary annual wage in an article written for *The New York Times Magazine*. Addressing himself to management opposition, the UAW leader wrote: "To businessmen who have been known to boast of their ability to meet payrolls and who, in times of strikes and picket lines, are extremely vocal about the 'right to work,' the annual wage proposal says, in effect: '. . . if private enterprise wants to stay private, it has to stay enterprising. If you won't accept a continuing commitment to employ, the government will have to move in.' "

Once the five-year contract with General Motors was signed in 1950, Reuther turned the UAW's growing resources to the task of fighting what undoubtedly became the bargaining battle of his lifetime.

"By 1951, the UAW was at last ready to begin its all-out drive for the guaranteed wage," wrote Nat Weinberg, one of the leading members of the union's "braintrust" that developed strategy for the years-long campaign. With typical thoroughness, Reuther first created a UAW study committee to go through the voluminous American and European literature on job security. The auto industry's historic hiring and layoff patterns, as well as state laws on unemployment insurance, also were scrutinized by the experts at Solidarity House, the new and modernistic Auto Workers' headquarters along the Detroit River. At the same time, according to Weinberg's account, the union began a campaign of "psychological warfare" through speeches, articles, radio-television appearances, and participation in debates before an impressive variety of audiences.

General Motors, Ford, and Chrysler inadvertently assisted the UAW cause, Weinberg wrote, by hiring tens of thousands of workers in the spring of 1953 and then discharging them a year later when the economy slowed. "This irresponsibility of the industry was the main target of the union's guaranteed wage drive," asserted Reuther's top economist. "The main purpose was not to get pay for idleness but to compel the industry, by imposing penalties for instability, to schedule steady employment for its workers, week by week throughout the year."

One of Reuther's forums was the *Annals* of the American Academy of Political and Social Science, in which he wrote early in 1951 that wage guarantees were the union's next objective. "It is more than a matter of economic justice to the wage earner," he asserted. "It is a matter of economic necessity to our nation, for freedom and unemployment cannot live together in democracy's house." Typically, he also made a simpler argument that any factory hand could grasp: "Corporation executives get paid by the year—why not a worker?"

Weinberg said the central idea of the demand ultimately embraced by the UAW—to link private layoff benefits with federally sponsored unemployment compensation—first was suggested by Murray Latimer in a study for the Office of War Mobilization during World War II. The union study committee, however, quickly ran into a potential snag. "Practically everybody in the country believed that the unemployment insurance laws would have to be amended to permit integration of private benefits and public benefits," Weinberg recounted. Many UAW officials felt that most states would reduce their payments by the amount of any benefits obtained from industry. If that happened, there would be no point in negotiating a guaranteed wage since the worker would not have improved his position and the company would be, in effect, wasting money that might have been used for other bargaining goals.

Leonard Lesser, director of the Auto Workers' Social Security Department, almost alone felt that state laws would permit the combination of payments the union was seeking, and he convinced Weinberg, who recalls: "I think we were able to persuade Walter fairly early in the game that it could be done but I remember going before our Board and being greeted with one helluva lot of skepticism."

By the time of the 1953 UAW convention, the study committee came up with a plan that was accepted, in principle, by the delegates. Then, in a move that recalled the appointment of a citizens' committee in the 1945-1946 General Motors strike, the union created a public advisory committee of leading economists to evaluate the UAW proposal and its probable impact on the public welfare. Harvard economists Alvin Hansen and Seymour Harris were two of the academicians who served on the panel, which led the UAW to revise some features of its plan in response to their criticism. Weinberg said the naming of the advisory group also helped convince the auto companies and the public that the union was serious about its demand. "The struggle for public opinion was important," he wrote later. "Public support for the union could help if a showdown battle with the corporations became necessary . . . [and] might make the government hesitate to intervene on the side of the companies."

Walter Reuther also prepared his troops—the Auto Workers' membership—for the coming fight. The guaranteed wage was placed on the agenda for local union meetings, regional and national conferences, summer schools, weekend institutes, and night classes. Rank-and-filers even helped to shape the plan, because, Weinberg said, they "raised many problems that had never been thought of by the many economists who studied the subject."

The UAW also was sending messages—albeit indirectly—to the major auto companies after the Big Three had rejected a proposal for joint study committees to discuss the overall problem of easing layoff hardships. This was "collective bargaining at long range," in Weinberg's lexicon, and he added: "We were feeding stuff out so management could be aware of our thinking and begin to develop their own thinking. Ford worked very seriously at it. They hired outside consultants and had one of their top financial people work on it. . . . Ford had made it crystal clear that there was going to be something in response to our demand."

At General Motors the reaction was entirely negative. GM board chairman Frederic Donner apparently was persuaded that yielding to the UAW on the issue might weaken and perhaps destroy the corporation. Under his direction, the GM negotiators prepared a 100-page reply to the wage guarantee plan that added up to a loud and clear "No!" Bargaining strategists for GM instead put forward an unusually rich ten-part offer. "It was a helluva package," said GM negotiator Louis G. Seaton. One provision would have subsidized factory workers' purchases of corporation stock but Reuther scorned the idea: "Hell, that's for the provident. I'm interested in the folks who can't take care of themselves." The GM plan was ridiculed by the union as a "wheel of fortune."

In giving broad approval to the guaranteed wage goal, the 1955 UAW convention had committed the union's full resources to the Reuther campaign. A strike fund of $25 million was in process of creation by virtue of a temporary increase in each member's dues from $2.50 to $7.50 a month until the objective was reached. George Meany, soon to become president of the AFL-CIO, endorsed the bargaining target in a speech to the UAW delegates. Armed with these evidences of support, the Auto Workers' negotiating team went into bargaining. GM's contract expired on May 29 that year and the Ford agreement ran out two days later, as arranged by the UAW five years before. "It had been decided to place the expiration dates of the contracts with these two giants close together so that the union could play one off against the other," Weinberg related.

General Motors clearly was determined to fight it out with the UAW to block any form of guaranteed wage and, secretly, was preparing a massive public relations campaign against the proposal, to be launched in the event of a strike. Ford's spokesmen also expressed dislike for the idea but seemed willing to consider the practical problems involved rather than take an ideological stand.

Even within the UAW high command, however, there was not unanimity on the bargaining goal. Vice-President Jack Livingston, head of the General Motors Department, was one who, by his own account, "was not enthusiastic." GM took heart when, at one negotiating session, Livingston pushed away from the table and asserted: "This is not my issue. This is Walter Reuther's issue."

Reuther decided to zero in on Ford as the target company, extending the GM contract for a week so the agreement at Ford's would expire first. He readily consented when Ford's top negotiators asked for time to prepare a counteroffer to the UAW's guaranteed wage demand. Having taken this as a hopeful sign, the Auto Workers' president was in for a shock. Following the delay, UAW negotiators assembled at the Leland Hotel in downtown Detroit to hear John S. Bugas, the chief Ford spokesman, read the company's proposal. Reuther told what happened:

> We had every reason to believe that they were going to give us a proposal . . . which was essentially another approach to doing what we wanted to do. To our complete surprise, John Bugas read the General Motors "wheel of fortune." Every word! The only thing that was changed was the date, and the Ford Motor Company name appeared. I was aware of this after John had read one page, although the document was quite thick. I said, "John, please don't insult our integrity and your integrity . . . when you know and I know that this is the General Motors Corporation proposal, which we rejected two weeks ago—and you haven't changed a word of it. You have a perfect right to change your mind. We do not question your right to stooge for the General Motors company. But I'd like to suggest that it's very bad policy and it will get you nowhere. You guys have got rocks in your head."

Nat Weinberg, who was present, recalled that the dialogue grew far more heated on this occasion, which soon became known as "Black Thursday" in auto union circles. "There was a lot of invective," he said. "It was pretty sharp and at times pretty personal. Our guys reacted sharply and the Ford Motor Company reacted to our reaction."

Reuther bluntly told Bugas: "You have just bought yourself a strike." He recited how long walkouts had started the decline of the Willys-Overland Company and had wrecked Chrysler's chances of overtaking Ford as the second-largest auto producer. Then, referring to what he considered Ford's slavish adoption of the GM offer, Reuther asked a question for which there was no answer: "How will you produce Fords on the Chevrolet assembly line?" Weinberg related:

> The union was relying on competition between the two companies. Production of automobiles was at record-breaking levels. If General Motors continued to operate while Ford was shut by a strike, Ford would lose customers and untold millions of dollars in profits to its competitors. It would continue to feel the

effects of a strike for years to come because it would lose sales of replacement parts for the cars not produced as a result of the strike. Many of its customers would be lost permanently since automobile buyers tend to purchase new cars of the same make as their old ones.

Bugas, responding to Reuther's charge, insisted that Ford had made an in-depth survey of workers in its plants that showed the rank and file favored management's offer by a margin of nine to one. Therefore, said Bugas, it was silly for the UAW to call a strike to secure benefits the members did not want when the union could have wage improvements desired by the membership without a fight. Reuther told his associates, "We'll box these guys, real quick." Earlier he had invited Henry Ford II to address the UAW's Ford Council, summoned to Detroit to act in the bargaining crisis. Declining, Ford had suggested that all company workers should have a chance to indicate their views on the management's offer. Reuther later recounted how he used Ford's suggestion to spring a trap on John Bugas:

> I never really enjoyed doing this to John, because I never really felt he was playing in our league on this kind of tactical stuff. . . . That doesn't stop me from doing it. . . . I said to John: "Will you agree to have a referendum vote of Ford workers . . . on our proposal? If they vote for yours, we'll sign a contract containing your proposal. If they vote for ours, we'll sign a contract with that. Since you say they want yours by nine to one, you're not taking any chances." Poor John! I thought he'd die.

The glum Ford executives caucused at their Dearborn headquarters. When Bugas returned to the bargaining table, the Auto Workers won an important preliminary battle. Ford withdrew its carbon copy of the GM offer and agreed to negotiate a settlement along the lines of the union demand.

Reuther proposed a "news blackout," a tradition in auto bargaining that eliminated daily statements on developments in order to avoid jockeying for public relations advantages. Bugas, however, pleaded an exception. Ford had contracted for full-page advertisements in major newspapers for the following weekend to promote its now-abandoned offer. It was too late to withdraw them. The UAW agreed, although unable to avoid chuckling at management's high-cost advocacy of a proposal that already was a dead issue.

Ford then presented what it termed a "supplemental unemployment benefit" plan, or SUB. It paralleled the UAW demand except that it provided lower benefits and greater restrictions on eligibility.

Reuther, by adroit leadership and masterful command of the negotiations, had split the united front established by GM and Ford and had won the unprecedented principle of a guaranteed annual wage. True, the Ford proposal contained some "real horrors" from the union's standpoint. But under strike pressure, the SUB plan was improved sufficiently to win UAW acceptance. From Reuther's standpoint it was only the first step down a long road: "What we are doing is laying a foundation for the kind of security we think automobile workers and their families are entitled to."

The Ford contract provided more a semiannual than annual guaranteed wage. Under its provisions, the company put five cents an hour into a fund that would be used to provide up to $25 a week to laid-off workers for up to 26 weeks. With unemployment compensation included, and that was a key to the whole plan, this would guarantee that an eligible worker would receive 65 percent of his normal take-home pay for the first 4 weeks of layoff and 60 percent for the remaining 22 weeks.

Next stop was GM, where the negotiators were in the dark on details of the union's new contract with Ford until Reuther provided them with a copy. The UAW chief recreated the dialogue:

GM: We're against what you have done.

REUTHER: You're not telling me anything new. You not only said "no" here but you said "no" at the Ford table. I think it's pretty scandalous when General Motors is able to dictate the collective bargaining posture of its major competitor. . . .

GM: We know that the ballgame is changed. But we can give you trouble by taking that SUB nickel and putting it on the wages. Your membership doesn't understand yet what you're doing.

If we put another nickel on there, they just might run over the top of you.

REUTHER: Why don't you do it?

GM: We don't think we can get away with it.

REUTHER: I can't think of a better reason for not doing it.

Lou Seaton of GM recalls: "We had all our top side looking at this SUB plan. We had eight or nine variations on it but the union was set in cement on the thing." After five days of crash bargaining General Motors announced it would accept the Ford SUB program: "We'll take a Chinese copy, even to the patch on the pants." Puzzled by the term, Reuther warily inquired what a Chinese copy might be. He was told it referred to "the ship captain who went to a Chinese tailor and said he wanted an exact duplicate of a pair of pants he was wearing, and got it—including the patch on the pants."

General Motors, Reuther learned, knew that Ford had hired experts to check the details of the SUB plan and was hoping Ford's men had done a good job. GM's Harry Anderson was quoted as saying: "I would like to congratulate Mr. Reuther for having gone to Ford first, because we never would have agreed to this otherwise. . . . This is the first time the president of General Motors Corporation has ever signed a contract that he didn't understand."

Less than three years later the SUB plan proved of enormous value to members of the auto union. More than $13 million in layoff benefits was paid to 877,000 UAW men and women during the 1958 recession, when car sales nosedived and the national unemployment rate climbed above 7 percent. Reuther, however, kept bargaining on SUB plan improvements until, in 1967 negotiations, the program approached what he regarded as the optimum level. Under the 1967 agreement a typical worker was entitled to receive 95 percent of his take-home pay for a maximum of 52 weeks, less a $7.50 weekly deduction that took account of the fact that a laid-off worker no longer bore the expense of commuting to work and eating lunches away from home.

In the auto industry, those who look critically upon SUB payments refer to "rocking chair money." And, indeed, disputes have arisen in some plants over who is entitled to get laid off first and collect the benefits. By 1970 Reuther believed the guaranteed wage posed a philosophical problem, at least in his industry: "I can visualize an ideal society somewhere, down the road of history, where maybe people will be fighting for the opportunities to work. . . . But I believe that in the framework of the economic and social structure in which we are functioning, and will be functioning for some time, there has to be some reward for gainful employment. . . . Therefore, when you're fighting for a guaranteed wage, I think you reach a point where you have to weigh, philosophically, its impact upon the value system within which you're functioning." In other words, the union had gone about as far as it could go without destroying the incentive to work.

As a curtain raiser for the 1958 negotiations, Reuther jolted the auto industry with a proposal that manufacturers reduce wholesale prices by at least $100 a car to help combat inflationary trends. If the cuts were made, he promised, the union would take that into account in shaping its bargaining demands. "The time has come—in fact it is long overdue—for a dramatic and electrifying step to prove to all concerned that democracy is capable of mobilizing on a voluntary basis the resources of wisdom and responsibility in management and labor needed to solve its economic problems," he declared.

The Big Three gave the latest "Reuther Plan" a fast brush-off. For General Motors, Harlow H. Curtice labeled the proposal "another publicity maneuver designed to divert public attention from the inflationary implications of your announced 1958 bargaining objectives." Henry Ford II wrote Reuther the plan was "an empty one and sidesteps your primary responsibility for the cost-price spiral." The unkindest cut came from L. L. Colbert of Chrysler, who asked: "Would it not be just as logical for the automobile industry to ask members of the UAW to take an immediate and sizable wage cut, which the companies would then 'take into consideration' in pricing their 1958 automobiles?"

Under pressure from intra-union rivals, Reuther adopted a shorter workweek as the UAW's next major bargaining goal. However, rising unemployment and slumping car sales made it obvious that this demand would be far too costly to be achieved in 1958 without lengthy strikes. Adroitly, Reuther shifted the union's sights to profit sharing as the top objective when contracts expired during the summer.

The "auto depression" hit hard in Detroit. Newsdealers in Cadillac Square peddled lists of job opportunities in California and a standard barroom joke referred to "Michigan on the rocks" as the most popular drink. The UAW itself was caught in the squeeze because dues income had fallen sharply. Reuther, agonizing with other union officers, decided to lay off more than 100 members of the UAW staff to cut expenses. Perhaps he took some of his frustration out on the automobile designers, because he told the International Press Institute: "Every year the cars get longer, the fins get higher, and they put enough horsepower under the hoods to fly them. . . . A man ought to be able to park his car in the same block in which he lives." He concluded that Americans buy cars for status, not for transportation alone, and surmised that consumers would buy new refrigerators every year if they parked them in front of their homes.

The bargaining climate being poor from Reuther's standpoint, he wanted only to extend existing contracts for a few months until the economy revived. Industry negotiators did not oblige him, however, but insisted on a two-year extension of current agreements. They were convinced the union's position was too weak to force any better deal.

Each side refused to compromise and the contract expiration date arrived. The UAW scorned organized labor's traditional "no contract, no work" slogan and decided to forego a strike until conditions had improved. "We are going to rock and roll all summer," declared Leonard Woodcock, the UAW's chief negotiator with General Motors. In turn, GM halted the checkoff of union dues but continued to honor other provisions of the expired agreement. At the plant level, labor-management relations actually improved, with fewer wildcat strikes. A GM man reports that "one little tough guy came in the first morning we ran without a contract, saluted and said: 'Yes sir, boss. You ain't going to get nothing to fire me on.' "

Reuther blamed GM for persuading Ford and Chrysler to put pressure on the union by forcing UAW members to work without a contract. But, he argued later: "It was one of the best things that ever happened to this union. They thought we were so reliant upon this automatic checkoff of dues that we would panic and they could bring us to our knees by threatening us with loss of the checkoff. And we said, 'We'll do it the old-fashioned way.' And we collected 98 percent of the dues in that period." A strike at the time, with nearly one million new cars in inventory, would have been disastrous, Reuther believed, and he was forceful in explaining why:

> They would have crucified us if we had gotten into this ideo-
> logical rut . . . this sheer nonsense of the labor movement say-
> ing "no contract, no work." Nothing could be more asinine and
> unrealistic than that kind of a slogan. I mean you use your eco-
> nomic power based upon a rational and intelligent evaluation
> of where you are and what the facts are. . . . You don't have
> an emotional commitment that says that on a given date . . .
> three years from now, no matter what the shape of the world is,
> we've got a policy of "no contract, no work." Nothing could be
> more asinine than that.

Nearly four months after the UAW contracts had expired in 1958, as new models were starting to roll off Detroit's assembly lines, the Auto Workers signed new contracts with the Big Three. They were not nearly as rich as the 1955 pacts, but the union had survived the no-contract test handily, thanks to Reuther's flexibility.

In the 1961 bargaining, Reuther succeeded in winning a profit-sharing plan from American Motors—an auto industry "first," which signaled tacit union recognition that if a small producer could not prosper, its factory hands could not realistically aspire to ever-higher wages and fringe benefits. The agreement guaranteed that stockholders would get the first 10 percent of profits, with the next 15 percent allocated to a fund for the workers. One-third of the fund would be used to buy American Motors stock, to be held in trust for the employes, and the rest would finance pension, insurance, and supplementary unemployment benefits. Leonard Woodcock exulted at the settlement and remarked, "If we could get the profit-sharing formula from GM, it would be like getting the keys to Ft. Knox after somebody had shot the guards."

The 1961 GM negotiations produced an impasse over the amount of relief time to be granted assembly line workers for visits to the toilet and attention to other personal needs. It led to a large-scale walkout labeled the "toilet strike," symbolizing the union's responsiveness to widespread rank and file complaints that year about working conditions.

Because of Reuther's generalship as a bargainer, UAW negotiating teams came to rely increasingly upon him in the critical final hours of talks. During marathon sessions his reserves of energy were so great that he was fresher by far than men who were years his junior. One of Reuther's stay-alert tricks was to brush his teeth at odd hours during negotiating breaks. He carried his own toothbrush for this purpose. Meeting with GM, he once rejected management-provided coffee and insisted the union would pay. Lou Seaton, dismayed by Reuther's freedom from fatigue, claimed the UAW leader's secret was to take a long "caucus with a couch" during recesses. The tireless Reuther insisted good conditioning accounted for his verve. Seaton also complained that General Motors' statements, labored over for hours, would not get one-tenth the public notice given to an offhand remark by Reuther. "Walter, he's press," Seaton sighed. Reuther hardly ever stopped needling his management adversaries. On his 54th birthday, spent at the bargaining table, the union chief was presented a small cake by Seaton. Newspapermen chipped in to buy a larger one and Reuther accepted it with a quip: "Like the GM offer, Mr. Seaton's cake was inadequate." Emerging from a gloom-filled conference with management a few hours before a strike deadline, Reuther was amazed to see his union colleagues enjoying themselves at the card table. "How can you characters sit there and play poker and have a damned good time and we're six hours away from a possible strike?" he demanded. One unionist leaned back and replied, "We just know you'll figure out the answer." As was his usual custom, Reuther did.

CHAPTER TWENTY-FIVE

Reuther Embattled

WALTER REUTHER'S SUCCESSES AT THE BARGAINING TABLE DID nothing to quiet the political conservatives who had long made him a favorite whipping boy. Indeed, his accomplishments seemed to inflame their imaginations. Republican Congressman Clare Hoffman of Michigan, author of many attacks on the UAW president, outdid himself: "In the opinion of many, Walter Reuther, because of his shrewdness, his intellectual ability, his adroitness and the power he wields, is far more dangerous to the security of the Republic and the liberty of the individual citizen than is Russia or any possible federation of Communist nations." A more moderate Republican, Sherman Adams, caught the fever and declared: "Mr. Reuther has been quoted as having said that he hopes to be President—in fact to be the Socialist President of the United States."

As the 1956 presidential nominating conventions drew near, *Time* named Reuther as one of the "Democrats' decisive dozen." However, the magazine quoted him as qualifying his fealty to the Party: "Citizen Walter Reuther will not support the Democratic Party nationally if that Party attempts to be all things to all men on civil rights."

Adlai Stevenson again won the Democratic presidential nomination, with support from the Michigan delegation and Reuther's blessing. Then came a surprising Stevenson announcement. He would abandon the tradition of selecting a running mate and let the convention decide between Senators Estes Kefauver and John F. Kennedy. Reuther and other labor leaders at the Chicago gathering were not prepared for this development. "Nobody had ever talked to us about Kennedy as a possibility," recalls Jack Conway, Reuther's administrative assistant at the time. "Up to that point we hadn't even looked at him seriously." Conway believes Stevenson hoped the delegates would nominate Kennedy but the UAW lined up behind Kefauver, considered more friendly to unions. The wide-open race cut short an Auto Workers' cocktail party as labor men dashed down a few drinks and fanned out to convention hotels to lobby for their candidate. "We worked our asses off," said Conway. The contest was so tight that, quite probably, the labor push gave Kefauver his hairline winning margin. Reuther also played an important role in winning AFL-CIO backing for the Democratic ticket, mustering enough Executive Council votes to overcome George Meany's opposition to any endorsement.

At a pre-election Senate hearing Republican Carl T. Curtis of Nebraska told Reuther, "You are the man that makes or breaks presidential aspirants in the Democratic Party." The UAW chief replied, "You are flattering me and I don't like that." Inevitably the Reuther name kept figuring in the campaign. Vice-President Richard M. Nixon, in pep talks to GOP workers around the country, referred to Reuther—not Stevenson—as "the man to beat." Nixon argued that Reuther, the "smartest labor leader in America," had the "big money" and the organizers capable of forging Democratic victories.

A month after Eisenhower defeated Stevenson for the second time, the Senate's Permanent Subcommittee on Investigations began exploring charges that high officials of the Teamsters Union had been misusing membership dues on a shocking scale. Dave Beck, then president of the Teamsters, was the initial target, but the inquiry was broadened in January 1957 with the creation of a Select Committee on Improper Activities in the Labor or Management Field. Popularly known as the McClellan Committee, after its chairman, Senator John L. McClellan of Arkansas, the panel eventually turned its spotlight on Walter Reuther and the United Auto Workers.

From the outset, Reuther studiously avoided the reaction of many labor colleagues who looked upon the work of the Committee as a clever attempt to discredit and hobble all trade unions. As early as 1945 he had made his position clear: "I do not believe we can protect the good name of the union movement by attempting to cover up the facts concerning . . . bad practices. I think it is much better to acknowledge such undesirable practices publicly and to act affirmatively to correct them." He said then that "compulsory

public accounting of union revenues and expenditures might help."
Now, in 1957, he was even more outspoken:

> American labor had better roll up its sleeves, it had better
> get the stiffest broom and brush it can find, and the strongest
> disinfectant, and it had better take on the job of cleaning its
> own house from top to bottom and drive out every crook and
> gangster and racketeer we find. Because if we don't clean our
> own house, then the reactionaries will clean it for us. They
> won't use a broom, they'll use an ax, and they'll try to destroy
> the labor movement in the process. . . .
>
> I say to the McClellan Committee: we will give you full sup-
> port and cooperation. Go after the crooks in the labor move-
> ment, but go after the crooks in management's side of the
> problem. When you find a crooked labor leader who took a
> bribe from a crooked employer, put them both in jail for about
> fifteen years and give them plenty of time to talk it over between
> themselves.
>
> The UAW is not perfect but I can say without fear of chal-
> lenge that we are clean and we are democratic. . . .

As a follow-up, Reuther circulated to all locals a directive ordering the removal of any officer who invoked the Fifth Amendment
protection against self-incrimination unless he provided "clear and
sufficient evidence that he is beyond a doubt not disqualified. . . ."
Because the order, approved by the Executive Board, shifted the
burden of proving innocence to the accused, the American Civil
Liberties Union charged that the UAW had "retreated from its customary defense of civil liberties and joined in the process of de-
grading the constitutional guarantee against self-incrimination."

Reuther described himself as "shocked and saddened" by the
initial findings of the Senate Committee and lashed out at Beck and
the Teamsters' crown prince, James R. Hoffa. "Beck's future as a
labor leader is behind him," he stated. As for Hoffa, if bribe charges
against him were upheld, he should "go to jail." Reuther began
pressing for suspension, then expulsion of the Teamsters from the
AFL-CIO and Meany was a willing ally. The truck drivers' union

and two others spotlighted by the Committee were expelled from the federation in December 1957.

Stern-faced John McClellan chose young Robert F. Kennedy to be his chief counsel. The Committee membership was divided evenly between Democrats and Republicans. One of its investigators, Pierre Salinger, later wrote:

> The one attempt to pervert the Committee for political purposes did, in fact, come from Republican members. Senators Barry M. Goldwater, Karl E. Mundt and Carl T. Curtis saw the hearings as a chance to smear Walter P. Reuther, president of the United Auto Workers. They spread the story around Washington that Bob Kennedy was "afraid" to look into Reuther's affairs because it might cost his brother the UAW leader's support for President. But Bob had a devastating answer. The one political appointee among our investigators was Jack McGovern, a hell-bent-for-leather Republican who had been hired at the urging of Senator Goldwater. Bob gave McGovern a free hand to delve into Reuther's affairs.

The Committee Republicans felt quite different about it, as they stated in their separate final report on the UAW inquiry:

> In the two UAW investigations which were conducted, the chief counsel divorced himself from these probes. Instead, in each instance one staff member was selected to conduct the investigation and assigned an entirely inadequate staff. . . .

With McClellan in the chair, Republican-directed public hearings began in the big Senate Caucus Room on February 26, 1958, and, continuing intermittently until September 1959, produced 32 days of often-conflicting testimony by 102 witnesses who filled a printed record of 2,572 pages. Walter Reuther was scheduled to be the first witness as the Republicans began their inquiry by looking into an historic Auto Workers' strike—one of the longest in American labor annals—against the family-owned Kohler Company of Kohler, Wisconsin. The Committee Republicans, however, insisted on departing from the panel's usual practice by going directly to accusatory testimony, refusing to hear Reuther. Already in Washington, Reuther found his own method of speaking his mind, and in particular of responding to charges of Committee member Barry Goldwater.

The Senator from Arizona and the UAW president had been feuding for months. At a Republican dinner in Detroit in January 1958 Goldwater had declared, "Walter Reuther and the UAW-CIO are a more dangerous menace than the Sputnik or anything Soviet Russia might do to America." Reuther replied by suggesting that each man choose three nationally prominent clergymen to investigate the validity of Goldwater's charge. If they found that the Senator was correct, Reuther promised, "I will voluntarily resign from the presidency of the UAW, the vice-presidency of the AFL-CIO, and from the labor movement entirely." Should the clergymen find in favor of Reuther, the labor leader suggested the Senator then search his conscience and decide whether he should remain in public life. Escalating the rhetoric, Reuther called Goldwater the nation's "number one political fanatic, its number one anti-labor baiter, its number one peddler of class hatred."

At a Caucus Room news conference, Reuther labeled the Senator a "political hypocrite and a moral coward" for refusing to hear his testimony. Taking the Senate floor, Goldwater replied: "In my section of the country when one calls a man a coward, he smiles. I could not tell whether Mr. Reuther was smiling or not, because he is such a coward he locked the door and would not let anyone in except members of the press." Goldwater said it was "typical of the lies that Reuther has been telling—I've called him a liar so many times I'm getting sick of it."

The strike against Kohler, the manufacturer of bathroom fixtures, had begun April 5, 1954, after months of fruitless bargaining on a first contract between the company and the United Auto Workers. Illegal mass picketing by the union had kept the plant shut for 54 days at the outset, until the courts stepped in. Violence between strikers and nonstrikers became commonplace. The company listed 402 alleged acts of violence or vandalism attributed to the UAW in the first year of the marathon walkout. The union leveled similar charges, accusing management of trying to break the union.

Two beatings of nonstrikers by members of the UAW Briggs Local imported from Detroit drew national attention and figured prominently in the Senate hearings. The two unionists, William Vinson and John Gunaca, testified that the local paid each of them $80 a week plus $7 a day expenses to assist in the strike. They said they never were given any specific instructions nor did they report to any union official. Senator John F. Kennedy, a Committee member, termed that "a regrettable way to run a strike or run anything."

On the evening of June 18, 1954, the 27-year-old Vinson was in Sopretto's Bar in Sheboygan Falls, a few miles from the Kohler plant, when William Van Ouwerkerk, a nonstriker, turned to Mrs. Van Ouwerkerk and said: "Let's get out of here. There is too many union people in here." Vinson, six feet three and a half inches tall and weighing 230 pounds, advanced on the 48-year-old nonstriker, who weighed 125 pounds. With a flurry of blows, Vinson smashed several of Van Ouwerkerk's ribs and punctured a lung. Arrested and convicted of assault, Vinson was sentenced to not less than one or not more than two years in the Wisconsin State Prison by Circuit Judge F. H. Schlichting. He actually served thirteen and a half months, during which time the UAW international and the Briggs Local each contributed $50 a week to support his wife and family. The union also met his legal expenses.

On the night of July 4, 1954, Gunaca and two other men drove to a Sheboygan Falls service station, where William Bersch, Jr., a nonstriker, was on duty. After an exchange of unpleasantries, Gunaca followed as Bersch entered the station and attempted to telephone the sheriff's office. Ripping the receiver from the wall, Gunaca knocked Bersch to the floor and kicked him. The station attendant lost consciousness. Bersch's father, who lived across the street, witnessed the assault and, grabbing a child's baseball bat from a parked auto, went to his son's assistance. Bersch, Sr., age 65, was beaten and stomped, suffering a broken vertebra. When the older man died a year and a half later, the Kohler Company contended the beating had contributed to the death, attributed to heart failure by the Bersch family doctor. A warrant was issued for the arrest of Gunaca, who had returned to Detroit, but Governor

G. Mennen Williams refused to extradite him until strike tensions eased, heeding a claim by Gunaca's union-hired lawyers that he could not get a fair trial in Sheboygan Falls.

Emil Mazey, the fiery secretary-treasurer of the UAW, stood behind Vinson and Gunaca, members of his old Briggs Local, although never claiming they acted properly. In Vinson's case, Mazey denounced Judge Schlichting for what he termed "obvious bias shown against organized labor" by the sentence given Vinson. Senate Republicans were not gentle with Mazey, accusing him of trying to intimidate the judge by organizing a boycott against Piggly Wiggly and Schlichting Food Markets, in which the jurist had financial interests. Mazey also was charged with encouraging lawlessness by extending legal and financial aid to Vinson and Gunaca. Goldwater, noting repeated whispered conversations between witness Mazey and the UAW's attorney, Joseph L. Rauh, Jr., complained.

> RAUH: I have been continually saying: "Don't get angry."
> MCCLELLAN: Let the chair make that official. Don't get angry.
> MAZEY: Does somebody have a tranquilizer pill?

Mazey's quick temper had given way earlier, as related to the Committee by Lyman C. Conger, chief executive of Kohler:

> CONGER: At the conclusion of my testimony yesterday afternoon, the situation arose that I feel called on to bring to the attention of this Committee. As I was leaving the witness stand here, Mr. Emil Mazey . . . approached me in a threatening manner . . . and unloosed against me such foul language that, in deference to this Committee, I would not repeat. . . .
> MCCLELLAN: If you want to have a quarrel with each other that is your business. But any attempt to intimidate, coerce or frighten witnesses . . . I shall regard, and I trust the Committee will agree with me, as an act of contempt of the United States Senate.

Rauh hastened to interject that the outburst had been prompted by an admission by Conger that Mazey was being shadowed by company-hired detectives.

Reuther, eager to testify, was given the opportunity on March 27, 1958, relating later that John Kennedy arranged for his appearance. Before the union leader took the witness chair, Goldwater remarked: "I find it stimulating. I wouldn't miss it for anything."

Drawing a sharp distinction between the UAW and some other labor organizations involved in the hearings, Reuther first presented a prepared statement emphasizing that all Auto Workers' witnesses were appearing voluntarily and "shall testify fully and freely without resort to the Fifth Amendment or any other constitutional privilege because we have nothing to hide." He also produced a letter he had written two months earlier to Robert Kennedy:

> Since as president of the UAW I will undoubtedly be involved in the Kohler hearings, I would feel much more comfortable if in advance of the hearings you would find it possible to assign a member of your staff to check into my personal financial affairs. I should be most happy to cooperate with such an investigation and will make available to your staff all of my personal financial records.

Although May Reuther, who handled the family's finances, grumbled at having to dig out old records, Reuther turned over to Carmine Bellino, the Committee's accounting wizard, copies of his income tax returns from 1942 through 1956, as well as bank statements, savings account records, and canceled checks from 1952 through 1957. Real estate transactions and U.S. Savings Bond investments also were detailed.

Reuther's salary had ranged from $1,730.88 in 1936 to $20,920.14 in 1957. Earnings from speeches and writings amounting to $11,290.96 had been turned over to a charitable, nonprofit Reuther Labor Foundation because the UAW chief was "firmly committed to the principle that he should live on the salary paid him by the union and that these honoraria are actually the result of his position in the labor movement. . . ." Bellino testified about Reuther's expense account practices:

> . . . He would submit expense accounts to his union at the per diem. . . . It ranged from $7.50 a day to $12 a day. I found in instances when he was . . . on business for the AFL [AFL-

CIO], during that period of time if he did accept the check from the AFL, he would not submit a bill to the union. Later on he found, at least his procedure was to turn in his check from the AFL to the union and elect to receive the lesser per diem figure from the union. . . . He would elect to receive the fee of $7.50 to $12 and turn in to the union the $40 or $50 per day per diem from the AFL.

. . . If anything, his hotel bills are audited very carefully. For instance, in one bill there was a valet charge of $1.50 or $1.75. That was stricken off. It was not paid by the union. It was charged to him personally. . . .

The accountant also found that the Auto Workers' president had invested about $1,000 in Nash-Kelvinator stock in 1948 and had sold it in April 1956 for $1,001.26. Labor writer John Herling sent a note to the witness table: "Reuther—the fox of Wall Street."

"I come before you this afternoon," Reuther testified, "not claiming that the UAW is a perfect organization. We have made mistakes, and we have attempted to profit by those mistakes. No organization made up of imperfect human beings can hope to achieve perfection. But I do believe that the record will show that we have consistently tried to find out where our shortcomings were, so that we could try to overcome them." Questioned about Vinson's attack on Van Ouwerkerk, he stated:

I think what Mr. Vinson did was reprehensible. I think Mr. Vinson did this union a great disservice. I think what happened with Mr. Vinson ought to teach our union that we need to do something about this kind of problem. . . . We need to do more to exercise a greater affirmative leadership and direction when local people come in.

As for Gunaca, Reuther gave this view:

. . . I think that Mr. Gunaca ought to be back in Wisconsin without another day's delay. I think that the prosecuting attorney in the Sheboygan District ought to agree . . . to try to work out another site. . . .

Put him where you know he can get a fair trial and then you wouldn't have an argument about it. There are other parts of

Wisconsin where they have good judges, and where they can draw a jury from a community.

But to try to insist that a man be tried in an atmosphere charged with hatred, suspicion, ill will, neighbor against neighbor, where a man doesn't talk to his own family except at a funeral, this is not a community where you can be certain to get a fair trial.

The controversy ultimately was resolved along the lines Reuther urged. After the Senate hearings, Gunaca returned to Wisconsin for trial in Chippewa Falls. He did not contest the assault charge and was sentenced to three years in prison, actually serving eighteen months.

Reuther, under questioning by Goldwater, was forced to admit that Mazey had a "low boiling point" and that his attacks on Judge Schlichting had been ill-advised: "I would not have used the language Mr. Mazey used, and therefore I disagree with the language he used."

The hearings did nothing to ease the Reuther-Goldwater feud. At one point the UAW leader quoted a television statement in which the Senator had said Kohler had a "right not to have a union if he can win a strike." Reuther went on:

. . . This is a fundamental question. Only the employes under the law of these United States can make a decision whether they want a union and which union. An employer cannot make that decision without violating the law.

I would like to know whether you think under the Taft-Hartley law a company can decide not to have a union and destroy that union? I maintain they can't.

GOLDWATER: I will tell you what, someday you and I are going to get together and lock horns.

REUTHER: We are together now and I would like to ask you right now—.

GOLDWATER: You save that.

REUTHER: I am asking a fundamental question.

GOLDWATER: Wait a minute, Mr. Reuther. You are not asking the questions, I am asking the questions. If you want to save that someday—.

REUTHER: I am seeking advice.

GOLDWATER: You come out to Arizona and enjoy the bright sunshine and clean air and save it for then.

Although the Senator acknowledged at one point that he had made extreme charges and used intemperate language in discussing the labor leader, the two men soon were at it again:

GOLDWATER: . . . I just want to advise Mr. Reuther of one thing. That he is going to continue to be attacked by me.

I am not attacking his union. I am going to attack Mr. Reuther because I don't believe in his economic or his political philosophy.

REUTHER: Attack me on the issues. . . .

GOLDWATER: I would suggest, Mr. Reuther, that you do the same and quit calling me a moral coward and a political hypocrite, a man that ought to see a psychiatrist and Lord knows what else you told the boys in the back room.

REUTHER: Senator—.

MC CLELLAN: Can you folks not get off somewhere and talk this out?

Senator Curtis also had sharp exchanges with the UAW president:

CURTIS: . . . Was it alleged . . . that some of the UE [United Electrical Workers] leadership was Communistic?

REUTHER: Oh, it was alleged . . . Senator Curtis. I happen to be—.

CURTIS: Just a minute, you answered the question and I have not yielded to you for a speech. . . .

REUTHER: Mr. Chairman, I am a very patient man but I am still an American citizen with certain rights and I am going to exercise them whether the Senator wants me to or not.

CURTIS: You are the only witness in this entire Republic of ours that comes here and attempts to dominate a committee. I shall ask the questions.

MC CLELLAN: Just one moment.

REUTHER: I never answered the question.

MC CLELLAN: Just one moment. There is not anybody going to dominate this Committee as long as I am in this chair. . . .

It had long since become evident from the questions of Republican members of the Committee that their aim was to explore the political role of the UAW. It was brought out, for example, that the union was paying 10 percent of the annual operating costs of Americans for Democratic Action. GOP senators also tried to picture the Auto Workers as one of the nation's most violent labor organizations. Reuther hit back in an exchange with Curtis:

. . . You take isolated newspaper clippings, pick up this, you pick up that.

And then you try to fabricate a conclusion. Just as Senator Goldwater the other day referred to 37 deaths and talked about the UAW; and when Senator Paul Douglas dug up the record, not one of these people was killed in a UAW strike.

Why did you associate it with the UAW?

This is part of the smear campaign. Our union has had less violence than most unions. That is why none of these 37 people who were killed were in our union. This is the attempt—the decision is: Reuther has got to be destroyed because his union is active in politics, and let's find some way.

We know Reuther didn't steal any money. We know Reuther hasn't got gangsters running his union. We know they kicked out the Communists. Now let's fabricate this theory of violence.

. . . The facts are that this union has worked hard to avoid violence. We have done everything in our power to discourage it.

CURTIS: All right.

REUTHER: But that doesn't change the fact that sometimes people being human are carried away by their emotions and they do things that are wrong, and we condemn that. When you say we are trying to obstruct justice, we are trying to corrupt justice, I am here to tell you you are wrong, and you can go on doing it. But you are wrong.

And if you think it will get you political votes, you go ahead, because you are fooling yourself. The people of this country are going to look at you and say: What are you doing about unemployment, what are you doing about farmers, what are you doing about schools? And these are the things that will determine the election issues in 1958 and 1960.

CURTIS: All right, Mr. Reuther. This isn't the first time you have cluttered up our records here with attacks upon members of the Committee. I repeat there is no other citizen in the United States that shows such disrespect for the Senate of the United States as you.

REUTHER: I might say that I have never been treated so disrespectfully as I have been treated by certain members of the Republican minority that sit here.

CURTIS: You answer the question and we will get along all right. The record is well established.

MC CLELLAN: This chair is not going to permit anybody to show disrespect and contempt for this Committee, knowingly; if any is being shown here, it hasn't penetrated me yet.

I think a witness has a right to answer. I would like for the witness—I don't mind telling him—to shorten his speeches and let's get along.

REUTHER: I would like to shorten this whole affair, Senator. . . .

After Reuther's three days of testimony the Committee turned its attention to a 1955 UAW strike at four Indiana plants of the family-owned Perfect Circle Company. The four-month walkout was climaxed by gunfire at one of the factories in which, according to witnesses, about half a dozen union demonstrators outside the gates and two nonstrikers inside were wounded. There was no agreement on who fired first but the UAW did produce a photograph of a man taking aim at demonstrators from a plant fire escape.

In 1959 Committee Republicans looked into a third UAW-related matter—the ethical standards of Richard T. Gosser, a UAW leader in Toledo who was an international vice-president of the Auto Workers. Witnesses testified that Gosser had been involved in conflict-of-interest situations, once selling property he owned in partnership with others to an affiliate of Toledo Local 12 when he was its president, and owning half-interest in a Toledo hardware store that did business with the local. It also became evident that Gosser enjoyed an affluence not normally associated with UAW officials. Republican members of the Committee found it "strangely significant to us that when Mr. Gosser appeared to become a potential target for our investigation that he suddenly was shorn of most of his authority by other leaders of the UAW and relegated to an inactive status under the guise of illness." Before the Gosser hearings were held, Reuther had told the Committee: "I happen to know Dick Gosser and I know he has made a great contribution to this union. He has made a great contribution to the city of Toledo. He is a decent, honorable citizen and I know he would not take a dishonest penny from anyone or any source."

The Select Committee's final report on the United Auto Workers was issued in March 1960, and it demonstrated the deep emotional and partisan cleavages that Reuther had inspired among members of the panel. The four Republican members—Goldwater, Curtis, Mundt, and Homer E. Capehart—issued a report of their own, as did Democrats McClellan, Kennedy, Sam J. Ervin, Jr., and Frank Church.

With John Kennedy openly contesting for the Democratic presidential nomination at the time the reports were prepared, the Republicans zeroed in on chief counsel Robert F. Kennedy:

> From the very outset of the UAW investigation, it became apparent that the Committee faced an awkward, if not impossible situation growing out of the natural conflict of interest situation in which its chief counsel found himself. When investigating unions other than those affiliated with the leadership of Walter Reuther, the chief counsel worked effectively and cooperatively with all members of the Committee—Democrats and Republicans alike. But whenever an investigation touched upon the domain of Walter Reuther, an altogether different procedure was followed. . . .

Chairman McClellan, joined by Ervin, offered a rebuttal:

> The testimony in these hearings, in our judgment, could have
> been developed more thoroughly and presented more effectively
> had the Republicans permitted the chairman to arrange and
> conduct the proceedings in accordance with his judgment, as
> had been done in all previous hearings.
>
> Criticism or a charge of failure to investigate these cases
> wholly lacks foundation and credibility. Walter Reuther . . .
> testified for three consecutive days. The Republicans were af-
> forded, and took advantage of, the opportunity to ask him and
> all of the other 101 witnesses any and all questions they desired.
> Every witness they requested was called. If they are unhappy
> and disappointed in the record they made, obviously, the Demo-
> crats are not to blame for their failure.

In their report the Republicans asserted that "violence and intimidation are essential parts of the Reuther formula for power."
They found a "clear pattern of crime and violence which has characterized and has generally been associated with UAW strikes."
Referring to the Kohler and Perfect Circle strikes, the GOP report
stated:

> The communities involved in these labor disturbances were
> actually under siege as though invaded by foreign mercenaries.
> In this case, however, the invaders were the arm-locked pro-
> fessional goons and thugs employed and imported by the UAW
> to enforce its dictates. . . .
>
> Furthermore, it is our opinion that the Committee could have
> secured ample evidence to prove that the pattern of crime and
> violence as devised and developed by the UAW is being increas-
> ingly imitated by other unions who have not remained unaware
> of the success of Reuther or his apparent immunity from the
> law.

The Gunaca case, said the Republicans, "demonstrates the political influence of Walter Reuther and the UAW in the state of
Michigan, influence so dominant that a goon may invade Wisconsin
and then return to Michigan expecting to find a haven from which
he could not be extradited for trial and punishment."

Committee Democrats termed the Kohler strike "a classic example of labor-management relations at its worst—where the community, the worker, and management all suffer and none gain." They were critical of both the UAW and the Kohler Company. But they said testimony in the Perfect Circle hearings had been too inconclusive to warrant solid findings.

(The Kohler strike formally ended September 1, 1960, after the National Labor Relations Board found the Kohler Company guilty of unfair labor practices and failure to bargain in good faith. Most strikers were offered their old jobs back and the company agreed to pay them $4.5 million in back wages and pension credits. Some issues were not resolved until 1965, following lengthy litigation. It had been a costly experience for all parties involved but the Auto Workers regarded it as a victory over a recalcitrant anti-union management. Said Reuther: "How many unions have the faith to stay nine years in the struggle and spend $12 million? Not many.")

The Republican members of the Select Committee reserved some of their strongest language for their findings on UAW matters in Toledo:

> The Gosser affair is of the same cloth from which the Hoffa pattern was cut. Yet, in our opinion, the Committee failed properly to investigate pertinent allegations. . . .
>
> We do not profess to have all the facts in our possession concerning corruption in the UAW. Nonetheless, with what we know about Richard T. Gosser, senior vice-president of the UAW, we cannot tell the American people that this union deserves a "clean bill of health." We have seen sufficient evidence during the Gosser hearing of kickbacks, terrorism, collusion with gamblers, conflicts of interest, destruction of records, misappropriation of funds, falsification of records, and evasive tactics to convince us that a thorough investigation of the machinations of this individual and others would produce criminality on a scale comparable to that which has been previously exposed by this Committee.

Committee Democrats concluded that the allegations that Gosser had "misappropriated union funds through real estate transactions,

or through salary kickbacks, were unsupported." However, they
wound up their findings by quoting a comment made by McClellan
during the hearings: "I want to say for the record that I have not
been overwhelmingly impressed with the veracity of either side. I
think I have spotted inaccuracies, and I am being charitable. . . ."
The chairman, stung by Republican claims that the Committee had
been remiss in not pursuing the Gosser inquiry far enough, set forth
his position separately:

> . . . The record is crystal clear that this was an investigation
> by the Republican members. They insisted on conducting their
> own independent investigation and withheld and kept secret
> from Democratic members of the Committee all material, docu-
> ments and information they procured until they presented it in
> testimony by witnesses at the hearings. . . .

Gosser subsequently was indicted on charges of violating federal
income tax laws. Convicted, he "retired" from the UAW. His case
bordered closer on corrupt stewardship of union affairs than any
other ever uncovered during the Reuther presidency. The Republicans on the Select Committee had labored mightily to find evidence that would justify equating Reuther and his Auto Workers
with the Becks and Hoffas of the labor movement. They fell far
short of their objective.

CHAPTER TWENTY-SIX

The World Stage

VERY EARLY IN LIFE WALTER REUTHER HAD DEVELOPED WHAT HIS father would have called a *Weltanschau,* or view of the world, that was far more sophisticated and internationalist than the outlook of most of his American contemporaries, either within or without the labor movement. He identified with the Social Democratic tradition of Western Europe, including its theme of global solidarity among workers, from an early age. When Walter and Victor traveled overseas in the early 1930's, they met with union leaders in Britain, Germany, France, and elsewhere who shared and bolstered their belief in the brotherhood of workingmen. It was with this background that they arrived late in 1933 at the Gorki auto plant in the Soviet Union. At first enthusiastic, the brothers later grew skeptical of the centralized decision making and Communist Party dominance they experienced. Once home, the Stalin-Hitler Pact of 1939 and the Soviet effort to sabotage the postwar Marshall Plan only hardened their contempt for the Kremlin dictatorship.

During the latter days of World War II the CIO had helped establish the World Federation of Trade Unions, welcoming Soviet delegations into the new organization. The AFL, which scorned the Russian "unions" as puppets of the Communist regime used only to control the work force, boycotted the WFTU. Three years later, after the Soviets had taken control of the world labor body and were using it to propagandize against the Marshall Plan, the CIO withdrew, to the applause of the Reuthers. AFL and CIO leaders then agreed to merge their differences at the water's edge and joined in creating the anti-Communist International Confederation of Free Trade Unions, with Walter Reuther as one of the CIO delegates.

Reuther believed that democracy must prove itself more effective in the pursuit of peace and elevation of the common man's living standards if it were going to compete with Communism on a global basis. "The chief weakness of American foreign policy," he asserted in 1948, one of the most frigid years of the Cold War era, "is the predilection of our State Department for dealing with anybody who will promise to hate Communism. It is fatal to resist Communism by courting reaction." Two years later he proposed a United Nations fund amounting to scores of billions of dollars "to help people help themselves to develop their material and economic resources in the building of a better life." Reuther returned to a very similar theme in a 1952 speech: "There is a revolution going on in the world. The Communists didn't start it. It is a revolution of hungry men to get the wrinkles out of their bellies. . . . The Communists are riding its back."

A short time later Walter Reuther became involved in furthering United States foreign policy, as a conduit for funds supplied by the Central Intelligence Agency. His role in transmitting $50,000 for a mysterious project in Europe was revealed in 1967 by Thomas W. Braden, who had been the CIA official assigned to deliver the money to UAW headquarters in Detroit. Braden's disclosures came at a time when the CIA's activities in subsidizing student organizations, labor unions, and cultural groups were under sharp attack.

Braden was motivated to write about the transaction, he later stated, because Victor Reuther had been accusing two high AFL-CIO officials, Jay Lovestone and Irving Brown, of accepting CIA funds to help counter Communist penetration of labor unions in Europe and Latin America. Braden implied in his article that the Lovestone-Brown operations indeed were financed by the intelligence organization—which was denied by the AFL-CIO—and he added:

> Victor Reuther ought to be ashamed of himself. At his request I went to Detroit one morning and gave Walter $50,000 in $50 bills. Victor spent the money, mostly in West Germany, to bolster labor unions there. . . . In my opinion and that of my peers in the CIA, he spent it with less than perfect wisdom, for the German unions he chose to help weren't seriously short of money and were already anti-Communist. The CIA money Victor spent would have done much more good where unions were tying up ports at the order of Communist leaders.

Braden said even later that, in distributing the cash, he had acted at the direct request of the late Allen W. Dulles, director of

CIA, and never learned exactly how it was spent. Victor, as the CIO's top representative in Europe, received other CIA funds for use in West Germany and the Middle East, Braden added.

Responding to Braden's article, Walter Reuther issued a statement acknowledging the union had received the $50,000 from the CIA courier and justifying the action:

> The labor movement of Europe in the postwar period was weak and without resources and was therefore especially vulnerable to Communist subversion. In this emergency situation, 15 years ago the union did agree reluctantly on one occasion to the request to transmit government funds to supplement the inadequate funds being made available by the United States labor movement. These monies were merely added to the trade union funds to intensify the education and organizational programs then under way in Europe. The content of the programs was in no way affected or altered.

After that point the Reuther and Braden versions began to conflict. Walter said Braden asked his brother to become an agent for the CIA, using his CIO position as a cover, following delivery of the money. The UAW statement said Victor "emphatically rejected" the proposal and that Philip Murray, then president of the CIO, agreed with the decision. Braden, however, insisted Victor never was asked to join the secret agency, adding that the younger Reuther "behaved as a responsible and patriotic American citizen in helping his government combat Communism in labor unions abroad."

Interviewed after publication of the Braden article, Victor Reuther refused to divulge any further details about how the $50,000 was spent, except to deny Braden's assertion that it was spent in West Germany: "It was for a very specific purpose, a very worthwhile purpose . . . direct assistance to a bona fide trade union group in Western Europe." Victor also said he was unaware of the source of the CIA money at the time. "I did not know—I do not believe Walter knew—it was Central Intelligence money." Braden, however, insisted that Walter Reuther was aware of his connection with the agency. He related that when he showed up in Walter's office with the cash, he had announced cryptically, "Here's the message for you," and had obtained a receipt for the funds.

Braden's well-publicized disclosure undercut Victor Reuther's allegations about CIA influence in the AFL-CIO. As one anti-Reuther member of the Federation's Executive Council said: "Who's complaining about the CIA? The guy who gets caught with the little black bag right in his own office."

Whatever his views at the height of the Cold War, Walter Reuther in 1967 rejected any thought of transmitting CIA funds. He called attention to the UAW's creation in 1962 of the Free World Labor Defense Fund, financed by earmarking the interest from the union's strike fund for international programs, then added:

> The CIA has a difficult and crucial role to play in helping defend the security of our nation. In our judgment, it can best serve this country and its free institutions, both private and public, by conducting its affairs in a manner that does not compromise the integrity nor put in jeopardy the independence of groups such as the labor movement and student organizations.

Victor Reuther said he wanted to expose "a very dangerous practice by Central Intelligence of trying to subvert bonafide non-governmental organizations. The Braden statements were designed to shut me up and also to create the false illusion that I personally, and the UAW, were as 'involved' as the AFL-CIO."

Reuther's foreign policy stands frequently put him at odds with George Meany, a hard-line anti-Communist who generally shared the Cold War outlook of Republican Secretary of State John Foster Dulles, particularly the Dulles hostility toward neutral nations such as India. Shortly after he became AFL-CIO president, Meany described India's Premier Jawaharlal Nehru and Yugoslav President Tito as "aides and allies of Communism in fact and in effect if not in diplomatic verbiage." A few months later Reuther began an eleven-day tour of India, apparently with the blessing of the Eisenhower administration, to make a case for American democracy. Speaking in New Delhi, Reuther dissented sharply from Meany's appraisal of Nehru, terming him "truly one of the great statesmen of the world." The UAW leader also distinguished his position from Meany's with these words: "Freedom's struggle in Asia will be won primarily in the rice fields and not in the battlefields. Like many Americans, I have felt that U.S. foreign policy in Asia has placed undue emphasis upon military power, military pacts and military alliances. This . . . has, in my opinion, tended to trade reliable democratic friends for doubtful military allies." An Associated Press dispatch from New Delhi said many knowledgeable Indians believed one of Reuther's main objectives was "to heal the wounds caused by Meany's speech." The Hindustan *Times,* a newspaper with close ties to Nehru, reported Reuther's tour was a "most welcome whiff of fresh air" that revived Indian faith in the United States.

Reuther made a similar impression in an appearance before the British Trade Union Congress in 1957, describing to a largely Socialist audience the gains achieved by American workers under a basically capitalist system. "No overseas visitor in living memory has made such an immense impact by his personality and tempestuous oratory," wrote a reporter for the *Daily Express.*

In the international field, Reuther faced an old adversary from the early days of auto unionism in Detroit. Jay Lovestone, who had advised Homer Martin and fought the Reuther brothers in the late 1930's, now was active as the head of a Free Trade Union Committee financed by several AFL-CIO affiliates. As its director, Lovestone ran his own intelligence network, supervised clandestine anti-Communist activities overseas, and lobbied before the United Nations. Reuther demanded that George Meany curb Lovestone, who once was described as "half cloak-and-dagger, half cloak-and-suiter" because of his ties with the garment unions in New York City. Lovestone was brought into AFL-CIO headquarters as a staff man but he and Reuther continued to clash over foreign policy issues at meetings of the Federation's Executive Council. It was largely a matter of style, rather than substance, that kept the old feud alive.

Appearing before a vast audience in Berlin at a May Day rally in 1959, Reuther lashed away at Kremlin "despotism" and declared:

"We shall stand with you in Berlin no matter how strong and cold the Soviet winds blow from the East." A more positive note was struck, however, as he added: "I can say in truthfulness that the only war in which the American people wish to engage is this war against poverty, hunger, ignorance, and disease. The promise of a world at peace, dedicating its combined resources to the fulfillment of human needs everywhere, will kindle the same hopes and warm response in the hearts of the Russian people as among the people in the free world."

Gradually, Reuther became the best-known American labor leader throughout the world, perhaps because his social democratic views coincided more closely with the outlook of foreign labor chiefs than did the more pragmatic, less imaginative rhetoric of George Meany. "I have no privacy anyplace in the world," Reuther once lamented. "It's a terrible thing." He recalled with chagrin how he and his wife May were reclining in a Venetian gondola, serenely listening to an open-air concert, when their peace was shattered by a shout from a nearby boat: "Hey, Mr. Reuther, can I see you at the hotel in the morning?" Reuther's reaction: "I felt like going over and upsetting his damned gondola." He also recalled a night in Copenhagen when labor union hosts arranged a free evening for the Reuthers. "I said to May, 'We've been liberated. Why don't we make the most of it?'" They window-shopped and walked through the city until well past midnight, all by themselves, and Reuther remembered: "It was the most wonderful evening. Nobody on our back."

In the international field, however, Reuther found it difficult to escape from controversy. When Soviet Deputy Premier Anastas Mikoyan visited the United States in 1959, he asked to see the headquarters of the American labor movement, only a block away from the White House. George Meany, consistent with his view that the Soviets stifled free trade unionism wherever possible, barred the door to the visitor from Moscow and Mikoyan had to settle for a glance through the lobby windows. Walter Reuther and three other AFL-CIO vice-presidents, however, invited Mikoyan to lunch at a nearby union building. Meany, rejecting an invitation to join the group, assailed Americans who "feel that they can meet the

Soviet challenge at the conference table," a pointed rebuke to Reuther. The UAW leader in turn defended his meal with Mikoyan as a necessary confrontation rather than an accommodation:

> I am told there is ever present danger that totalitarian leaders, unaccustomed to soliciting or heeding the views of others, may underestimate the mood and determination of free people to resist encroachment on their rights. For this reason I thought it wise to tell Deputy Premier Mikoyan to his face during his visit in America that on the question of safeguarding the rights of free Berlin and securing a Germany united in freedom and democracy, the American people are more united than on any other issue. . . . The Soviet Union has made great industrial progress and the Soviet workers have won more bread but they have not won more freedom. We in the free world want both bread and freedom.

Labor reporter John Herling's account of the Reuther-Mikoyan lunch indicated it was a rugged exchange, with the American denouncing the Soviets for their repression of the 1956 Hungarian revolt and their role in fomenting a crisis in Berlin. "American trade union leaders understand the Communists better than American capitalists," Reuther was quoted as telling Mikoyan. Countering Meany's criticism, Senator John Sherman Cooper, the Kentucky Republican, said Reuther performed "a major service for peace" by his plain talk to the Kremlin's number two man.

The confrontation with Mikoyan, however, was only a curtain raiser for a similar clash between Reuther and Soviet Premier Nikita S. Khrushchev in the fall of 1959. Learning of Reuther's efforts to arrange a meeting with Khrushchev, Meany put a resolution before the AFL-CIO Executive Council that assailed the Soviet dictatorship. It was a deliberate move to cut the ground from under the UAW president. Reuther proceeded with his plans anyway, setting up a dinner in San Francisco where the AFL-CIO convention would be in progress during Khrushchev's visit to that city. Unexpectedly, Reuther asked the AFL-CIO high command to endorse the dinner but was overwhelmingly rebuffed, picking up only two votes in addition to his own. Some labor leaders who accepted Reuther's dinner invitation voted against him, including Emil Rieve: "I think it's wrong for the Executive Council to endorse a dinner with the head of the Russian state but if I want to have dinner with him, that's my business."

Joined by half a dozen labor chiefs, Reuther sat down to break bread with Khrushchev, a few aides, and interpreters on the evening of September 20, 1959. The dinner, which lasted five hours, began on a light note with Reuther telling the visiting Premier that his chair had to be moved slightly to avoid a table leg: "Even though I have shifted you to the right, Mr. Chairman, I assure you there is no political significance to it." Khrushchev laughed, declaring that his faith in Communism could not be shaken so easily. The conversation turned to the hard life of coal miners in the Soviet Union, Great Britain, and the United States:

REUTHER: One thing we must do, most of all, in the future is to harness the atom for peace and get all of the miners out of the earth.

KHRUSHCHEV: Our scientists tell me we are approaching that.

REUTHER: This is a venture in which we favor a mutual effort to pool the abilities and scientific knowledge of all nations.

KHRUSHCHEV: A very noble goal.

That was one of the few conflict-free exchanges of the evening. The editor of *Pravda,* Pavel Satyukov, reminded Reuther that the Communist Party publication had printed the full text of the UAW president's most recent statement about rising unemployment in the United States. "We didn't change a word," the Soviet editor said. Reuther quickly responded. "No, you wouldn't, because that report on unemployment would reflect upon us. Why didn't you publish my May Day speech of this year in West Berlin?"

From that point, the discussion turned into a verbal duel between the roly-poly Khrushchev and the articulate ex-Socialist from Detroit. An example:

KHRUSHCHEV: The United States exploits the wealth of other countries, underdeveloped countries, for profits. . . . We do not exploit any country, we only engage in trade.

REUTHER: You exploit the workers of East Germany.

KHRUSHCHEV: Where did you dream that up?

REUTHER: If you don't exploit them, why should three million of them cross the border into West Germany?

KHRUSHCHEV: You are feverish. [Several voices speak at once.]

REUTHER: Do you have credentials to speak for the workers of the world?

KHRUSHCHEV: Do you have credentials to poke your nose into East Germany?

Moments later, the Soviet leader shouted at Reuther: "You have been spoiled by everyone bowing down, by everyone cringing and crawling. . . . I, as a former miner, have to say that I pity you as representing the working class but your thinking is not of the working class." Joe Curran, the ham-handed former sailor who heads the National Maritime Union, broke into the table-pounding exchange to assert: "We ought to talk sense here and we're not talking sense yet. I don't want to be confused with statesmen. I am a worker speaking for workers and I'm pretty sure the rest of the guys here do."

Reuther began again, saying, "I grew up in a working-class home in West Virginia—" but Khrushchev interrupted, waving his hands, causing the auto union leader to inquire, "Is he afraid of my questions?" The Russian shot back, "I am not afraid of the devil and you are a man." Pressing for answers, Reuther fired questions about the independence of Soviet labor unions and received another rebuff when Khrushchev replied loudly, "Why poke your nose into our business?" Undaunted, Reuther replied, "Freedom is everybody's business—" but again he was interrupted by his dinner guest, who by now was red-faced and shouting. "We call what you represent —capitalist lackeys!" exploded the Premier. Reuther innocently responded, "Every time I ask a question he has no answer for, he gets angry."

Taking the offensive, the burly Soviet visitor called attention to the movie, *Can Can*, which he had seen being filmed at a Hollywood studio. He stood, turned his back to the table, bent downward and flipped his coat in a crude burlesque of the chorus girls. "This is a dance in which girls pull up their skirts. This is what you call freedom—freedom for the girls to show their backsides. To us, it's pornography. It's capitalism that makes the girls that way." Reuther, as much a moralist as anyone, replied weakly, "Perhaps it was a stupid movie."

Pausing only for translation, the disputants continued for hours until a calmed-down Khrushchev finally concluded: "You have your point of view; we have ours. They are irreconcilable. . . . We did not come to this meeting to aggravate our relations. They are bad enough as they are." A moment later he told Karl Feller, president of the Brewery Workers Union, to "drink your beer" when Feller asked again about the exodus of workers from East Germany to the West. Reuther wound up the stormy session by tossing a copy of American wage rates at his Russian adversary and asking rhetorically, "How can he say these people are wage slaves exploited by capitalism?"

The confrontation made page-one news in the United States and around the world, but Reuther's role did not draw universal applause. Murray Kempton, an old admirer of the UAW president, felt the exchange of insults was rather disgraceful. Jay Lovestone, probably reflecting Meany's thinking, asserted: "Walter is his own worst enemy. . . . This was a mistake, and for Khrushchev a bonanza. . . . I don't think Reuther knew he got screwed until he was eight months pregnant."

Shortly after Khrushchev's return to Moscow, the Soviet press ran a story about Reuther's "marriage" while he was working in Russia, in what seemed to be a clear attempt to discredit him. Reuther reacted by telephoning his wife to assure her the Soviet report was pure propaganda.

During the summit conference at Vienna in 1961, President John F. Kennedy recalled to Khrushchev the Soviet chief's meeting with Reuther in San Francisco two years earlier. Without smiling, the Russian replied, "We hung the likes of Reuther in Russia in 1917." For his part, Reuther had hardly been the gracious host, later complaining that his dinner guest "blew his stack three or four times—he abused me." Subsequently he was more charitable, telling Soviet newsmen in 1965 that "Khrushchev's great contribution was that he opened the door and let a little light in" to the Soviet Union from the world outside.

When Reuther went to Japan in 1962 to urge inter-union solidarity for higher wages there, Communist-led protesters greeted him with signs reading, "Go Home, Walter Reuther" and "Capitalist Spy." Some jabbed him in the ribs and others rocked his taxicab, shouting, "Yankee imperialist," but Reuther was not hurt. His Japanese visit was part of his effort, which began in the 1950's, to raise the wages of auto workers around the globe. "The day of the purely U.S. auto corporation is gone forever," he observed. "Profits know no patriotism. . . . Twelve major auto manufacturers . . . rule a worldwide industry employing two million workers. . . . Technologies are the same and corporate policies are uniform, yet the workers are divided by national differences in social policies and in trade union custom and development. This is a division we must bridge."

Chrysler Corporation, according to Reuther, was a good example of the trend. As late as 1962 about 98 percent of its output was manufactured in the United States or Canada, but in the five subsequent years the figure dropped to 77 percent as the American firm bought French Simca and a British auto maker. Plants were added in sixteen additional countries.

Global corporations, Reuther warned, could produce in the lowest wage areas and sell the cars where the highest profits could be made, with a corresponding threat to American wages and working conditions.

At Reuther's instigation, delegates representing workers in General Motors, Ford, and Chrysler plants in fourteen countries met to consider what to do about it. "Only as we can overcome the efforts of these giant international corporations to divide their workers in different countries can we find answers to these common problems," Reuther argued. The delegates formed worldwide councils to protect the right to organize and move, on a long-range basis, toward uniformity of wages, working conditions, and other benefits. One immediate objective was a sharing of information about contract terms among the labor organizations because, as Reuther phrased it, "When a GM worker discusses a problem at the bargaining table, . . . he ought to know precisely what GM is doing about that kind of problem in every other part of the world." He termed the resulting joint statement of the delegates the "Declaration of Detroit" and looked upon it as an historic breakthrough in trying to forge international solidarity among auto workers.

History of another kind, and lesser order, was made in 1966 when Victor Reuther made a sentimental return journey to the Gorki auto plant where he and his brother had labored more than three decades earlier. Victor renewed acquaintance with Vladimir Vladimirski, a co-worker who had been promoted to superintendent of the tool room. Said Victor: "I saw many of the machines that Walter and I worked on 31 years ago. Interestingly, they still wore the little plaques with the American flag and an inscription in both Russian and English saying that these machines were presented by the people of the United States as economic assistance to the people of the Soviet Union. I was really pleasantly surprised that, despite the ups and downs of our relationship with the Soviet Union during those years, that they had not removed those plaques."

1957—Valentine Reuther in a happy time with his son, Walter. *UAW Solidarity*

1961—During contract negotiations with General Motors Walter Reuther sits beside Leonard Woodcock (second from left), UAW vice president and director of the union's General Motors Department. In the foreground is Louis Seaton, then personnel vice-president of GM. (Woodcock succeeded to presidency of the UAW after Reuther's death.) *UAW Solidarity*

1961—Eleanor Roosevelt and Walter Reuther.

1963—Walter Reuther and James B. Carey (right), president of the International Union of Electrical, Radio and Machine Workers of America, welcome President Kennedy to AFL-CIO convention in New York City.

1964—President Johnson and Walter Reuther en route to UAW
convention in Atlantic City. *Wide World*

1965—Walter Reuther with Martin Luther King Jr., in Selma, Alabama. *Declan Haun/Black Star*

1965—Walter Reuther with Archbishop John Cody of New Orleans, later John Cardinal Cody of Chicago, at St. Mary's College in New Orleans where Reuther received an honorary LL.D. degree. *Dennis Cipnic/Black Star*

1968—In California, Walter Reuther and Vice-President Hubert H. Humphrey talk with Ted Watkins, a UAW staff representative on leave to work full time with the Watts Community Union. *Gene Daniels/ Black Star*

1968—Reuther introduces Senator Robert F. Kennedy to UAW convention in Atlantic City. *UAW Publications*

1968—Testimonial dinner in Detroit marks the establishment of a Walter P. Reuther chair in the Peaceful Uses of Atomic Energy at the Weizmann Institute of Science in Rehovoth, Israel. Left to right: Senator Philip Hart, Mrs. May Reuther, Walter Reuther, and Israeli foreign minister Abba Eban. *UAW Publications*

1966—Walter Reuther and retired auto workers at retirees' meeting in Detroit. *UAW Solidarity*

Walter Reuther testifying before a congressional committee.

At their 60th wedding anniversary, Valentine and Anna Reuther, seated, are surrounded by their children (left to right) Theodore, Christine, Roy, Victor, and Walter on the porch of the family home in Wheeling, West Virginia. *Courtesy of Victor Reuther*

The Reuther brothers—Victor, Walter, and Roy—in their later years.

The United Farm Workers' building in Delano, California, is named in honor of Roy L. Reuther, who died in 1968. Roy's son, Alan, and Walter Reuther are holding the memorial plaque as Cesar Chavez (right), director of the UFW Organizing Committee, looks on. Young man in black shirt (left) is William Wolfman, UAW staff member who died in the same plane crash that claimed Walter and May Reuther. *Gene Daniels/Black Star*

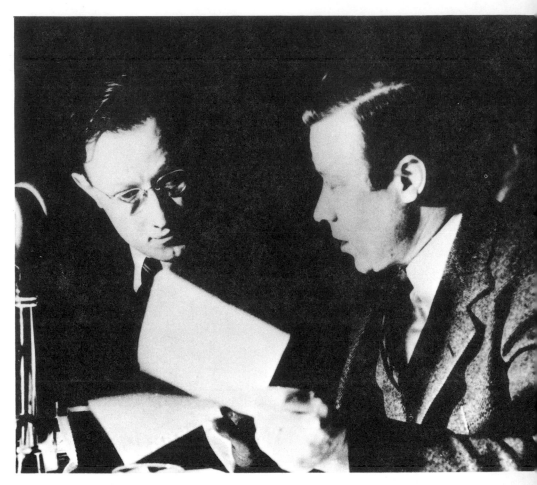

Victor and Walter consulting together during Walter's famous debate
with C. E. Wilson. *Courtesy of Victor Reuther*

May and Walter Reuther. *AFL-CIO News*

CHAPTER TWENTY-SEVEN

New Frontier

WITH THE APPROACH OF THE 1960 POLITICAL SEASON, A "REUTHER for President Committee" was organized in New Jersey, and a separate group, "Reuther in '60," set up shop in New York to promote the UAW chief as a prospective Democratic nominee. Embarrassed as much as he was flattered, Reuther felt compelled to send a special letter to all auto union locals: "I am not in any way interested in running for or holding any office. I have said this publicly many times before, and I repeat it now with all the emphasis at my command."

Officially, Reuther was neutral in the heated contest for the Democratic nomination. Sixteen months before either party held its national convention, the Auto Workers staked out a hands-off position that Reuther publicly honored but, as time passed, privately skirted: ". . . The UAW has not—nor will we—endorse a candidate for the presidential nomination of any party. This is properly the responsibility of the delegates who make up the conventions of both parties. Any news reports which state or imply anything to the contrary of the foregoing statement are without foundation in fact."

In Reuther's mind the dream of "political realignment" lingered, although he recognized that the likelihood of such a development was waning. In a television interview with ABC News, he said again that he "would like to put Dixiecrats in the Republican Party where I think they belong." He went on to echo his phrases of a decade or more earlier: "The day must come . . . when political parties stand for things and have discipline and internal integrity. . . . Then you can vote for the party that has the program and the policy that you believe in and you will get what you vote for."

Behind the scenes two UAW men were members of a Democratic steering committee that was trying to arrange a relatively harmonious nominating session—a convention that would not repel the television viewers of America by presenting a poor electronic "image." This effort, which involved representatives of all the possible contenders, was prompted by a widespread feeling that lame-duck Party chairman Paul Butler had delivered the convention machinery to Adlai Stevenson in 1956. As Jack Conway, still serving as Reuther's principal assistant at the time, explained his part in the operation, a second factor was at least equally important:

> In '56 they wouldn't even let Herbert Lehman or Paul Douglas have the floor, you know. It was a disgrace. And old Sam Rayburn chaired that convention and he looked like Mussolini. It was just the God-awfullest public impression. . . . We were concerned about the fact that this is an age of television and if you look like a bunch of bums, you're reacted to like a bunch of bums.

Conway and UAW vice-president Leonard Woodcock were members of the steering committee. Others included Theodore Sorensen, Mike Feldman, and Paul Ziffren. The result of their labors was broad agreement on convention rules and the choice of telegenic men who would be in the camera's eye: a Westerner for keynoter, a Southerner as convention chairman, and an Easterner to head the platform committee.

In the running for the presidential nomination were John F. Kennedy, Hubert H. Humphrey, Stuart Symington, Adlai Stevenson, and Lyndon B. Johnson. Reuther, although his ties with Humphrey and Stevenson were close, had also become friendly with Kennedy during the hearings of the Senate's Labor-Management Rackets Committee. Joseph L. Rauh, Jr., the Auto Workers counsel at the hearings, remembers that "whenever we were in trouble, we'd look up and Jack Kennedy would be walking in." Rauh even wondered if the Committee counsel, Robert F. Kennedy, was in wireless communication with his older brother and summoned him at appropriate moments. In any case, the union lawyer thought John Kennedy "was a real saint towards the UAW." Reuther did not consider that a determining factor in presidential politics, however.

As the pre-convention primaries progressed, with Kennedy and

Humphrey the principal contestants, Reuther leaned increasingly toward the younger man from Massachusetts because in him he saw a winner whose philosophy would not run counter to that of the Auto Workers. Humphrey, quite naturally, felt a bit slighted by his friend and believed his record entitled him to UAW support. Rauh, a Humphrey supporter at the time, believes Reuther "didn't go for Hubert because he felt that was kind of a useless gesture and the kind of thing you let idealists do. . . . You don't go for the guy who is not going to win." Even so, when Kennedy shoved Humphrey out of the race by winning the crucial primary in West Virginia, Reuther stepped in to help raise funds for the financially stricken loser.

After that decisive race, the leader of the Auto Workers continued to maintain a neutral stance in public, but privately he now had no doubt that Kennedy was the logical choice. "We were clearly for Kennedy very early," recalls Douglas Fraser, a UAW stalwart. After Humphrey's withdrawal, he says, Reuther "talked long and hard to Stevenson . . . to talk him out of the running." The union chief was convinced the alternative to Kennedy was Lyndon Johnson, the powerful Democratic leader of the Senate who was considered suspect on a number of the UAW's litmus paper tests, including civil rights. After Johnson in 1959 had helped Southerners block a reform of Senate Rule 22, which would have eased passage of civil rights legislation, Roy Reuther publicly berated Robert G. (Bobby) Baker, then Johnson's assistant, for conspiring with his boss to "corrupt" freshman Democratic senators elected with the help of campaign contributions from organized labor; the first-termers had split eight to seven against the reform plan.

The UAW also was dismayed that Johnson had not publicly supported Medicare proposals. Thus when another LBJ assistant, George E. Reedy, was assigned to attend a Midwest Democratic conference in Detroit, with the hope of enlisting Auto Workers' aid for Johnson's candidacy, he found there was little he could do but "go around, shake hands and drink with my old friends."

On June 8 the Washington *Star* quoted Kennedy as saying he

hoped to have Reuther's public endorsement in advance of the Democratic convention, opening July 11. Reuther did not oblige, but four days before the first convention session, he and a number of other major labor leaders met and privately agreed their efforts should be exerted in Kennedy's behalf. One who did not join the compact was James B. Carey, then president of the International Union of Electrical Workers and a strong Symington supporter. When Reuther urged Carey to "overcome anti-Catholic prejudice and support Jack Kennedy," the Roman Catholic Carey had a joking retort: "Listen, you damn Protestant—."

More than 40 UAW members were delegates to the convention, and the *Wall Street Journal* reported that Reuther, although not a delegate, was the most influential labor leader at the Los Angeles meeting.

Reuther and Rauh tried at this point to persuade Humphrey to line up with them behind Kennedy. Simultaneously, they importuned Kennedy to accept Humphrey as his running mate. "We really thought we were going to get it for Hubert—but we reckoned without Hubert," says Rauh. Conway agrees: "We had essential agreement with Kennedy that when he was nominated, Humphrey would be his choice for Vice-President. He was prepared to do that but Humphrey was unprepared." Because of his own past associations and pressure from Senate colleague Johnson, Humphrey gave Stevenson an eleventh-hour endorsement. Kennedy and many others felt Humphrey had thus placed himself in the stop-Kennedy camp, a loose coalition that, had it succeeded, would probably have delivered the presidential nomination to Lyndon Johnson.

Although the UAW people had become convinced Kennedy would be a first-ballot winner, Johnson's all-out move disquieted them. "Lyndon came on strong," recalls Conway. "He lined up Humphrey, he lined up the Stevenson people, he lined up favorite sons. . . . The theory they were operating on was that if they could stop [Kennedy] on the first ballot, they could break away delegates and nominate Lyndon Johnson."

Having failed in their effort to sew up the vice-presidential nomination for Humphrey, Reuther and his associates held a series of discussions about an alternative candidate. Symington, they decided, would bring greatest strength to the ticket and contribute most toward Party unity. They agreed, too, that Senator Henry Jackson of Washington would also be acceptable. LBJ did not figure in their calculations.

On July 14, after Kennedy had won first-ballot nomination with the solid support of UAW delegates, a labor group called on the candidate to discuss the second spot on the ticket. Included in the delegation were Reuther, Conway, Alex Rose of the Hatters Union, and AFL-CIO counsel Arthur J. Goldberg. To the shock and dismay of his visitors, Kennedy announced he felt obligated to offer the vice-presidential nomination to Johnson. He argued that the Senate leader had made a very powerful race, that he enjoyed widespread support, and that if Johnson felt alienated from Kennedy he could do great damage to the candidate during a scheduled post-convention special session of Congress. Still dumbfounded, the labor men suggested that perhaps an offer could be made to Johnson in a form that would encourage a rejection. Kennedy had decided, however, to make a bona fide offer to his defeated rival.

The news of Kennedy's intentions traveled fast. Leonard Woodcock, a member of the Michigan delegation, and Mildred Jeffrey of the UAW staff had a leisurely lunch at the Biltmore while the conference with Kennedy was in progress. Returning to the Statler-Hilton, they learned of the unexpected choice from Rauh. "Tears were literally rolling down his cheeks," Woodcock remembers. May Reuther also wept at the news and Jim Carey, in the words of one UAW man, "just blew his mind" and seemed ready to jump from a hotel window. Woodcock, a fervent Kennedy partisan, relates:

> I must confess I was shocked. I went upstairs to Walter's suite and people were sitting around in almost stunned silence. . . . I finally said, "Well, goddamit, I was a delegate in '52 and I voted for John Sparkman. And Lyndon Johnson isn't John Sparkman and Texas isn't Alabama. This is not the end of the world."

Dave Dubinsky then telephoned Alex Rose, who reported on the conversation: "Dave thinks this is great. Who's the genius who thought of this?" Dubinsky's call "finished picking us up off the floor," says Woodcock.

Although the unionists in Reuther's suite fell into line behind Kennedy's decision, the selection of Johnson held the potential for sparking an ugly floor fight. Governor G. Mennen Williams of Michigan, never as close to Reuther—or as beholden to him—as many suspected at the time, was bent on forcing a roll call on the Johnson nomination. So were Rauh and other members of the District of Columbia delegation. Moreover, George Meany was totally unreconciled to Johnson and wanted the AFL-CIO Executive Council to back him up with a public statement.

In a closed caucus of the Michigan delegation, Woodcock carried the ball against Williams. He turned sentiment around and, on a voice vote that drew a handful of "nays," Michigan gave its support to LBJ. A floor fight that could have seriously damaged Party unity—and had great impact on the national television audience—was averted, even though Williams and others shouted their disagreement during the subsequent voice vote in the convention hall.

That evening Meany convened the Executive Council of the labor federation, insistent on a policy pronouncement condemning the Johnson nomination. Goldberg and Reuther counseled against such an action. Conway states: "Reuther did the job. . . . Walter prevailed in blocking the Council from issuing a statement of condemnation. And all it required was two and a half hours of plain goddam hard work. What he did, in effect, was beat Meany down. And once he'd beat Meany down, that Council never does anything that Meany doesn't want to do."

On August 3, with the convention concluded, Reuther flew to Hyannisport for a conference with Kennedy and remained several days. Asked by reporters to state his attitude toward LBJ on the ticket, he replied that Johnson had clearly pledged to support the entire Democratic platform and "that is good enough for me." Reuther gave the candidate a seven-page memorandum on high unemployment and, in Kennedy's phrase, they had "a most useful talk." Reuther later recalled the Hyannisport visit:

> The first morning he and I had a long bull session. He and I were on the phone with Lyndon Johnson, who was down at the ranch. That afternoon Jack had some things to do and he said, "Why don't you go swimming with Jackie?" . . . She was carrying their second child, as I recall. After we went swimming for a while, we lay on the beach there. She said, "You know, I want to talk to you about this whole business of security and privacy." So we had a long, long talk. . . . I said to her: "This is going to be the area in which you pay the biggest price. . . . You are making the decision, as an adult, and so is Jack. But your kids aren't making the decision. You really have to work, and work hard, to have your children lead as nearly normal a life as possible. Everywhere you turn you're going to be a prisoner. You will take over the White House, if Jack wins the election, but they will take over your lives— the security people. It's a terrible thing. This is going to be the most difficult problem for you." We spent a couple hours lying there in the sand talking about these things. I often have thought back . . . my God, how true these things we talked about turned out to be. It's a terrible thing to have somebody on your back all the time.

The Reuther brothers and the Auto Workers campaigned harder for the Kennedy-Johnson ticket than any other segment of organized labor. Roy Reuther, head of the UAW's Citizenship Department, was the only representative of an AFL-CIO union to attend a voter registration meeting called by Robert F. Kennedy. Subsequently he took a leave of absence from the union to become co-director of the Democratic Party's 1960 voter registration committee.

The Republican presidential nominee, Richard M. Nixon, was very mindful of the role of the Reuthers in the campaign and tried to make something of it. In a statement issued in Texas a few days before the balloting, Nixon termed Walter Reuther a "labor leader turned radical politician" and predicted that if Kennedy was elected, Reuther would "have a lot to do with calling the tune in the White House." Said Nixon: "I can think of nothing more detrimental to this nation than for any President to owe his election to, and thereby be a captive of, a political boss like Walter Reuther." The UAW chief replied that Nixon "makes the mistake of believing that the American people are easily fooled by reckless charges and distortion."

At the 1962 UAW convention President Kennedy responded to a welcoming ovation and jocularly acknowledged his debt to the Auto Workers: "Last week, after speaking to the Chamber of Commerce and the presidents of the American Medical Association, I began to wonder how I got elected. And now I remember."

Although Kennedy and members of his staff consulted frequently with Reuther, they by no means became UAW captives. Only one member of the Auto Workers, Jack Conway, joined the administration, and his assignment was not exactly exalted. Conway served as deputy administrator of the Federal Housing Administration and owed his job primarily to his own executive talents rather than labor backing. Kennedy in 1962 rejected a Reuther suggestion that Conway be named Undersecretary of Labor and gave the nomination to California union official John Henning. On patronage matters of concern to labor, Kennedy deferred to George Meany.

Following the abortive Bay of Pigs invasion of Cuba, Kennedy did ask Reuther to set up a private committee to seek release of the invaders being held captive by the Castro government. The idea was to ransom the men by providing Cuba with American-made farm implements, purchased through public donations. Reuther named a bipartisan Tractors for Freedom Committee, which included Eleanor Roosevelt and Milton Eisenhower. The rescue effort failed, however, when Castro told a Reuther emissary, Pat Greathouse of the UAW, that he wanted heavy earth-moving machinery, not simply the farm tractors that agricultural economists who accompanied Greathouse recommended as potentially the most useful to Cuba's farming populace. Contributions were returned and the Committee was disbanded.

Reuther's continuing interest in Washington affairs was evidenced in April 1962—seven months before the off-year election—when, on behalf of the AFL-CIO Industrial Union Department, he invited all members of Congress to join him for cocktails and steak at the capital's Mayflower Hotel. Two Cabinet officers, 35 senators, and 167 House members—including 55 Republicans—showed up and listened to a 43-minute Reuther speech on the problems of the time. Joked one union man: "After all, Reuther had a joint session of Congress. I knew he couldn't resist a State of the Union Message." Meany, invited belatedly, did not attend.

"We have a good President," said Reuther in advance of the elections, "but we need a much better Congress if the President . . . is going to be liberated from his congressional prison." In the view of the UAW leader, the legislative program sent to the Capitol by Kennedy represented a promising if not wholly adequate beginning. "But," he declared, "that program has been blocked and watered down and compromised. . . . Our job is to go out and arouse the people of America."

Almost simultaneous with word of the 1962 election results—close to a standoff in partisan terms save for a Democratic gain of four Senate seats—came sorrowful news for Reuther. Eleanor Roosevelt, his friend and patron, was dead. For more than two decades Walter and May Reuther had gone to Hyde Park, New York, each summer to spend a few days with the widow of the President who had diverted him from the path of orthodox Socialism in 1936. When the two Reuther daughters were old enough, they had gone along, too. Anna Roosevelt Halsted remembers these visits: "Walter Reuther and Mother, despite a generation gap, had mutual concerns about humanity throughout the world. When they met, no time was wasted in reminiscence as they laid plans for further action. May and I sat by fascinated, but with a certain awe."

In 1962 the Reuthers paid a September call on "Mrs. R," as Reuther called the former first lady. He found her virtually bedridden but eager to do more than her failing health would permit.

Her physician told Reuther, "She will not cooperate any more," and asked him to intervene. Mrs. Roosevelt promised Reuther she would try to remain abed—a difficult undertaking for one who, in Reuther's words, "always had a great sense of social obligation" when she had house guests. Recalling an earlier weekend, when a Reuther visit coincided with a birthday party for Franklin D. Roosevelt, Jr., the labor leader said:

> She had about 35 guests, mostly relatives. They had a very close sense of family. They fought like hell but they had a very close sense of family. And this woman . . . felt that she was personally responsible for every single one of those guests. . . . On Saturday—the birthday party was on Saturday afternoon— this woman not only wrapped a little gift for every guest but wrote a little poem for every guest in her longhand. This is a measure of this really wonderful human being.

During the 1962 visit Mrs. Roosevelt insisted that Reuther take her to church on Sunday morning. "I think you're too ill," he replied. "You really ought to stay home." Also visiting was President Roosevelt's uncle, David Delano, a man in his nineties, and Mrs. Roosevelt said, "But Uncle David has to go and I feel that I must go with him." Reuther finally agreed he would take the two of them to church provided his hostess promised to return to bed immediately thereafter. She promised, and they went, sitting in the family pew at the front of the church, with no one around them. It was a "high" Episcopal parish and, to Reuther, the ritual was "more Catholic than the Catholic Church." In the past Mrs. Roosevelt had always given him her elbow when he was supposed to stand, sit or kneel. This time she and Uncle David fell asleep. "I don't know when to get up and when to get down" Reuther recalled. "And I hear a lot of noise back there. I figure something's happening. I went through the damnedest experience. . . . And finally it's over and I get Mrs. R and Uncle David back home. . . . The next time she was in that church, it was her funeral. We were the last house guests she had before she died."

Mrs. Roosevelt died on November 7, 1962. Her burial on the

grounds of the Hyde Park estate was witnessed by men whose public service spanned the years between her husband's New Deal and the New Frontier of John F. Kennedy. Standing side by side were Kennedy, Dwight D. Eisenhower and Harry S Truman. Barely a year later, Kennedy, too, was dead and Lyndon Johnson, one of F.D.R.'s protéges in the 1930's, was President.

CHAPTER TWENTY-EIGHT

The Great Society

THE DAY AFTER JOHN F. KENNEDY WAS ASSASSINATED, PRESIDENT Lyndon Johnson telephoned Walter Reuther to make a personal appeal: "I need your help." The chief of the Auto Workers, although grieving and troubled, pledged his wholehearted support. The result in the months and years that followed was a close collaboration between Reuther and the Texan he had opposed three years earlier. In the words of one UAW official, the two men became "big armpit buddies." Within months a conservative polemicist, J. Evetts Haley, could write with a measure of accuracy that "now nobody seems to move in and out of the White House with greater ease than the arrogant radical, Walter Reuther."

Johnson's "Great Society" legislation was greeted with almost total enthusiasm by the labor leader. Indeed, Reuther contributed to framing the LBJ proposals and, according to one of Johnson's principal assistants, was a key architect of the Model Cities program, behind which the Auto Workers mounted an intensive lobbying campaign.

"President Johnson relied on Walter quite a bit—in foreign policy and civil rights—for both advice and support . . ." states former Vice-President Hubert Humphrey. ". . . Johnson's domestic legislative policy was just what Walter Reuther had hoped and prayed for. He was consulted [on that program] as often as any man outside government."

Most Reuther visits to the White House were unannounced and unpublicized. Sometimes he was with the President for two or three hours. At other times Johnson conferred with him by telephone. Humphrey met Reuther often for breakfast or late night talks at Washington's Statler-Hilton Hotel. He says: "Most every liberal Democrat respected Walter Reuther and he had a good deal of influence with them. He had an evangelical zeal about him. It was always business." Humphrey felt that "Walter's fun was really his conversation and most of it related to politics and unionism."

In dealing with Reuther over the years, he decided: "I'd rather hear him speak an hour than hear some people yawn. . . . I got a lot of education from him."

Reuther was an early supporter of Johnson for election in 1964 and, at the Democratic convention that August, played an important and controversial role as an agent for the President in an emotion-packed contest over the seating of delegates from Mississippi. The state's old-line Democrats were sending a lily-white delegation to Atlantic City, where a challenge was promised by the Negro-dominated Freedom Democratic Party of Mississippi. Johnson's men first proposed to seat the Jim Crow delegation, give the Freedom Democrats floor privileges but no votes, and adopt a new rule to ensure racially mixed Southern delegations at future conventions. Joseph L. Rauh, Jr., acting as counsel for the Freedom Democrats, countered with a proposal that both groups be seated, and he claimed sufficient support to force a floor fight on the question. Fearing a Southern walkout should the issue reach the floor, Johnson called Humphrey, who was a key figure in efforts to find a harmonious solution, with instructions: "You get ahold of Walter Reuther and see if he can help you." Johnson was banking on Reuther's broad influence within the Democratic Party, his unquestioned credentials as a champion of Negro rights, and the fact that Rauh was the UAW's general counsel at the time. Contacted during negotiations with General Motors, Reuther insisted he could not leave. Humphrey pleaded with him and, relenting, the UAW president reached Atlantic City in a chartered plane shortly after midnight on August 25. He went directly into a night-long meeting with Humphrey, Walter Jenkins, and other presidential lieutenants. At sunrise the group emerged with a compromise proposal. "Without his help," Humphrey believes, "I don't think we would have been able to put it together."

Rauh learned about the plan from Reuther, whose telephone call he took in a public phone booth surrounded by reporters and photographers. It was the original LBJ proposal except that two Freedom Democrats specified by name—Aaron Henry and Ed King—would be given votes in the convention. Rauh appealed for a delay in presentation of the plan to the Credentials Committee so he could confer with Henry. Reuther said he would do what he could but insisted, "This is the way it's going to be." He was emphatic in demanding that Rauh accept the compromise, delay or no delay. The attorney, irate at what he considered Reuther's heavy-handed pressure, emerged from the booth to be confronted by the press. "Who was it?" he was asked. "A pretty girl," he replied.

Rauh was convinced the compromise would fail because both Henry and King represented the intellectual, middle-class faction within the Freedom Democratic Party. He felt that Fannie Lou Hamer "had to be seated representing the poor sharecropper." He wanted time and the opportunity to convince Reuther and the other Johnson representatives that replacement of King, a white, by Mrs. Hamer would be an acceptable solution. No delay was granted, however, and, facing heavy White House pressure, Rauh's supporters on the Credentials Committee lost their appetite for forcing a showdown on the convention floor. "Every hour we were losing them," the attorney reports. "I'd get a call and they'd say, 'Sorry, Joe. . . .'" He contends that one woman on the Committee was informed by Edmund G. (Pat) Brown, then Governor of California, that her husband would not get a judgeship if she voted with Rauh, and that unusual pressure from Washington was exerted on another: "They had the Secretary of the Army call this guy, who was a teacher in the Canal Zone, and fire him if he didn't leave me. He told the Secretary of the Army to go fuck himself, right on the telephone. That's how hot it was. . . ."

The Freedom Democrats did not accept the Humphrey-Reuther compromise but instead staged a sit-in on the convention floor while Mississippi's old-line Democrats walked out. It was the very kind of televised demonstration Johnson had insisted on avoiding. Rauh, although hardly a dispassionate observer, felt afterwards that:

> . . . A lot of history might have been different. . . . With the exception of Mrs. Hamer for Ed King, this was the perfect offer . . . had it been properly handled. Had Reuther gotten off the

"muscle" and onto the sensible operation, we could have done it. . . . Walter made the greatest mistake of his life in thinking that the way you run something like this is with muscle instead of with thought and care. . . . Lyndon was running this through Walter.

Humphrey takes a quite different view of Reuther's role: "He was a practical man, and there are very few practical liberals who know how far to go. He was a born negotiator—he knew when to settle—and he never had to worry that somebody would charge that he was selling them out." Rauh, of course, did feel betrayed.

Reuther and Rauh were agreed on one point at Atlantic City. Hubert Humphrey was their choice for the vice-presidential nomination. Even Reuther and George Meany could agree on that.

The Democratic campaign that culminated in the record-smashing defeat of Republican Barry Goldwater began with a mass rally on Labor Day in Detroit's Kennedy Square. Walter Reuther preceded Lyndon Johnson to the rostrum and talked until the President, a man of scant patience, was visibly restive.

Despite Reuther's close identification with the Democratic Party, and his exertions on its behalf, old Socialist Norman Thomas was convinced even in the mid-1960's that Walter and his brothers still favored Socialism with a capital "S." Recalling events dating back to the 1930's, he related:

> I've been nicely lectured by both Walter and Victor of not being far enough left, yet under the stress of circumstances Walter and more or less his brothers came around to the position that the way to advance . . . was to work within the orthodox labor movement and to support first Roosevelt and then other Democratic presidents, that they get more for their union that way. Walter, for instance, for a great many years—not so much now—took rather elaborate care to have no personal contact with me—no letters in his file, I think, not because he wasn't still my friend but because he thought it was the tactics that he had to follow to get what he wanted for the union.

Walter Reuther certainly had the interests of the auto union in mind as he worked in close tandem with Johnson and his Democratic predecessors. However, Reuther's interests in the areas of legislation and social reform ranged far beyond the conventional interests of trade unionism and were not circumscribed by any lingering attachment to the doctrinaire ideology of the Socialist Party. He sought his vision of progress wherever he could find it.

Unlikely as the Johnson-Reuther collaboration might have seemed a few years earlier, the two men worked well in harness. Occasionally, however, the UAW leader was rebuffed in urging a faster pace for the "Great Society" and ultimately he became disenchanted with the Vietnam War. In October of 1965, however, Reuther was as firm as Meany in his support of the intervention in Southeast Asia. The UAW Board formally applauded the Johnson policy of "insuring against Communist military victory while holding forth the hand of unconditional negotiation." When Paul Schrade, the union's top man in California, persisted in criticizing Johnson's Vietnam policy, Reuther called him on the carpet a couple of times, arguing that it was embarrassing to have a regional director opposing union policy supported by a majority of the membership.

Reuther usually was on Johnson's side, at home and abroad. When the International Longshoremen's Association balked at handling American wheat bound for the Soviet Union, the UAW chief pointedly asked the ILA president, Thomas W. (Teddy) Gleason, if he were "trying to become Secretary of State." Reuther was equally blunt in opposing a New York subway strike, while arguing for practical machinery to redress worker grievances in such cases: "We cannot live in a situation where a few workers who are denied their equity can paralyze an entire community. Workers should be able to get justice in the absence of strike action."

Where the interests of his own union were involved, Reuther occasionally trimmed his crusading sails. It seemed odd, for example, to find him "hanging back in Detroit" and sending a written statement to a congressional committee investigating auto safety while his old foe, Jimmy Hoffa of the Teamsters, appeared in person. Jerry F. Ter Horst, chief Washington correspondent of the Detroit *News,* suggested Reuther wanted to avoid questioning about shoddy assembly work performed by UAW members.

The interests of the membership and the economic health of the domestic auto industry were twin concerns that Reuther never overlooked, no matter how far afield he ranged in his reforming zeal. He was acutely conscious that the industry had to prosper if its workers were to prosper.

These considerations prompted the UAW chief in 1965 to submit to President Johnson yet another "Reuther Plan." Concerned about the impact of import competition, particularly from Volkswagen, Reuther proposed that the major American auto makers be permitted to set up a joint venture corporation that would produce a "people's car" directly competitive in size and price with Volkswagen. By pooling resources to turn out a single economy model, Reuther argued, the domestic industry could turn back the import threat and increase its sales and profits, employment of auto workers would be increased, and the nation's balance of payments position would be strengthened. Johnson was impressed and ordered a high level study. The idea was abandoned only after Attorney General Nicholas deB. Katzenbach told the President it would conflict too sharply with the Clayton antitrust law.

In one area—civil rights—Reuther never permitted himself to be influenced by persistent and vocal opposition to his activities by a substantial minority of the UAW's membership. From the outset of his union career, and before that as a City College student, he worked for racial equality. An early member of the National Association for the Advancement of Colored People, Reuther told the organization's 1957 convention in Detroit:

> I've often thought—why is it that you can get a great nation like America marching, fighting, sacrificing, and dying in the struggle to destroy the master race theory in Berlin and people haven't got an ounce of courage to fight against the master race theory in America? . . .
>
> I want to say to these people in Congress that they have been on the longest sit-down strike in the history of America—80

long years. We think it's about time they terminate that sit-down strike on civil rights and turn out some legislation.

Under Reuther's leadership the UAW repeatedly cracked down on local unions practicing discrimination. With his backing, the convention that elected him president set up a Fair Practices and Anti-Discrimination Department and authorized elaborate machinery for handling racial problems. Reuther's Auto Workers hired more Negro staff officials than any other union, although it was 1962 before Reuther sponsored the first Negro, Nelson Jack Edwards, elected to the Executive Board.

Throughout the sixties Reuther supported with his marching presence, his words, and his union's dollars a whole series of civil rights and minority group causes. He was a leader of the massive 1963 civil rights "March on Washington"—the one climaxed by Martin Luther King's memorable speech, "I have a dream." The Kennedy administration originally had feared disruptive sit-ins at the Capitol but Reuther and others, with close cooperation from Kennedy aides, planned and executed a peaceful and effective assembly of 200,000 at the Lincoln Memorial. Before the march, Reuther clashed with Meany over AFL-CIO policy toward the demonstration. At Meany's urging, the Federation's high command approved a hands-off policy statement and Reuther fumed: "That resolution is so anemic it will need a transfusion to get to the mimeograph machine."

Two years later Reuther and his wife May were marching again —with Martin Luther King at Selma, Alabama, and with James H. Meredith in Jackson, Mississippi. At Selma the union leader climbed on a cane-bottom chair and delivered one of the shortest speeches of his career, just three minutes in length: "The struggle will be carried on until every American can share in the blessings of human dignity. . . . Let us take heart, our cause is just and human justice will prevail." At Jackson the Reuthers walked the final five miles of Meredith's route, the segment many observers feared would produce physical attacks on the demonstrators.

Reuther also was the first major labor leader to dramatize the cause of Cesar Chavez and his Mexican-American grape pickers in

California. He went to strike headquarters at Delano, bringing inspiration and UAW funds to the impoverished, then-obscure band of farm workers. His appeals to George Meany to make a similar journey were rebuffed because, as the AFL-CIO president later explained, he looked upon Reuther's trip as press agentry.

To the head of the Auto Workers, the fight for minority rights meant more than grape strikes and showpiece demonstrations. In 1964 he launched the Citizens' Crusade Against Poverty, winning an Executive Board pledge of a million dollars in the effort to mobilize nongovernmental support for the impoverished. Scores of prominent citizens, including heads of large corporations, joined him in the undertaking. In a statement marking the opening of a Crusade-sponsored "Poor People's Convention" in Washington in 1966, Reuther warned that "reason will yield to riots and bitterness will yield to bloodshed" unless more were done for the least privileged of society. Criticizing Lyndon Johnson for not asking larger anti-poverty appropriations, he declared, "When you trim your sails before a fight you make a tactical mistake." Reuther himself came in for criticism because he did not attend the meeting. Sargent Shriver, then director of the Office of Economic Opportunity, did so and, when hoots drowned out his speech, left the hall declaring he would not "participate in a riot." One labor leader, suspecting Reuther had anticipated disorder, was irate that the head of the Auto Workers had not appeared with Shriver to deliver his own scheduled speech.

Within the year, Reuther's warnings of riots and bloodshed came to pass in his own city. As parts of Detroit burned and citizens fell before gunfire in 1967, LBJ and Governor George Romney sparred warily over the dispatch of federal troops to put down the riot. The city's mayor, Jerome Cavanaugh, asked Reuther to intercede. Wanting to "save the city," the union leader telephoned the White House and talked to Supreme Court Justice Abe Fortas, who was helping Johnson deal with the crisis. The troops were sent.

Reuther's reaction to the riot was to join his bargaining table adversaries in creating a New Detroit Committee that hoped to do locally what the Citizens' Crusade was attempting on a national scale. One of the Committee's first goals was passage of fair housing legislation. Twice during the autumn of 1967 Reuther joined Henry Ford II and General Motors board chairman James Roche on special plane flights to Lansing to conduct personal lobbying. "It was the damnedest conglomeration of power you ever saw in your life," declared one participant. "It was business power, labor power, money power." However, the legislature defeated the bill, 55 to 47, and within days Detroit's black power leaders, who apparently spoke for a minority of the city's Negroes, were calling the New Detroit Committee a failure. Aiming special scorn at Reuther, they argued he was "paternalistic" and unwilling to "deal with indigenous residents as equals." They said: "Walter Reuther has attempted to dictate to the black community ever since the UAW came to power. He has been a Jekyll and Hyde—a liberal around the country, and in Detroit, where he tried to control political power, he is a ruthless despot." Sixteen months earlier, Reuther had been dropped from the list of nominees for the national board of the NAACP by "Young Turks" who stated they were seeking "more militancy." Running nationally on an independent slate, he was reelected, receiving more votes than any other candidate.

If Reuther was dismayed by the sniping, he gave no sign of it. At his behest a distinguished Citizens' Board of Inquiry into Hunger and Malnutrition was created and, after a nine-month study financed by the UAW, asserted that at least ten million Americans were suffering from chronic hunger and malnutrition. The Agriculture Department's commodity distribution program was branded a failure and its food stamp program a "nightmare for the hungry." The Board reported that food programs were reaching only 18 percent of the poor, and not the poorest of the poor at that, while the Agriculture Department was turning back money to the Treasury. As a result of Reuther's initiative, congressional investigations were held, hunger became a national issue, and reforms were instituted.

When the Negro garbage collectors in Memphis struck in 1968, Reuther was there. The labor chief reported to the union's convention a few weeks later:

What do you think these workers were fighting for? They were paid $1.60 an hour for hard, miserable, disagreeable work. And the mayor of that city, who was living in the eighteenth century, was arguing with the federal mediator that it should take a worker five years to get the going rate of $1.80 an hour because, he said, it takes five years to learn the skill to empty a garbage can.

I stood before 50,000 workers . . . and I said, "I serve notice upon the mayor of Memphis and the people who have to make this decision that they will not starve these sanitation workers into submission."

On behalf of the UAW, we laid $50,000 on the line to demonstrate we meant business. And that was an important factor in shifting the whole attitude of the people in positions of power and responsibility in the Memphis government and they finally worked it out.

Now, after I got back a few days later, I got some criticism from some of the membership of this union and I will bet the last nickel I have that the people—there weren't many who wrote me these critical letters—did not understand where *we* came from.

Who helped us back in 1936 and 1937 when we were being beaten up and shot at, when our offices and our cars were being blown up by gangsters hired by the corporations? Who helped us? The coal miners whose wages were not one-third of our wages today. The Clothing Workers, they gave us the money to help build our union. . . .

If we are to preach the gospel of democratic performance, then we must narrow the gap between what we preach and what we practice in this great country of ours.

First of all, because we do understand that human freedom is indivisible, no one is truly free until everyone is free. We must work together to make our nation whole, not make it the same, nor put it into the narrow restrictive mode of conformity, but to build a united nation, a united people within the framework of the splendor of human diversity. This is what is so exciting about America. . . .

I believe that men of good will must work together to find the answers. The answers will not be found in a contest between black power and white supremacy. . . . What we need is the

power of human solidarity, the power built upon our common
humanity, because the only differences there are are only skin
deep. Inside we are all exactly alike. We are all children of God.

For all his intensity and his profound concern about problems
facing the UAW and the nation, Reuther found time to relax—
woodworking, fishing, playing tennis.

The family home near Rochester, Michigan, provided Reuther
with unending do-it-yourself projects. Working there with a power
saw in 1966, he sliced off the tip of a finger. Carpentry also occupied him at a very modest vacation home he and May purchased
on the west coast of Florida near Fort Myers. There the union
leader found solitude and an opportunity to avoid the strict security
measures imposed on him following the 1948 shooting. A Detroit
labor reporter once ambled onto the property unnoticed by Reuther
or Billy Wolfman, his young bodyguard. "Walter and Billy," according to the reporter, "were up on the roof. Walter said: 'Billy,
move that over here. Billy, let me have the hammer. Billy, now
hit her there, Billy.' I stood there for about three minutes during
which . . . I could have set fire to the goddam shed and burned
them out."

Assistant Irving Bluestone once ended a vigorous round of tennis
with Reuther by confessing, "I've had enough." The older man
responded, "I was waiting for you to say that." He had been too
proud to quit. Because Reuther had a weak backhand, the result
of his shotgun injuries, friendly opponents volleyed to his forehand.

When traveling in territory known for fresh water fishing, the
UAW president often carried a collapsible rod in his luggage. On
one expedition along the Mississippi, he prized a catch so much
he had it stuffed and arranged to have it shipped to him by air
freight. Returning to union headquarters, he boasted about his
trophy and promised that all doubters could inspect it. When days
passed and the shipment did not arrive, Reuther began calling the
airlines. Finally, after the package was located, an airline man
telephoned the good tidings and asked Reuther what could be
in the box to prompt so many calls from a man of such importance.
"My reputation's in that box," he was told.

During 1968, however, there was little joy for Walter Reuther. His brother Roy died of a heart attack, his friends Martin Luther King and Robert F. Kennedy were assassinated, and his own inability to achieve the large goals he had set for himself and the labor movement drove him in frustration out of the AFL-CIO.

Two years younger than Walter, Roy died on January 10 in a Detroit hospital. The most gregarious of the brothers, he was, as one labor man put it, "the only guy in the Reuther family that George Meany really liked." Another said: "He took everybody's problem as his own. Walter used to send him to all the funerals. He was doing that all the time. And it would get to him because he took it all to heart. He liked everybody and everybody liked him." Walter was profoundly saddened by the death. He and Roy had been particularly close.

The tragedies that befell the King and Kennedy families also touched Walter Reuther deeply. He marched in Dr. King's funeral procession in Atlanta. And when Senator Kennedy was shot in Los Angeles, he hurried there, then followed the body to New York City where he joined the honor guard that stood by the casket in St. Patrick's Cathedral. The Senator had been the only one outside the family to sit with Walter at Roy's funeral.

Had Kennedy lived, Walter Reuther might have supported him for the Democratic presidential nomination in 1968. Although Humphrey felt that Reuther was "basically loyal to me," the union chief never indicated his choice for the nomination to his UAW colleagues. He did become increasingly disturbed about the Vietnam War, one of Kennedy's major issues. Appearing on "Meet the Press" in September 1967, Reuther declared:

> If I were the President I would, I believe, be willing to cease the bombing of the North in the hope that that might give us the basis for new initiatives in trying to get to the conference table, because I believe over the long pull there are no military solutions to the economic, social, and political problems of Asia and that freedom must win that fight over tyranny in the rice fields and not in the battlefields.

Reuther, who eventually lent his name to a committee of moderate "doves" who sought "Negotiations Now," was in no way sympathetic to the presidential aspirations of Senator Eugene McCarthy, the first and most outspoken of the peace candidates. Following President Johnson's withdrawal and Kennedy's murder, the UAW hierarchy was solidly for Humphrey.

At the ill-starred Democratic convention in Chicago, Humphrey and Reuther collaborated in trying to develop a "middle-ground position" for a party-uniting platform plank on Vietnam. Recalls Humphrey: "I was on the telephone all day Friday and Saturday prior to the convention with Dave Ginsburg, Ken O'Donnell, and Ted Sorensen. I had cleared a compromise plank with a number of people in government but administration forces torpedoed it. I was for it, Walter was for it—the President turned out not to be." Reuther ultimately went along with the Johnson-tailored resolution that won adoption. So did Humphrey.

By 1968, Humphrey felt, "Walter's orientation became more Democratic Party and less with ADA. . . . He became disillusioned with ADA because it became less realistic about social issues and was concentrating almost exclusively on the anti-war issue."

Humphrey received substantial Auto Workers' help in his 1968 campaign against Richard Nixon. Although the Republican nominee made a major effort in Michigan, aided on the stump by Governor Romney and World Series heroes of the champion Detroit Tigers, Humphrey carried the state by 222,417 votes out of 3,306,250 cast. It was one of the Democratic candidate's better showings in an election he lost by a national popular vote margin of seven-tenths of one percent. It may be one reason he believes that Walter Reuther "exercised more power than any Senator—and I think he did more good than most of us."

CHAPTER TWENTY-NINE

The Changing Union

THE ENORMOUS CHANGES THAT OVERTOOK AMERICAN SOCIETY IN the 1960's confronted Walter Reuther with a series of challenges that tested his flexibility and gift for innovation. In UAW-organized shops, skilled tradesmen demanded more than they felt they were getting under his leadership. The gap between the aging Reuther and the auto union's youthful membership kept him hustling to retain his place at the head of the parade. And the old radical found himself in sharp disagreement with the tactics of the new breed of radical youth and black revolutionaries.

As a young man working for Henry Ford, Reuther had belonged to Detroit's blue collar elite, the skilled craftsmen who fashion tools and dies, make models, and perform other precision tasks. By 1967 about 115,000 of these "aristocrats of labor" belonged to the UAW and were complaining loudly that their wage rates were falling behind the scales of old AFL craft unions by $3 to $4 an hour. "Are we a nickel and dime union?" one grumbled.

With the Big Three contracts expiring on September 6, 1967, Reuther recognized that he must offer special concessions to his skilled trades constituency. If nothing were done, he feared, the result might be a union-splitting revolt and perhaps even the establishment of a rival organization vying for NLRB recognition to represent skilled workers. Just such a group, the Society of Skilled Trades, had been formed following the 1955 industry settlement but the auto union and the auto makers had formed a common front to block the Society's effort to gain bargaining rights.

Reuther knew that palliatives would not be accepted by the rebellious craftsmen of 1967, although the UAW did give them their own slick monthly magazine, *New Technology*, and a "status symbol" lapel pin. Far more important, the UAW Executive Board promised the skilled tradesmen the right to veto any agreement emerging from negotiations. Addressing a special Skilled Trades Conference, Reuther declared:

No group of workers has a right to say, "I, as a member of
the UAW, want special privilege," because we will not extend
special privilege. But a worker with a special problem has a
right to say, "I want my union to deal with my special problem," and we will do that in 1967.

As part of its bargaining preparations, the auto union hired a
New York polling organization, Oliver Quayle & Company, to
make an exhaustive study of the membership's contract goals. The
UAW also opened a health club for the Solidarity House headquarters staff, but denied published reports that its objective was
to get its negotiators in trim. At any rate, GM's Lou Seaton approved, declaring, "We like to bargain with healthy people."

Industry offered the Auto Workers a three-year contract with
increases in wages and fringe benefits totaling 55 to 60 cents an
hour during the three years. This was far short of the union demand for a package amounting to at least 90 cents. Negotiations
produced no movement on either side and the union, backed by
a strike fund of $67 million, shut down the year's target company,
Ford, on September 6. Of the 160,000 strikers, 20,000 were
skilled workers. Because it promised to be a long and costly walkout, Reuther and all members of the UAW's Ford Department
staff went off the payroll. The rest of the professional staff took
a voluntary 25 percent pay cut. Coming at the start of the 1968
model year, the strike cost the corporation heavily, too, and Henry
Ford II was not pleased. Terming the walkout "totally unjustified
and completely unnecessary," he declared, "Because we would not
accede to the unconscionable demands of a powerful union, we
are paying a stiff penalty."

After seven weeks Ford capitulated and offered a settlement
that, in money terms, closely approximated the union's "unconscionable demands." Providing an estimated 91 cents an hour in
wages and fringes over three years, it represented, in Reuther's
words, "the largest wage increase that our union has ever negotiated
with a major corporation." The historic feature in the eyes of the
union president, however, was achievement at last of a true guaranteed annual wage.

The big question was whether the proposed pact would win the approval of the skilled workers, voting in a referendum of their own. Unless they gave their support, the strike would continue. The settlement terms provided that the craftsmen would get an immediate wage increase of 50 cents an hour, compared with a 20-cent hike for production workers. To gain this and other concessions, Reuther had agreed to put a three-year ceiling of 18 cents an hour on automatic cost-of-living pay boosts—a major concession in view of subsequent strong inflationary trends born of the Vietnam War. There was a "catch-up" provision to restore inflation-eroded buying power at the end of the contract term, however.

The night before the skilled tradesmen were to vote, Reuther touted the contract during an hour-long television broadcast aimed at union members in Michigan. Estimating the settlement's cost to Ford at between $700 million and $800 million, Reuther warned that "if you strike for three more months, it is our judgment there will be no substantial improvement in this contract." He emphasized, "I tell you that we have squeezed and squeezed and squeezed." Six disgruntled skilled tradesmen raised a war chest of their own and purchased half an hour of television time immediately following the Reuther broadcast. They argued that rejection of the accord "would give Brother Reuther the ammunition to go back" and get a better agreement.

Reuther prevailed. The skilled men voted for the contract by a margin of nearly three to one while production workers gave it nine-to-one approval. However the settlement did not end discontent in the ranks. At the 1968 UAW convention, skilled workers were prominent in a minority faction that campaigned to make the union "more democratic." Although they had an inviting slogan, "One man, one vote," they could muster only 293 delegates— 10 percent of the total—on a test of strength. Nevertheless, theirs was the best organized, best financed, and most active campaign against Reuther policies since he had captured firm control of the union machinery in 1947.

The very fact of the convention challenge to Reuther's leadership demonstrated that the United Auto Workers, even in its maturity, was a changing union that could not afford to be content with the status quo. Neither could Reuther indulge in complacency, although it was evident that, for the moment at least, his intra-union critics could not come close to threatening his position and power.

The auto union had crossed many a mileage marker since Walter Reuther had been elected in 1936 to its first autonomous Executive Board. The historic first agreement with General Motors, for example, had been typed on a single page, whereas the 1967 contract ran to 477 pages. The nature of the UAW membership also had been altered dramatically over the years. By 1967 at least half a million members had retired and get-togethers were being planned by the "Florida Sun Coast Council of Retired UAW Members." Some active unionists by then were attending union-sponsored lectures on "Fundamentals of Investing." More than half the membership had signed their checkoff cards since 1962 and had little or no knowledge of the sacrifices and physical assaults that had been endured by the men who had created their union.

Walter Reuther, an old radical, found himself labeled a member of the "Establishment" by some of his younger union brothers. His reply:

> Obviously, the UAW is an established organization. We're not struggling for our very survival. . . . I have been in the state of continuous revolt against the status quo, and I equate the status quo with the Establishment. What the labor movement has got to do is try to find a way to, in effect, have a working relationship with the Establishment—because it bargains with the Establishment; it obviously deals with the government, and that's part of the Establishment. It can't pretend the Establishment doesn't exist and it can't act as though it has no contact with it. It obviously has to have. It has to have a working relationship with the Establishment.
>
> But the labor movement ought not to become absorbed in the Establishment. It has to consciously know while it's working with the Establishment—and, in effect . . . is a part of the Establishment in *that* relationship—it must be the instrument of constructive and creative social change. If the labor movement

is not an instrument of social change, it is nothing. And when it fails to be that kind of a creative, constructive instrument for social change and is just dealing with pressure group things —getting more—then I think it fails totally in its responsibilities.

Reuther had firsthand knowledge of the "youth rebellion," and he talked about it: "My youngest daughter doesn't surprise me anymore. Because I now have made up my mind that she is a part of a different generation that's living in a different world than I am. And I don't expect her to behave like I used to behave. I made up my mind to that. You understand, she shocks me—but she doesn't surprise me."

Yet Reuther, uncertain just how to handle the youthful members of his union, and disturbed about the young radicals on campuses and in the streets, could not fathom why some of the supposedly enduring values he cherished were being challenged by such groups as Students for a Democratic Society:

> I can remember a time when I was considered very radical and revolutionary because . . . I led a successful fight at Wayne University [his old City College] against the ROTC. And now the SDS kids think that's a brand new idea. Excepting I think the thing that's wrong with the SDS kids, as I told them in the last confrontation I had with some of them, number one, they think that you can solve things by violence and I believe that violence is counterproductive . . . and doesn't solve any problems. And secondly, I said, we sat down in the plants. And if there was a university administration that said, "We won't talk to you, we won't meet with you," and you tried every avenue of approach and they were all blocked, . . . then I could understand why you might want to sit down in the administration building until they would talk to you. . . . We sat down because they wouldn't talk to us. And when they did talk to us, we did not have any nonnegotiable demands. We had all negotiable demands. And you're sitting down because you don't want to talk. And when you do talk you have nonnegotiable demands and the first one is for the president of the university to be fired. Now, I said, that's crazy. And I said we knew what we were fighting for—and you only know what you're fighting

against. And that's not good enough. You have no moral right to destroy something unless you think you've got something better to put in its place. And I said that's the difference between what we did when I was a young radical going to the university and what you're doing. And that's a fundamental difference.

Whether one would call him a radical or an Establishment man, Reuther never lost his awareness of change and the need to meet it. An attempt to revive some of the union's do-or-die spirit of the 1930's absorbed much of his time during the last years of his life. He conceived, and brought to reality, a UAW Family Education Center on the shores of Black Lake in northern Michigan. Reuther's objective was to carve out of virgin land an attractive, comfortable union "spa" to which a young Auto Workers' activist and his entire family could retreat for a combination vacation-indoctrination session. Noted Philadelphia architect Oskar Stonarov, who designed Solidarity House, laid out the plans for the $18 million project and Reuther threw himself into the work with such gusto that his associates gossiped he had contracted a bad case of "Black Lake fever." He even went around the property marking trees he wanted preserved.

Joe Rauh, among others, applauded the effort of Reuther and the Auto Workers to come to grips with the "generation gap." He felt the UAW was "the one union that's faced up to the problem . . . instead of just bemoaning the fact that the ones who didn't go through the union struggles don't have the same loyalties."

Reuther also recognized that younger UAW members were not as Depression-conscious as their predecessors. There had been a time, not long ago, when auto workers always welcomed overtime. But that was when lengthy unpaid layoffs were common and a factory hand faced economic pressures to earn while he could. The New Breed, Reuther decided, should be given a choice between overtime and having a date or bowling with the wife. He reasoned this way:

> . . . We're going to be talking about overtime, which I think is a very, very serious problem in our kind of industrial society. And I've been saying that if a worker goes to work for the

General Motors Corporation . . . he, in effect, goes to work knowing that he is going to . . . accept a certain discipline of that workplace. . . . That isn't something that he finds out by surprise. He knows that that's a condition of his employment. But he takes the job under the generally accepted national work pattern of an eight-hour day and a 40-hour week. And whenever the needs of production, or the desire of the company, require the extension of that work discipline beyond the eight hours or beyond 40 hours, it is my contention that that then begins to infringe upon the free hours that a worker has, in which he has not contracted to accept this arbitrary discipline . . . and therefore he should have a voice in whether or not he is willing to accept that discipline. . . . And the foreman shouldn't to able to say to him, "Well, we are going to work tonight two hours overtime, and if you've got something scheduled with your wife, that's just too damn bad because you're working and you'd better be on your job or you're gonna get penalized." Well, I don't think the foreman has a right to interfere in the nonworking hours of that worker and his family. . . . I can assure you that the attitudes of the corporations will not be in the same spirit. Why? Because this takes on the gut issue with them about their right to run the plants. Well, what about the worker's right to run his life in the nonworking hours?

Protecting a union man against overtime would have made Reuther a laughingstock in the days when he was an Auto Workers' pioneer. In fact, it was a notion alien to virtually all labor leaders even in 1970. On the other hand, Reuther never understood nor fully appreciated many of his labor colleagues, as they did not understand or appreciate him. Squabbling interminably with the AFL-CIO, he contended that many union leaders had "*made it* and they are very comfortable, and when you try to get people to do things that disturb their comfort, . . . they're not going to feel very pleasantly about you." He said the trouble with the labor movement was that some of its functionaries had come to "look upon it as their private property." He added: "It happens to belong to 12 or 15 million Americans. It's theirs. It doesn't belong to me or anybody else."

In and out of his own union, there were those who argued that Reuther did look upon the Auto Workers as his private property. One such critic was B. J. Widick, a radical, a former auto worker, and a former member of the UAW staff, who wrote in his 1964 volume, *Labor Today*: "Reuther operates the UAW with an air of infallibility, and with the iron grip of an infallible man. The top AFL-CIO leaders know how Reuther runs his union, and how the international union Executive Board has been reduced to a 'rubber stamp' body. Consequently, Reuther's moralizing in the union movement has an air of hypocrisy to them."

Yet it was Reuther who, in 1957, took a gamble that no other union president had ever risked. He created a Public Review Board of distinguished private citizens to hear any complaints that he or the Executive Board had erred, been capricious or otherwise strayed from the path of pure justice in handling intra-union squabbles involving disciplinary or other formal action. Creation of the blue-ribbon panel was his way of saying, with a flair for the dramatic that was his trademark, "This is a clean, democratic union." And the Review Board, it should be added, ruled against Reuther personally when it felt the UAW chief had been in error.

In his first years as president, while strident factionalism continued, Reuther did act—when he felt he had the power to overwhelm and not simply outvote his opponents—to revise UAW convention procedures for the benefit of his own Caucus. His justification was his fervent combat against Communist infiltration and a desire to end once and forever the internal struggles that more than once had threatened to tear the union apart. As a sympathetic labor historian, Walter Galenson, subsequently recorded: "Convention rules make it difficult for policies not sanctioned by the administration to be raised and discussed. The method of selecting international officers renders minority representation unlikely." Another writer noted that opposition elements did not find places on convention committees and that the Reuther rules virtually precluded roll call votes. On the other hand, wrote Jack Steiber in *Governing the UAW*, "This has not prevented long and heated discussion on a variety of issues and even the defeat of some committee recommendations by the convention. The administration encourages full debate and discussion and uses delegates' views as a sounding board to test rank and file sentiment on controversial issues. On a few occasions the administration has withdrawn or modified its original proposals because of delegates' reactions. . . ." Within the Executive Board it was Reuther's practice to take soundings, even straw votes, to make certain in advance that his position would claim a substantial majority. When the votes were not forthcoming, he was prepared to compromise. Asked in advance of the union's 1970 convention about a likely new anti-Reuther campaign of the type mounted two years earlier, he responded: "If we're not ahead of them, maybe they ought to be leading the parade."

As the union grew, Reuther faced administrative problems never envisioned in the early days. The Auto Workers' staff, for example, decided it needed a union within a union to represent its interests in dealing with the high command. Appalled at the outset, Reuther ultimately accepted with good grace the wishes of his "employes," and a Staff Council came into being to bargain with the Reuther "management." At headquarters the numbers involved were not inconsiderable. In fact, a joke spread through labor circles that, as the Solidarity House payroll approached 1,000, Secretary-Treasurer Emil Mazey was asked how many worked there and replied, "About half of them."

The Auto Workers' treasury grew to such proportions that investing the funds safely became a problem for Mazey. The San Francisco National Bank, for example, closed its doors in 1965 when the UAW held $3 million worth of the bank's certificates of deposit. The union was forced to settle for 52 cents on the dollar. A second bank failure, in Detroit, put another dent in the UAW treasury but Richard T. Frankensteen, who had become a corporation president, observed that Mazey "was in good company" because a number of blue chip industrialists suffered with him. It was a far cry from the 1935-1936 period, when Walter Reuther had to borrow gasoline money from his wife so he could drive to organizing meetings and when he opened the first West Side Local

office on borrowed funds. Dave Miller, a retired Auto Workers'
pioneer, recalled: ". . . Three of us stood on a corner in this city
in 1935 and he [Reuther] told us he had found a room that could
be rented for $10 a month for a headquarters for the organizing
drive on the West Side of Detroit. And between the three of us
we didn't have $10."

More important to the union's long-range future than a couple
of bank failures was the rising tide of expectations in black com-
munities and among black workers. Reuther and his colleagues in
the UAW hierarchy collaborated with the auto makers to help
meet the expectations—even as the Auto Workers became the first
major union target of organized black revolutionaries.

An innovative UAW concept, limited substitution of a "juniority"
system for the traditional seniority rights of older workers in
layoff periods, grew directly out of a cooperative industry-union
effort to train and find jobs for the hard-core unemployed among
young black workers. The training and hiring went smoothly
enough in most instances. By early 1969, for example, Ford had
hired 13,000 such workers. However, a dip in production prompted
the company to return 1,500 of the young men to the streets. To
Reuther and other Auto Workers' leaders, this represented economic and social waste. First of all, it had cost more to prepare
the new black employes for their jobs than had been the case with
most whites hired for similar assignments. Equally important, there
was a real danger that the laid-off blacks would return to lives of
idleness and never be reclaimed as productive members of the work
force.

In March 1969 director Ken Bannon of the union's Ford Department held a news conference to announce that the UAW would
be talking to the company about an inverted job protection plan—
juniority—as a promising method of salvaging the newly trained
blacks. Because it had been the practice of Ford and other auto
makers to operate on a last-hired/first-fired basis, the UAW was
proposing that workers with high seniority, who were thus eligible
for the virtual equivalent of a guaranteed annual wage, be permitted
to volunteer for layoff so young Negroes could remain on the

payroll. When Ford and other manufacturers balked at the proposal, Reuther expressed his discouragement:

> It seems to me that the industry, from a purely narrow operations policy matter, ought to see the wisdom of that. It's costly as hell to break in new workers, and it's more costly to take a hard-core guy and help him. . . . And so we don't understand why they're so narrow and rigid and unimaginative about this. . . . Why do people resist things because they're new? . . . I think we'll have to talk to them about this at the bargaining table. I think it would be good for the country, and I think it would be good for them.

It was ironic that the Auto Workers, with a civil rights record unsurpassed by any other labor organization, became the whipping boy of several black revolutionary groups in 1968-1969. Initially, the challenge to the union was from more moderate elements such as a National Ad Hoc Committee of Concerned Negro UAW members, headed by a vice-president of Ford Local 600. One of its principal objectives was a greater voice for blacks in union affairs. Emphasizing that Reuther's integrity and commitment were not at issue, the Committee stated: "It is precisely because of our faith in your integrity and commitment that we seek to resolve these matters with you at the conference table, rather than, as many powerful voices have suggested, take the issue to the streets and the public press." Although Reuther had a number of meetings with representatives of the group, some of the union's Negro membership felt that too little progress was being made. They cast their lot with the small Detroit-based League of Revolutionary Black Workers.

Active in about a dozen plants, the League announced that "all-out war has been declared on Uncle Tomism in order for us to kill racism" in the auto industry. Workers entering the River Rouge plant were handed leaflets attacking "that racist Walter Reuther" and "white racist pigs." There were instances of violence, and the union hit back at the League as "this group of extremists and racial separatists" which it said "has sought to spread terror among both white and black workers." Douglas Fraser, head of the UAW's Chrysler Department, told labor writer Harry Bernstein of the Los Angeles *Times*: "These people do scare me, I admit it. But I'll be damned if I will back away from the UAW position that there is just no such thing as a black solution to problems any more than there is a white solution. We have to work together."

For thirty years the union had been spreading the racial brotherhood gospel through its policies, in its publications, and in speeches by its leaders—yet white prejudices persisted in the membership. Marcellius Ivory, first Negro elected a regional director of the Auto Workers, was convinced, however, that the integrationist efforts had borne considerable fruit. "We probably could not get a white majority for neighborhood integration," he conceded, "but we have achieved a large measure of on-the-job democracy. Whites would vote almost unanimously, even by secret ballot, to work alongside blacks in the factories and to have integrated union or company bowling teams or golf clubs—as long as these activities are not in the neighborhoods where they live."

By the end of 1969 Walter Reuther felt the campaign of the revolutionaries to create a separate black faction with the union had "tapered off to the point where it's very unimportant." He said: "It was a problem for a period of time . . . and then they got themselves into trouble because of their commitment to violence and their malice. They believe in terrorism. And they stabbed some people in supervision and workers in the plant, and got in trouble. And I think the workers . . . began to realize that that kind of tactic is nonproductive and counterproductive and cannot solve their problems. Plus the fact that . . . the overwhelming majority of black workers in our organization really believe that our union tries to do something about these problems. I mean, they know the leadership of this union has been in this struggle from the very beginning." At the union's 1970 convention Reuther gave reporters his explanation why he and the Auto Workers had been singled out by the revolutionaries: "When you are in favor of destroying the system, the worst enemy is anyone who is trying to make the system work and make it responsive to human needs."

CHAPTER THIRTY

Reuther *v.* Meany

A DECADE AFTER THE 1955 MERGER OF THE AFL AND CIO, THE nation's labor leaders assembled in San Francisco, generally jubilant over the flood of "Great Society" legislation and looking ahead to seven more years of Lyndon B. Johnson's presidency. Only a few of the union officials were deeply disturbed by the escalation of the war in Vietnam or anticipated the inflationary surge that was just over the horizon. Within the Federation, AFL-CIO president George Meany clearly was in command, overshadowing Walter Reuther and every other labor figure. Combining force of personality with shrewd political infighting, Meany had made his office a mighty power center in Washington. His peers at the 1965 conclave, including Reuther, unanimously approved a resolution of tribute:

> The AFL-CIO has never been stronger and more united than it is today and there is not the slightest reason to doubt that its strength and unity will wax still stronger in the years ahead. It is universally recognized in the AFL-CIO and in the nation that the greatest contribution—immeasurable in its influence and indispensable to our success—has been the courageous and determined leadership of the president of the AFL-CIO, George Meany.

Privately, Reuther was sharply critical of Meany's leadership during the ten years since they had jointly wielded a huge gavel to open the first convention of the merged federation. Their relations rarely had been trouble-free and, more than once, the two strong-willed men had clashed so heatedly that another split in the labor movement had seemed inevitable. In the first months of merger Meany had startled labor's elite by shouting at Reuther, "I don't trust you!" Friends had to talk the Auto Workers' leader out of resigning his AFL-CIO vice-presidency on the spot. The merits of India's Prime Minister Nehru soon became another prickly issue, with Meany and Reuther arguing for nearly two hours at an Executive Council meeting—an unlikely forum—over Nehru's policy of neutrality.

The hostility may have been rooted in their ancestry and upbringing. Meany, son of an Irish-born plumber in turn-of-the-century New York, grew up with a devotion to the craft union that equalled his attachment to the Roman Catholic Church. Reuther, product of a strict German Lutheran home in West Virginia, was raised in the class-struggle tradition of Socialist Eugene V. Debs. While Meany loved to relax over a martini, a cigar, and a game of gin rummy, Reuther shunned liquor and preferred the lonely leisure of the cabinetmaker to the camaraderie of the card table.

Even so, they might have been more compatible except for their common concern with the control of power—and each other. From Meany's standpoint, Reuther was forever plotting ways to advance himself and his programs without regard for the consequences to the labor movement. From Reuther's point of view, Meany was obsessed with protecting his job and failed to take the lead in forcing social change. Their disputes, like all family quarrels, became more bitter than conflicts with others outside the labor movement. A Reuther sympathizer said: "Walter was a crusader and idealist. Meany is a business trade unionist who was annoyed when new ideas and proposals for dramatization of issues were advanced. His immediate, automatic response was one of massive inertia."

The February 1959 meeting of the AFL-CIO Executive Council in San Juan, Puerto Rico, clearly showed the extent of hostility between them. The location itself was a calculated rebuke to Reuther by Meany. A year earlier, expressing annoyance with the custom of holding winter Council sessions in luxurious Miami Beach, Reuther had won grudging approval from his colleagues to conduct the following February's meeting in Washington. David Dubinsky, then head of the Ladies' Garment Workers, chided Reuther at the time, declaring: "You don't like to mix business and pleasure. All right. But I do!" During the intervening year Meany quietly arranged for Puerto Rico's governor, Luis Muñoz Marín, to invite the AFL-CIO hierarchy to San Juan early in 1959, assuring the labor leaders of a place in the sun as usual, despite Reuther's best efforts.

When the San Juan session opened, Meany was absent, fighting off a cold, and Reuther alarmed some old AFL unionists by seeking to occupy the chair reserved for the AFL-CIO president. In addition, as chairman of the Economic Policy Committee, Reuther won tentative approval for a dramatic labor "March on Washington" to protest against high unemployment and demand effective counteractions by President Eisenhower. When Eisenhower was asked about the plan at a news conference the following day, he drew laughter by noting that it came from the "sunny beaches" of Puerto Rico, far from the centers of heavy unemployment. Stung by the President's remark, Reuther noted sharply that he had opposed meetings in Florida and other resort areas but was outvoted by his AFL-CIO colleagues. "Mr. President," he retorted, "I have spent no time on the sunny beaches of Puerto Rico nor have I been with you and your many big business friends on the golf course, the duck blinds, and the quail hunts."

Meany, hearing belatedly about the proposed march, frowned on the thought of a mass demonstration in the streets, fearing that Communists and other radicals would take advantage of the occasion for propaganda purposes. Angrily, he demanded that the Economic Policy Committee reverse itself. Reuther refused, threatening to resign as chairman if Meany persisted. Eventually a compromise "Unemployment Rally" of very limited size was endorsed by the Executive Council, giving Reuther a half-a-loaf victory in the contest of wills.

The UAW chief was dealt another setback when he attempted to rally leaders of the old CIO unions to defend Jim Carey, the volatile president of the Initernational Union of Electrical Workers, against a Meany rebuke. In a furious barrage of epithets, Meany had ordered Carey to take a seat at the far end of the Executive Council table. To Reuther, this was shameful treatment of the former secretary of the CIO and he sought a united-front reproach to Meany for employing verbal brutality. It never quite came off, perhaps because, as one former CIO attorney put it, "Jim has blown his stack with almost everybody. . . . I don't think too many people were very upset at seeing him on the receiving end." Although Reuther's CIO caucus met for hours one evening to voice dissatisfaction, it did not take any concerted action.

Later, at the 1959 convention of the AFL-CIO, the caucus met again to consider criticism of the Federation's civil rights record. Al Hartnett, who was the number two man in Carey's union, later said Reuther privately agreed to support the attack but gaveled Hartnett down when he tried to speak on the subject during floor debate.

Reuther was ready and willing, however, to be critical of Meany and the building trades unions on the eve of the 1961 AFL-CIO convention in Miami Beach. In a widely publicized speech before the Industrial Union Department, he declared that prolonged division over jurisdictional claims threatened to destroy the five-year-old federation. "We merged but we did not unite," Reuther stated, advocating new machinery to settle disputes over job rights of competing unions. Earlier, in the spring of the year, he had convened a meeting of former CIO union officials to discuss a series of allegations against the craft unions. Events reached the point where Secretary of Labor Arthur J. Goldberg, appearing before the AFL-CIO building trades convention, felt compelled to appeal strongly for labor unity. Aware of the strong anti-Communist feeling in the audience, Goldberg declared; "Nothing would please Khrushchev more than to have a split labor movement in the United States, fighting within itself, rather than fighting to build a better free world."

Meany established a five-man committee, including Reuther and headed by Machinists' Union president Albert J. Hayes, to come up with a new program to deal with inter-union disputes. Privately, the AFL-CIO president felt that a case-by-case analysis would show that the issues "did not warrant the heat that was being generated," as a top aide put it. With Reuther and Hayes working together, the panel majority proposed outside arbitration of disputes over job rights, with court enforcement of the arbitrator's award if necessary. This was anathema to the building trades, which dearly prized jurisdictional claims, and Meany believed the Hayes proposal could not get sufficient support to win adoption.

Presiding over an extraordinary night session of the Executive Council, Meany called for Hayes' report and then, after it was delivered, moved to set it aside and consider a compromise plan. Bristling, Reuther pulled his papers together, stood up and said to his friends, "C'mon, let's get out of here." There was a dramatic pause. Could this be the much-feared split in the AFL-CIO? Joe Beirne, president of the Communications Workers, quickly spoke up: "Wait a minute. We're not through. We've got work to do." Finding himself without any CIO allies for a walkout, Reuther sat down. Using the Hayes report as a basic document, the Council members shouted, cajoled, and compromised through the long night.

Hours later, a proposal was drafted to set up a modified form of arbitration, with an appeals provision, to deter encroachments on established bargaining units. The proposed penalties were revised to eliminate automatic expulsion, regarded as too severe by critics of the Hayes plan. "What's the use?" Reuther asked, not yet reconciled. "It doesn't matter what you do the building trades won't buy it anyway." Challenged, Meany said simply, "Let's see." One by one, he called the roll of craft union presidents on the Council and each accepted the compromise plan. The outcome was a sharp reversal for Reuther in the internal power struggle. Emerging weary but triumphant at four o'clock in the morning, Meany had preserved the hyphen in the AFL-CIO.

A sign of Meany's irritation with Reuther was the failure to include the UAW president on an AFL-CIO escort committee for President Kennedy at the 1961 convention. The nonappointment was regarded by many delegates as a deliberate snub, despite a disclaimer by Meany.

Other irritants arose to mar the Meany-Reuther relationship, even during a long period of *detente* that extended from 1962 through 1965. Kennedy and the late Adlai E. Stevenson became involved in one of the behind-the-scenes struggles early in the

"New Frontier" days. Reuther was in line to become a member of the United States delegation to the United Nations, to serve under his old friend Stevenson, who apparently asked Kennedy to make the appointment. When Kennedy checked with Meany, the AFL-CIO leader refused to grant his consent and the idea was dropped. Meany said later he would have agreed if Reuther had made the request through the AFL-CIO. Neither Reuther nor any other labor leader was named to the U.N. delegation while Stevenson served at the world organization.

A similar impasse occurred when the elevation of W. Willard Wirtz to Secretary of Labor left a vacancy in the undersecretary's post in 1962. Writing Kennedy directly, Reuther recommended his former aide, Jack Conway, but again the President checked with Meany and found the proposed appointment had not been cleared through AFL-CIO headquarters. "Conway's out," Kennedy said, and he later named another union man to the number two position at the Labor Department. "If Walter had spent five minutes on the telephone, Conway could have become undersecretary," Meany told a visitor later. Reuther felt Meany would veto Conway or anyone identified with the UAW for that post, however. In a crunch, Kennedy deferred to Meany, who had reached the pinnacle of labor power.

Another blowup came when Meany vetoed Reuther's choice of Ralph Helstein, president of the Packinghouse Workers, for a seat on the Executive Council in 1962. It was Reuther's contention that the old CIO unions had the right to name anyone to fill a vacancy caused by the death or resignation of a former CIO man. Meany, however, decreed that Helstein's union was not entirely free of Communist influence at the time, despite Helstein's efforts to control the situation. Reuther rallied his CIO caucus behind his nominee but Meany mustered a majority to block the election. At a later meeting, sensing a split in CIO ranks, Meany pushed through Shipbuilders' president John Grogan over Reuther's opposition. Three years later Helstein was acceptable to Meany and joined the Council by a unanimous vote.

Jack Conway helped smooth over some rough spots in the

Meany-Reuther relationship, largely by working closely with Lane Kirkland, a trusted associate of the AFL-CIO president. "Some problems were worked out simply by taking them as a problem rather than a cause, a flaming, factionalist cause," Kirkland recalled later. "I think Jack Conway was a realist. . . . His own view was that so far as Reuther's own aspirations were concerned, they would be better served this way."

In a move viewed as a peace gesture to his old antagonists in the building trades, Reuther agreed to drop objections by industrial unions to legislation that would expand picketing rights on construction sites. "I think he made a real effort . . . to make himself acceptable to the other unions within the Federation," said an AFL-CIO observer. During the annual winter sessions in Miami Beach, Reuther muted his grumbling about conspicuous consumption, while never spending time around the swimming pool playing gin rummy; he preferred movies, followed by an ice cream sundae, for his resort recreation. One year, however, Reuther and his staff booked rooms in a motel, believing it to be more modest and lower-priced, but the cost turned out to be slightly higher than at the hotel where most Executive Council members stayed.

Reuther's relations with Meany became "almost affable" during that period, and a Detroit newspaperman reported early in 1963 that they enjoyed "a whole week of togetherness without a fight, without hardly a cross word." Each man was critical of the other in private conversation, however. Reuther once declared that Meany was "a hundred years behind the times," and Meany, asked if Reuther were honest, replied brusquely, "*Dollar* honest."

The AFL-CIO president of course was not unaware of Reuther's prominence in the public eye. During a labor meeting in New York, Meany and William F. Schnitzler, heavy-set secretary-treasurer of the AFL-CIO at the time, were walking with Reuther through a hotel lobby. "Look, there's Walter Reuther!" one woman exclaimed to a friend. "Yes, but who's that with him?" the friend asked. "His bodyguards, of course," came the reply, while Meany chuckled to himself.

As Meany approached his 70th birthday, many observers believed Reuther was his heir apparent. A. H. Raskin, labor writer for *The New York Times,* wrote, "When Meany does leave his post, Reuther is the man most likely to succeed." Reuther, however, saw one major drawback: "One of the tragedies of being president of the AFL-CIO is that you're cut off from the main function of the labor movement and that's collective bargaining. . . . I don't think I'm about to be drafted and I'm not about to launch a campaign to bring that about." Early in 1964 Meany said he had no thought of retiring but would not exclude Reuther from a list of qualified successors.

When Meany addressed the UAW convention in 1964, he discovered that the union had just adopted a rule forbidding anyone to run for office after his 65th birthday. "We are trying to avoid the mistakes that many other unions have made," said the 56-year-old Reuther in urging approval of the 65-and-out amendment to the UAW constitution. The timing seemed to be a not-so-subtle reminder to Meany, then 69, who told newsmen he objected to compulsory retirement for union officers. Reuther, an aide said, "was rather embarrassed" that anyone would think that the UAW rule was directed against the AFL-CIO chief.

The following year Reuther alienated his old CIO friend, Jim Carey, by publicly advocating a merger of the UAW and the Carey-led International Union of Electrical Workers. Reuther argued that a UAW-IUE consolidation would be a practical step to resolve "an overlapping collective bargaining situation." It also would have provided a haven for Carey, who was in deep trouble with his membership, but Carey angrily rejected the merger proposal. Referring to 1964 surgery Reuther underwent for removal of a lung tumor, Carey quipped, "When Walter has an operation, the knife winds up in my back." Elsewhere within the disintegrating "CIO caucus" there was bitterness about filling several Executive Council vacancies. "Walter was dealing fast with everybody," an AFL-CIO official reported. "A lot of them told him to go to hell for the first time."

An obvious sign of discontent was Reuther's failure to win the votes of the Textile Workers' Union of America in his otherwise routine reelection as an AFL-CIO vice-president in 1965. Insiders knew that he had been "cut" by William Pollock, president of the textile union, who believed Reuther had reneged on a promise of support for Pollock's elevation to the Executive Council. Several other union presidents resented Reuther's constant speechmaking at Council meetings. A staff member recalled a room-service breakfast with Reuther and two other Council members when "in the middle of the scrambled eggs Walter jumps up, starts pacing and makes a speech in his hotel room." Others felt he showed poor judgment on when and how to conduct internal battles.

From Reuther's standpoint, his former allies were moving away from him into Meany's camp because they had lost some of their fighting spirit. "What happened was that the CIO guys got absorbed," he contended later. "Our guys more and more accommodated themselves to a status quo relationship and that was a great disappointment to me." When other labor leaders urged him not to be so insistent on pressing for change, so he could win Meany's blessing as the AFL-CIO crown prince, Reuther replied: "That's all very fine but I won't like myself. I have to live with me every day. I'm not interested in being president of the AFL-CIO under circumstances in which I cannot be true to the things I believe in."

Outwardly there was harmony at the AFL-CIO convention in 1965. Reuther and UAW vice-president Leonard Woodcock worked behind the scenes to revise a proposed resolution on the Vietnam War that they felt was far too militaristic. Meany's aides consented to a clause endorsing the principle of a negotiated settlement and, in return, Reuther threw his support behind President Johnson's escalation of the war. When Meany denounced student anti-war demonstrators in the balcony of the convention hall as "kooks" for belittling Secretary of State Dean Rusk, only UAW secretary-treasurer Emil Mazey rose to assail the administration's war policy. Following Mazey to the rostrum, Reuther asserted, "Lyndon Johnson is just as concerned about peace as was Jack Kennedy, because he too can understand that peace transcends every other question." The AFL-CIO delegates approved another two-year term for Meany, although he was 71 years of age and hobbled by an arthritic hip that forced him to use a walking cane. Reuther, 58 at the time, had made a good recovery from the chest surgery of a year earlier and was in excellent health.

Early in 1966 Meany entered a New York City hospital for a major operation on his afflicted hip—high-risk surgery for a man of his age but offering the possibility of pain-free movement again. Together with his wife May, Reuther went to see Meany following the successful operation. "We spent two hours, had a delightful conversation," Meany reported to an aide. "They were extremely friendly."

The era of good feeling ended abruptly in the summer of 1966. The first irritant, so far as Meany was concerned, was a Los Angeles *Times* interview with Victor Reuther in which Walter's brother charged that AFL-CIO overseas operations, particularly in Latin America, were a front for the Central Intelligence Agency. Victor was sharply critical of Jay Lovestone, who had become Meany's chief foreign policy adviser. According to the AFL-CIO president, Walter Reuther soon gave assurances that he had reprimanded his brother for being "way out of line" and indicated disagreement with the allegations.

A few days later the election of an obscure Polish Communist named Leon Chajn as chairman of the annual conference of the International Labor Organization in Geneva opened one of the more sizzling chapters in the Reuther versus Meany saga. The U.S. workers' delegate to the meeting, Rudolph Faupl, was aghast. Chajn was the first Communist ever chosen to head the ILO, and Poland, whose government he represented, had been cited repeatedly by an ILO committee for denying the right of workers to form labor unions.

Faupl, who had been recommended by Meany but appointed to his post by President Johnson, placed a transatlantic call to Meany's office and reported that he planned to walk out of the meeting as a protest against Chajn's election. "If I were in your position I would do the same thing," Meany told Faupl, cautioning him, however, not to withdraw from the ILO itself. With this backing, Faupl and his advisors boycotted the remainder of the June session.

Reacting sharply, Reuther dispatched a letter to Meany on June 9, 1966, which arrived at the Washington *Post* before the AFL-CIO president had a chance to see it. The UAW Executive Board, Reuther wrote, deplored Faupl's walkout as "unwise, undemocratic, contrary to established AFL-CIO policy, and unauthorized by any AFL-CIO body with authority to change that policy."

Interpreting the letter as a direct challenge to his leadership, Meany summoned the Executive Council to an emergency meeting to solicit a vote of confidence. The session began with the Federation president recalling that he first read Reuther's charges in the newspaper, and asking, "Walter, don't you know there's such a thing as a telephone?" Before long, the two men were pounding tables and shouting curses in their stormiest confrontation in years. "It got hot, very hot," said a participant. Joe Curran, president of the National Maritime Union and a veteran of many a waterfront scrap, twice had to call for order. At one point Meany accused his redheaded critic of uttering a "damnable lie." In the showdown, the Council voted 18 to 6 to support the ILO walkout. Asked by a reporter if he felt the episode raised any question about Reuther's qualifications to succeed him, Meany grinned impishly and replied, "I haven't any great interest in that because when that time comes, I won't be around."

Another result of the meeting was a vote to investigate Victor Reuther's charge that a Meany-backed development program in Latin America was supported by the CIA. In turn, Reuther called for a special meeting to review all of the AFL-CIO's policies in the foreign affairs field. Many observers wondered why he was bent on forcing a showdown on issues that seemed remote to the average American workingman.

Jack Conway, who was Reuther's liaison man with Meany, related that the UAW leader began getting requests from Vice-President Hubert Humphrey, Senator Robert F. Kennedy, and other officials expressing concern about discussion of the CIA's alleged ties with labor unions. The intelligence agency apparently feared that embarrassing disclosures might result. As a consequence, Conway said, Reuther and Meany reached an understanding that the issue would not be raised at the next meeting of the Executive Council in August 1966. Lane Kirkland, Meany's top aide, recalled that the matter was discussed but said no commitment was made about removing it from the agenda.

When the August meeting began, the Latin American program of the AFL-CIO was the first item considered. Victor Reuther was rebuked, although not by name, for linking it with the CIA. "It was a double cross" by Meany, according to Conway, who added: "That event made it impossible for those two men ever to trust each other. . . . It was downhill all the way from that point."

The Council met in Washington in November of that year to review its foreign policy statements, at Reuther's request, but to the amazement of his colleagues, Reuther did not show up for the discussion. "Walter's often left his fight in the dressing room but this time he never left the dressing room," jibed one of Meany's men. Reuther said later that he attended a special meeting of the UAW Executive Board where, he contended, "his time would be best spent."

The breach was widening. As 1966 drew to a close, Reuther issued a sweeping denunciation of the AFL-CIO and its leaders in these words: "The AFL-CIO lacks the social vision, the dynamic thrust, the crusading spirit that should characterize the progressive, modern labor movement. . . . The AFL-CIO suffers from a sense of complacency and adherence to the status quo."

David Dubinsky, who was on good terms with both Meany and Reuther, attempted early in 1967 to act as a peacemaker. Telephoning from Florida to UAW headquarters in Detroit, Dubinsky set up a meeting with Reuther. Before it could be held, however, Reuther resigned from the AFL-CIO Executive Council and other UAW officers quit Federation committee assignments, severing most official ties between the auto union and the AFL-CIO. In a 6,000-word letter to UAW locals, Reuther condemned Meany for running the AFL-CIO with a heavy hand, shutting off dissent, and acting as if he owned the labor movement. Yet Reuther added, "UAW members may be assured that the leaders of their union are not engaged in political maneuvers or power drives or personality contests, nor are they motivated by personal considerations."

In reply, the AFL-CIO Executive Council declared it was ready to listen to any complaint or proposal in the usual forums of the labor movement or at a special convention. "We are not, however, prepared to act upon the basis of a kaleidoscope of ever-changing allegations and demands, expressed through press releases, public speeches, or circular letters," it added.

One charge particularly irked Meany. Reuther had accused the AFL-CIO of spending "not a dime" to help striking grape workers in California. Checking with his auditors, Meany insisted the Federation had contributed $1.5 million in cash at the time the UAW leader spoke. It was true that Reuther first proposed the farm worker organizing drive. At one point, Meany persuaded the AFL-CIO high command to abandon the campaign. The emergence of Cesar Chevez as a leader of the grape workers brought renewed interest from Reuther, who appeared on a picket line in Delano, California, late in 1965 to give his moral support, later bolstered by financial contributions, to the farm worker campaign.

In a series of public letters running up to 8,500 words in length, Reuther castigated his fellow labor leaders in the early months of 1967. He also proposed a $90 million, six-year organizing drive, more centralized bargaining, a $15 million national labor defense fund, and changes in the AFL-CIO decision-making machinery.

Although Reuther served notice he would fight for his program at the AFL-CIO convention in December 1967, the Auto Workers' president did not appear. Negotiations with General Motors were at a "critical stage," he said, requiring that he remain in Detroit. His later demand for a special convention was granted by the AFL-CIO brass only on condition the UAW would be bound by the decisions of that body—a condition unacceptable to the auto union.

From that point it was simply a matter of time—about three months—before Reuther pulled his union out of the Federation on July 1, 1968. In a biting letter ten days later, Meany accused Reuther of running out on a fight following a two-year campaign of "vilification." It was a bitter parting.

There was blame for both of the leading figures following the withdrawal of the UAW. Meany, according to some analysts, should have tried to give Reuther a larger role in the AFL-CIO and made a greater effort to be conciliatory during the opening phases of the dispute. "Meany's weakness is his strength," commented one perceptive union president. As for Reuther, many agreed with a Detroit editorial writer who had asserted long before, "The young man never has shown a fondness for playing second fiddle in anybody's orchestra." Labor writer A. H. Raskin said of the Meany-Reuther clashes, "The downward spiral of their relationship culminated in a series of schoolboy-like jousts . . . almost all of which wound up badly for Reuther and none of which was calculated to contribute anything notable to the general advancement of labor." The late George Harrison, a veteran labor leader, attributed the feud to "leadership conflict" and observed: "I think Reuther thought that Meany would retire. When he didn't, Reuther got annoyed." When this appraisal was brought to Reuther's attention early in 1969, he laughed and made this reply:

> I never wanted Meany's job. What is Meany's job? It's got nothing to do with collective bargaining. I don't know whether he could lead a poverty crusade, or the fight on health care. I know I can lead these fights as president of the UAW, because our guys respond. I wouldn't want to hold the hand of reluctant labor politicians. I'm action-oriented and the UAW is the place where the action is. This is why I think I've got the best job in the American labor movement and I'm very happy with it.

About a month after his formal break with the AFL-CIO, Reuther founded a new "Alliance for Labor Action" with an unlikely partner, the International Brotherhood of Teamsters. A decade before, Reuther had joined with Meany to expel the Teamsters from the AFL-CIO on charges of corrupt domination.

Now the UAW idealist was signing a pact with the union, whose president, James R. Hoffa, was serving a federal prison sentence for jury tampering. By early 1968, however, it appeared that Hoffa never would resume active control of the truck union and Frank Fitzsimmons, who had known Reuther from the early days of the labor movement in Detroit, was running the Teamsters.

The two giant unions claimed a combined membership of close to four million and they recruited two smaller organizations, the International Chemical Workers and the National Council of Distributive Workers, during the first year of the Alliance's existence. A "Declaration of Purpose" in Reuther's rhetoric pledged the organization to a wide variety of trade union and social welfare goals, including coordinated organizing campaigns and the formation of "community unions" for the poor and the blacks.

In a sense, the Alliance gave Reuther a larger power base while providing the Teamsters, still trying to live down the villainous image of them created by the Senate investigation of the 1950's, a form of respectability.

The organization was slow to get going. It took nearly a year to arrange the first conference of the ALA, bringing together UAW and Teamsters leaders from across the nation for a get-acquainted session in Washington. "We have not come together to divide the labor movement," Reuther insisted. "We have come together to revitalize the labor movement." In sharp contrast to the AFL-CIO leadership, Reuther and Fitzsimmons took strong stands against the Vietnam War. Also, the ALA fought the deployment of the anti-ballistic missile. In general, the new organization took a somewhat more radical or militant position on social welfare issues than did the Meany-led federation.

Gradually, the Alliance began to move. It picked Atlanta as the target for its first comprehensive organizing drive, winning eleven bargaining rights elections in a row. Community unions were aided in the Watts neighborhood of Los Angeles and in other urban and rural poverty areas. Although the pace was not nearly as rapid as Reuther desired, he was not discouraged. In mid-1969 he boasted, "We have been accomplishing more reform in the AFL-CIO from outside than when we were in it."

CHAPTER THIRTY-ONE

Finale

WALTER REUTHER DID NOT SLOW HIS PACE AS HE NEARED THE sundown of his career. According to his closest associates, he displayed more vigor than ever as he mounted a new series of crusades from his walnut-paneled office in Solidarity House. He became chairman of a "Committee of 100" to advocate a system of national health insurance. Unveiling a 1970 "Reuther Plan," he urged a law requiring military contractors to put one-fourth of their profits into a fund to finance conversion to post-Vietnam production. As in many instances, the odds were against him but the "forever optimist" refused to concede defeat.

Reuther's durable interest in mass-produced, low-cost housing for the urban centers of America led him into open warfare with the AFL-CIO building trades unions, which effectively control most of the jobs on major government construction projects. Reuther charged that craft unions were far too rigid about jurisdictional claims, discouraging the use of modern technology, and that they exerted monopoly power to raise wage rates far beyond any increases in productivity. His experience as the contractor on the Black Lake Family Education Center, where eight strikes by building unions delayed completion, only confirmed his long-held views.

During most of 1969 craft unions negotiated pay increases averaging 15 percent a year, sharply raising the expectations of skilled tradesmen in the UAW and other industrial organizations. Reuther protested: "The uneconomic settlements in the construction industry . . . represent the single most destructive, negative, complicating factor in the industrial wage picture in America. . . . You're dealing here with monopoly situations . . . and there are no external economic disciplines in that labor market." Anyone wanting to put up an office building in New York City, he said, must pay the New York scale for building craftsmen or forget the whole idea. By contrast, a manufacturer of television sets could shift production to another area or another country if he felt New York wages were too high.

The American labor movement, Reuther argued, needed to develop a national wage policy to guide union negotiators, rather than continue with the AFL-CIO's traditional hands-off attitude toward bargaining demands and settlements. "When the building trades act irresponsibly, that affects the whole labor movement," he fumed, "yet George Meany doesn't even know what you mean when you talk about this. Now it's not because he's a mean old man. It's because he belongs in another period of human history." As Reuther explained his proposal, it would not require that everyone get the same wage or the same wage increase. But a "rational wage policy," he suggested, would prevent widely varying settlements for each labor market or each craft.

"When we had some of the strikes at Black Lake in our building program up there," Reuther said heatedly, "I had some of the building trades bitching the other guys because they had made a pattern and the other guys wouldn't take it. And they were bitching each other. . . . Every little empire makes its own wage policy." Eventually, he predicted, such practices would prove self-destructive: "Unless something is done about this, the cost of construction is just going to continue to escalate and . . . the only people in America able to build will be the federal government, because it has unlimited taxing capability, or giant corporations who just push it onto the consumer. Everybody in between is just going to get lost."

As the 1970 auto negotiations approached, Reuther devoted himself to shaping the union's demands. Although the number of unsold cars was mounting, along with unemployment, he developed a costly package that won overwhelming approval at the UAW convention. It included a generous early retirement demand that would permit auto workers to collect $500-a-month pensions after 30 years on the job, regardless of age. In his keynote address the 62-year-old Reuther spoke in vibrant tones: "We are without question the strongest and most effective industrial union in the world.

. . . We have taken on the most powerful corporations in the world . . . and we have prevailed."

Of the Vietnam War, Reuther said: "It has divided this nation. It is wasting our resources that we need at home and it is tarnishing our moral credentials in the world. . . . But I want to make it clear that . . . we condemn those Americans who burn the American flag and march behind the Viet Cong flag. We reject the concept that says in order to be anti-war you have to be anti-American. That kind of reckless attitude, we believe, is destructive and counterproductive."

Ten days after Reuther spoke, President Nixon sent American troops into Cambodia. In the tumultuous college demonstrations that followed, four students were killed by National Guard troops at Kent State University in Ohio. Reuther's reaction was to draft a statement of protest and seek the aid of industrialists, clergymen, educators, and other prominent Americans to form a new coalition against international and domestic violence. Sharply criticizing the President for the move into Cambodia, Reuther wrote: "If there is one thing to be learned from the tragedy of Vietnam it is that democracy is the system of government least capable of being transplanted at the point of a bayonet. As the war is widened, so are the divisions within our country. . . . We share the view that the highest form of patriotism and human morality is to insist that America end the tragic war and loss of life in Southeast Asia and devote our energies and resources to building a more just and humane society at home."

Although he could not know it at the time, the document became a final testament to the depth of Reuther's feeling against the fighting in Southeast Asia.

Discouraged by world and national events, Walter and May Reuther prepared to enjoy some quiet moments of solitude at the UAW's Black Lake Center, carved out of the northern Michigan wilderness with the aid of their old friend, architect Oskar Stonorov of Philadelphia. "This is a thing of beauty where man and nature can live in harmony and where the human spirit can be enriched,"

Reuther had said. A friend called the woodland retreat a "Camelot, a Garden of Eden" for the auto union president.

Routinely, the UAW chartered a Lear Jet from Executive Jet Aviation Corporation to fly the Reuthers, Stonorov, and Walter's bodyguard-nephew, William Wolfman, from Detroit's Metropolitan Airport to the airfield at Pellston, Michigan, where a union car and driver waited to take them to Black Lake. Stonorov and Reuther wanted to review the progress of construction for the last time before the June dedication of the camp.

The sleek, two-engine jet, with veteran pilots George Evans and Joseph Karaffa at the controls, raced down the runway at Detroit's airport, taking off at 8:44 on Saturday evening, May 9, into a steady rain. It was not the best flying weather—an 800-foot ceiling with scattered clouds as low as 400 feet—but both pilots and passengers had made the flight together safely many times before when conditions had been far worse. Evans, who had more than 7,000 hours of flying time, navigated by instruments as he headed the jet northward from Detroit. Twenty-six minutes after takeoff he was in radio contact with the tower at Pellston's Emmet County airfield and received the latest word on the weather: cloud ceiling at 800 feet, easterly winds at ten miles an hour, light rain with visibility of seven miles. "I've got the airport in sight," Evans announced at 9:28, and turned on the bright landing lights on each wingtip.

Slowing sharply from his cruising speed, the pilot brought the plane down through the inky darkness. With the airport only three miles away, however, the jet slammed into the top of a 50-foot elm tree. Wood flew into both engines, causing a double flame-out, and Evans was powerless to control the aircraft. It smashed into the ground, skidding through a stand of pine, leveling foot-thick trunks, and exploding into a ball of fire.

No one escaped from the flaming wreckage. At 9:33 that night Walter and May Reuther died, their bodies scorched beyond recognition.

News of Reuther's fate sent shock waves around the world.

UAW officers assembled at Solidarity House, numbed by grief, and proclaimed a week of mourning for the 1.8 million members of the union. In ·Washington, George Meany was awakened before dawn and stated: "This is tragic news. Walter Reuther had made a unique and lasting contribution to the auto workers, the American labor movement, and the nation. We had disagreements but we worked well together as well. . . . All of the labor movement will join in mourning his death." From the White House, President Nixon saluted his old adversary with these words: ". . . A deep loss not only for organized labor but also for the cause of collective bargaining and the entire American process. He was a man who was devoted to his cause, spoke for it eloquently, and worked for it tirelessly. . . . Even those who disagreed with him had great respect for his ability, integrity, and persistence." At the United Nations in New York, Secretary-General U Thant said: "The world has lost a wise, courageous, and statesmanlike humanitarian. . . . He was a man who had deep feeling for all people." In Detroit, Henry Ford II added, "His tough-minded dedication, his sense of social concern, his selflessness, and his eloquence all mark him as a central figure in the development of modern industrial history."

In a voice heavy with emotion, Victor Reuther spoke to 800 UAW officials and staff members at Solidarity House. "It will be difficult," he acknowledged, "but we will all have to wipe away the tears and pick up the tools again to complete the unfinished tasks."

Now that he was gone, the editorial writers who had questioned his politics or his bargaining programs were generous in their praise. The conservative Detroit *News* said: "While he talked a lot, he also did a lot." The Washington *Star* proclaimed: "This nation will miss Walter Reuther . . . a moralist and an idealist . . . eloquent on the subject of economic justice."

In Detroit, flags were flown at half staff on city buildings and at the headquarters of General Motors, Ford, Chrysler, and American Motors. Thousands of mourners filed past the plain oak coffins of Walter and May Reuther in the Veterans' Memorial Building, opened from eight o'clock in the morning until ten o'clock at night so workers on all shifts could pay their final respects. Many came in UAW jackets or work clothes. A railroad man hesitated, telling the doorkeeper: "I'm not in his union. I wish I was. But he left all of us a better world. So it's all right if I say goodbye to him, isn't it?"

The funeral was conducted in the Henry and Edsel Ford Auditorium, a reminder of Henry Ford's determined campaign to prevent unionization of his plants in the 1930's. Cabinet officers, United States senators, industrialists, rank and file workers filled the hall in what was described as the largest gathering of dignitaries in Detroit history. Auto assembly lines stopped for three minutes as the service began. Thousands of truck drivers, members of the Teamsters Union, halted their vehicles for a similar silent tribute.

An estimated 30,000 UAW members remained away from work on the day of the funeral, sacrificing a day's pay out of respect for their leader. And the workers also mourned May Reuther, a quiet, serene woman who had always been at her husband's side during the long years of struggle and the moments of triumph. She had filled their Rochester home with pottery and modern paintings to complement the walnut furnishings that Walter designed and built. His causes were her causes and she once remarked, "I guess if we had to do it over, Walter and I would live our lives in much the same way."

Reuther had been aware that he was nearing the end of his career. In a letter to Louis G. Seaton of General Motors, written a few days before the plane crash, the UAW president noted Seaton's retirement and added, "My own retirement is not too far down the road."

The funeral service was simple and prayerless. A recording of "He's Got the Whole World in His Hands," sung by Marian Anderson, was the only reference to God in the 75-minute ceremony. Eleven speakers eulogized Reuther, each symbolizing an area of his concern. Among the eulogists were Senator Philip A. Hart of Michigan, Whitney Young of the National Urban League, John Gardner of the Urban Coalition, Ivar Noren of the International Metalworkers Federation and Sam Brown a national youth leader. Dave Miller, a white-haired union veteran of 79, spoke movingly about the early days. "Men listened to him, loved him, followed him, trusted him," said Miller. "His voice was the call to the conscience of man."

Perhaps the most eloquent tribute to Walter Reuther's achievements came from Mrs. Martin Luther King, Jr., who declared:

> Walter Reuther was to black people . . . preeminently the most widely known and respected white labor leader in the nation. The secret of his success with blacks was that he was there in person when the storm clouds were thick. We remember him in Montgomery. He was in Birmingham. He marched with us in Selma and Jackson, Mississippi, and Washington. And he was in Memphis. Only yesterday, there he was once more in Charleston, South Carolina, the leader of a million and a half workers giving personal support to a strike of only 400 black women. . . . We shall all miss him because we are all better off—black and white—as beneficiaries of his creative life. . . . He spent his life fighting the fight of the whole world.

Dr. Durward B. Varner, chancellor of the University of Nebraska, recalled his friendship with his former Michigan neighbors:

> The leaders of industry knew Walter Reuther in the heat of the bargaining room. . . . I knew May and Walter Reuther in the warm glow of their gaily decorated home at the Christmas season where we exchanged simple gifts: Texas pecans from our family, Grandmother Reuther's homemade wine from theirs.

Irving Bluestone, Reuther's close associate for more than a decade, delivered the final tribute:

> Walter's deeds mark him a giant among men but, above all, he was of and for the people. . . . They always called him "Walter," not "Mr. Reuther." . . . Walter and May have not died. They live on in the hearts and minds of those of us who, like them, look not to yesterday but the bright tomorrow.

Softly, the audience began singing an old labor song, Walter Reuther's favorite, a hymn to a Wobbly martyr. His family knew the verses well:

I dreamed I saw Joe Hill last night,
Alive as you and me.
Says I: "But Joe, you're ten years dead."
"I never died," says he.

Hubert Humphrey and Edward M. Kennedy added their voices:

And standing there as big as life
And smiling with his eyes,
Joe says, "What they forgot to kill
Went on to organize."

Henry Ford II and the General Motors excecutives sang the un-familiar words:

"Joe Hill ain't dead," he says to me.
"Joe Hill ain't never died.
Where working men are out on strike,
Joe Hill is at their side."

Secretary of Labor George Shultz and George Romney, Secre-tary of Housing and Urban Development, joined in:

"From San Diego up to Maine,
In every mine and mill,
Where workers strike and organize,"
Says he, "You'll find Joe Hill."

Three thousand voices blended in a muted farewell:

I dreamed I saw Joe Hill last night,
Alive as you and me,
Says I: "But Joe, you're ten years dead."
"I never died," says he.
"I never died," says he.

Sources

<small>HOPEFUL OF ADDING AN EXTRA DIMENSION TO OUR BIOGRAPHY OF</small>
Walter P. Reuther, we decided when we undertook the project in 1967
to place special emphasis on interviews with Reuther, his relatives, his
friends and union associates, and his enemies and critics. Our first debt
therefore is to the scores of individuals who agreed to grant us interviews, most of which were tape recorded. Although associates of Walter
Reuther told us at the outset he preferred that a biography be deferred
indefinitely, the late president of the Auto Workers granted a series of
interviews, all of them taped and some exceeding two hours in duration.
Among those who also agreed most generously to a series of interviews
were Walter's brother Victor, his sister Christine, and such longtime
Reuther associates as Frank Winn, Jack Conway, Leonard Woodcock
and Joseph L. Rauh, Jr.

Nearly all other interviews also were conducted on a face-to-face
basis, although a very few were accomplished by telephone or, in just
one instance, an exchange of written questions and replies. Others who
cooperated with us included:

Willoughby Abner, George F. Addes, Kenneth Bannon, Jack Barbash,
Merlin D. Bishop, Irving Bluestone, Tom Braden, Joseph A. Califano,
Jr., James B. Carey, David Dubinsky, Evelyn DuBrow, Billie Sunday
Farnum, Kenneth J. Fiester, Henry C. Fleisher, Clayton W. Fountain,
Richard T. Frankensteen, Douglas Fraser, Neil Gilbride, Joe Glazer,
Arthur J. Goldberg, Nat Goldfinger, John Grimes, Paul Hall, Thomas E.
Harris, George Harrison, Al Hartnett, Hubert H. Humphrey, David R.
Jones, Robert Kanter, Lane Kirkland, Edwin A. Lahey, William H.
Lawrence, Richard T. Leonard, John M. Livingston, Joseph Loftus,
Frank Lombardo, Jay Lovestone, Emil Mazey, Justin McCarthy, George
Meany, Saul Miller, William M. O'Brien, Patrick J. Owens, Jacob
Potofsky, George E. Reedy, Anna Reuther, Archie Robinson, Stephen
Schlossberg, Paul Schrade, Louis G. Seaton, Donald Slaiman, Frank
Swoboda, Norman Walker, Joseph Walsh, Nat Weinberg, Michael F.
Widman, and Albert J. Zack.

Although the volume is authorized neither by the United Auto Workers nor by members of the Reuther family, the authors owe particular
debts to Frank Winn and Victor Reuther for, between them, reading the
entire manuscript and offering extensive and invaluable comments and

suggestions. Of course, Winn and Victor Reuther are in no way answerable for the contents, which is the responsibility of the authors.

Thanks also are due Larry George of Pacific Grove, California, who zealously and effectively carried out research assignments on the West Coast.

We also are grateful to the staff of the Labor History Archives at Detroit's Wayne State University which, in some future year, will provide researchers with an enormous fund of information about the career of Walter Reuther and the affairs of the UAW. The Archives is the official repository for the papers and records of Reuther and the union, and also houses an extensive oral history of the Auto Workers' union and its late chief. Unfortunately, very little of this material has been available. However, we found valuable documents in public collections bearing the following designations: Homer Martin, Henry Kraus, George Lyons, Daniel Gallagher, Edward Levinson, Richard T. Frankensteen, George F. Addes, R. J. Thomas, Bud and Hazel Simons, Ray Speth, United Auto Workers—General Motors Corporation, and UAW Public Relations Department—Ford Motor Company Series.

The newspaper reference section of the Library of Congress is due a bow for preserving a microfilm file of the Moscow *Daily News,* including the 1933–35 issues published while Walter and Victor Reuther worked and traveled in the Soviet Union. We made extensive use of the file, providing, we believe, the first Western publication of the writings of the Reuther brothers in the Soviet press during their stay at Gorki. We also are grateful to the library staff of the Detroit *News* for giving us free access to the very extensive Reuther-UAW files there.

Use of printed *Proceedings* of union conventions was essential to our task. These are cited in the Chapter Notes that follow. With the help of the library staffs of the UAW, AFL-CIO and Department of Labor, we located transcripts of all UAW conventions and pertinent sessions of the CIO, the AFL and the successor AFL-CIO.

A number of federal government documents or transcripts were of great value. Tom Healy helped obtain the "Official Report of Proceedings before the National Labor Relations Board, Case No. VII-C-61 in the Matter of Ford Motor Company and International Union, United Automobile Workers of America," and *Decision and Order: United States of America Before the National Labor Relations Board in the Matter of Ford Motor Company and International Union, United Automobile Workers of America, Case No. C-199—Decided August 9, 1939* (Washington: Government Printing Office, 1939). Other useful documents included: *Investigation of Un-American Propaganda Activities,*

Hearings Before a Special Committee on Un-American Activities, House of Representatives, Vols. 1, 2, 3, 7 and 11 (Washington: Government Printing Office, 1938–1940); *Annual Report, Special Committee on Un-American Activities, House of Representatives,* January 3, 1939 (Washington: Government Printing Office, 1939); "Amendment to Answer (Exhibit No. 1-P) in the Matter of Ford Motor Company and International Union, United Automobile Workers of America, Case No. VII-C-148 Before the National Labor Relations Board, May 22, 1941"; transcript, "United States of America v. Harry Renton Bridges, Henry Schmidt and J. R. Robertson, in the District Court of the United States for the Northern District of California, Southern Division," 1950; *Investigation of Organized Crime in Interstate Commerce, Hearings before the Special Committee, United States Senate, 82nd Congress, First Session,* Part 9 (Washington: Government Printing Office, 1951); *Hearings Before the Select Committee on Improper Activities in the Labor or Management Field, 85th Congress, Second Session, Parts* 21–25 (Washington: Government Printing Office, 1958); *Hearings Before the Select Committee on Improper Activities in the Labor or Management Field, 86th Congress, First Session,* Part 58 (Washington: Government Printing Office, 1960); *Final Report of the Select Committee on Improper Activities in the Labor or Management Field,* Part 2 (Washington: Government Printing Office, 1960).

Remarkably, despite his long prominence, Walter Reuther heretofore had been the subject of only two biographies, although a third volume combined a recounting of his early career with a history of the development of the UAW. Perhaps the most useful, although published years before the others is: *The UAW and Walter Reuther* by Irving Howe and B. J. Widick (New York: Random House, 1949). For a more recent and sympathetic view, see a volume written primarily for young people: *Walter Reuther* by Fred J. Cook (Chicago, New York, London: Encyclopaedia Britannica Press, 1963). The third is a critical portrait: *Walter Reuther: The Autocrat of the Bargaining Table* by Eldorous L. Dayton (New York: The Devin-Adair Company, 1958).

The authors consulted several hundred books in the preparation of this volume. However, the following selected bibliography lists only those cited in Chapter Notes and excludes references mentioned above.

ALINSKY, SAUL, *John L. Lewis, an Unauthorized Biography.* New York: G. P. Putnam's Sons, 1949.

AMRINE, MICHAEL, *This Awesome Challenge.* New York: G. P. Putnam's Sons, 1964.

BENNETT, HARRY H., *We Never Called Him Henry*. New York: Gold Medal Books, 1951.

BUDENZ, LOUIS F., *The Techniques of Communism*. Chicago: Henry Regnery Company, 1954.

BURNS, JAMES MacGREGOR, *Roosevelt: The Lion and the Fox*. New York: Harcourt Brace and Co., 1956.

CALKINS, FAY, *The CIO and the Democratic Party*. Chicago: The University of Chicago Press, 1952.

CARTER, RICHARD, *The Doctor Business*. Garden City: Doubleday & Co., 1958.

CATTON, BRUCE, *The War Lords of Washington*. New York: Harcourt, Brace and Co., 1948.

CUBBAGE, MOYNE LEROY, "A Rhetorical Study of Walter Philip Reuther on Matters of Public Policy." Unpublished doctoral dissertation, University of Michigan, 1961.

DAVIS, ELISABETH LOGAN, *Mothers of America*. Westwood, N.J.: Fleming H. Revell Co., 1954.

DE TOLEDANO, RALPH, *RFK: The Man Who Would Be President*. New York: G. P. Putnam's Sons, 1967.

EVANS, ROWLAND, and NOVAK, ROBERT, *Lyndon B. Johnson; The Exercise of Power*. New York: New American Library, 1966.

FOUNTAIN, CLAYTON W., *Union Guy*. New York: The Viking Press, 1949.

FRISCH, MORTON J., and DIAMOND, MARTIN, eds., *The Thirties*. DeKalb, Ill.: Northern Illinois University Press, 1968.

GAER, JOSEPH, *The First Round*. New York: Duell, Sloan and Pearce, 1944.

GALENSON, WALTER, *The CIO Challenge to the AFL*. Cambridge: Harvard University Press, 1960.

GITLOW, BENJAMIN, *The Whole of Their Lives*. New York: Charles Scribner's Sons, 1948.

GOLDBERG, ARTHUR J., *AFL-CIO Labor United*. New York: McGraw-Hill Book Co., 1956.

HALEY, J. EVETTS, *A Texan Looks at Lyndon*. Canyon, Texas: Palo Duro Press, 1964.

HARDMAN, J. B. S., and NEUFELD, MAURICE F., *House of Labor*. Englewood Cliffs: Prentice-Hall, Inc., 1951.

HARRIS, EVELYN L. K., and KREBS, FRANK J., *From Humble Beginnings*. Morgantown, W.Va.: West Virginia Labor History Publishing Fund, 1960.

ICKES, HAROLD L., *The Secret Diary of Harold L. Ickes,* Vol. II. New York: Simon and Schuster, 1954.

John L. Lewis and the International Union, United Mine Workers of America. Washington: United Mine Workers, 1952.

JOSEPHSON, MATTHEW, *Sidney Hillman: Statesman of American Labor*. Garden City: Doubleday & Co., 1952.

KEMPTON, MURRAY, *Part of Our Time*. New York: Simon and Schuster, 1955.

LASKY, VICTOR, *JFK, The Man and the Myth*. New York: The Macmillan Co., 1963.

LEVINSON, EDWARD, *Labor on the March*. New York: University Books, 1956.

McDONALD, DAVID J., *Union Man*. New York: E. P. Dutton & Co., 1969.

McDOWELL, EDWIN, *Barry Goldwater: Portrait of an Arizonian*. Chicago: Henry Regnery Co., 1964.

MILLIS, WALTER, ed., *The Forrestal Diaries*. New York: The Viking Press, 1951.

PERKINS, FRANCES, *The Roosevelt I Knew*. New York: The Viking Press, 1946.

PHILLIPS, CABELL, *The Truman Presidency*. New York: The Macmillan Co., 1966.

REUTHER, WALTER P., *Selected Papers,* edited by Henry M. Christman. New York: Pyramid Books, 1964.

ROOSEVELT, ELLIOTT, ed., *F.D.R.: His Personal Letters, 1928–1945,* Vol. I. New York: Duell, Sloan and Pearce, 1950.

ROOSEVELT, FRANKLIN D., *The Public Papers and Addresses of,* Vols. 3 and 5. New York: Random House, 1938.

SALINGER, PIERRE. *With Kennedy*. Garden City: Doubleday & Co., 1966.

SCHLESINGER, ARTHUR M., JR., *The Vital Center*. Boston: Houghton Mifflin Co., 1949.

SCHLESINGER, ARTHUR M., JR., *The Coming of the New Deal*. Boston: Houghton Mifflin Co., 1959.

SHOGAN, ROBERT, and CRAIG, TOM, *The Detroit Race Riot, a Study in Violence*. Philadelphia and New York: Chilton Books, 1964.

SORENSEN, CHARLES E., with WILLIAMSON, SAMUEL T., *My Forty Years With Ford*. New York: W. W. Norton & Co., 1956.

SORENSEN, THEODORE, *Kennedy*. New York: Harper & Row, 1965.

STIEBER, JACK. *Governing the UAW*. New York: John Wiley and Sons, 1962.

SWARD, KEITH, *The Legend of Henry Ford*. New York: Rinehart & Co., 1948.

TAFT, PHILIP, *Organized Labor in American History*. New York: Harper & Row, 1964.

TRUMAN, HARRY S, *Memoirs,* Vol. 2. Garden City: Doubleday & Co., 1956.

VELIE, LESTER, *Labor U.S.A.* New York: Harper & Brothers, 1959.

WHITE, WALTER, *A Man Called White*. New York: The Viking Press, 1948.

WIDICK, B. J., *Labor Today*. Boston: Houghton Mifflin Co., 1964.

Chapter Notes

ONE   *Father and Son*

Principal sources were members of the Reuther family who, in separate interviews, described their forebears and the Wheeling home environment. Those interviewed were Walter P. Reuther (referred to as WPR in subsequent "Notes"), Victor G. Reuther, their mother Anna, and their sister, Christine Reuther Richey. Valentine Reuther's trade union and Socialist Party activities are recounted in *From Humble Beginnings* by Harris and Krebs, pp. 68f. WPR's paper route, athletic interests, and toe accident are covered in *Walter Reuther* by Cook, pp. 24ff. His mother told of his throwing the pills out the window. WPR described his bakery experience (see *Proceedings, American Bakery and Confectionary Workers,* 1962, p. 298). Information on Anna Reuther came, in part, from *Mothers of America* by Davis. Victor Reuther's evaluation of the father's concern for social justice is quoted from *A Rhetorical Study of Walter P. Reuther* by Cubbage, and Valentine Reuther's collective bargaining philosophy was reported in "Reuther: F.O.B. Detroit," *Fortune,* December 1945.

TWO   *The Die Leader*

WPR told of his arrival in Detroit, his subsequent hiring by Ford, his interest in aviation, his investments, and his 1932 Socialist campaign activities. Cooperative living arrangements in Detroit, some details of the 1932 campaign, and City College episodes were related by Victor Reuther. Merlin Bishop discussed the 4-C Club, communal living experiences, and the campaign in detail, and WPR told of his indecision about a career at the 1962 convention of the American Bakery and Confectionary Workers (see convention *Proceedings*). Reference to WPR's lack of interest in baseball is from *Part of Our Time* by Kempton, p. 269. Cook, in his *Walter Reuther,* recounts picketing of segregated swimming pools, the impact of double pay cuts at Ford, and WPR's feeling of liberation after his firing.

THREE   *Europe 1933*

WPR told in an interview of being hired for work in Gorki, as well as efforts on his behalf by John Rushton. He also provided considerable information about his and Victor's activities in Wheeling before departure and about their experiences in Western Europe before entering the Soviet Union. The example of their underground courier work is quoted from Cook's *Walter Reuther,* p. 55. WPR discussed this subject with the authors in more general terms. The itinerary of the brothers during their first weeks in Germany and WPR's statement on the motivation for the trip are from *Official Report of Proceedings Before the National Labor Relations Board,* Case No. VII-C-61, in the matter of Ford Motor Company and the UAW, pp. 150f. There is considerable material on Ford's dealings with the Soviets in Chapter 15 of *My Forty Years With Ford* by Sorensen. Merlin Bishop's recollections, including unattributed passages relating to Roy Reuther, were given in an interview. Virtually all other material is from interviews with Victor Reuther.

FOUR   *Russian Adventure*

Victor Reuther was the principal source, through an interview and subsequent memo to the authors. Of great value, too, was the file of the Moscow *Daily News* for 1934–1935. WPR's letters to the English-language publication appeared January 9, January 12, March 8, and October 4, 1934. Victor's letter was published February 11, 1935. Other items gleaned from the Moscow *Daily News*: resolution of Gorki tool and die workers, February 28, 1934; chastisement of the head of the foreign department at the Molotov plant, March 16, 1934; interview with WPR, May 4, 1934; editorial concerning *udarniks,* January 1, 1935. The Sorensen quote on his own consulting work in the Soviet Union is from *My Forty Years With Ford,* p. 4. WPR's statement about the importance of getting Moscow's ear to promote action on complaints is from "Reuther: F.O.B. Detroit," *Fortune,* December 1945. His comment to Khrushchev concerning his Soviet stay is from his *Selected Papers,* p. 252. *Trud's* attack on WPR appeared in translation in the Detroit *News,* October 30, 1959. The *News* editorial was published the following day. WPR's account of secret police arrests at Gorki is quoted from Cook's *Walter Reuther,* p. 60. The summation by WPR of his Soviet experience appeared in "What Does Walter Reuther Want?" by Jack Alexander, published in *The Saturday Evening Post,* August 14 and 21, 1948. His account of the Yangtze flood was quoted in *The New York Times,* March 26, 1944. Cook, pp. 65f, tells about the clubbing of starving Chinese and the Reuthers' return to the United States. Additional information about the final leg of the world tour is from interviews with WPR and Victor Reuther.

FIVE   *Open Shop Town*

The state of unionization in Detroit in the early 1930's is described in Schlesinger's *The Coming of the New Deal,* pp. 139–47. Leon Henderson's report is quoted by Cook in *Walter Reuther,* p. 70, and the assembly line pace is discussed in *The UAW and Walter Reuther* by Howe and Widick, p. 21. Richard T. Frankensteen gave a general description of working conditions and the extent of union organization in an interview. The history of Ford's labor relations, including the $5-a-day wage and the threatened Wobbly strike, is recounted in Sward's *The Legend of Henry Ford,* pp. 46–52. Early AFL efforts at auto organizing are related in *Organized Labor in American History* by Taft, p. 485. The Howe-Widick volume, p. 29, describes the impact of Model T discontinuance. The Chevrolet assembler quoted is Frank Lombardo, from an interview. Mazey's activities were recorded in *Part of Our Time* by Kempton, p. 272. The account of the Ford hunger strike is from Sward, pp. 231–38. Howe and Widick, p. 94, discussed the Briggs strike and Ford's reaction to it, as well as the AFL's ineptness in auto organizing.

Frankensteen told of his experiences at Chrysler in an interview. The Roosevelt quote is from his *Public Papers and Addresses,* Vol. 3, p. 167. The AFL grievance against the Auto Labor Board is recounted in Josephson's *Sidney Hillman,* p. 375. Results of the poll were analyzed by Howe and Widick, pp. 49f, and they also described the wildcat strike wave. The role of John L. Lewis in the formation of the CIO, and his encounter with Hutcheson, are related in Chapter 4 of Alinsky's *John L. Lewis.* In an interview, WPR told of his presence at the CIO founding. FDR's attitude toward exclusive representation and his belated endorsement of the Wagner Act are described in *Roosevelt: The Lion and the Fox* by Burns, p. 219. Schlesinger, p. 113, quotes Sloan's reaction to the Wagner Act, and Burns, p. 220, appraises Roosevelt's alliance with labor. Alinsky, p. 177, tells of Lewis's role in the 1936 election and his claim on the New Deal. The FDR quote is from his *Public Papers and Addresses,* Vol. 5, p. 339. The Alinsky quote is from his Lewis biography, p. 102.

SIX   *Reuther Organizes*

Major sources were interviews with WPR, Victor Reuther, and Merlin Bishop, as well as the *Proceedings* of the UAW's 1936 convention in South Bend and a memo written by Bishop for his own records shortly after the Kelsey-Hayes strike was concluded. A report of the NLRB on UAW charges against the Ford Motor Company (Case No. VII-C-61) also provided information on WPR's activities after returning from abroad. Brookwood Labor College was described by Frank Winn in an interview. Cook's *Walter Reuther*, p. 74, tells of WPR's courtship, marriage, and wedding trip, and May Reuther's description of their meager diet was quoted by *Time*, June 20, 1955. Martin's complaints about Dillon were found in letters in the Homer Martin Collection, Labor History Archives, Wayne State University. Winn described the climate in South Bend. WPR's reminiscences about his arrival there can be found in the 1962 *Proceedings*, p. 299, of the American Bakery and Confectionary Workers, which also contains his account of the local union election. WPR told of his illicit credential in an interview. The *Proceedings* of the 1936 UAW convention carry transcripts of his speeches: on vice-presidents and fat jobs, p. 48; on Hearst, p. 76; on AFL jurisdiction, p. 176. Green's membership figure, p. 21 of *Proceedings*, was challenged by Winn. The dispute over endorsement of FDR was recounted in an interview by a Washington labor reporter who attended the convention. The accounts of the protest against WRP's election is from the *Proceedings*, pp. 164f, as is that of his defense by Martin, pp. 168ff and 247.

WPR, in an interview, described the opening of his organizing office. His description of a worker's life is from the preface to Levinson's *Labor on the March*. He told of his last tool and die job in addressing the UAW's 12th Skilled Trades Conference, March 17, 1967. The quote about the organizing climate is from Cook, p. 83. Frankensteen's enrollment is recounted in Kempton's *Part of Our Time*, p. 281. Victor Reuther told of his hiring by Kelsey-Hayes in an interview. Taft's *Organized Labor in American History*, p. 493, discusses the Bendix strike. The Bishop memo, together with details he supplied in an interview, provided the basis for the account of the Kelsey-Hayes strike. George Edwards' description is from a copy of the UAW newspaper published immediately after the strike. Frankensteen, in an interview, told of Hoffa's assistance and gave details of the settlement. Winn's comment is from an interview. The lyrics of "Solidarity" are quoted from Schlesinger's *The Coming of the New Deal*, p. 416.

SEVEN   *Flint*

The comparative strength of GM and the UAW are discussed in Alinsky's *John L. Lewis*, pp. 105f, and Levinson's *Labor on the March*, pp. 151f. Auto wage rates were compiled by the National Industrial Conference Board and reported in *The New York Times,* January 6, 1937. Ickes' appraisal of Lewis is from his *Secret Diary,* Vol. II, p. 92. Howe and Widick discuss the assembly line in their *The UAW and Walter Reuther,* p. 19. The anonymous worker's complaint was reported in *The New York Times,* February 1, 1937. Levinson gives a detailed account of the November sit-down, p. 175, and Cook's *Walter Reuther,* pp. 85f, details Knudsen's view of negotiations. Alinsky, pp. 110f, describes the Martin-Knudsen meetings and Lewis' irritation with Martin. *The New York Times,* December 29, 1936, reported the Cleveland sit-down and, December 31, the Fisher 1 strike. The homespun song is from Levinson, p. 152. Most of the strike developments are taken from daily accounts in *The New York Times,* as are the Lewis quotes about tyrannical employers. FDR's reaction is from Perkins' *The Roosevelt I Knew,* p. 322. Pressman's reaction to the judge's GM holdings is from Alinsky, p. 116. The Sloan reply to UAW demands was quoted in *The New York Times,* January 5, 1937, with Martin's rejoinder in the next day's edition. Father Coughlin's statement was in *The New York Times,* January 2, 1937. Kempton in *Part of Our Time,* p. 284, describes the atmosphere in the plants. The "Sit Down!" song is from Levinson, p. 179. The skit was found in the Henry Kraus Collection, Labor History Archives, Wayne State University. Bishop recalled his teaching duties in an interview.

Sources for the "Battle of Bulls' Run" were Victor Reuther, in an interview, accounts in *The New York Times,* and Levinson, pp. 156f. The song celebrating the episode was found in the Kraus Collection. Bishop Gallagher's reaction was reported in *The New York Times,* January 12, 1937. Lawrence related his account of the false armistice in an interview. Lewis' plea for Roosevelt's help, and FDR's reply, is described by Josephson in *Sidney Hillman,* p. 480. Ickes' view is from his *Secret Diary,* Vol. II, p. 55, and the Adams epigram is from *FDR: His Personal Letters, 1928–1945,* Vol. I, p. 648. Alinsky, p. 124, describes the ending of the glass strikes. Roy Reuther's plan to capture Chevy 4 is dramatized in Kempton, pp. 286f, and WPR added details, including his direction of the barricade builders, in an interview. The letter to "Emma" is in the Kraus Collection, as is the ungrammatical note that follows. Velie in *Labor U.S.A.,* p. 147, tells how Lewis dared Murphy to use violence to oust the strikers. Josephson, p. 410, reports on FDR's compromise efforts. WPR's pass is preserved in the Hazel and Bud Simons Collection, Labor History Archives. Alinsky, p. 139, tells of Lewis' annoyance at mention of the AFL. The account of settlement is from the United Mine Workers' publication, *John L. Lewis and the UMW,* p. 91. The triumph was hailed as labor's greatest by Josephson, p. 412. Winn described Martin's confused condition in an interview. Alinsky's appraisal is from his Lewis volume, p. 97. Clay Fountain told of his elation in *Union Guy,* p. 60. Howe and Widick, p. 62, told of the subsequent sit-down fever in Michigan.

EIGHT   *Bloody Rouge*

The account of WPR's flight over the Rouge is based on an Associated Press account in *The New York Times,* April 17, 1937, and the recollections of Frank Winn, a participant in the project, are from an interview. Winn also contributed background material on the overpass battle and the repeat demonstration at the Rouge on August 11, 1937. Material on Henry Ford's attitude toward organized labor as reflected in his newspaper interviews, in the *Ford Almanac,* and in "Fordisms" is from *Decision and Order,* United States of America Before the National Labor Relations Board in the matter of Ford Motor Company and the UAW, Case No. C-199, decided August 9, 1939. Virtually all material on preparations by the UAW and Ford for the May 26 demonstration, and on the combat itself, is from the NLRB's *Decision and Order* and, to a greater extent, from *Official Report of Proceedings Before the NLRB,* Case No. VII-C-61, in the matter of Ford Motor Company and the UAW; the latter is the complete transcript of overpass hearings held in Detroit in July 1937.

Denials by Bennett and Cameron of any Ford involvement in the violence are from *The New York Times,* May 27 and July 22, 1937. *Time's* overpass account was published June 7, 1937. Colombo's questioning of WPR is from the *Official Report of Proceedings,* pp. 150ff. The account of the intraunion struggle over WPR's plan to lead the August 11 Rouge demonstration is based on minutes of Executive Board meetings August 10 and 11 in the George F. Addes Collection, Labor History Archives; on the Detroit *News* of August 12 which carried texts of statements by Martin and the Reuther group, and on an interview with Frankensteen. The demonstration itself was chronicled in the Detroit *News* and *The New York Times* of August 12. The *Times* editorial appeared two days later.

NINE   *The Leaping Parson*

Early biographical material on Martin is from his obituary in *The New York Times,* January 24, 1968, and from *Time,* October 11, 1937. The letter to friend Scott is in the Homer Martin Collection, Labor History Archives. Frank Winn and Merlin Bishop gave their recollections of Martin in interviews. *The New York Times* reported on the Flint factional dispute, April 19 and 20, 1937, and the wildcat situation, July 18 and 21 and August 3, 1937. Winn's comment is from a memo to the authors. Galenson's appraisal of the Unity-Progressive split is from his *The CIO Challenge to the AFL,* p. 168. Leonard's memories on this and other matters dealt with are from an interview. Pre-convention caucuses of 1937 were reported in *The New York Times,* July 19, 1937. Accounts of the convention and its immediate aftermath appeared in *The New York Times,* August 23–31, 1937. WPR talked about his unity plea to the convention in an interview. Fountain discusses the convention and many other events dealt with in the chapter in *Union Guy.* Dubinsky's recollection of WPR's alliance with the Communists is from an interview. WPR's convention defense of Ganley appears in the official *Proceedings,* p. 106. The Stark discussion of WPR's ties with the Communists appeared in *The New York Times,* November 27 and 28, 1937. A clipping of WPR's contribution to the Ternstedt *Flash* was found in the R. J. Thomas Collection, Labor History Archives.

Much of the material on Jay Lovestone is from interviews with him and Winn, supplemented by reference to Gitlow's *The Whole of Their Lives.* Victor Reuther, in an interview, recalled the post-convention firing of himself and other organizers; there also were accounts of this in *The New York Times,* September 24 and 30 and November 28, 1937. The incident in which Martin pulled a revolver on union men was reported at length in an Associated Press dispatch in *The New York Times,* October 1, 1937, and in *Time,* October 11, 1937. The authors also interviewed a Washington labor writer who was present. The first UAW attempt to influence Detroit politics was reported in *The New York Times,* November 1–4, 1937, and the Detroit *News,* October 6 and November 8, 1937. WPR's statement on his primary victory appeared in the Detroit *Times,* October 6. Winn's account of WPR's loose attachment to the Socialist Party is from a 1958 memo to Galenson, quoted in *The CIO Challenge to the AFL,* pp. 150f. Victor Reuther's account is from an interview, as is the recollection of Communist efforts to recruit the brothers. Infighting over the GM agreement is based largely on Galenson's account. The Communist double cross of Victor at the Michigan CIO Council convention is drawn principally from interviews with him, WPR, Leonard, and Frankensteen. Also of help was *Union Guy* and materials in the Dan Gallagher Collection, Labor History Archives.

TEN   *Letter from Gorki*

The account of the invasion of WPR's home is based on interviews with Victor Reuther and Frank Winn and the narrative in Cook's *Walter*

Reuther, pp. 107ff. WPR's own story of the delayed arrival of police and his subsequent discovery that he was to have been murdered is from *Hearings Before the Select Committee on Improper Activities in the Labor or Management Field,* United States Senate, Part 25, p. 10060. The account of Victor's dinner invitation from one of the assailants is from WPR's testimony before the Senate Labor Committee, quoted in *Commonweal,* June 10, 1949, and repeated in substance in *Hearings Before the Select Committee,* p. 10115. Testimony before the Dies Committee is from *Investigation of Un-American Propaganda Activities* with, in sequence, the following pages cited: 2188, 1607, 1532, 1653, 1658f, 1248, 1286f, 1254, and 1289. WPR's NLRB testimony is from the *Official Report of Proceedings Before the NLRB,* Case No. VII-C-61, in the matter of Ford Motor Company and the UAW, p. 138. McCuistion's testimony is from the Dies Committee record above, p. 6742. WPR's rebuttal appeared in the Detroit *News,* November 4, 1939.

The New York Times, July 8, 1937, told of the "Vic and Wal" letter appearing in *The Detroit Saturday Night.* The text as used is from Dayton's *Walter Reuther, The Autocrat of the Bargaining Table,* pp. 50ff. The WPR-Colombo exchange is from the *Official Report of Proceedings,* p. 156. The Luhrs testimony is from the cited Dies Committee record, p. 1661. Victor Reuther discussed the letter, and its use against the brothers, in an interview. *The Saturday Evening Post* footnote was quoted in the Detroit *News,* September 5, 1956. The Howe-Widick quote is from their volume, *The UAW and Walter Reuther,* p. 192, and the Farnum quote is from an interview. *The New Republic,* October 6, 1958, discussed the Rumely ad in the *Wall Street Journal.* Rauh and Victor Reuther talked to the authors about the Humphrey-McClellan exchange of correspondence. Photocopies of the letters were obtained from Joseph Walsh, former UAW publicity director.

ELEVEN   *Martin's Fall*

The account of Frankensteen's alliance with the Communists is based on interviews with him and Frank Winn, as well as papers in the George F. Addes Collection, Labor History Archives. For Martin's move against Frankensteen, see *The New York Times,* May 11, 1938. The "confidential" Socialist Party report referring to WPR is in the Henry Kraus Collection, Labor History Archives. *The New York Times,* June 14, 1938, reported the attempted Unity coup. Martin's suspension of UAW officers and subsequent developments were reported by *The New York Times* on virtually a daily basis beginning June 14, 1938. The Lewis statement after meeting with WPR and others appeared July 15, 1938.

Reporting of the trials of suspended officers commenced July 26. Purloined Lovestone correspondence first appeared in the *Daily Worker,* August 4–6, 1938. The account here is based on files of the *Daily Worker, The New York Times* of August 7, and an interview with Lovestone. WPR's mission to Dubinsky was recalled by Winn. Much subsequent material is from *The New York Times,* August 10–26, 1938, although the account of the Hillman-Murray intervention is based on Josephson's *Sidney Hillman,* p. 457. WPR's delayed departure from the Socialist Party is recounted in *The UAW and Walter Reuther* by Howe and Widick, p. 195.

Virtually all the narrative of events leading to the rival special conventions is based on reports in *The New York Times.* Exceptions: the anecdote of a reporter being held by the heels was supplied by a former Detroit labor reporter; some subsidiary material on violence during the period is from Galenson's *The CIO Challenge to the AFL,* p. 168; Dubinsky discussed his support of Martin in an interview. The account of the Cleveland convention is based on daily reports in *The New York Times* and the *Proceedings* (for the verbal battle between WPR and Frankensteen, see pp. 101ff), as well as interviews with WPR and Frankensteen. WPR recounted his view of voting strength and his deal to become head of the GM Department in return for supporting Thomas. The attitude of Lewis toward WPR was related in interviews by Lovestone and Justin McCarthy, editor, United Mine Workers *Journal.* Widman gave his assessment of Martin in an interview.

TWELVE   *Renaissance*

Frank Winn was a principal source on the 1939 tool and die strike. Fountain's *Union Guy,* p. 108, also discusses the union's dilemma at GM. Leonard Woodcock, in an interview, reported on precarious conditions in the UAW at the time. WPR's explanation is from a GM Strike Bulletin dated July 6, 1939, in the United Auto Workers-General Motors Collection, Labor History Archives. *The New York Times* reported picket line incidents at Pontiac and Cleveland on, respectively, July 11 and 31, 1939. WPR gave his estimate of the first auto labor contracts in an interview. Louis G. Seaton, a management negotiator who was present, recounted the WPR-Wilson exchange in an interview. The Detroit *News,* September 3, 1948, told of the "commissar" dispute with Knudsen. The text of WPR's planned broadcast is in the UAW-GM Collection cited. Stark's assessment of the settlement appeared in *The New York Times,* July 5, 1939, and WPR used the "renaissance" phrase in an interview. Galenson's *The CIO Challenge to the AFL,* pp. 175f, lists the series of UAW victories. Martin's resignation was recorded in *The New York Times,* April 27, 1940, and Ford's generosity toward him was reported by Harry Bennett in his *We Never Called Him Henry,* p. 116.

Michael Widman was the CIO man who directed the Ford drive because of internal rivalries within the UAW, as he related in an interview. WPR's recollections come from his *Selected Papers,* p. 179, and Cook's *Walter Reuther,* p. 72, tells of his sign language communication. The account of the Ford worker fired for smiling is from *The UAW and Walter Reuther* by Howe and Widick, p. 93. Bannon related organizing anecdotes in an interview. The Dallas episodes were reported in *The New York Times,* April 20, 1940, and Ford's defense of its conduct at the Rouge plant appears in Exhibit 1-P in NLRB Case VII-C-148, dated May 22, 1941. Edsel Ford's attitude is described in Sorensen's *My Forty Years with Ford,* p. 259. Widman told of his conversation with Lewis. Josephson's *Sidney Hillman,* p. 524, reports the Ford contract award, and Upton Sinclair's aid is described in *The Thirties* by Frisch and Diamond. Bannon told of Communists in the Ford drive and the surprise strike of April 1, 1941. Widman gave his view of the shutdown in an interview. White's *A Man Called White,* p. 147, and contemporary newspaper accounts describe the racial clashes that erupted, as do Howe and Widick, p. 104. The authors also benefited from a Frank Winn memo on the subject. Galenson, p. 184, gives the outcome of the Ford vote. Henry Ford's reaction is recounted by Sorensen, pp. 268ff, and Cook, p. 124, notes Ford's legal position. Widman, Leonard, and Winn, in separate interviews, told of the surprising turnabout by Bennett.

THIRTEEN   *Prelude to War*

UAW actions prior to Roosevelt's third-term nomination were reported in *The New York Times,* July 11, 1940. Debate on the pro-FDR resolution at the St. Louis convention of the UAW is recorded in *Proceedings,* pp. 426ff. Material on the dictatorships resolution is from *Proceedings,* pp. 292ff, and *The New York Times,* August 4, 1940, in which the Stark quote appeared. *The New York Times,* August 6, 1940, also reported disqualification of totalitarians from union office. WPR's Executive Board gains and the subsequent purge were related by Leonard Woodcock in an interview. Attacks on WPR as GM director and the Board's vote of confidence were reported in the Detroit *News,* October 10, 1940. The Lewis attack on FDR is from Josephson's *Sidney Hillman,* pp. 487f. In an interview, Frank Winn told of the meeting of the West Side Local's Executive Council. UAW reaction to Lewis and the meeting with Roosevelt was in *The New York Times,* October 28, 1940. The WPR radio campaign speech is from the Detroit *News,* October 31, 1940. The account of the 1940 CIO convention is from the *The New York Times,* November 22 and 23, 1940; Galenson, *The CIO Challenge to the AFL,* p. 638f; and Taft, *Organized Labor in American History,* p. 533. The report of GM mediation is from *The New York Times,* April 12, 18, 23, 25 and 27 and May 1, 16, and 17, 1941. Gallup Poll on strikes was reported in *The New York Times,* January 5, 1941.

The account of the Allis-Chalmers strike is based largely on reporting by *The New York Times,* with WPR's quote on Babb from Galenson, p. 189. Budenz gave his view of the strike in his *The Techniques of Communism,* p. 31. *The New York Times* again was the principal source on the North American strike but Mazey told of the bean field meeting in *Proceedings* of the 1941 UAW convention, p. 263, and Frankensteen recounted the Mortimer firing in an interview. Victor Reuther told of the Plymouth Local's resolutions when interviewed.

WPR's draft case was reported in the Detroit *News,* March 6, April 29 and 30, and May 5, 8, 20, and 29, 1941. Anderson's view on the subject is from the 1941 *Proceedings,* p. 702, and WPR's reply is from the same source, pp. 713f. The *Fortune* assessment is from "The Gas-Engine Union," November 1941. Victor Reuther talked of Addes in an interview, as did Woodcock and Frankensteen. The latter also told of his vacation trip with WPR and their common convention program. The account of the Allis-Chalmers delegation fight is from the Frankensteen interview, *The New York Times* of August 6 and 14, 1941, and *Proceedings,* pp. 303, 326f, and 419. Stark reported the WPR-Frankensteen split in *The New York Times,* August 8, 1941, and Mazey told of Haywood's intervention in an interview. The Michener debate is from *Proceedings,* pp. 249ff, 253, 420, 440, 423, and 432f; also from *The New York Times,* August 9 and 12, 1941. Michener's testimony is from "Transcript, United States of America v. Harry Renton Bridges, Henry Schmidt, and J. R. Robertson, 1950," pp. 3671, 3673, 3675, 3706, and 3786. Text of the anti-Communist constitutional amendment is from *Proceedings,* p. 688. The debate is reported in the same source, pp. 689, 692f, 700, 259, 689, 702f, 713, and 734; also in *The New York Times,* August 15, 1941. Material on the Addes-Leonard contest is from interviews with Woodcock and Leonard and from *Proceedings,* p. 742. Woodcock told of WPR's close call in Executive Board balloting and recounted the movie theater scene. *The New York Times* reported on Board gains by the WPR faction, August 16, 1941. *Business Week's* assessment appeared August 23, 1941. *The New York Times* told of the pay raise, August 14, 1941. The Pearl Harbor anecdote is from a memo to the authors from Frank Winn, and also from Kempton's *Part of Our Time,* p. 292.

FOURTEEN   *500 Planes a Day*

WPR told of the genesis of the "500 planes" program in an interview. Victor Reuther cited the Gorki parallel in a separate interview. Preparation of the plan is detailed in George R. Clark's "The Strange Story of the Reuther Plan," *Harper's,* May 1942. WPR told about approaching Thomas with the idea. Murray's presentation to FDR is from *The New York Times,* December 24, 1940. WPR's quote mentioning "England's battles" is from the Detroit *News,* December 23, 1940. Excerpts from "500 Planes A Day" are from WPR's *Selected Papers,* pp. 2ff. Jouett's initial rebuttal appeared in *The New York Times,* December 24, 1940. Clark in *Harper's* cited columnist backing, and WPR told about conferring with Roosevelt. Jouett's second rebuttal is from *The New York Times,* January 27, 1941. WPR's letter to *The New York Times* appeared earlier, January 23, 1941. Other items from the same newspaper: auto industry reaction, January 1; Gallup, January 4; staff writer assessments hostile to the plan, December 29, 1940, and January 5, 1941; hostile editorial, January 31, 1941; Roosevelt news conference and WPR's reaction, December 28, 1940; WPR's meeting with New Dealers, December 30, 1940; Associated Press rejection report, January 2, 1941; WPR and Lovett, January 4, and his tour in the military plane, January 22. The WPR-Knudsen anecdote is from Dayton's *Walter Reuther,* p. 127. Knudsen's Senate testimony is quoted by Catton in *The War Lords of Washington,* p. 70. Clark recounted the meeting with Knudsen and Hillman, and Joseph L. Rauh, Jr., told the Coy anecdote in an interview.

WPR's December 13 speech is from *The New York Times,* December 13 and 14, 1941. His House testimony is quoted in Michael Straight, "The Automobile Conference," *The New Republic,* January 19, 1942. The Knudsen-Hillman news conference was reported in *The New York Times,* January 6, 1942. Catton's comments on the WPR plan is from his book, pp. 98 and 110, as is the Donald Nelson anecdote, p. 91. WPR's remarks to GM delegates appeared in *The New York Times,* February 8, 1942. Accounts of the WPR-Wilson debate are largely from the Detroit *News,* March 31 and April 1, 1942; *Business Week,* April 4, 1942; an interview with Victor Reuther, and *The New York Times,* March 22 and April 1, 1942. The Detroit *News* editorial appeared April 2. Keller's testimony is from *The New York Times,* September 16, 1945, and Graham's reaction was related by Rauh in an interview. *Fortune's* kind words were in "Reuther: F.O.B. Detroit," December 1945.

FIFTEEN   *The War Years*

WPR recalled his wartime experiences in an interview. He talked about his plan to take down the White House fence, and about breaking engine and tank gun production bottlenecks. His remarks on arming workers were quoted in *The New York Times,* February 23, 1942. *The New York Times* also reported the Sunday pay dispute, February 2, 6, and 9; March 21 and 29; April 9, and September 18 and 28, 1942. Thomas on Congress and the income ceiling proposal is from *Proceedings* of the 1942 UAW convention, p. 18. WPR's convention remarks are from the same source, pp. 394f; his second for Addes, p. 297; and the Addes second for WPR, pp. 299ff. The delegate revolt is reported in *The New York Times,* August 7 and 8, 1942. The source for the Sunday pay battle at the convention and the subsequent meeting with FDR and his order on the subject is from the same publication, August 5, 28, and 29 and September 10, 1942.

The New York Times reported on Roy Reuther's WPB job September 10, 1942, and told of Victor Reuther's wartime assignment April 1, 1942. WPR's cited article in *The New York Times Magazine* appeared December 13, 1942. He told of various federal job offers, including Roosevelt's proposal, in an interview. The possible Army commission was discussed in the Detroit *News,* December 20, 1944. Establishment of the UAW Washington office was in *The New York Times* on February 11, 1943, and subsequent WPR activities in that connection on February 25 and June 20, 1943. The same newspaper told of his 48-hour week plan, January 17 and February 11, 1943. WPR's own interview account of the expedition to Camp Atterbury was supplemented by Associated Press dispatches in *The New York Times,* March 22 and 23, 1943.

Racial tensions in Detroit and WPR's role in trying to ease them are discussed in Howe and Widick, *The UAW and Walter Reuther,* pp. 219ff, and in the Detroit *News,* April 12, 1943. Also see White's *A Man Called White,* pp. 234f, and White's quote, p. 217. The report of WPR at Northwestern High School is from *The Detroit Race Riot* by Shogan and Craig, pp. 86f. The account of initial skirmishing on piecework is from *The New York Times,* May 1, 1943; an interview with Frankensteen; and the Detroit *News,* May 14, 1943. *The New York Times* reported the convention fight on piecework, October 8, 1943. The "Ballad of the Gruesome Twosome" is quoted from Fountain's *Union Guy,* p. 163f. The rival song was found in the Dan Gallagher Collection, Labor History Archives. The Addes-Leonard vote is from *Proceedings* of the 1943 UAW convention, as is the result of the WPR-Frankensteen contest. *The New York Times* appraised the Executive Board lineup, October 10, 1943, and the Thomas-Addes anecdote was related by John M. Livingston in an interview.

WPR discussed the *Normandie* project and his relations with the Roosevelts, as well as reciting the Thomas-FDR anecdote, in an interview. The caucusing anecdote came from an interview with Stephen Schlossberg. *The New York Times,* September 12, 1944, reported on violence at the Grand Rapids convention, and in succeeding issues on the fight over the no-strike pledge. Frankensteen's criticism of the WPR compromise is from *Proceedings* of the 1944 UAW convention, p. 158. In an interview WPR discussed at length the Leonard candidacy and his own political troubles. Frankensteen and Leonard gave their own accounts in separate interviews. The roll call results are detailed in *Proceedings,* pp. 411 and 419. WPR's conversion plans and his debate on the 30-hour week are from *The New York Times,* May 1, 1943; May 7, 1944; January 15, 1944; March 17 and 26, 1944, and September 16, 1945. WPR told of the portable foxhole in an interview. The Matt Hammond quote is from Howe and Widick, pp. 128f, and the Thomas quote from *The New York Times,* July 20, 1945.

SIXTEEN   *On Strike at GM*

The economic brief filed with federal agencies in June 1945 is described in *The UAW and Walter Reuther* by Howe and Widick, p. 129. Big business resistance to union demands at the New York meeting of industrialists is recounted in Phillips' *The Truman Presidency,* p. 121. Howe and Widick, p. 127, report the wartime rise in living costs and wages; also Truman's wage-price order, WPR's reaction to it, and the Davis statement, pp. 143 and 150. Fountain's *Union Guy* recounts GM's rejection of WPR's proposal and gives the Wilson quote, p. 173. A UAW pamphlet, "Purchasing Power For Prosperity," provides statistics on a GM worker's earnings. The WPR quotation supporting his demand is from Fountain, p. 185, and *The New York Times Magazine* article is reprinted in his *Selected Papers,* pp. 11ff. The Romney-Reuther debate is mentioned, p. 5, in a looseleaf "Contract Negotiations—Chronology," provided by General Motors Corporation. WPR's message to the locals is from the UAW-GM Collection, Labor History Archives. Howe and Widick, p. 131, describe the "one-at-a-time" strategy, and GM's "Chronology" details the presence of newsmen at the opening of negotiations (p. 6) as well as the corporation's newspaper advertising campaign (p. 7).

The multiple correlation analysis is taken from the UAW pamphlet,

p. 56, and Wilson's longer workweek proposal is mentioned in the GM "Chronology," along with the "skunk" epithet, p. 39. Fountain, p. 179, reported the exchange over prices and Dayton's *Walter Reuther,* p. 121, reprinted the debate over sharing the wealth. WPR's quote on reactionaries is from the Detroit *News,* October 28, 1946, and the strike vote is from GM's "Chronology," pp. 8f. Truman's statements in a speech of October 30, 1945, are quoted in the UAW's "Purchasing Power" document, p. 2.

Most of the information regarding bargaining developments was taken from accounts in *The New York Times* or the factual record kept by GM. White's *A Man Called White,* p. 217, describes the citizens' committee. The memo to Thomas came from Lincoln Fairley on December 8, 1945, and is in the R. J. Thomas Collection, Labor History Archives. Murray's attitude is reported by Howe and Widick, p. 141, and the Lewis quote is from Taft's *Organized Labor in American History.* The UAW news release of December 18, 1945, is in the Thomas Collection.

The accounts of Reuther's vow to wage "the damnedest fight," as well as the discussions of the dispute over the presidential fact-finding panel and GM's walkout, are from the corporation "Chronology" of strike events, pp. 19 and 21f. *The New Republic* editorial on WPR appeared January 7, 1946. His mobilization of strike support is documented in the collections of the Labor History Archives. Joseph L. Rauh, Jr., told in an interview of arranging for tax deductibility of strike donations. The Thomas criticism of the walkout was found in *Proceedings* of the 1946 UAW convention, pp. 147f. The report of WPR's outrage over the UE settlement is from *Time,* February 25, 1946. The letter from the angry welder, Frank Freeman, is in the Thomas Collection. Truman's attitude is reported in *The Forrestal Diaries,* pp. 143f. The union aide quoted in the final paragraph is Frank Winn, in a letter to the authors.

SEVENTEEN   *Battle on the Boardwalk*

Main episodes in this chapter are taken from *Proceedings* of the UAW's 1946 convention. WPR's attitude toward the contest was described by Frank Winn in a letter to the authors. Leonard Woodcock added his recollections of the 1946 Reuther-Thomas battle in an interview; his account included the contemplated alliance with Addes that did not materialize. Addes's report on the union's money troubles was reported in the Detroit *News,* March 22, 1946. The fist fights were described in Cook's *Walter Reuther,* p. 156. The hotel manager's appeal is in *Proceedings,* p. 156, and the Addes' warning on rowdyism, p. 283. The estimate of Communist strength was made by Howe and Widick, *The UAW and Walter Reuther,* p. 150, and they cite the reason for WPR's anti-Communism on p. 151. The Reutherites' quacking and its target were recalled by Winn in a letter to the authors. Thomas' anti-intellectual comment was reported in the Detroit *News,* March 26, 1946, and Howe and Widick, p. 108, tell of the Thomas preference for poker over productivity charts. Lahey's appraisal of WPR is from *The New Republic,* April 8, 1946; Winn set down a contrasting assessment in a letter to the authors. James B. Carey gave his memories of the 1946 convention in an interview, as did Richard Leonard, who recounted WPR's approach to Murray. The CIO president's words are from *Proceedings,* pp. 95ff, and WPR's implied criticism of Murray is from Howe-Widick, p. 164. Criticism of the GM strike appears in *Proceedings,* p. 145, as does the proposal for a Reuther-Thomas debate, p. 140. Dubinsky's role is discussed by Fountain in *Union Guy,* p. 193, and was recounted by Dubinsky in an interview. Fountain's description of the Communist sex plot is from his volume, p. 195. Cook, p. 160, relates the pre-balloting confrontation between WPR and Thomas. The commotion on the platform is described by Fountain, p. 196, and was discounted by Woodcock in an interview. The Detroit *News* reported the post-balloting conversation between WPR and Thomas, March 28, 1946. WPR's unity plea is from *Proceedings,* p. 218. The membership of Local 50 is mentioned on p. 50 of the convention record. Frankensteen told of his decision to leave the UAW in an interview. WPR's pledge to isolate the Communists was reported by the Detroit *News,* March 31, 1946.

EIGHTEEN   *Purge*

Jack Conway supplied much information on 1946–1947 developments in an interview. He described the union's financial plight and the $250,-000 loan. The hostile Executive Board was described in the Detroit *News,* April 21, 1946. Howe and Widick give a good account of the factional "nightmare" in their *The UAW and Walter Reuther,* including the Communist-written resolution, p. 163. Cook's *Walter Reuther,* p. 162, cites the withholding of WPR's signature from paychecks as a political bargaining device. Howe-Widick, pp. 165f, tell of infighting over the Allis-Chalmers fight. Conway related how WPR men swept CIO offices in the Midwest and Nat Weinberg recalled in an interview how UAW typists took sides. Walter White's role is described in his autobiography, *A Man Called White,* p. 335. Conway discussed Murray's role in the factional dispute and linked it to the campaign against Communists in the CIO. Thomas' complaints about WPR and Wyndham

Mortimer's suggested strategy for dealing with WPR can be found in the R. J. Thomas Collection, Labor History Archives. Howe and Widick, p. 151, report the testimony before the House Committee on Un-American Activities and WPR's reaction to it. Fountain's *Union Guy*, p. 204, tells of the 1947 bargaining setback for WPR. Major sources on the proposed merger of the Farm Equipment Workers and the UAW were interviews with Conway and John Livingston. The pro-Thomas observer quoted is Richard Leonard, from an interview. WPR wrote about the anti-Communist drive for *Collier's* in 1948 and the article is reprinted in his *Selected Papers,* pp. 19ff. The smear campaign and WPR's rebuttal is described by Howe and Widick, p. 169, and Fountain, p. 212. Conway told of the meeting with Murray. WPR wrote about the Ford Local 600 contest for delegates in the *Collier's* article. The Thomas quote is from a UAW news release of September 21, 1947, from the Thomas Collection, Labor History Archives.

The 1947 UAW convention *Proceedings* is the principal source for the outcome of the election contest. Murray's words are recorded in Jack Stieber's *Governing the UAW,* p. 13. Murray's remarks about patting WPR's "red locks" are quoted in Dayton's *Walter Reuther,* p. 177. Fountain, p. 215, recounts WPR's acceptance speech. His pay raise was reported in the Detroit *News,* November 15, 1947. The Wechsler article appeared in *Harper's,* March 1948. Taft's appraisal is from his *Organized Labor in American History,* p. 571. The Buffalo unionist interviewed is Frank Lombardo. The Detroit *News,* March 18, 1948, recorded the firing of Communists from the UAW staff, and the Henry Ford visit, December 5, 1947. In interviews, Conway and Arthur J. Goldberg gave information on the anti-Communist drive in the CIO. WPR's 1952 appraisal of Communist influence was reported in the Detroit *News,* December 8, 1952.

NINETEEN   *Shotguns and Dynamite*

Pre-shooting threats were reported in the Detroit *News,* April 21, 1948, as was WPR's shooting, his hospitalization, and the initial search for the assailant, May 21–23, 1948. Anna Reuther's urgings that her son abandon union work are described in Cook's *Walter Reuther,* p. 169. WPR's statement that the union would go forward is from Fountain's *Union Guy,* p. 225. Efforts to protect WPR and his brothers were outlined by Conway in an interview. WPR told of the change in his life style in an interview. Conway and WPR gave details of the recuperation and nerve surgery. The account of the Victor Reuther shooting is from Cook, pp. 171f, and *Time,* June 6, 1949. WPR told of his mother's reaction in an interview. The dynamite incident is reported in *Time,* January 2, 1950. WPR's move to the country was recounted by Conway and WPR told of using carpentry as therapy. The Lucido-Scroy disappearance is from the Detroit *News,* January 6, 1954. Bolton's arrest and acquittal is from Dayton's *Walter Reuther,* pp. 198f. Conway discussed auto plant gambling as well as the Briggs beatings and the Mazey-Bishop rivalry.

The Perrone-Renda ties to the Stove Works and Briggs are detailed in *Investigation of Organized Crime in Interstate Commerce,* Hearings Before the Special Committee, United States Senate, 82nd Congress, First Session—Part 9. The report of the trial and firing of Bishop is from the Detroit *News,* March 7, 1951, which in the same edition and on the following day told of Bishop's 1947 arrest with Perrone. Mazey testified about the hiring of UAW investigators and his suspicion of DeLamielleure in *Hearings Before the Select Committee on Improper Activities in the Labor or Management Field,* Part 22, pp. 9042 and 9055. The Detroit *News* disclosed results of its "Secret Witness" plan, January 10, 1954. The same publication reported the Immigration Service raid on the Stove Works, February 11, 1951. Kefauver Committee testimony can be found in the cited *Investigation of Organized Crime,* pp. 5, 124, 130, and 160f.

Developments relating to the Canton Bar and DeLamielleure are from the Detroit *News,* August 23, 1951, and January 10, 1954. Conway told of the drive to organize the Stove Works. Supplementary information came from *Business Week,* June 16, 1951, and the Detroit *News,* November 26, 1951. The latter also reported Perrone's loss of the haulage contract. The report of Perrone's trial and parole is from the Detroit *News,* December 6, 1951; April 25, 1965, and August 7, 1953. Henderson's search for Ritchie and subsequent reward negotiations were reported by the Detroit *News,* February 17 and 18, 1954, and January 12, 1954. Mazey testified about the negotiations in the cited *Hearings Before the Select Committee,* pp. 9044f.

O'Brien's announcement of a "solution" to the WPR shooting is from the Detroit *News,* January 6, 1954. Ritchie's statement was made public by O'Brien and published following the Canadian's flight of January 8, reported in the Detroit *News* of January 9, 1954, and *The New York Times,* January 10, 1954. Ritchie's capture and the collapse of extradition efforts were reported in the Detroit *News,* January 13 and February 19, 1954. The Detroit *News* reported punishment of the guards, February 16, 1954, and told of the statute of limitations extension, April 15, 1954. The Renda suit and its outcome were given in the Detroit *News,* April 25, 1965. Winstead's fate is from *Business Week,* April 26,

1958, and Dayton, p. 205. Mazey testified about DeLamielleure and the Teamsters in *Hearings Before the Select Committee,* p. 9055. The account of the bombing of Perrone is from the *News,* April 25, 1965, which also told of Ritchie's perjury conviction. WPR summed up his attitude toward the search for his assailants in an interview.

TWENTY   *Politics*

Schlesinger's quote is from his *The Vital Center,* p. 268. WPR talked about officeholding in an interview. Victor Reuther, in a separate interview, discussed his school board race. Murray's remarks are quoted from Joseph Gaer's *The First Round,* p. 61. Gaer, pp. 150, 152, and 631, also is the source for the Luce-Hillman exchanges. Wayne County registration figures were reported in *The New York Times,* October 23, 1944. The quoted Johnson associate is George E. Reedy, from an interview. The Michigan Commonwealth Federation is discussed in *The UAW and Walter Reuther* by Howe and Widick, pp. 273f, and Fay Calkins' *The CIO and the Democratic Party,* p. 115. Victor Reuther's third-party statement appeared in *Common Sense,* December 1945. People's Party activities were reported in *The New York Times,* May 5, 1946. The WPR quote on Socialism is from "Reuther: F.O.B. Detroit," *Fortune,* December 1945, as is the succeeding one on realignment. WPR's discussion of labor parties is from Goldberg's *AFL-CIO: Labor United,* p. 215. Material on WPR and the ADA is from an interview with Joseph L. Rauh, Jr.

Calkins, pp. 114ff, is the source on formation of the Michigan Democratic Coalition. Woodcock was interviewed by the authors. Material on the coalition's battle with Hoffa is from Velie's *Labor U.S.A.,* pp. 32 and 71f, and Widick's *Labor Today,* p. 152. The Murray-Truman anecdote appeared in the New York *Post,* February 16, 1959. WPR's Detroit *News* interview on Truman appeared June 6, 1948. The associate cited next is Rauh. The meeting in WPR's basement was reported by Jack Conway in an interview. Victor Reuther discussed with the authors his brother's attitude toward Eisenhower and Douglas. Rauh talked about the ADA board meeting. WPR on Truman to Wechsler is from *Time,* May 24, 1948. The March Executive Board actions are related in Howe-Widick, p. 276, and Fountain's *Union Guy,* pp. 229ff. The *Free Press* interview with WPR appeared April 4, 1948. UAW endorsement of Truman is mentioned in Howe-Widick, pp. 276f. Conway discussed UAW campaign efforts and told of WPR's receiving the election results. The Wallace complaint about WPR is from *The New York Times,* October 18, 1948, and WPR's post-election statement is

from the Detroit *News,* November 5, 1948, which reported his meeting
with Truman, December 15, 1948. Howe and Widick, p. 277, discuss
the inauguration eve conference. Hoffa versus the Democratic coalition
is from Velie, p. 72, and Calkins, pp. 114 and 120ff. Calkins, pp. 133f,
also is the source for the Williams' recount victory. WPR's account of
his meeting with Moody is from an interview. The DeToledano quote
is from his *RFK, The Man Who Would Be President,* p. 101. The Woodcock quote is from an interview. WPR's Senate testimony is quoted in
his *Selected Papers,* p. 141. Rauh told of WPR and Stevenson in an
interview. The Barkley affair is described in a memo to the authors from
Frank Winn and one to Winn from WPR. Truman's quote is from
Volume II of his *Memoirs,* p. 495. The account of WPR and Nixon is
from *Selected Papers,* p. 47, as is the concluding quotation, p. 45.

TWENTY-ONE   *Bargaining Pioneer*

Principal sources were WPR and Louis G. Seaton in interviews. Day-
to-day bargaining developments are reported in the General Motors
mimeographed notebook entitled "Chronology—Contract Negotiations,"
and from the daily press. The value of the escalator clause was reported
in the Chicago *Daily News,* May 8, 1968. Wilson's statement on the
1948 agreement is from a GM news release dated June 2, 1948. WPR's
arguments for pensions are from his *Selected Papers,* p. 33. Joe Glazer
told in an interview of writing the pension song. Douglas Fraser also
was interviewed. Nat Weinberg spoke of the link between pensions and
Social Security in a 1956 speech to the International Metalworkers Federation, privately printed by the UAW. The *Fortune* quotes are from
the issue of July 1951. Jack Conway discussed the "living document"
theory in an interview. McDonald's criticism is from his autobiography,
Union Man, p. 238.

TWENTY-TWO   *The Visionary*

Leonard Woodcock told of "500 Plans" in an interview. Widick in
Labor Today, p. 77, reports the arrangement with Mrs. Roosevelt. The
housing-rail plan is in WPR's *Selected Papers,* pp. 13ff. His subsequent
presentation of the plan to the Senate Banking Committee is discussed
in *The New Republic,* February 28, 1949, and in Dayton's *Walter
Reuther,* p. 183. WPR on central city decay is in *Selected Papers,* p.
276. His writing of the slum rebuilding plan was related by Stephen
Schlossberg in an interview. The source of WPR's ideas is explored in
Stieber's *Governing the UAW,* p. 91, and Cubbage's *A Rhetorical Study,*

p. 177. The Weinberg autobiography is quoted by Stieber, pp. 112f. WPR's Peace Corps idea is in *Selected Papers,* p. 158, as is his speech about the paralyzed young man and Wilson's bull, pp. 35f. WPR on Blue Shield is from Carter's *The Doctor Business,* pp. 257ff, and Stieber, pp. 116f. WPR on the purpose of his speeches is reported by Cubbage, p. 175, as are WPR's subsequent quotes, p. 176; Victor Reuther on his brother's talks, p. 181; WPR on the importance of speechmaking fervor, p. 186; the Civic Opera House anecdote, p. 187, and the plateau observation, p. 206. Walsh's remark is from an interview. Cubbage again was the source for WPR on prepared texts, p. 178; WPR's habits in making speech notes, pp. 184f, and WPR on repetition of speech themes, p. 175. Winn assessed "the speech" in a memo to the authors. WPR's flexible car-pricing idea was quoted in *Business Week,* June 16, 1956, and discussed by Sylvia Porter in the Detroit *Free Press,* June 7, 1956. WPR's tour of the Ford Cleveland plant was reported in the Detroit *News,* June 22, 1953. His automation discussion and plan is from *Selected Papers,* pp. 119 and 157ff. WPR talked of economic planning at the 1965 AFL-CIO convention and his remarks are from the convention *Proceedings,* p. 300. The memo-redrafting anecdote appeared in *Time,* June 20, 1955, and the one involving Mike Wallace, in *Holiday,* December 1959. WPR on his own verbosity is in the text of his "Opening Remarks" to the 1968 UAW convention.

TWENTY-THREE   *Road to Merger*

Major sources were the *Proceedings* of the 1952 CIO convention and interviews with WPR, George Meany, Arthur J. Goldberg, James B. Carey, and Thomas E. Harris. WPR's 1946 denial of interest in the CIO presidency appeared in the Detroit *News,* November 10, 1946, and William Green's comment is from the same publication, April 30, 1948. Harris described Mike Quill's efforts for Haywood and Albert J. Zack told of WPR's approach to Beirne. WPR commented on McDonald in an interview and Harris discussed Haywood's accent. Goldberg summed up anti-Reuther criticism, and John Livingston told of the Oil Workers' ploy. Zack recalled the cactus-caucus joke, the McDonald-Reuther exchange, and the inflation of voting totals. Accounts of the roll call results, Haywood's reaction, the Carey resolution, Rieve's introduction, and WPR's acceptance speech are from *Proceedings,* pp. 469–83. Joseph L. Rauh, Jr., recalled WPR's labor unity hopes in an interview. The *Wall Street Journal,* November 9, 1953, reported the Woodworkers' honors. Harris told of dividing the restaurant check and repeated WPR's off-color story. Joseph A. Loftus recalled the airborne staff conference.

WPR's comments on McCarthy appeared in the Detroit *News,* August 4 and 19, 1953. Harris analyzed the problems of running a labor federation. Nat Goldfinger, in an interview, was critical of WPR's leadership of the CIO. WPR's troubles with McDonald are described in John Brophy's recollections, p. 1021, in the Oral History Collection, Columbia University. Meany described his exchange with Raskin, as well as his warning to WPR about "sniping." Carey related the hotel room anecdote. Meany's brevity as contrasted with Reuther's free-flowing oratory is contrasted in Velie's *Labor U.S.A.,* p. 19. The arrangement for naming top AFL-CIO officers was described by Goldberg. The account of the Industrial Union Department is from Goldberg's *AFL-CIO: Labor United,* pp. 98ff. WPR's pledge is from *The New York Times,* December 9, 1955.

TWENTY-FOUR   *The Annual Wage*

Primary sources were WPR, Nat Weinberg, and Louis G. Seaton in interviews. Weinberg also provided a copy of a paper he gave at the International Metalworkers Federation meeting in Paris in the summer of 1956, which provided additional details. GM's record of bargaining developments in their looseleaf notebook, "Chronology—Contract Negotiations," also was helpful. Roosevelt's 1936 reference to annual earnings is from his *Public Papers and Addresses,* Volume V, pp. 498f. WPR's 1945 article on the subject appeared in the September 16 issue of *The New York Times Magazine.* His article in the *Annals* appeared in Vol. 274, March 1951, pp. 64–74. Seaton told of WPR's reaction to the stock purchase proposal, as well as GM's view of the annual wage demand. Paul Schrade, in an interview, described Livingston's attitude. Jack Conway recounted the 1955 impasse at Ford and the "Black Thursday" result. WPR and Seaton recalled the "Chinese copy" expression. The price reduction proposal is from *The New York Times,* August 18, 1957, and the account of the manufacturers' rejections is from Detroit newspapers of the following week. WPR's ridicule of American cars was quoted in the Detroit *News,* April 17, 1958. Leonard Woodcock and Seaton discussed the 1958 bargaining in interviews and WPR commented on the union strategy.

TWENTY-FIVE   *Reuther Embattled*

Hoffman's attack on WPR is recorded in the *Congressional Record,* August 2, 1955. The Adams' remark was reported in the Detroit *News,* October 26, 1956. The *Time* account appeared June 18, 1956. Jack

Conway, in an interview, told of UAW efforts on Kefauver's behalf, and the Executive Council action was reported in the Detroit *News,* August 29, 1956. The exchange with Curtis is from WPR's *Selected Papers,* p. 136. Nixon's quote on WPR is from the Detroit *News,* September 25, 1956. WPR on corruption in 1945 was quoted in *House of Labor* by Hardman and Neufeld, p. 175. His 1957 comments are from *Selected Papers,* pp. 161f. *The New York Times,* October 13, 1957, reported Civil Liberties Union criticism. WPR's comment on Beck and Hoffa is from the Detroit *News,* March 24 and May 22, 1957. The Salinger quote is from his *With Kennedy,* p. 27. The Republican rebuttal is from *Final Report of the Select Committee on Improper Activities in the Labor or Management Field,* Part 2, pp. 321f. This volume also is the source for the account of separate Republican and Democratic findings on the Committee's investigation of the UAW. Companion volumes, *Hearings Before the Select Committee,* etc., Parts 21, 22, 23, 24, 25, and 58, contain the complete transcript of the UAW inquiry and are the source for the account of the hearings. WPR's testimony begins on p. 9958 of Part 25 and is complete in that volume. Goldwater's "Sputnik" comment appeared in the Detroit *Times,* January 21, 1958. His feud with WPR is reported in the Detroit *News,* February 2 and March 9, 1958, and McDowell's *Barry Goldwater,* pp. 123ff. WPR, in an interview, told of John Kennedy's role in arranging for his testimony and of the note from Herling. His comment on the cost of the Kohler strike is from the transcript of his address to the 12th UAW Skilled Trades Conference, March 17, 1967.

TWENTY-SIX   *The World Stage*

Many of WPR's foreign policy statements are reprinted in his *Selected Papers,* which also includes a transcript of his confrontation with Khrushchev. Josephson's *Sidney Hillman,* pp. 638–51, reports CIO involvement with the World Federation of Trade Unions and the subsequent establishment of the International Confederation of Free Trade Unions. The transfer of CIA funds is discussed in a statement in *The New York Times,* May 8, 1967, a follow-up to Braden's article in *The Saturday Evening Post,* dated May 20 but made public before that time. Braden also discussed the incident in an interview, as did Victor Reuther. Paul Hall was the AFL-CIO Executive Council member who made the "black bag" remark in an interview. The clash with Meany over Nehru was reported in the Detroit *News,* April 6, 1956. Widick's *Labor Today* tells of British praise for WPR and antagonism between Lovestone and Victor Reuther. The description of Lovestone came from the late Edwin

A. Lahey. WPR told the gondola anecdote and Copenhagen walking story in an interview. He also justified his meeting with Mikoyan, in *Selected Papers,* p. 236. Goldfinger related Rieve's position on the Khrushchev meeting in an interview. Lovestone also gave his view in an interview. Irving Bluestone told how WPR telephoned May Reuther about the "marriage" story. McGill wrote about the trip to Japan in the Detroit *News,* January 15, 1963. WPR's view on global corporations appeared in the UAW newspaper, *Solidarity,* May 1968. Victor Reuther provided a copy of the "Declaration of Detroit," along with union pamphlets explaining its significance. He described his return to Gorki in an interview.

TWENTY-SEVEN   *New Frontier*

WPR for President moves and his disavowal are from the Detroit *News,* April 28, 1959, as is the UAW neutrality statement, March 14, 1959, and the realignment statement, September 5, 1960. Jack Conway told of the pre-convention steering committee in an interview, and Joseph L. Rauh, Jr., was the interview source of the account of John F. Kennedy and the McClellan Committee, and of WPR and the Humphrey presidential bid. Douglas Fraser discussed in an interview Reuther's approaches to Stevenson after West Virginia. The Roy Reuther-Bobby Baker episode is from *Lyndon B. Johnson: The Exercise of Power,* by Evans and Novak, p. 202. Reedy told of his Detroit experiences in an interview. The WPR-Carey anecdote was related by Carey in an interview. Rauh and Conway told of WPR's efforts in behalf of Humphrey for Vice-President, and Conway discussed the Johnson presidential attempt, Symington for Vice-President, and Kennedy's announcement to labor leaders that his running mate would be LBJ. Leonard Woodcock told of Rauh weeping at the news, and in a separate interview Paul Schrade recounted the reactions of May Reuther and James B. Carey. Woodcock described the scene in WPR's suite and the Dubinsky call to Rose. Conway told how Woodcock turned sentiment in the Michigan delegation, and described WPR's joust with Meany over an endorsement. The Detroit *News,* August 3, 1960, reported WPR's visit to Hyannisport, and in an interview he told of his conversation with Jacqueline Kennedy. Roy Reuther's role in the campaign is related in Stieber's *Governing the UAW,* pp. 110f, and the Washington *Star,* January 11, 1968. The Nixon-WPR exchange was reported in the Detroit *News,* November 4, 1960. Sorensen's *Kennedy,* p. 439, tells of the President at the UAW convention. Conway and Frank Winn related the Tractors for Freedom effort, and *Business Week,* April 14, 1962, reported the WPR party for

Congress. WPR gave his reaction to JFK and the Congress in addressing the 1962 convention of the Bakery and Confectionary Workers (see *Proceedings,* p. 308). WPR, in an interview, told of his visits to Mrs. Roosevelt at Hyde Park, and Anna Roosevelt Halsted gave her memories at a Washington, D.C., memorial service for WPR and May Reuther, May 1970.

TWENTY-EIGHT   *The Great Society*

LBJ's call to WPR is described in Amrine's *This Awesome Challenge,* p. 40. The Haley quote is from his *A Texan Looks at Lyndon,* p. 212. Joseph A. Califano, Jr., in an interview, told of WPR's role in the Model Cities Program. Hubert H. Humphrey, in an interview, told of WPR's relations with him and Johnson; he and Joseph L. Rauh, Jr., recounted the Freedom Democrats dispute. Thomas gave his statement on the Reuthers in 1965 for the Oral History Collection, Columbia University. The UAW's Vietnam policy statement is from the Detroit *News,* October 22, 1965, and Paul Schrade, in an interview, told of being called on the carpet. The account of the ILA wheat boycott is from the Detroit *News,* February 19, 1964, and the same publication is the source for WPR on subway and other government disputes, January 17, 1966, and WPR's absence from auto safety hearings, June 6, 1966. WPR's views on free trade are from a transcript of the NBC "Meet the Press" broadcast, September 24, 1967, and Stephen Schlossberg told of the "People's Car" in an interview. WPR's remarks to the NAACP is from his *Selected Papers,* pp. 167ff. For the material on UAW and the Negro, see Stieber's *Governing the UAW,* pp. 122ff. Dubinsky in an interview and Sorensen's *Kennedy,* p. 504, discussed the March on Washington. In an interview WPR told of his support for Chavez, and the Detroit *News* reported on WPR in Selma, March 16, 1965; the Meredith march, June 27, 1966, and the Citizens' Crusade Against Poverty, April 14, 1966. An official of another union who did not want to be quoted also was a source on the Citizens' Crusade. Schlossberg told of WPR's intervention to get troops to control the Detroit riot, and an Associated Press dispatch in the Washington *Post,* January 9, 1969, reported the anti-WPR remarks of Negro militants. Reference to WPR and the NAACP Board is from AP in the Detroit *News,* September 20, 1966, and a memo to the authors from Frank Winn. WPR and hunger is from the *Post,* April 23, 1968, and he gave his views on the Memphis strike and civil rights in his "Opening Address" to the 1968 UAW convention. The Detroit *News,* February 7, 1966, reported on WPR's slicing off a finger. Patrick J. Owens recounted the Florida anecdote, Irving

Bluestone provided the tennis stories, and Winn told the fishing trophy anecdote, in interviews. The account of Roy Reuther's death, and the attendant quotes, are from *The New York Times,* January 11, 1968. Humphrey and Jack Conway, in interviews, related WPR's pre-convention activities in 1968. The endorsement of LBJ and his stop-the-bombing suggestion is from the "Meet the Press" transcript. Conway told of WPR and Negotiations Now, and Humphrey recalled his collaboration with WPR on a Vietnam plank.

TWENTY-NINE   *The Changing Union*

Disquiet among skilled tradesmen in 1967 was discussed in *Newsweek,* September 18, 1967, and their 1955 rebellion in Widick's *Labor Today,* p. 191. WPR addressed the Skilled Trades Conference on March 17, 1967. The hiring of Quayle was reported in the Detroit *News,* March 19, 1967, and industry's contract offer in *The New York Times,* August 30, 1967. Patrick J. Owens told of the UAW health club in an interview. WPR's removal from the payroll and staff pay cuts were detailed in an interview by Stephen Schlossberg. The report of Ford's reaction to the strike is from *Newsweek,* above, and the settlement offer from the Washington *Post,* October 23, 1967. A day later the *Post* reported on rival TV appeals to the membership, as did *Time,* November 3, 1967. The *Wall Street Journal,* May 10, 1968, carried a lengthy account of the 1968 convention challenge to WPR. In an interview WPR discussed the youth rebellion, student radicals, overtime problems, and comfortable union leaders. The Rauh quote is from an interview. Widick's "infallibility" quote is from *Labor Today,* p. 186. Galenson's observations are from the introduction, p. viii, of *Governing the UAW,* and Stieber's are from the same volume, pp. 54f. WPR's comment on challengers is from an Associated Press interview in the Washington *Star,* September 1, 1969. Willoughby Abner discussed the staff union in an interview and Schlossberg retold the Mazey joke. The Washington *Post,* December 25, 1968, reported the San Francisco bank failure, and Richard T. Frankensteen talked about the Detroit bank failure in an interview. Miller reminisced at the WPR memorial service in Detroit, May 15, 1970. The *Post* told of the juniority plan, March 13, 1969, and WPR talked about it in an interview, as he did about black revolutionaries. His convention news conference was quoted in the Washington *Post,* April 23, 1970. Bernstein reported on the revolutionaries in the Los Angeles *Times* of June 10, 1969. Report of the Ad Hoc Committee's efforts was in *The New York Times,* October 1, 1968.

THIRTY   *Reuther versus Meany*

In addition to interviews with WPR and Meany, the authors relied on the recollections of one of their number, William J. Eaton, who began news coverage of the AFL-CIO from Washington in 1957. The lengthy Administrative Letters issued under WPR's name in late 1966 and early 1967, together with the AFL-CIO's rebuttal pamphlet entitled, "To Clear the Record," also were consulted. The AFL-CIO resolution, No. 224, is from its 1965 convention *Proceedings,* p. 650. Velie's *Labor U.S.A.,* p. 17, records Meany's outburst and WPR's reaction. The India debate was reported by the Detroit *News,* May 3, 1956. Meany described the detour to Puerto Rico. Eaton recalled infighting over the unemployment march and Thomas Harris, in an interview, appraised the Carey sentiment. Hartnett related the 1959 episode in an interview. The 1961 feud over jurisdictional disputes was described by Lane Kirkland in an interview. Goldberg's remarks are from the Detroit *News,* December 1, 1961. Kirkland gave Meany's reaction and the chronology of the late meeting, including WPR's role. Eaton recalled WPR's absence from the Kennedy escort committee and Meany told of the UN incident and the Undersecretary of Labor nomination. The fight over Helstein was covered by Eaton. The togetherness quote is from Asher Lauren in the Detroit *News,* February 24, 1963, and the same newspaper, August 18, 1963, reported WPR's harsh estimate of Meany, whose comment on WPR was originally reported to Eaton by the late Lyle C. Wilson. The lobby anecdote was told by Al Zack in an interview. Raskin's estimate is from *The Atlantic Monthly,* October 1963, and WPR's view was expressed in an interview broadcast by Detroit radio station WXYZ, May 12 and 19, 1963. Eaton recalled Meany's appearance at the UAW convention at which the mandatory retirement rule was adopted. The Carey-Reuther clash was reported in the Detroit *News,* February 10 and 17, 1965. Saul Miller, in an interview, told of other hostility from old CIO colleagues. Eaton recalled the feelings of the Textile Workers, and Nat Goldfinger recounted the breakfast speech in an interview. Leonard Woodcock, in an interview, discussed revision of the Vietnam resolution (also see 1965 AFL-CIO convention *Proceedings,* pp. 560ff.). Kirkland told of WPR's hospital visit to Meany and the Los Angeles *Times* interview with Victor Reuther. Meany recounted his conversation with WPR on the subject. The account of the ILO episode is taken from the AFL-CIO "white paper," which contains WPR's letter. Eaton covered the confrontation meeting. Conway and Kirkland were interviewed about the controversy over CIA connections. Meany described Dubinsky's peace overtures. Paul Hall commented on Meany's weakness and the editorial appeared in the Detroit *News,* December 3, 1952. Raskin's appraisal is from *The Atlantic Monthly,* above. Harrison gave his views in an interview.

THIRTY-ONE   *Finale*

This chapter is based in large part on an interview with WPR in August 1969. William J. Eaton attended the UAW convention in May 1970 and WPR's quotes at the meeting are from a transcript of his "Opening Remarks." The Cambodia statement, never publicly distributed, was supplied by Stephen Schlossberg. The account of the plane flight and crash is from the Detroit *News* and an article on air crashes by James Weighart in the New York *Daily News,* May 25, 1970. Eulogies quoted also came from newspaper accounts. John Reuther, Victor's son, reported the Solidarity House message of his father. The quotes from mourners are from the Detroit *News* and the Detroit *Free Press.* Funeral statements were published by the UAW and lyrics of "Joe Hill" were printed in the funeral program.

Index